# John Adams and Thomas Jefferson

## Creating the American Republic

GERARD W. GAWALT

ISBN-13: 9781495360473
ISBN-10: 1495360474
Library of Congress Control Number: 2014902033
CreateSpace Independent Publishing Platform
North Charleston, South Carolina

Dedication

For George A. Billias, Gerald N. Grob and David G. McCullough
whose writings are models for all other historians.

# Contents

# Acknowledgements

Jeffery Flannery, head of the Manuscript Division Reading Room of the Library of Congress, and Manuscript Division staffers Patrick Kirwan and Bruce Kirby were indispensable to the writing of this book. Special thanks to Michael Hill, author and researcher, for his encouragement, advice, and research assistance; and Bruce Slawter and James Hutson for engaging in thoughtful discussions on Adams, Jefferson and republics. Speacial thanks to Sara Georgini, Papers of John Adams Project; Kelly Cobble, Curator, Adams National Historical Park; special thanks for assistance to Jack Robertson, Foundation Librarian, and especially Anna Berkes, Research Librarian, and Gaye Wilson, Research Historian, Jefferson Library, Thomas Jefferson Foundation; Colby O'Connor and Mark Santangelo, Fred W. Smith National Library.

A special thanks to Rich Shaner, a National Park guide, who went above and beyond to provide a tour of Adams's birthplace and John and Abigail's first home.

Heartfelt thanks and affection to my best friend and wife, Jane Cavanaugh Gawalt, for helping me through yet another historical project.

# Introduction

*"Many are the evils of a political life, but none So great as the dissolution of friendships, and the implacable hatreds which too often take their place."*
BENJAMIN RUSH TO THOMAS JEFFERSON, FEBRUARY 1, 1811

The rivalry and the friendship of John Adams and Thomas Jefferson were both born in the cauldron of the American Revolution and nurtured by shared experiences, the flames of ambition, clashing political philosophies and festering factions during the founding of a new nation.

This is the story of the intertwined lives of two men who planned and plotted together, led a revolution together, declared independence together, served as American ministers abroad together, and worked together to put the new federal government on its feet. These colleagues and quondam friends became bitter rivals even enemies before finding peace and a renewed friendship in retirement and old age.

Adams's belief that Jefferson had become a Jacobin and Jefferson's belief that Adams favored a monarchical for government are the keys to understanding their rivalry and the bitter politics in the first decade under the new federal constitution.

Both men were patriotic revolutionaries or traitors depending on your point of view. Both men no doubt believed Edmund Burke's warning: "The greater the power, the more dangerous the abuse." Both men saw danger in the concentration of power and were firm believers in a republican government for the United States. Adams envisioned a strong national government controlled by a commercial/professional elite with the support of artisans and farmers. Jefferson envisioned a national confederation of strong states controlled by landed gentry with the support of artisans and small farmers. Neither man supported universal manhood suffrage for white men-never mind universal suffrage for all people who have reached their eighteenth birthday. Both men burned with a steady high-intensity flame of ambition. In politics both men tried to define each other in stark terms. Adams became an Anglophobic monarchist and Jefferson became an infidel Francophile. Both men would have been shocked at the diverse democratic republic that now is the United States.

Both men became convinced that the other was part of a conspiracy that would lead to civil war, a divided nation or a military counter-revolution. Both men blamed each other for leading factions or political parties.

Adams and Jefferson had clear visions of the new United States as a federal republic. How they defined "federal republic" grew increasing different as they struggled to establish the United States, establish the place of the United States in the international arena, and to create a new national government under a new federal constitution.

Adams considered Jefferson his close friend. Jefferson considered Adams a colleague or acquaintance, but not his close friend. Not like Madison was Jefferson's close friend. Jefferson did not suffer the same sense of betrayal that Adams did, when political philosophies, ambition, and competing factions forced a series of political clashes.

Principle, ambition, and pride were contributors to their successes and their failures. Both men experienced the bitter and the sweet. This is their story.

Their relationship ebbed and flowed as colleagues, competitors, and friends. Adams more than Jefferson mistook collegiality for deep friendship. They were indeed friendly at points in their lives, but once they collaborated on writing the Declaration of Independence their plans for a Republican government for the United States steadily moved apart. In the vernacular of today, these friends and rivals might be called frenemies.

Judging from their backgrounds there were few similarities between our two protagonists--Jefferson and Adams.

One was the product of a hardscrabble New England small farm and a religion that abhorred debt and loved hard work. One was imbued with the southern slave culture in which masters could be "petty tyrants." Both were lawyers, but only Adams loved the inherent confrontation of the legal system. Jefferson's enlightened worldview emanated from books. Adams used books to tame the chaos of life and help steer the ship of life through the dangerous shoals that constantly threatened.

One was short with a softness that covered inner steel. The other was tall and spare looking strong and commanding. Adams did not shy from direct confrontation whether personal or political. Jefferson shied away from direct confrontation, preferring to act through intermediaries. Some might say Adams was simply irascible. Both men had more than "a spice of ambition." Some might say Jefferson had a passive aggressive personality. Jefferson always hoped that the future would solve all problems without any personal sacrifice--slavery would end, Great Britain would stop impressing seamen, and his personal debt would be erased. Adams believed that only hard work and personal sacrifice could achieve lofty goals and personal independence. Adams had few friends. Jefferson had many friends. Adams was never known as a ladies man. Jefferson cultivated many women friends on both intellectual and physical levels.

Both men regularly made hollow protests against holding public office and pleas seeking a return to the quiet life on their farms. Each burned with desires for fame, fortune, and power, although in true eighteenth century style they publicly disclaimed such aims or motivations.

Some say, Jefferson and Adams were like a cobra and a mongoose locked in combat. Others say they were like two vipers competing for the same prey or even two scorpions in a bottle. Others say they were two idealists with opposing visions for the United States. Some say they were firm friends. Others say they were faux friends. Certainly they were colleagues, competitors and correspondents.

Everyone says they were two men essential to the founding of the United States.

George Washington was the indispensable founder of the United States. He was the ultimate pragmatist. Adams and Jefferson were ideologues who fought to define the parameters of the American Republic. They were unable to provide the definitive answers, but they established the boundaries and tensions of the debate for centuries to come. They sought to answer the questions that we are still debating in our political theory and public policy forums.

They engaged in both famous and infamous campaigns for the presidency in 1796 and 1800. They were both party candidates and sectional candidates. Madison and Jefferson had painted Adams as a representative of New England

commercial interests beginning with his appointment as America's peace negotiator in 1779. Jefferson was the first presidential candidate to benefit from the
three-fifths rule, which counted three-fifths of the slave population in devising
proportional representation in the House of Representatives and the Electoral
College. Both men benefited from the political manipulation of the selection
of "independent" presidential electors.

Both Adams and Jefferson were highly motivated by political principle
and political ambitions. Both men had visions of the new American republic. Neither man wanted to create an American monarchy. Jefferson feared
monarchy and aristocracy. Adams feared democracy. While Adams admired
the British monarchical-parliamentary system of government, he wanted
a freely elected, balanced government for the United States with a strong
executive, legislature and judiciary. While Jefferson was a Francophile and
an admirer of French aristocratic culture, he wanted an American republic
where the national legislature played the most prominent role and there were
term limits, a weak executive, and a Bill of Rights limiting the authority of
the government. Both men believed the president should be the leader of
the national government, but Jefferson believed his term in office should be
limited. Both men believed that they could apply the true meaning of the
Federal Constitution.

It is hard to imagine at this point in time, how fragile the American
Republic was in the first decades of its life. No republic had succeeded in governing a large geographic area with a diverse population. No one knew who
should be the final arbiter of the constitution-the executive, the judiciary, the
legislature, or the people through a continual series of national constitutional
conventions. The role of the state governments in a national federal government had yet to be determined. Not everyone equated the United States with
her/his country. Jefferson, for example, continually referred to Virginia as
"my country."

Sectional politics was already firmly established. Adams had suggested
Jefferson write the Declaration of Independence because he was not a New
Englander. Adams was continually thought to represent the New England
commercial interests as an American minister in Europe. Jefferson was the
representative of the southern agricultural interests. Both men feared the rising power of the western territories and feared that they would form their

own republic. In their presidential campaigns Adams's strength rested on a unanimous New England. Jefferson benefited from the three-fifths rule, which gave the southern slave states a minimum of twelve additional congressmen and hence presidential electors.

In 1800 no one knew for sure which direction the nation would take. Would it split into three or more nations? Would a strongman overturn the republican government and establish a dictatorship or establish himself as a monarch? Would the rich and wellborn establish an aristocracy and create a republic in name only? All this was up for grabs when Jefferson and Adams waged two presidential campaigns that they believed would determine the course of the American Republic.

Often their letters do not reflect their true thoughts or plans leaving historians to guess at their real meanings or to simply conclude that they were inclined to write what the recipient wanted to hear or that they were simply manipulative or disingenuous. Adams was more prone to written outbursts. Adams was more open than Jefferson. For the most part Adams (often to his detriment) wrote exactly what he was thinking. But even Adams admitted in a famous February 3, 1821, letter to Jefferson that he refused to take public stands against slavery for political expediency. "I constantly said in former times to the Southern Gentlemen, I cannot comprehend this object; I must leave it to you. I will vote for forceing no measure against your judgements. What we are to see, God knows, and I leave it to him, and his agents in Posterity."

By his own admission Jefferson's correspondence was drastically affected by his political life. His work as secretary of state forced him "to deny myself the satisfaction of all private correspondence." During the 1790s he virtually ended his correspondence with his friends in France because, as he told Madame de Corny in an April 23, 1802, letter, he feared that his political opponents would use his correspondence as additional proof that he favored the French nation to the detriment of the United States. And in 1799 and 1800 Jefferson warned his correspondents, even his family members, that he was curtailing written personal communications because he feared that his political opponents would open them and seize on their contents to damage his chances during the hotly contested presidential election of 1800. More than talent was necessary for both Adams and Jefferson to succeed in the revolutionary maelstrom. They

Gerard W. Gawalt

were both willing to go far from home to serve their country. Other men of equal talents and abilities, such as James Warren of Massachusetts and George Mason of Virginia, refused to leave their localities and limited their roles in the revolution and the formation of a new nation. Adams and Jefferson, despite their denials, eagerly seized opportunities to serve as delegates to Congress in Philadelphia, foreign ministers in Europe, and officials in the new federal capital.

Both men were highly educated, well traveled and sophisticated for the eighteenth century. Both men wrote extremely well but still had their own spelling and grammatical quirks. Jefferson's written conversations were more circumspect and tailored to the recipient. In comparison to Adams he conversed with a wider range of men and women. Metaphors spilled out of his pen like water through a sluice gate during a spring flood. In the days of television and radio the ever-glib Jefferson would be considered the master of the thirty-second sound bite. Adams was the more forthright conversationalist both in written and spoken form. For that reason, Adams tended to grate on people, more than the smooth talking man from Monticello. Neither would be mistaken for a rough-cut farmer or backwoodsman.

Although Adams and Jefferson differed politically, they both held traditional personal beliefs. Both men believed in a paternalistic family life. Adams, for example, tried to determine his daughter's choice of a husband. Jefferson lectured his daughters on the need to be subservient to their husbands. Both their spouses played their traditional roles, although Abigail certainly pushed the envelope. Jefferson voiced his belief that wives should tolerate alcoholic even abusive husbands. Neither man could envision women actively participating in politics, although Adams certainly consulted with his wife and Jefferson exchanged political information with a number of women. They may have led the American Revolution against Great Britain, but they did not espouse revolution in their homes.

A study of the two men together allows us to study the interrelationship of their personal and professional lives and their vastly different personalities, experiences and backgrounds.

They also are prime examples of the twisting turns of historical interpretation.

For most of the more than two centuries since the adoption of the Declaration of Independence Jefferson was hailed as an iconic founder and leading intellectual of the nation. Now his reputation is in disrepute.

Over the same period Adams was known as an irascible conservative and the pretentious cousin of the famous Adams—Samuel. Now Adams is hailed as an iconic founder and leading intellectual of the revolutionary era.

Adams famously asked Jefferson in a July 30, 1815, letter. "Who shall write the history of the American revolution? Who can write it? Who will ever be able to write it?"

Jefferson's answer was not very encouraging. "Nobody; except it's external facts. All it's councils, designs and discussions, having been conducted by Congress with closed doors, and no member, as far as I know, having even made notes of them, these, which are the life and soul of history must for ever be unknown."

Fortunately, Adams and Jefferson kept enough of their diaries, notes, and letters to crack open their windows into the history of the American Revolution and their own lives.

Everyone interested in history and culture during the founding of the United States should be grateful to both Adams and Jefferson for carefully preserving their public and private papers. Now they chiefly reside at the Massachusetts Historical Society and the Library of Congress. We have tens of thousands of letters, diaries, journals, sketches, notes and documents for both men. Their letters have been widely reprinted in multiple documentary projects of single volumes, multiple volume sets, and individual letters in print and online. For these reasons I have attached no section of letters, but I have quoted frequently from their letters to allow readers access to their invaluable thoughts in their own words.

Although Jefferson apparently destroyed his correspondence with his wife Martha, Adams saved more than 1100 letters exchanged by him and his wife, Abigail. Fortunately, Adams and Jefferson preserved their letters to each other. In cold numbers, John wrote 189 letters to Thomas, while Jefferson wrote only 149 to Adams. As a double bonus, Abigail and Thomas also corresponded—27 by Abigail and 24 by Thomas. In a broader sense the value of this correspondence is incalculable for anyone trying to understand the relationships of these people and their impact on creating the United States. Their letters open windows into the innermost thoughts of two of the major actors on the stage of America's founding.

To understand their story is to understand the creation of the American Republic.

# Time Line, 1735-1826

---

1735
October 30 (October 19 Old Style)
John Adams is born in Braintree (now Quincy), Massachusetts to John Adams and Susanna Boylston.

1743
April 13 (April 2 Old Style)
Thomas Jefferson is born at Shadwell Plantation in Goochland (now Albemarle) County, Virginia to Peter Jefferson and Jane Randolph.

1751
Adams begins studies at Harvard C ollege.

1754
May 28
French and Indian contingent defeated by George Washington's militia and Indian allies at Jumonville Glen, Pa.
June 10
Colonial delegates and Indian representatives meet in Albany, N.Y.; Benjamin Franklin presents Albany Plan for American Union.
July 3
Washington surrenders to French at Fort Necessity.

1755
Adams graduates from Harvard College.

July 9
British led by General Edward Braddock defeated by French and Indian allies near present day Pittsburgh, Pa.

1756
Adams begins legal studies with Samuel Putnam.

1757
August 17
Peter Jefferson dies, leaving a widow and eight children, including fourteen-year-old Thomas, the eldest son.

1759
November 6
Adams passes the bar examination and soon begins legal career in Braintree.

1760-1762
Jefferson attends the College of William and Mary in Williamsburg, Virginia.

1761
George III crowned King of Great Britain.
May 25
John Adams Senior dies.

1762
Jefferson begins the study of law with George Wythe.

1763
Britain and France sign Treaty of Paris ending the French and Indian/Seven Years' War.
Pontiac's War flares in the Ohio River valley.
October 7
Proclamation establishing a boundary line along the Appalachian Mountains beyond which Euro-American colonists cannot claim land or settle announced by British government.

1764

October 25

John Adams and Abigail Smith marry.

1765

Jefferson passes the Bar examination.

March 22

British Parliament passes an act requiring purchase of stamps to be affixed to newspapers, documents, playing cards, licenses and other items.

May 15

Quartering Act requiring Americans to provide food and housing for British soldiers in private houses in peacetime becomes law.

July 14

John and Abigail's daughter Abigail is born.

August

Adams writes Braintree Instructions protesting taxation without representation.

October 7-25

Stamp Act Conference meets in New York to protest taxation without representation.

1766

Jefferson travels, to Annapolis, Philadelphia and New York.

March 18

Stamp Act repealed by British Parliament. Declaratory Act stating Parliament's right to make all laws for the colonies passed.

1767

Jefferson begins legal practice while living at Shadwell.

June 29

British Townshend Acts imposing new import taxes on glass, paint, lead, paper, and tea are passed by Parliament.

July 11

John and Abigail's son John Quincy is born.

1768

April

Adams family moves from Braintree to Boston.

Circular letter opposing British revenue acts passed by provincial legislatures.

December 28

John and Abigail's daughter Susanna is born.


1769

May

Jefferson begins seven years of service in the Virginia House of Burgesses and Assembly.

American provinces adopt Non-importation Agreements.


1770

February 1

Jefferson's home, Shadwell, is destroyed by fire.

February 4

John and Abigail's daughter Susanna dies.

March 5

British troops fire on a Patriot crowd killing five and wounding six in the Boston Massacre.

Adams serves as defense attorney for British troops accused of murder.

Adams is elected a representative to the state assembly, the General Court, where he serves for four years.

May 29

John and Abigail's son Charles is born.


1771

April

Adams family moves back to Braintree.


1772

January 1

Jefferson marries Martha Wayles Skelton.

September 15

John and Abigail's son Thomas is born.

September 27

Thomas and Martha's daughter Martha is born.

November

Adams family moves back to Boston.

1773

December 16

Boston Tea Party takes place.

1774

Plans circulate for an annual "general congress" of the colonies to meet in Philadelphia.

January 14

Sally Hemings is among the 135 slaves inherited by Martha Jefferson from her father John Wayles.

April 3

Thomas and Martha's daughter Jane is born.

May

Port of Boston closed by British.

June 17

Adams elected delegate to Continental Congress.

Adams family moves back to Braintree.

July

Jefferson drafts A *Summary View of the Rights of British America* proclaiming America's right to control its governance.

September 5

Adams attends First Continental Congress.

October 26

Adams leaves Philadelphia.

1775

March 27

Jefferson is elected a delegate to Continental Congress.

April 19

Fighting between British Army and American Minutemen breaks out at Concord and Lexington.

May 10

Congress reassembles and Adams returns to Congress.

June 15

Washington appointed commander of American army.

June 21

Adams and Jefferson first meet when Jefferson begins service in the Continental Congress in Philadelphia.

Jefferson helps draft a declaration "Setting Forth the Causes and Necessity of Their Taking up Arms."

July 21

Adams elected to Massachusetts Council.

August

Jefferson and Adams return home.

September

Thomas and Martha's daughter Jane dies.

September 15

Adams returns to Congress.

October 2

Jefferson returns to Congress

October 15

Adams appointed chief justice of the Massachusetts Superior Court of Judicature.

December 8

Adams leaves Philadelphia.

December 28

Jefferson leaves Philadelphia.

December 31

American forces defeated at Quebec City.

1776

January 9

Thomas Paine's *Common Sense* is published.

February 9

Adams returns to Congress.

March 17

British evacuate Boston.

March 31

Jefferson's mother, Jane Randolph Jefferson, dies.

April

Adams's *Thoughts on Government* is published.

May 14

Jefferson returns to Congress.

June

Jefferson and Adams lead drafting of the Declaration of Independence.

Adams appointed head of Continental Board of War and Ordnance.

July 4

Declaration of Independence is adopted.

July 12

Jefferson begins service on committee drafting Articles of Confederation.

September 3

Jefferson departs Philadelphia for Monticello and returns to Virginia Assembly.

September 11

Adams attends peace conference with Lord Richard Howe.

September 26

Congress appoints Jefferson a commissioner to represent the United States abroad, but Jefferson declines.

Washington's army flees New York City.

October 12

Adams returns to Braintree.

December 12

Congress flees to Baltimore.

December 20

Congress reconvenes in Baltimore.

December 26

Washington leads Americans to victory at Trenton, N.J.

1777

January

Washington's Army goes into winter quarters at Morristown, N.Y.

February 4

Adams returns to Congress.

February 10

Adams resigns as chief justice of Massachusetts Superior Court.

Jefferson fails to return to Congress but continues attending the Virginia Assembly.

Jefferson submits A Bill for Establishing Religious Freedom in Virginia House of Delegates.

March 4

Congress leaves Baltimore for Philadelphia.

May 28

Thomas and Martha's unnamed son is born.

June 14

Thomas and Martha's unnamed son dies.

July 11

John and Abigail's daughter Elizabeth is stillborn.

September 11

British army defeats General Washington's army at Brandywine Creek clearing the way for British army to enter Philadelphia.

September 19

Adams flees Philadelphia with Congress for Lancaster and York, as British army moves in.

September 30

Congress convenes in York, Pennsylvania.

October 17

British army surrenders at Saratoga, N.Y.

November 10

Adams returns to Braintree to resume legal practice.

November 15

Articles of Confederation sent to the states for ratification.

November 27

Congress appoints Adams a commissioner to negotiate an alliance with France.

1778

France signs treaties of amity and alliance with the United States.

February

Adams leaves for France.

August 1

Thomas and Martha's daughter Mary is born.

August

Franco-American forces defeated at Rhode Island.

September

Congress dissolves joint commission and appoints Franklin as sole minister to France.

1779

June-August

Adams returns to Massachusetts.

Jefferson submits a Bill for the More General Diffusion of Knowledge in Virginia House of Delegates.

June 1

Jefferson is elected governor of Virginia.

August 2

Adams arrives home from France and helps draft the Massachusetts Constitution.

September-November

Adams is appointed minister to negotiate treaties of peace and commerce with Great Britain and sails for France.

1780

May 12

American forces suffer worst defeat of the war with surrender of Charleston, S.C.

June

Adams authorized to negotiate with Holland.

Adams's draft of Massachusetts's constitution is adopted with few alterations.

June 2

Jefferson is re-elected governor of Virginia.

November 3
Thomas and Martha's daughter Lucy (the first) is born.

1781
March 1
Articles of Confederation formally approved by last required state and goes into effect.
June
Adams named one of five commissioners to negotiate peace with Great Britain.
British force nearly captures Jefferson at Monticello.
July
Jefferson flees to Bedford County and drafts Notes on the State of Virginia.
Adams sets off for Holland.
August
Jefferson returns to Monticello.
September 15
Thomas and Martha's daughter Lucy dies.
October 17
British surrender at Yorktown effectively ends the military aspect of the American Revolution.

1782
April 22
Adams received as American minister to Netherlands.
Netherlands formally recognizes United States.
Thomas and Martha's daughter Lucy (the second) is born.
September 6
Jefferson's wife Martha dies.
November
Jefferson is appointed a commissioner to negotiate peace.
November 30
Adams and other American commissioners sign Preliminary Articles of Peace in Paris.
December 27
Jefferson arrives in Philadelphia.

1783

April 1.

Congress withdraws Jefferson's appointment as peace commissioner.

April 12

Jefferson leaves Philadelphia.

June 6

Jefferson elected delegate to Congress.

September 3

Adams signs Treaty of Paris concluding the American Revolution, and Congress cancels Jefferson's appointment as peace commissioner.

November 4

Jefferson attends Congress in Princeton, N.J.

December 4

Jefferson attends Congress in Annapolis.

1784

March 1

Jefferson proposes eliminating slavery in western territories by 1800.

May 3

Jefferson leaves Congress.

May 7

Jefferson, Adams, and Franklin appointed commissioners by Congress to negotiate treaties of amity and commerce with twenty-three European and African nations.

June 20

Abigail sails from Boston to join John in France.

July 5

Jefferson sails from Boston to join Adams and Franklin as American ministers in Europe.

August

Jefferson arrives in France.

October 13

Thomas's daughter Lucy dies.

1785

February 24

Adams named first American minister to Court of St. James.

March 7

Jefferson appointed Franklin's replacement as Minister Plenipotentiary to France.

March 20-28

Washington hosts Mt. Vernon Conference.

May 26

Adams arrives in London as Minister Plenipotentiary to Great Britain.


1786

March-April

Jefferson joins Adams in England for a tour of the countryside; the King of Great Britain snubs Jefferson. Jefferson and Adams try to negotiate commercial treaties with Tripoli and Portugal.

June 12

John and Abigail's daughter Abigail marries William Stephens Smith.

August

John and Abigail Adams go to Holland for signing of treaty with Prussia.

August-October

Jefferson meets and falls in love with Maria Cosway, vivacious wife of noted British

artist, Richard Cosway.

September 11-14

Delegates to the Annapolis Convention call for a national convention at Philadelphia to address deficiencies in the Articles of Confederation.

Shays' Rebellion gains strength in Massachusetts.


1787

January

Adams publishes first of three volumes of *A Defence of the Constitutions of Government of the United States of America*.

March-June

Jefferson tours southern France and Italy.

May-September

Federal Constitution is written and adopted in Philadelphia.

June 26

Thomas's daughter Mary arrives in London on her way to Paris.

1788

March-April

Jefferson tours Holland and neighboring countries.

April

Adams family leaves England.

June

Adams arrives in Boston.

Adams elected delegate to Congress.

1789

March

Adams elected vice-president with 34 out of 69 votes.

April 21

Adams begins duties as the first vice-president of the United States.

April 30

Washington inaugurated as first president under the Federal Constitution.

May 5

Jefferson attends opening of French Estates-General.

July 14

French rioters attack Bastille.

September

Twelve amendments to the federal constitution sent to the states for ratification.

September 26

Senate confirms Jefferson as Secretary of State.

September 28

Jefferson's leaves Paris to return to Virginia.

October

President Washington tours New England.

November 23

Jefferson reaches Norfolk, Virginia.

1790

Thomas and Sally's unnamed child is born and dies.

February 14

Jefferson accepts appointment as secretary of state.

February 23

Jefferson's daughter Martha marries Thomas Mann Randolph, Jr.

March 21

Jefferson arrives in New York and begins work as secretary of state.

July

Capital relocated to Philadelphia and Congress approves funding and assumption of revolutionary war debts.

November

Adams and Jefferson relocate to Philadelphia.

December 6

U.S. Congress convenes in Philadelphia.


1791

February

National Bank is established.

March 24

President Washington embarks on tour of southern states.

May-June

Jefferson and James Madison undertake tour of northern states.


1792

Adams is candidate for vice-president.


1793

February 13

Adams is re-elected vice-president with 77 out of 132 votes. Jefferson receives four electoral votes.

April 22

President Washington proclaims American neutrality.

December 31

Jefferson resigns as secretary of state.

1794

July

President Washington leads troops against Whiskey Rebels.

August 29

Adams's son Charles marries Sally Smith.


1795

August 14

Jay Treaty ratified by Senate.

October 5

Thomas and Sally's daughter Harriet is born.


1796

April 21

House approves funding for Jay Treaty.

December 7

Adams receives 71 electoral votes and Jefferson 68 electoral votes making them president and vice-president.


1797

February 8

Electoral vote officially counted.

March 4

Adams inaugurated as second president of the United States and Jefferson sworn in as vice-president of the United States.

June

Adams sends special three-man mission to France.

July 26

Adams's son John Quincy marries Louisa Catherine Johnson.

October 13

Jefferson's daughter Mary (Maria) marries John Wayles Eppes.

December 7

Thomas and Sally's daughter Harriet dies.

1798
XYZ Affair with France.
Quasi-War with France.
April 1
Thomas and Sally's son Beverly is born.
June-July
Alien and Sedition Acts pass Congress.
Adams appoints George Washington and Alexander Hamilton to command American Army.
September-October
Jefferson drafts Virginia and Kentucky Resolutions.

1799
Thomas and Sally's unnamed daughter is born.
December 14
George Washington dies.

1800
Adams and Jefferson wage fierce presidential election.
Jefferson drafts manual of parliamentary practice for the Senate.
Thomas and Sally's unnamed daughter dies.
May
Adams fires "Cabinet" members Timothy Pickering and James McHenry.
October
John and Abigail Adams become first presidential family to occupy the new president's house in Washington, D.C.
November 30
John and Abigail's son Charles dies.
December 3
Electors cast their votes for president and vice-president.
Jefferson and Burr each win 73 electoral votes to Adams's 65.

1801
February 17
House of Representatives chooses Jefferson over Burr for president.

March 4

Jefferson inaugurated as third president of the United States.

Adams returns to Massachusetts.

March 18

Adams reaches home.

May 22

Thomas and Sally's daughter Harriet is born.

August

Jefferson begins naval war against Barbary pirates.

1802

Adams begins his autobiography.

1803

January 18

Jefferson requests funds for Lewis and Clark Expedition.

February 23

Supreme Court reaches decision in Marbury v Madison.

April 30

Jefferson's ministers in France conclude a treaty with France purchasing the Louisiana Territory.

July 4

News of the purchase of Louisiana Territory is announced.

1804

April 17

Jefferson's daughter, Mary Jefferson Eppes dies.

July

Abigail Adams and Jefferson begin exchange of letters.

July 12

Alexander Hamilton dies after being shot by Vice President Aaron Burr.

December

Jefferson is elected president and George Clinton is elected vice-president with 162 electoral votes.

1805
January 19
Thomas and Sally's son Madison is born.
March 4
Jefferson is inaugurated president for second term.
May 16
Adams's son Thomas marries Ann Treat Harrod.

1806
Jefferson begins construction of his octagonal summerhouse, Poplar Forest, in Bedford County.
April 18
Non-Importation Act passes Congress.

1807
January 17
Aaron Burr arrested and later charged with treason.
July
American ports closed to all British ships.
December
Non-importation Act becomes effective.
Embargo Act passes Congress.

1808
May 21
Thomas and Sally's son Eston is born.

1809
February 16
Non-Intercourse Act passes Congress to replace Embargo Act.
March 4
Jefferson's second presidential term ends.
James Madison is inaugurated as fourth president. Jefferson returns to Virginia.

1812

January 1

Adams writes to Jefferson and begins renewal of old friendship.

June 18

United States declares war against Great Britain.

1813

August 15

John and Abigail's daughter Abigail dies.

1814

Jefferson begins work to establish the University of Virginia.

August 24

British burn United States capitol.

1815

February 17

War of 1812 officially ends.

April

Jefferson's library is transported to Washington.

1817

October 6

Cornerstone laid for Central College, later the University of Virginia.

1818

August

Jefferson, Madison, and Marshall agree to establish a university at Charlottesville.

October 28

Abigail Adams dies of typhoid fever.

1819

January 25

University of Virginia granted charter.

1819-1820
Jefferson compiles The Life and Morals of Jesus of Nazareth.

1820
November-December
Adams attends Massachusetts Constitutional Convention.

1821
January 6
Jefferson begins his autobiography.

1823
Jefferson makes last trip to Poplar Forest.

1825
February 9
John Quincy Adams elected president of the United States in House of Representatives.
March 7
University of Virginia opens to students.

1826
July 4
Adams and Jefferson die.

# Personal Foundations

DURING THE CHILDHOODS of John Adams and Thomas Jefferson, the American colonies were firmly within the British Empire. The idea of an independent United States of America was a radical fantasy. But the process of psychological and political revolution would track the lives of John Adams and Thomas Jefferson. Indeed, they would be among the founders of the new American republic. Surely their parents could not and perhaps would not want to have envisioned their sons' life courses. Yet, today centuries after their births, our lives are still deeply affected by the thoughts and actions of these two men who were born Britons and helped birth the United States of America.

Jefferson and Adams were in many ways a study in contrasts. One was a tall angular Southerner and the other was a Northerner of middling height tending toward the rotund. Their vocal accents clashed. Their religions were different. Jefferson was one of the largest slave owners in Virginia and therefore the American provinces. Adams abhorred slavery and the slave trade. Adams farmed at most 600 acres. Jefferson's plantations covered several thousand acres. Even though Adams and Jefferson lived over 500 miles apart that distance cannot begin to measure the distance between Adams's small farm/artisan experience, and Jefferson's large plantation lifestyle.

Jefferson was the thoughtful listener who spoke well but infrequently. Certainly, he was a man with a controlled and controlling personality. In contrast to the stereotypical New Englander, Adams was cordial, outgoing, quick to anger and outspoken. Adams's cordiality could lead him to happily greet a loyalist from Massachusetts while serving as American minister to Great Britain. After being greeted effusively by Adams, Jonathan Sewall, an exiled Massachusetts loyalist, reportedly declared. "Adams has a heart formed for friendship, and susceptible of its finest feelings."

Jefferson was slow to anger, but could hold a grudge for a lifetime. Both men were principled men of enormous ambitions. When they were born, no one would have predicted the paths of their lives and the incredible impact the intersection of their paths would have on their lives and the live of their nation.


## CHILDHOOD

Thomas was not even a gleam in Peter Jefferson's eye when John Adams was born on October 30, 1735 in the quiet village of Braintree, Massachusetts to Deacon John Adams and Susanna Boylston Adams. Later, brothers Peter and Elihu joined young John.

John Senior was a shoemaker and a farmer, who served as a town selectman, militia lieutenant and deacon of the Congregational Church. In short, he was a pillar of small town New England. The Adams family was not of high social standing. They were community stalwarts, but Boston was the big city and Virginia was another country. John would teach his son few social skills. The son would become a bad card player, cut a poor figure on the dance floor, would not be good at small talk, and would be awkward in "high society." Both father and son were born small farmers and the son always seemed to be cleaning his boots.

John made kind, even loving remarks about his father in his autobiography. "My Father by his Industry and Enterprize soon became a Person of more Property and Consideration in the Town than his Patron had been. He became a Select Man, a Militia Officer and a Deacon in the Church. He was the honestest Man I ever knew. In Wisdom, Piety, Benevolence and Charity In proportion to his Education and Sphere of Life, I have never seen his Superiour." About his death Adams wrote. "Nothing I can say or do, can sufficiently express my Gratitude for his parental Kindness to me, or the exalted Opinion I have of his Wisdom and Virtue."

As the eldest son John received one-third of his father's estate "which consisted in a House and Barn such they were and forty Acres of Land. He Left me one third of his personal Estate."

Susanna, the daughter of Peter and Ann White Boylston, came from of a well-to-do professional family in Brookline where the family mansion still stands on the street now memorializing the family name. To young John she would always be his "honored and beloved mother." Despite her claims to a higher social standing than her small farmer/artisan husband, she could not read or write. She would not make that mistake with her children.

John's father died during an influenza outbreak in 1761. John wrote kindly of his father describing him as "a man of strict piety, and great integrity; much esteemed and beloved wherever he was known, which was not far, his sphere of life being not extensive."

Five years later his mother married John Hall. Young Adams was not pleased with his mother's choice and said nothing in his autobiography. But how many sons are truly pleased when their mother remarries? A proud Susanna Boylston Adams Hall did live until her son became president of the United States.

Peter Jefferson, like John Adams Sr., was said to have married above his social level, when Jane Randolph from one of the most powerful families in Virginia became his wife on October 3, 1739. And like Susanna she brought little but herself and her family connections to the union. In his autobiography Jefferson said little about his mother, but made a snide comment about her family ancestry. "They trace their pedigree far back in England and Scotland, to which let every one ascribe the faith and merit it deserves."

Thomas was the eldest son and third child when he was born on April 13, 1743 at Shadwell, a 1400-acre plantation in what is now Albemarle County, Virginia. Seven more children would be born to Thomas and Jane.

Readers are left to wonder about Thomas's relationship with his father after viewing the unemotional account of Peter's death in Thomas's autobiography. "He died, August 17th, 1757, leaving my mother a widow, who lived till 1776, with six daughters and two sons, myself the elder. To my younger brother he left his estate on James River, called Snowdon, after the supposed birth-place of the family: to myself, the lands on which I was born and live."

That Jefferson and Adams were the eldest sons in their families proved profitable because they both inherited the lion's share of the their father's estate.


## INTELLECTUAL PURSUITS

Young John and Thomas both started their educations at home.

Their parents taught them the fundamentals of reading, writing and arithmetic and the basics of civilized life.

Adams moved on to attend a common school in Braintree, where he did badly, disliked the teacher, Joseph Clearly, and longed to spend his days in the fields as a farmer or as he later admitted going "on the marshes to kill wild fowl, and to swim." His father saw a different future for the bright young boy. In his autobiography Adams claimed that he wanted to quit school and farm alongside his father, telling him he did not "love Books and wished he would lay aside the thoughts of sending me to Colledge." But his father insisted he return to school with another teacher, Joseph Marsh, who operated a "private academy" which was "within three doors of my father's house." Marsh turned his student's intelligence into education, and John "Began to study in Earnest." Soon he was prepared for Harvard College. A fifteen-year old John passed the entrance exam and his father, envisioning a future minister, sold ten acres of land to pay for his son's tuition.

Adams discovered a love of books and study at Harvard and a dislike for the prospect of the ministry. With his mother's blessing Adams set off in 1755 to Worcester where he taught school for a year. Then, his mind filled with thoughts of politics and government, he became an apprentice lawyer to James Putnam in 1756. For the next two years he continued teaching and reading black letter law. Inspired by the presence of British troops marching through Worcester and all the excitement of the French and Indian War, Adams was proud to be an Englishman.

Two years later his legal education completed, he returned to Braintree a newly minted lawyer "beginning life anew."

Jefferson began his formal education with tutors in a little schoolhouse on Tuckahoe Plantation, which overlaps Goochland and Henrico counties. Jefferson reported in his autobiography that my father "placed me at the English school at 5 years of age and at the Latin at 9. where I continued until my father's death." Jefferson then left the tutelage of Rev. William Douglas and in 1758 entered the school of Rev. James Maury, whom Jefferson called "a correct classical scholar."

In 1760 Jefferson began two years of undergraduate study at The College of William and Mary where Dr. William Small "fixed the destinies of my life." Jefferson then moved on to five years of studying law with Professor George Wythe in Williamsburg.

Even after founding the University of Virginia, Jefferson advised his grandson Francis Wayles Eppes through a September 16, 1821, letter to his father John that attending college would be very useful but obtaining a college degree was "certainly not worth the sacrifice of a single useful science."

Both men acquired large libraries, which they actually used. Eventually Jefferson acquired over 6000 volumes, which he sold to the government in 1815 after the British had burned the capitol and the Library of Congress in 1814. Jefferson's 1814 library has now been reassembled at the Library of Congress. Jefferson used the twenty-three thousand nine hundred and fifty dollars that he received to pay some of his ever -present debts and to begin a new library of several thousand books.

Upon hearing that Jefferson's library would be part of the Library of Congress, Adams wrote of his envy in an October 23, 1814, letter to Jefferson. "By the Way I envy you that immortal honour: but I cannot enter into competition with you for my books are not half the number of yours: and moreover, I have Shaftesbury, Bolingbroke, Hume, Gibbon and Raynal, as well as Voltaire."

"I cannot live without books," replied Jefferson. "But fewer will suffice where amusement and not use, is the only future object."

Adams too had a connection to the Library of Congress signing the legislation in 1800 to "purchase such books as may be necessary" for a Library of Congress.

There were more than 3200 books in Adams's library. Both men received copies of hundreds of books by admirers and authors who hoped they would write a letter of thanks to be used as an endorsement.

Gerard W. Gawalt

Adams complained or bragged (take your choice) that he was over-whelmed with gifts of books. "My Friends or Enemies continue to overwhelm me with Books. Whatever may be there intension, charitable or otherwise, they certainly contribute, to continue me to vegetate, much as I have done for the sixteen Years last past," commented Adams in a May 18, 1817, letter to Jefferson.

Adams's use of his books cannot be denied because he constantly wrote comments in the margins and marked key passages. His comments in one book (Mary Wollstonecraft's *French Revolution*) alone came to over 12,000 words. Adams gave his 3200 books to the town of Quincy for the use of townsmen and students at Adams Academy, which he encouraged. Adams's plan for continued public use of his books went awry as the books were stored in a town-building basement for more than one hundred years. In 1894 they were donated to the Boston Public Library where they are still available for scholars.

Adams's study in Peacefield is easily the most impressive room in the house. It was there he suffered his fatal stroke while listening to one of his granddaughters read to him aloud.

Jefferson seldom wrote in the margins of his books, but his constant ana-lytical comments in written conversations testify to the depth and breadth of his reading. Both men read extensively and delighted in telling each other and their friends about their latest discovery or their new analysis of both the clas-sics and the modern.

Both men also believed, like Cicero and Caesar, that a general or liberal education was necessary and "proper for a free citizen." In practice, this meant that education was designed for the children of prosperous white citizens who were the future leaders of the country.

Although Adams was briefly involved with Jefferson and Washington in plans for the wholesale immigration of professors from the University of Geneva in 1795 to form a national university in the District of Columbia, he had no plans for the reform of higher education.

Jefferson hailed as one of his greatest achievements the furtherance of education. In the 1780's he drafted a bill for "the diffusion of knowledge" in Virginia. It would have created a complex system of public education. Designed for children of free men, the bill proposed some education for girls but concentrated on providing education for boys who would become the leaders of a free republic. Education was "the true corrective of constitutional power," according to Jefferson.

To that end he spent years of his retirement fostering the birth of the University of Virginia and then planning and overseeing its development. Some friends argued that he might have been better off concentrating on the business side of his plantations

In pushing for legislative action, Jefferson created an image of lost Virginia sons in a January 22, 1820, letter to William Jarvis. "If our legislature does not heartily push our University we must send our children for education to Kentucky [Transylvania College] or Cambridge [Harvard College]. The latter will return them to us fanatics and tories, the former will keep them to add to their population." Jefferson got his charter and his money for the University of Virginia.

Both men excelled at the art of letter writing in an age when letters were the only sure means of long distance communication. In many ways the eighteenth century was the golden era of letter writing. The work of Laurence Sterne, Eliza Haywood, Montesquieu and Samuel Richardson brought letter writing into the realm of true art. Jefferson and Adams undoubtedly saw themselves as part of this grand epistolary tradition.

When it came to writing for the public, Adams was far superior in many ways to Jefferson. Jefferson often asserted that he never wrote essays for public consumption. His only book, *Notes on the State of Virginia,* remains a classic and is considered by many historians as the best eighteenth century account of that state.

Adams, on the other hand, was a prolific writer turning out newspaper essays at a prodigious rate. He kept a daily diary and wrote an introspective autobiography. His three-volume book, *A Defence of Constitutions*, his pamphlet *Thoughts on Government* and his best-known series of newspaper essays, "Discourses on Davila" were outspoken arguments for a balanced form of government for the new American republic.

In their later years, both men sought to preserve their writings for posterity and used their autobiographies to buff and puff their reputations and roles in history.

Gerard W. Gawalt

## MARRIAGE AND FAMILY

John had known his distant cousin Abigail Smith when she was a child, but since he was nearly a decade older he no doubt paid little attention. John first began to "really" notice young Abigail in the summer of 1759 when she was a girl of 15. She has been described as the young girl reading quietly in the corner while her more vivacious sisters attracted most of the attention. We cannot now say what a young man of twenty-four really thought of this girl on the cusp of womanhood. Enough of the bright, intelligent, attractive and always engaging woman of the future shone through to keep young John returning to the Rev. William Smith's house on Penn Hill.

Abigail's mother, Elizabeth Quincy Smith, opposed her daughter's marriage to "a country lawyer." Upon hearing of her October 1, 1775, death, John dared offer "my opinion" on his mother-in-law in a query to Abigail. "Were not her Talents, and Virtues too much confined to private social and domestic Life?" he asked in an October 29, 1775, letter. Should not she have shared these with the wider world in acts of charity and concern, John wondered. Abigail made no written reply.

John and Abigail were married on October 25, 1764 by the bride's father. Fertility was not a problem. Nine months later a daughter, Abigail, appeared, followed by five more children. Three sons, John Quincy, Thomas and Charles, and Nabby survived to adulthood. Thomas and Charles lived troubled alcohol fueled lives and failed at careers in the law. Thomas finished his life as a foreman on John's farms, a small town officeholder, and "a brute in manners and a bully in the family," according to his nephew, Francis. John Quincy would be the first presidential son to rise to that office. Two other daughters Elizabeth and Susanna would not live beyond their first year.

In his autobiography, Adams assured everyone that even though he "was of an amorous disposition" from an early age, "No Virgin or Matron ever had cause to blush at the sight of me, or to regret her Acquaintance." Perhaps with Jefferson or Alexander Hamilton in mind Adams wrote: "My Children may be assured that no illegitimate Brother or Sister exists or ever existed."

During John and Abigail's courtship and marriage, they engaged in a remarkable exchange of letters. They often wrote under pseudonyms, Lysander, a Spartan naval hero, and Diana, goddess of the hunt and birthing.

The pseudonyms seemed to free them to open their minds and hearts. Their letters were sometimes serious, sometimes playful, sometimes flirtatious, sometimes critical, sometimes steamy and filled with the longing that only long separations can evoke from a couple full of lust and love. Both can be seen in a September 30, 1764, letter John wrote as Lysander. "O my dear girl, I thank heaven that another fortnight will restore you to me—after so long a separation. My soul and body have both been thrown into disorder by your absence, and a month or two more would make me the most insufferable cynic in the world." Adams continued. "But you who have always softened and warmed my heart, shall restore my benevolence as well as my health and tranquility of mind."

Their correspondence is remarkable not only for its length and breath, but also because it survived. So many times when a spouse died, the survivor, for example Jefferson, destroyed their personal correspondence.

John's travels to distant courts necessitated a courtship correspondence, even though John and Abigail lived only a few miles apart. For the entire period of the American Revolutionary War John and Abigail were apart more than they were together. At one point in 1782 Adams broke down. "I must go to you or you must come to me. I cannot live, in this horrid Solitude," cried John in frustration. Two years later, Abigail finally joined John in France. They never spent long years apart again.

Jefferson's relationships with women were complicated to say the least. At best he was attracted to women with whom he could not commit to a permanent relationship. His first love was Rebecca Burwell, who was already engaged. Then he tried to seduce Elizabeth Moore Walker, wife of his best friend and neighbor John Walker. Next he became infatuated with his friend John Page's wife, and even proposed to Page that the three of them could live together in some sort of ménage a trois. His wife Martha was a widow, but after her death he became enthralled with a series of women. Elizabeth House Trist, the daughter of the operator of his boarding house in Philadelphia, was married to a former British officer who was off in the Mississippi River territory. After her husband died she remained a friend for life, often living at Monticello. Maria Cosway, the love of his life in France, was married to Richard Cosway, a portraitist. They remained corresponding friends for life. Sally Hemings, Jefferson's slave and almost certainly his wife's half sister, could and would bear his children but could never marry Jefferson. Yet despite these varied sexual experiences he was no Thomas Thistlewood preying on any woman in this path.

When Jefferson did marry, he entered into a complicated family situation. His chosen bride Martha Wayles Skelton was a widow with a young son, who died shortly before their marriage. Although it was not unusual for a man to marry a widow, Martha came from a complex family. Her father John Wayles was married three times. Martha was the only surviving child of John Wayles and his first wife Martha Eppes who died a week after giving birth to Martha. Wayles married two more times and after this third wife died, he took as his mistress his slave Betty Hemings. Wayles and Hemings had six children. Among them was Sally who like her mother would become the mistress of her master. When John Wayles died in 1773, Jefferson's wife Martha inherited thousands of acres of land, dozens of slaves including Sally, and large debts. Jefferson spent decades trying to pay the debts of his lawyer/slave dealer father-in-law while enjoying the fruits of his wife's inheritance.

Jefferson, in his autobiography said as little about his wife as he did his mother. "On the 1st of January, 1772, I was married to Martha Skelton, widow of Bathurst Skelton and daughter of John Wayles, then twenty-three years old." About her death, he was a little more emotional. ""I had, two months before that, lost the cherished companion of my life, in whose affections, unabated on both sides, I had lived the last ten years in unchequered happiness."

Jefferson and his wife Martha were the parents of six children. Martha, Mary, and Lucy lived beyond infancy, but young Lucy died of whooping cough when she was two. Jefferson later described his children as a "rich treasure." Jefferson and Martha's two surviving daughters, Martha and Mary (Maria) married their cousins, Thomas Mann Randolph (Described by Jefferson as a "young gentleman of genius, science, and honorable mind.") and John Wayles Eppes.

Like her mother, Martha died of septicemia or debilitation brought on by multiple pregnancies following the birth of young Lucy.

Thomas and Martha copied out a moving sentimental passage from Laurence Sterne's novel *Tristram* Shandy while Martha lay dying in September 1782.

"Time wastes too fast: every letter I trace tells me with what rapidity life follows my pen. The days and hours of it are flying over our heads like clouds of windy day never to return more. Every thing presses on—and every time I kiss thy hand to bid adieu, every absence which follows it, are preludes to that eternal separation which we are shortly to make!"

Family tradition and some oral reports agree that Jefferson promised his wife on her deathbed that he would not remarry and make her children step-children-a fate she had no doubt found very distressing as a child. Jefferson did not remarry, but established a long-term relationship with his slave and his wife's half-sister, Sally Hemings. Jefferson's relationship with Sally has long been a point of contention, but solid evidence has led most people to the con-clusion that Sally and Jefferson had a sexual, perhaps even a loving relation-ship. The depth of the emotional attachment is not known, but they had six children. The four children to survive beyond infancy all received Jefferson family names: Eston, Madison, Beverly, and Harriet. Jefferson never formally acknowledged the relationship or his paternity, although all four children but not Sally were ushered into freedom by Jefferson.

## Physical Surroundings

Adams was born in a modest saltbox style frame house built in 1681 sitting on six acres in the northern precinct of Braintree, which in 1792 was incor-porated into the town of Quincy. In 1744 the elder John Adams purchased a second saltbox style house just 75 feet away from his own house. When Deacon John died in 1761, young John Adams inherited this "1744 house" and the sur-rounding forty acres. When John and Abigail married in 1764 they moved into this modest house featuring two rooms downstairs and two rooms up with a lean-to kitchen added on to the back. A parlor and John's office filled the front two rooms of the first floor. Later described by John as "my pretty little farm" or jokingly, my "Lilliputian Plantation."

As the years went by and business prospered Adams purchased small par-cels of land. When his brother Peter moved on to his new wife's farm, John purchased the remaining fifty-three acres of the family homestead and the buildings including the 1681 house.

All of John and Abigail's children were born there in what John called "my humble House." Abigail's thrift and skillful management of the family funds and farms were the secrets to Adams's economic prosperity. As Jefferson remarked to Madison in a May 25, 1788, letter. "His pecuniary affairs were under the direction of *Mrs Adams*, one of the most estimable characters on earth, and the most attentive & honorable economists. Neither had a wish to lay up a copper, but both wished to make both ends meet." Jefferson was only partially correct. Abigail had an eye to their future prosperity.

In 1787 thanks in no small measure to Abigail's financial management, they were able to purchase a nearby stately manor home of seven large rooms with several smaller servant rooms that had been built in 1731 as a summer home by a wealthy American Tory and Jamaican sugar planter, Leonard Vassall. In 1787 while minister to Great Britain John Adams purchased the house called Peacefield from Leonard Vassall Borland, descendant of the prominent loyalist family who settled in Bristol, England after the war. The house came with three barns, a wood house, a corncrib and eighty-eight acres. And it was conveniently located a little over a mile from the older Adams homes. After a decade Abigail became tired of the size of the house after living in mansions in Paris, London, New York, Philadelphia, and Washington, D.C. and added a two and one-half story kitchen and servants quarters to the Georgian styled house.

Now located in the midst of busy urban Quincy, it is difficult to imagine the rural small town atmosphere surrounding the Adams homes and farms in the eighteenth century.

Adams decided to "lay fast hold of the Town of Braintree and embrace it." So in an August 27, 1787, letter he directed Abigail's uncle, Cotton Tufts, to purchase any piece of land "that adjoins upon me, which is offered to Sale, at what you shall judge an Advantagious Price, especially Salt Marsh & Woodland."

By 1789 their land holdings totaled 446 acres, but then Adams added 30 acres in 1790, and 20 acres in 1791. Abigail had also inherited half of an 86-acre farm in Medford and purchased 1650 unimproved acres in Vermont. In 1800 flush with money after receiving a presidential salary of $25,000 for four years, the Adams added a large two and one-half story wing on the east end of the house called Peacefield. The house remained in the Adams family until 1947 when it became a national park.

Jefferson was born at Shadwell, a one and one-half story frame house constructed by his father around 1737 and named for the English home parish of Peter Jefferson. Jefferson spent little time at Shadwell, because his family moved to the Randolph plantation of Tuckahoe when he was two and remained there for nine years. Shadwell burned on February 1, 1770, while Jefferson was away on legal business. Jefferson later built a smaller house on the site for his mother and her slaves.

Fortunately, Jefferson had already planned to move his home to the top of a nearby hill, Monticello.

Jefferson later gave a glorified description of the hill Monticello to Maria Cosway, the woman he became infatuated with while minister to France. This oft quoted paragraph from his famous Head and Heart letter of October 12, 1786 reflects his idealized view. "And our own dear Monticello, where has Nature spread so rich a mantle under the eye? mountains, forests, rocks, rivers. With what majesty do we there ride above the storms! How sublime to look down into the workhouse of nature, to see her clouds, hail, snow, rain, thunder, all fabricated at our feet! And the glorious Sun, when rising as if out of a distant water, just gilding the tops of the mountains, and giving life to all nature!"

There he built a small brick building, later called the South Pavilion. When Thomas and Martha were married they moved into this small brick building with a shingled roof, living primarily on the second floor with a kitchen below. Jefferson's house on Monticello was under construction for over thirty years because he kept enlarging and improving the Palladian symmetrical style brick and frame house. Family members and visitors alike complained that it was in a state of constant construction. As finally finished in 1810, Monticello was a large (101 feet by 84 feet) three-story brick house with two-long largely underground dependency wings. Monticello has been considered one of the architectural gems of America.

Jefferson began construction on Poplar Forest a summer retreat in 1806 on nearly five thousand acres near Lynchburg in Bedford County, Virginia. After his presidency Jefferson made one to two trips per year to the Palladian style brick house--sometimes to escape the many visitors and family members at Monticello and other times to supervise his labor force on his most productive land. Designed by Jefferson Poplar Forest was the first octagonal house built in the United States. It has sides that measure twenty feet and porticos to the north and south.

Neither the homes of Jefferson nor Adams could have competed with the contemporary English country estate houses or the palatial town houses in London and Paris with which both men were so familiar. Even when Jefferson's Monticello reached twenty-one rooms it paled when compared to the hundred-room country houses of the English and French landed nobility. Adams's farm, large by New England standards, was denigrated by the visiting Rochefoucauld-Liancourt's 1799 report that "no Paris advocate of the lowest rank" would be caught dead living there.

Even Abigail complained to her daughter when they returned from England in 1788, that her house was so small it "feels like a wren's house."

Jefferson imagined his own little agricultural village in the image of the Roman or British gentry. Slaves, indentured servants and hired hands provided house servants, carpenters, coopers, sawyers, weavers, distillers, tanners, curriers, and field laborers to carry out the extensive operations of the plantations. Economic autonomy would ensure political independence, in Jefferson's view. It was an illusion sustained in the face of chronic crop failures and dependence on foreign merchants for the sale of cash crops and the purchase of refined manufactured goods.

Adams and Jefferson liked farming and found much comfort and little profit in tilling the soil. Seldom was either a hands on farmer until they retired from public office. Jefferson had overseers and hundreds of slaves to work his thousands of acres. Adams had his wife Abigail to oversee the work of a few farm laborers on his farm. At times Adams employed five or more hired hands and oxen to harvest crops, such as barley, potatoes, corn, oats, and hay, and for clearing his land of trees and rocks. Upon returning home in 1788 from his years in Europe and London, Adams remarked to an English friend. "It is not large, in the first place. It is but the farm of a patriot."

Adams tried some of the new farming innovations, but he was not an experimenter on the level of Jefferson. Farmer Adams planted clover and grasses in his fields and was convinced that good manure for the fields was the key to success. Adams tried growing hemp as a possible cash crop. Adams even wrote a scientific paper on "making Experiments, upon Soils and Manures, Grains and Grasses, Trees and Bushes."

Jefferson was very much interested in crop rotation to preserve the soils and enlarge the yields. Jefferson advocated contour plowing and even helped develop a plow that reduced erosion on the Piedmont hills. Jefferson grew or tried to grow hundreds of varieties of fruits, vegetables, shrubs, trees and other vegetation. Jefferson helped introduce Merino sheep in Virginia as a way to improve the production of American made woolens.

Adams, more than Jefferson, was a hands on farmer and gardener. Riding his horse to observe plantation operations Jefferson seldom dirtied his hands, while Adams seemed to enjoy being up to his elbows and knees in his manure pile. When it came to the physical activity of felling trees, collecting seaweed for fertilizer, sowing and harvesting the crops, digging ditches for his ha-ha (the au courant fencing by ditching) Adams was right in there along side his hired hands. Jefferson was more director than physical participant. Even in his beloved vegetable and flower gardens slaves did the real work.

Like most absentee gentleman farmers, much of his farming pleasure resided in Adams's imagination, as when he wrote to Abigail in January 1794, while serving as vice-president in Philadelphia. "I begin to think all time lost that is not employed in farming; innocent, healthy, gay, elegant amusement! Enchanting employment!" Adams no doubt ended this muse when he closed the letter and returned to the business of government and politics.

Adams jokingly suggested in 1801 changing the name of his farm from Peacefield to Stony Field, which would be much more descriptive of a New England farm. Adams, like Jefferson, was so attached to the soil, that when Abigail suggested in 1790 they sell land and put the money into government bonds, he refused, holding "his faith in land as true wealth."

Thanks to Abigail and to a natural frugality, Adams's farms were profitable and he never suffered from the financial indebtedness of Jefferson. The Virginian was chronically in debt. Not even the hundreds of thousands of dollars he received in government salaries could overcome his repeated renovations of each of his residences, his love of expensive wine, books, fine clothes, and exuberant entertaining. Not even the labor of hundreds of slaves and even their selective sale could save the improvident Jefferson from constant heavy indebtedness.

Even though Adams was not as "wealthy" as Jefferson, his financial status was certainly more secure. This was due in no small part to the hundreds of thousands of dollars he received from public offices and to Abigail who was the real manager of their farms, money, and rental properties.

Adams's practical mind kept his focus on crops rather than gardens, remarking in this diary that the formal British gardens were "Ostentations of Vanity." Both Adams and Jefferson were surprised and disappointed to find large numbers of common American plants in the best British gardens when they toured them while serving as American ministers to Great Britain and France.

Jefferson did develop large gardens at Monticello in emulation of the large gardens he had seen in England and France, but not so Adams.

But Adams did maintain the long triangular beds lined by boxwoods surrounding fruit trees at the old Vassall house. Adams happily noted in a May 1, 1817, letter to his grandson-in-law John P. DeMint. "You would be pleased to see the pretty Figure your Peach Trees and Cherry Trees make in my Garden." And the descendants of a White York rose brought back from England by Abigail in 1788 still flourish at the Old House.

Both men hailed small farmers as the backbone of an "agrarian republic" of independent freemen. Both supported agricultural societies and awards for successful innovative farming.

Adams had relatively small flower and vegetable gardens. Small plots of grass marked the front of his houses. Classical flower gardens laid out in rectangles bordered by boxwood hedges stood behind the houses. Lilacs and other flowering bushes delineated the entrances to the house. Large orchards of peaches, pears and apples stood nearby. Even the vines shading the porch on Peacefield provided concord grapes for the kitchen. Fenced vegetable gardens provided rhubarb, strawberries, potatoes, beans and root crops. Adams like Jefferson received some exotic plants, such as African pumpkins and peppers from Constantinople, but he did not seek them out, as did Jefferson. Stonewalls divided his fields and marked his boundaries.

Jefferson's gardens were huge compared to those of Adams. He told his friend, Madame de Tessé that he had always favored the planting of trees and "scarcely ever planted a flower in my life", but when he retired "I believe I shall become a florist" because "the labours of the year, in that line, are repaid within the year." He told John Barnes in 1809, that my "gardens added wonderfully to my happiness." Now famous for his thousand foot garden terrace,

Jefferson was content for most of his life with a more modest planting area. Not until he retired from the presidency in 1809 did he have time to develop his large flower and vegetable gardens. Supplied with seeds and plants from friends in the United States and Europe, Jefferson's Monticello came to resemble a botanical garden.

Jefferson corresponded widely with men and women about farming and plants. He collected American plants and seeds and shipped them to Europe. His friends, in turn, sent him similar objects from their own gardens. Rice seeds received from Europe, for example, failed in Virginia but flourished on his friends' lands in Georgia.

"Botany is the school of patience," he counseled Madame de Tessé in an April 25, 1788 letter.

However, Jefferson and Adams seldom discussed agriculture with each other in their hundreds of letters. One exception was Jefferson's May 25, 1795, letter during his self-imposed absence from national political office. "We have had a hard winter and backward spring. This injured our wheat so much that it cannot be made a good crop by all the showers of heaven, which are now falling down on us exactly as we want them. Our first cutting of clover is not yet begun. Strawberries not ripe till within this fortnight, and every thing backward in proportion. What with my farming and my nail manufactory I have my hands full. I am on horseback half the day, and counting and measuring nails the other half. I am trying potatoes on a large scale as a substitute for Indian corn for feeding animals. This is new in this country, but in this culture we cannot rival you." Adams, who planted potatoes for human as well as animal consumption, did not respond.

The expeditions of Lewis and Clark and Zebulon Pike provided Jefferson with a bonanza of plants from the western plains and mountains with which to experiment.

While most of the seeds and plants went to Bernard McMahon and William Hamilton in Philadelphia, Jefferson kept some of the Mandan tobacco, currants, prairie flax, Osage oranges, the flowering pea of Arkansas, the yellow Arikara bean, snowberries, and the yellow lily from the Columbia River valley which were planted at Monticello.

Adams received neither seeds nor plants from the Lewis and Clark Expedition, and it does not appear he was the least bit interested.

Gerard W. Gawalt

Jefferson spent hours recording the success or failure of new crops, valued seeds, and the productivity of his slaves in his farm book. He had many records of prospective profits, but few of real expences. If records could make a man wealthy, Jefferson would have died a rich man rather than a debtor.

Both Jefferson and Adams sought to manage their plantations or farms in a profitable manner. Thanks to his wife Abigail Adams was more successful than Jefferson. Both men's establishments were representative of the wealthy segment of society in Massachusetts and Virginia.

Despite all of Jefferson's innovative ideas and botanical experiments, his plantation farming methods were frozen in time. "Gangs" of slaves led by overseers and drivers continued to grow crops in the traditional inefficient ways with rudimentary farming equipment and relying too much on human power. Overseers who were often paid a percentage of the tobacco crop were extremely reluctant to try new methods or even abandon tobacco cultivation for grain crops that would deplete the soil less quickly. Large plantations with hundreds of acres of land discouraged many of the innovative techniques used on smaller European farms to improve the soils and fertilize the crops.

Jefferson, more than Adams, sought personal autonomy through economic independence and a self-sustaining farming operation. Their gentlemanly life-styles, however, were only sustained by infusions of cash from public salaries and, in the case of Jefferson, periodic sales of slaves and increasingly heavy mortgages and debts.

## SLAVERY

When Jefferson and Adams drafted the document declaring, "all men are created equal," they set a standard that has forever since become both a goal and a test. For centuries these words have been a clarion call to men and women throughout the world to seek political and social equality and freedom. Neither man was able to transfer this enlightened principle of the equality of all humanity into political or social reality. For Jefferson this phrase has become proof of a slaveholder's hypocrisy. To their credit they enunciated this ideal and raised the flag of equality. To their detriment they were never able to put their words into action. When they lived and when they died, racism and sexism remained cultural and political realities in the United States and the world.

Adams was no stranger to slavery, even though he did not own any. The slave trade was a staple of New England commerce and hundreds of slaves lived and labored in New England. Closer to home Abigail's family had owned two slaves as servants when John married into the Smith family. When her father died in 1783 he gave his slave Phoebe her freedom if "she chuse it" or she could live with Abigail or one of her sisters. Abigail oversaw her freedom according to her wishes and her father's will. When Abigail sailed for Europe in 1784, Abigail left her father's former slave Phoebe and her husband William Abdee to live in her and John's house and be supplied from the Adams family farm.

John said in 1819, "I have, through my whole life held the practice of slavery in such abhorrence, that I have never owned a negro or any other slave, though I lived for many years in times, when the practice was not disgraceful, when the best of men in my vicinity thought it not inconsistent with their character, and when it cost me thousands of dollars for the labor and subsistence of free men, when I might have saved by the purchase of negroes at times when they were very cheap." He decried it as "an evil of colossal magnitude."

But he defended the rights of slave owners in New England courts. Most notable was the case of Newport v. Billing heard at the Hampshire Superior Court in Springfield in 1768. The plaintiff, Amos Newport, sued for freedom but Adams successfully convinced a jury that the plaintiff was indeed the slave of Joseph Billings. In a March 21, 1795, letter to the historian Jeremy Belknap, Adams reported that he was "concerned in several Causes in which Negroes sued for their Freedom (omitting the fact that he represented the masters) and incorrectly remembered "I never knew a Jury by a Verdict, to determine a Negro to be a Slave."

When he helped draft the 1779 Massachusetts Constitution, he did not argue for the outright abolition of slavery. He preferred the process of gradual emancipation. But his friend and colleague, William Cushing, sitting as chief justice of the Massachusetts Supreme Court, ruled in 1783 that slavery violated the state constitution. Much later in an April 8, 1810, letter to Colonel Joseph Ward, Adams would condemn slavery as a "foul contagion in the human character."

Gerard W. Gawalt

After 1774 when his wife inherited 135 slaves, Jefferson controlled or owned roughly two hundred slaves. Over the course of his life he owned more than 600 slaves. Those were the people who labored for Jefferson's happiness. Jefferson's sales and occasional runaways kept the number fairly constant. Although Jefferson often referred to his slaves as "my family," he sold ninety slaves to raise money and gifted seventy-six slaves to his daughters and sisters in the decade after the American Revolution. Jefferson never engaged in commercial slave dealing as his father-in-law John Wayles had done, but he often sold slaves when he needed money or to dispose of a recalcitrant slave. Occasionally Jefferson had more humanitarian reasons, as when he sold Brown Colbert so he could reunite with his wife, or purchased Ursula's husband, John Granger. "Nobody feels more strongly that I do the desire to make all practicable sacrifices to keep man and wife together who have imprudently married out of their respective families "(i.e. their master's holdings), wrote Jefferson to Randolph Lewis on April 23, 1807. The dark side of this wish was the rewarding of slaves who married within the family and the punishment of slaves who did not.

Whether Jefferson treated his slaves well is immaterial to the larger issue. Still there is clear evidence that Jefferson's slaves fared no better than most. Slaves, even children, were regularly whipped if they were truant from work, misbehaved, ran away, or defied their owner and his overseers. Runaways or rebellious slaves were severely punished and sold. Miscegenation was normal, whether it was consensual or not. There is no bright side to slavery in Jefferson's plantation world.

Jefferson asserted in his autobiography that he tried to secure passage of a bill in 1769 that would have given slave owners unfettered rights to free their slaves. The measure, which was actually submitted by Richard Bland, failed amidst the "grossest indecorum."

Within a year Jefferson made a plea for the individual rights of freedom for all men, black or white. As the lawyer to Samuel Howell who was suing Wade Netherland to secure his freedom, Jefferson argued "everyone comes into this world with a right to his own person and using it at this own will." The court ordered Howell, the son of an enslaved mixed race mother, to remain in servitude even though his grandmother had been a free white person.

Jefferson drafted a paragraph for the Declaration of Independence condemning the British for encouraging slavery and the slave trade. The Congress removed this paragraph during its revisions.

Jefferson introduced the bill in the Virginia Assembly that made it in 1778 the first state to ban the importation of slaves from Africa. By 1807 when the Federal Government banned the importation of slaves during Jefferson's administration, every state except South Carolina had followed Virginia's example.

Jefferson wrote his strongest denunciation of slavery while hiding from British troops in a small house on his Bedford County lands in 1781. In what was later called "Notes on the State of Virginia," Jefferson condemned "The whole commerce between master and slave" as "a perpetual exercise of the most boisterous passions, the most unremitting despotisms on the one part, and degrading submissions on the other." "Indeed," concluded Jefferson, "I tremble for my country when I reflect that God is just: that his justice cannot sleep forever."

On the political stage neither Adams nor Jefferson was willing to directly confront the existence of slavery, but Jefferson did oppose its expansion. On March 1, 1784, Jefferson proposed to abolish slavery in the Northwest Territories by 1800. Congress removed this from Jefferson's proposed Northwest Ordinance. This would be the high mark of Jefferson's anti-slavery actions.

While in Europe he claimed to have proposed a plan that would have freed all children born to slaves after 1800. The only action supported by the evidence is a letter to Madison proposing that Madison draft a bill to that effect but not to involve him. At the same time he was defending his inaction to the French writer, Jean Nicolas Démeunier, in a June 26, 1786, letter. "The moment of" freeing slaves "with success", argued Jefferson, "was not yet arrived, and that an unsuccessful effort, as too often happens, would only rivet still closer the chains of bondage, and retard the moment of delivery."

Jefferson could always find a reason to continue to hold "those who labor for my happiness" in bondage.

Jefferson insisted in a January 26, 1789, letter to the Englishman Edward Bancroft, "To give liberty to, or rather, to abandon persons whose habits have been formed in slavery is like abandoning children." In other words slavery was a never ending, self-perpetuating continuum.

Gerard W. Gawalt

Closely following the political crises leading to the Missouri Compromise of 1820, Adams revealed his fears and feelings on slavery to Jefferson in a famous February 3, 1821, letter. "Slavery in this Country I have seen hanging over it like a black cloud for half a Century. If I were as drunk with enthusiasm as Swedenborg or Wesley, I might probably say I had seen Armies of Negroes marching and countermarching in the air, shining in Armour. I have been so terrified with this Phenomenon that I constantly said in former times to the Southern Gentlemen, I cannot comprehend this object; I must leave it to you. I will vote for forceing no measure against your judgements. What we are to see, God knows, and I leave it to him, and his agents in Posterity."

Jefferson did not reply. But in an even more well known August 25, 1814, letter to his neighbor and protégé Edward Coles who challenged Jefferson to join with him in freeing his slaves in the territory north of the Ohio River. Jefferson excused his failure to act and passed the "enterprise" to "the young." My views "on the subject of slavery of negroes have long been in possession of the public, and time has only served to give them stronger root. The love of justice and the love of country plead equally the cause of these people, and it is a moral reproach to us that they should have pleaded it so long in vain, and should have produced not a single effort, nay. I fear not much serious willingness to relieve them & ourselves from our present condition of moral & political reprobation. From those of the former generation who were in the fullness of age when I came into public life…I soon saw that nothing was to be hoped. Nursed and educated in the daily habit of seeing the degraded condition, both bodily and mental, of those unfortunate beings, not reflecting that that degradation was very much the work of themselves & their fathers, few minds have yet doubted but that they were as legitimate subjects of property as their horses and cattle." Jefferson asserted. "I may say till I returned to reside at home in 1809, I had little opportunity of knowing the progress of public sentiment here on this subject. "Jefferson rationalized that "I had always hoped that the younger generation receiving their early impressions after the flame of liberty had been kindled in every breast" would be different. But, Jefferson concluded, they had not made the progress "towards this point I had hoped."

Jefferson hoped for a plan of "gradual extinction" of slavery through a long term of staggered emancipation based on birth dates. Because slavery has rendered them "as incapable as children of taking care of themselves" and when freed "they are pests in society by their idleness, and the depredations to which this leads them."

Now, Jefferson pleaded "this enterprise is for the young; these are the only weapons of an old man." Jefferson even chided Coles who planned to move to the Northwest Territory and free his slaves. "Are you right in abandoning this property, and your country with it? I think not." Rather Coles should stay in Virginia and fight for "this doctrine truly Christian." In 1819 Coles moved to the Illinois Territory and freed his slaves.

Even when Jefferson was apparently offered money by his old "friend" Tadeusz Kosciuszko, a veteran of the American Revolution and a Polish freedom fighter, to free his slaves, he found ways to delay the decision and ultimately turn it aside.

Jefferson recognized the threat to the union posed by slavery and the fight over its expansion into the western territories. During the 1820 fight over the admission of Missouri as a slave state into the union, Jefferson warned it was "like a fire bell in the night" that could sound "the knell of the Union." Foreseeing secession looming, he told Adams: "But the Missouri question is a breaker on which we lose the Missouri country by revolt, what more, God only knows."

Adams too recognized the danger but hoped the Missouri Question "will follow the other Waves under the Ship and do no harm."

The abolition of slavery was certainly beyond both men's capabilities and almost beyond their comprehensions.

The next year they continued their debate. Jefferson wrote on January 22, 1821. "The real question, as seen in the states afflicted with this unfortunate population, is Are our slaves to be presented with freedom and a dagger? For if Congress has a power to regulate the conditions of the inhabitants of the states, within the states, it will be but another exercise of that power to declare that all shall be free. Are we then to see again Athenian and Lacedemonian confederacies? To wage another Peloponessian war to settle the ascendancy between them? Or is this the tocsin of merely a servile war? Surely they will parley awhile, and give us time to get out of the way."

Then Adams, despite his hatred "of that foul contagion in the human character, Negro slavery," confessed in his February 3 reply to his lifelong avoidance of the issue of slavery in the political arena. "Slavery in this Country

I have seen hanging over it like a black cloud for half a Century. If I were as drunk with enthusiasm as Swedenborg or Wesley, I might probably say I had seen Armies of Negroes marching and countermarching in the air, shining in Armour. I have been so terrified with this Phenomenon that I constantly said in former times to the Southern Gentlemen, I cannot comprehend this object; I must leave it to you. I will vote for forceing no measure against your judgements. What we are to see, God knows, and I leave it to him, and his agents in posterity."

Jefferson perhaps summarized the conundrum the best. "But, as it is, we have the wolf by the ears, and we can neither hold him, nor safely let him go. Justice is in one scale, and self-preservation in the other."

Even if Jefferson had the will to free all his slaves, he didn't have the means. He had no other means of settling his debts of more than $100,000 than the sale of his slaves. Moreover, under Virginia law Jefferson's estate would have had to guarantee payment for their support, training/education and land for farming. Washington may have had the will and the money, but Jefferson did not. He could have led them to freedom like Edward Coles but he did not.

In the end Jefferson, who would call slavery "a hideous blot," could only muster the will to free several members of the Hemings family, most of who were related to his wife and/or himself. He did free all of his and Sally Hemings's children. Jefferson provided funds for Harriet and Beverly to "run away." Madison and Eston gained their freedom in his will. His overseer Edmund Bacon reported that people were saying when Harriet ran away that Jefferson "freed her because she was his own daughter." Even when asked in a March 26, 1792, letter from his friend Benjamin Rush, to manumit or sell a slave of his to the woman's husband, John Hall, there is no evidence of action by Jefferson.

It is not remarkable that Jefferson freed his own children or relatives of his deceased wife. What is remarkable is that Jefferson, like many slave masters, kept his children and relatives enslaved for years and years.

And within the next generation hundreds of thousands of Americans would die when the volcano of slavery could no longer be suppressed and politicians, like Adams and Jefferson, could no longer pass on the responsibility of abolishing slavery to future generations.

# RELIGION

Organized religion did not play a significant role in the personal life of either Adams or Jefferson—their political lives were another question. In form Adams was a Congregationalist and Jefferson was an Episcopalian. In practice Jefferson and Adams were creatures of the Enlightenment and religion was more a subject for intellectual debate than sincere worship either within or outside of an institutional structure.

While in the Continental Congress the men clashed over a day of prayer and fasting. Adams, of course, favored the plan, while Jefferson opposed it and seemed to denigrate Christianity. According to Benjamin Rush's later recollection, Adams castigated Jefferson saying I have "never known a man of sound sense and genius that was an enemy to Christianity." It would not be the last time they would disagree.

One Enlightenment principle both men would agree on and champion was the principle of freedom of worship or religion without governmental interference. Jefferson considered his drafting a Virginia statute to provide freedom of religion one of his greatest achievements. In 1779 Adams drafted a clause for the Massachusetts constitution of 1780 that declared that it was "the duty" of everyone to worship "The Supreme Being, the great creator and preserver of the universe" and that no one should be "hurt, molested, or restrained in his person, liberty, or estate for worshipping God in the manner most agreeable to the dictates of his own conscience."

At nearly the same time, Jefferson had drafted a Virginia statute of religious freedom in 1777 that was submitted to the legislature on June 12, 1779, and was finally adopted by the Virginia Assembly on January 16, 1786. Jefferson, too, insisted that no one should be compelled to attend or support a religion and that "all men shall be free to profess, and by argument to maintain, their opinions in matters of Religion" without suffering physical or financial harm or diminishing "their civil capacities." Moreover, a 1777 broadside supporting Jefferson's proposal argued that "forcing him to support this or that teacher of his own persuasion is depriving him of the comfortable liberty" and to "compel a man to furnish contributions of money for the propagation of opinion which he disbelieves is sinful and tyrannical."

Gerard W. Gawalt

Jefferson was proud of America's religious freedom, writing to Roman Catholic Maria Cosway on January 31, 1803 that she need not fear for Catholics in America: "all religions here are equally free and equally protected by the laws, and left to be supported by their own votaries, in some places the Catholic is better off than other sects." He refused to support institutional religion, testily responding to his friend Margaret Bayard Smith on August 6, 1816, that ministers have resented the Virginia Act of Religious Freedom and therefore labeled him "Atheist, Deist or Devil." But Jefferson continued I "have ever thought religion a concern purely between our god and our consciences, for which we are accountable to him, and not to priests."

Jefferson believed in a lower case "god" and as he grew older in an afterlife. An occasional churchgoer, Jefferson did his duty as vestryman. Two things are certain about Jefferson and religion. He opposed the concept of an established church and fought the power of religions' institutions. When it came to religion he was a democrat.

In 1819 and 1820 Jefferson spent days compiling a story of Jesus' life and moral teaching by cutting and pasting from printed New Testament texts to produce a religious book attuned to enlightenment sensibilities. Jefferson's "The Life and Morals of Jesus of Nazareth" excluded all references to miracles, the resurrection, atonement for sins on the cross and other claims of his godliness. He relegated all parts that could not be explained by his "reason" to "the dung-hill." The resulting bound scrapbook, often referred to as the "Jefferson Bible," provided Jefferson with a ready reading book that has beguiled historians and religious scholars.

Whatever Jefferson's religion, neither his religion nor his enlightened morality led him to overcome his paternalistic culture to intervene on behalf of his daughter, granddaughters and sister against their alcoholic and violently abusive spouses. Not to mention the moral issue of slavery or intrigues with married women.

Whether Jefferson can be considered a Christian or simply an Enlightenment deist is still the subject of considerable debate.

When pushed to declare an adherence to Christianity or any particular form of religion, Jefferson would refuse to be categorized, as he explained in his August 6, 1816, letter to Margaret Bayard Smith. "The priests indeed have heretofore thought proper to ascribe to me religious, or rather antireligious sentiments, of their own fabric, but soothed their resentments against the Act of Virginia for establishing religious freedom, they wished him to be thought Atheist, Deist or Devil, who could advocate freedom from their religious dictations. but I have ever thought religion a concern purely between our god and our consciences, for which we were accountable to him, and not to the priests. I never told my own religion, nor scrutinized that of another." "But," continued Jefferson, "this does not satisfy the priesthood. they must have a positive, a declared assent to all their interested absurdities. my opinion is that there would never have been an infidel, if there had never been a priest." In short, as to his religious beliefs, "I shall leave them, as heretofore to grope on in the dark." And still we do.

Born and raised a New England Congregationalist, Adams might have become a minister after his Harvard education. However, he never really gave it serious consideration. Later in life he remembered in this autobiography that his experience with ecclesiastical debates in the house of Deacon Adams convinced him that he was too contentious for a preacher. "I saw such a spirit of dogmatism and bigotry in clergy and laity, that if I should be a priest I must take my side, and pronounce as positively as any of them, or never get a parish, or getting it must soon leave it." But a litigating lawyer, that was just his cup of tea.

Adams's doubts started early and remained throughout this life. In a February 22, 1756, diary entry Adams mocked the idea that if everyone followed the dictates of the bible life would be grand: "What a Utopia; what a Paradise would this region be!" As to "The church of Rome" their opinion that "no man can be saved out of their church" was a "dreadful opinion" made under the "influence of ignorant or wicked priests." On that score Adams and Jefferson were in agreement.

While a delegate to Congress in Philadelphia Adams would attend church at least once sometimes three times on a Sunday. But he was a man at an intellectual buffet, sampling services by Roman Catholics, Presbyterians, Anglicans, Methodists, Baptists, Quakers and German Moravians. His diaries are filled with his comments on ministers, music, and ceremonies. Like an anthropologist, Adams reported to Abigail on his attendance at St. Mary's Catholic Church. He found the service awesome and "affecting," while "the dress of the priest was rich with lace." Still his Congregational background led him to pity "the poor wretches fingering their beads, chanting Latin, not a word of which they understood." Still, he was clearly curious.

Many scholarly and popular writings have been devoted to analyzing the religion of these men. Jefferson's religion or lack of religion has drawn more than its share of criticism and adulation ever since his presidential campaign of 1796.

Later in life both men would devote many hours and long letters to discussing religion with each other and with others.

Adams considered himself a firm Protestant, but for long periods of time did not regularly attend church. When his dear daughter Nabby died, Adams affirmed to Jefferson in a September 14, 1813, letter that "my religion" is "the love of God and His creation, delight, joy, triumph, exultation in my own existence." Adams continued. Calvinists "will say, I am no Christian: I say Ye are no Christians: and there the Account is ballanced. Yet I believe all the honest men among you are Christians in my Sense of the Word."

By April 19, 1817, Adams could assert to Jefferson. "Without Religion this World would be Something not fit to be mentioned in polite Company, I mean Hell." Jefferson responded that the world would be better without "Sectarian dogmas" but "if the sublime doctrines of philanthropism, and deism taught us by Jesus of Nazareth in which all agree, constitute true religion, then, without it, this would be, as you again say, 'something not fit to be named, even indeed a Hell'."

When elected a delegate to the Massachusetts convention of 1820 to revise the very constitution he had drafted four decades earlier in 1779, Adams found the energy to attend and put forward an amendment offering religious freedom for all in the state and a separation of church and state thereby undoing the established church system he had supported in 1779. In a February 3, 1821, letter to Jefferson, Adams attributed part of his failure to his poor performance in debate where "I boggled and blundered more than a young fellow just rising to speak at the bar." Despite Adams's failed proposal, Jefferson congratulated him in a January 22, 1821, letter on having "had health and spirits enough to take part in the late convention of your state and for his attempt to "advance liberalism" and "get back to the freedom it enjoyed 2000 years ago."

Jefferson told Adams that his own faith "is known to my God and myself alone. Its evidence before the world is to be sought in my life; if that has been honest and dutiful to society, the religion which has regulated it cannot be a bad one."

And in truth, only their God and themselves knew the faith of Jefferson and Adams.


## HEALTH AND DIET

Adams was a bit of a hypochondriac –Jefferson not so much. Both men suffered migraine headaches when stressed. Adams's health was also prone to break down during periods of stress and hard work. In his autobiography, Adams reported that in 1770 the pressure of overwork and trying the Boston Massacre cases "exhausted my health, brought on pain in my breast and complaint in my lungs" forcing him to leave Boston and return to Braintree where "the fine breezes from the sea" and "daily rides on horseback" revived his health. Again and again Adams would fall victim to headaches and "nervous fever."

It appeared Adams would keep bad health hovering overhead, in case he needed an excuse. On October 9, 1781, after a grueling but failed effort to secure loans from Holland, Adams wrote to Abigail he had been suffering from "a nervous fever of a dangerous kind, bordering on putrid. It seized upon my head in such a manner that for five or six days I was lost." When he was appointed American minister to Great Britain, Adams wrote to a friend Richard Cranch, in an April 27, 1785 letter "although my Health is dear to me, the Public Peace, and Prosperity are dearer." In a January 20, 1796, letter Adams informed Abigail that he was "heir apparent" to Washington, but worried to Abigail that his health might not sustain him in the presidency.

John was an inveterate pipe and cigar smoker throughout his life. What adverse effect it had on his health is not known. Certainly everyone, particularly women, inhaled enough smoke from wood fires to equal a heavy smoker.

Jefferson too suffered from migraines, the after effects of his broken wrist suffered in France, an occasional kidney stone or prostate problem, and chronic colitis in later years. In general he enjoyed fine health, according to the testimony he gave Benjamin Hawkins in a February 23, 1803, letter. "I retain myself very perfect health, having not had 20 hours of fever in 42 years past.

I have sometimes had a troublesome headache, and some slight rheumatic pains, but now sixty years old nearly, I have little to complain of in point of health as most people."

Some of his good health could be attributed to his practice of bathing his feet in cold water every morning, according to Jefferson. But he was not a fan of a cold bath each day.

Adams did not like exposure to cold air while sleeping. When Adams and Franklin shared a room while on a diplomatic mission to New York during the revolution, Franklin opened the window in their room when they retired. Adams, reportedly, got up and closed it. Franklin told Adams he would suffocate without fresh air. Adams told Franklin he "was afraid of the evening air." Finally Adams agree to go to bed with the window open as Franklin continued to belabor Adams with his theories of colds and fresh air.

Jefferson but not Adams was a big fan of exercising for good health. Adams did, however, admit to horseback riding and sea breezes restoring his health after the Boston Massacre trials. Jefferson was particularly fond of walking and horseback riding. And by all accounts he sat a horse extremely well. He told David Howell in a December 15, 1810, letter "I give more time to exercise of the body than of the mind, believing it wholesome to both." He urged his children and young relatives not to sacrifice health for learning. Once telling his daughter Martha not "to consider yourself as unemployed while taking exercise." However, he warned his nephew Peter Carr, in an August 15, 1785, instruction against games. "Games played with the ball & others of that nature, are too violent for the body & stamp no character on the mind." Wonder what he would have thought of modern football or hockey! Instead he recommended "the gun. While this gives a moderate exercise to the body, it gives boldness, enterprise and independence to the mind." Jefferson added. "Let your gun therefore be the constant companion of your walks."

Despite occasional bouts of bad health, Adams and Jefferson each managed to live a full life and reach an envious old age. But in the years just before death an intestinal illness, probably colitis, and prostate problems laid Jefferson low, and hearing hindered his conversational skills. As Adams neared his eightieth year he suffered from rheumatism, the loss of his teeth, blindness and palsy.

Jefferson was a lover of fine food and wine. Adams—not so much.

Still when Adams was American minister to Great Britain, Jefferson wrote Abigail on January 21, 1785, asking her to tell John "I had before ordered his Madeira and Frontignac." Six months later Adams was ordering even more wine. In a June 7, 1785, letter to Jefferson, John cut back on his wine order because of a British limits on imports. "For Mercy Sake stop all my Wine but the Bourdeaux and Madeira, and Frontenac. And stop my order to Rouen for 500 Additional Bottles. I shall be ruined, for each Minister is not permitted to import more than 5 or 600 Bottles which will not more than cover what I have at the Hague which is very rich wine and my Madeira Frontenac and Bourdeaux at Auteuil." Jefferson later took the cask of wine at Auteuil off Adams's hands. Wow! Adams was not all hard cider and birch beer.

Still he did like hard cider every morning. Adams jokingly told his friend and cousin, Zabdiel Adams, in a July 23, 1763, letter. "Give me Bacon, and Cyder and Book and Girl and Friend, and I will frisk it, like a Lambkin among the Clover." Sounds like a recipe for a happy life.

Some say Jefferson became enamored of French food when he was minister to France. But Jefferson had even employed a French cook when he was a member of the Confederation Congress in Annapolis in 1783. When he went to France, he brought along his slave James Hemings to be trained in the cooking of French pastries and food. When he returned he brought along his French butler and cook, Adrien Petit, to manage his household and kitchen.

Recipes for delicacies, like Pêche Flambée, were scattered in Jefferson's personal papers. His plan for a macaroni maker is famous. When traveling in northern Italy he acquired a pasta maker. He became such an aficionado of macaroni and spaghetti that when he returned to Virginia he experimented with more than twenty different varieties of tomatoes for his sauces.

Books have been written about Jefferson and his love of wine. For Jefferson wine was good and bad. On the good side he enjoyed a wide variety of expensive wines and he encouraged the growth of wine quality grapes in Virginia. On the bad side his expenditures for wine and his failed efforts to grow wine quality grapes contributed to his financial ruin.

When Jefferson ordered wine it was always "the best possible." In one month at the President's House he served 207 bottles of Champagne to 651 guests. During his first term in office, Jefferson spent 7597 dollars on wine. Even with a salary of 25,000 dollars per year, this was extravagant. President

Jefferson instructed a complaining James Hoban to dig a sixteen-foot deep wine cellar under the President's House. No doubt the British appreciated the wine cellar when they sacked the President's House in 1814.

Jefferson encouraged Philip Mazzei, the Italian liberal and scientist, to settle in Virginia and produce wine. In fact, Mazzei did purchase a plantation in Virginia. The winemaking operation failed and ultimately Jefferson "borrowed" the money from the sale of Mazzei's property.

Jefferson was constantly asking his correspondents in France, Italy, and the United States to send him grape cuttings that he might try to improve the local Virginia wines. In 1807, for example, Jefferson added 287 rooted vines of 24 European grapes to the varieties planted in his two vineyards. He hoped to make wine that was "doubtless as good" as European, but he was never successful in producing a wine at Monticello. Many of his grapes, both local and European, were table grapes. He was, however, a major experimenter of growing European grapes, most of which succumbed to diseases such as black rot and phyloxera.

Nearly two hundred years would pass before Virginia wine vintners achieved the success envisioned by Jefferson.

# Revolution In The Mind And
# In The Street

*"The Revolution was effected before the war commenced. The Revolution was in the minds and hearts of the people....The radical change in the principles, opinions, sentiments, and affections of the people, was the real American Revolution."*
JOHN ADAMS TO HEZEKIAH NILES, FEBRUARY 13,1818

*"The God who gave us life gave us liberty at the same time."*
THOMAS JEFFERSON, *SUMMARY VIEW*, 1774

THE AMERICAN REVOLUTION emerged from the intellectual and political turmoil following British and American victory in the French and Indian War. At the end of the war the French and Spanish were defeated and the British flag flew over virtually all of North America east of the Mississippi River. Peace brought the promise of freedom from fear of frontier attack. Economic prosperity followed from the western frontier to the fishing banks of Newfoundland and Nova Scotia. Freed from the threat of hostile French, Spanish and Indian forces, Americans now were confronted with political conflict with a new enemy-their imperial masters in London who saw new opportunities to ensure Americans remained in the British empire and paid their "fair" share of imperial expenses.

Americans, like Adams and Jefferson, were emboldened to resist new British colonial policies that raised issues of inequalities of power, political rights and individual freedoms. The application of British authority, regulations and commercial restrictions that were borne as necessary when facing

Gerard W. Gawalt

the threat of French forces, now seemed like unnecessary oppressions. In the afterglow of victory, Americans were not willing to bear ANY burden.

With Americans feeling free to resist British assertions of power, and the British feeling free to impose new imperial demands on the Americans the stage was set for conflict.

The revolution began in the minds of Americans, but the revolution of the mind had physical consequences as Americans openly and sometimes violently opposed Great Britain's new assertions of control and taxation. The right to representation, political independence, separation of church and state, nationalism, slavery, closure of the frontier, increased taxation, commercial restrictions, use of the military in civil unrest, individual freedoms and judicial independence were some of the salient issues that would boil up in the revolutionary cauldron of Britain's American colonies.

Neither Jefferson nor Adams led any troops to victory in the Revolution, but they were there to stir the cauldron and fan the flames of rebellion. Their fame rests squarely on molding "the principles, opinions, sentiments, and affections of the people."

There is an old saying that all politics is local. There should be a parallel saying that all politicians begin on a local level. Such was certainly the case of Adams and Jefferson. Both men also built on the political foundations laid down by their fathers.

John's father was a selectman, a militia officer and a church deacon-in short a pillar of the community. Thomas's father was a county justice (an equivalent to a selectman) and an official county and state surveyor—in short a pillar of the community.

Jefferson made his first foray into elected office in 1769, successfully being elected to the House of Burgesses where he would serve for seven years.

Politics was not for him, Adams told a friend, Zabdiel Adams, in a July 23, 1763 letter. Instead of politics "Give me Bacon, and Cyder and Books and Girl and Friend, and I will frisk it, like a Lambkin among the Clover, whether H-t-n [Hutchinson] or O-t-s [Otis] or neither of them, are in or out of Power." But fortunately, he did not stick to his joking renunciation of politics.

In 1765 John began his political office holding as a surveyor of the highways in Braintree and then a selectman in 1768. After moving to Boston in 1770 he moved up to be a member of the Massachusetts House of Representatives.

But by the next year he had abandoned his Boston legal and political offices to return to Braintree, where he and Abigail no doubt felt more at home and better able to raise a growing family. Adams determined to avoid politics and concentrate on his business affairs-telling his diary on November 21, 1772. "Above all Things I must avoid Politicks, Political Clubbs, Town Meetings, General Court etc." This was an empty resolution.

Both men were immersed in revolutionary politics before they ventured onto the public stage. Neither man had fought in the French and Indian War, but they understood the implications of the French defeat and the removal of the French threat from the American frontiers.

Both no doubt realized the defeat of the French freed the Americans from a foreign threat and made them less dependent on British military power. So the imposition of British authority was all the more frustrating. Victory was supposed to bring benefits not involuntary burdens.

First, came the Proclamation of 1763. Few Americans were willing to accept the 1763 proclamation prohibiting Americans from settling west of the Appalachian Mountains. Instead of the war bringing greater opportunities in the west, there would be none. What was the point in defeating the French and their Indian allies if their enemies were to be awarded the spoils?

Then came a new blow. Great Britain wanted the American colonies to help pay off the British debt from the war and to help pay the £200,000 maintenance of the 10,000 British regular troops stationed in America. One of the soldiers' chief jobs was to prevent American colonists from exploiting their western victories and another was to intimidate the Americans into obeying the British trade restrictions and monopolies. And the British Exchequer George Grenville was shocked when Americans rebelled against paying taxes imposed by the Stamp Act of 1765! Can you imagine?

The Stamp Act, the first direct tax imposed by Parliament in the colonies, taxed every sheet of paper used by newspapers, in the courts or in the course of business. Opposition flared up and down the American colonies.

Jefferson played no role in Virginia's adoption of fiery resolutions against the Stamp Act. Although Jefferson was a law student of Wythe when he helped prepare the Virginia denunciation. When Patrick Henry introduced resolutions in the House of Burgesses opposing the Stamp Act and declaring that Virginians were "not bound to yield Obedience to any Law" imposing taxes, unless passed by the House of Burgesses, Jefferson was listening at the door. Jefferson reported in his autobiography. "When the famous Resolutions of 1765, against the Stamp –act, were proposed I was yet a student of law in Williamsburg. I attended the debate, however, at the door of the lobby of the House of Burgesses and heard the splendid display of Mr. Henry's talents as a popular orator." Jefferson soon left Williamsburg for home and left colonial agitation behind him.

Adams threw himself into the colonial uprising by writing newspaper articles, drafting opposition resolutions for the Braintree town meeting, and attending private planning sessions and public meetings denouncing the Stamp Act.

Adams condemned the Stamp Act in a newspaper essay, A Dissertation on Canon and Feudal Law. The Stamp Act Adams argued was part of "design" to strip us in a great measure of the means of knowledge" and "to introduce the inequalities and dependencies of the feudal system, by taking from the poorer sort of people their little subsistence, and conferring it on a set of stamp officers, distributors, and their deputies."

In his September 24, 1765 instructions to Braintree's delegates to the Massachusetts General Court, Adams denounced taxation without representation and the juryless Admiralty Courts that would enforce the Stamp Act. "We have always understood it to be a grand and fundamental principle of the constitution that no freeman should be subject to any tax to which he has not given his own consent." In December Adams denounced the Stamp Act to the governor and provincial council.

At the end of a year of turmoil Adams exulted in his diary on December 18: "The year 1765 has been the most remarkable of my life. The enormous engine fabricated by the British Parliament for battering down all the rights and liberties of America, I mean the Stamp Act, has raised and spread through the whole continent a spirit that will be recorded to our honor, with all future generations." Adams continued. "The People, even to the lowest Ranks, have become more attentive to their Liberties, more inquisitive about them, and more determined to defend them, than they were ever before known or had occasion to be."

Neither Jefferson nor Adams contemplated traveling to New York to attend the colonial "congress" called to protest the Stamp Act. In fact Virginia was not one of the nine states that met in New York from October 7 to 25, 1765. James Otis, Oliver Partridge and Timothy Ruggles, who served as chairman, represented Massachusetts. The delegates to this national assembly adopted a Declaration of Rights and Grievances that asserted the sole right of colonial assemblies to impose taxes, and claimed all the rights of Englishmen, including trial by jury and representation in Parliament.

The repeal of the Stamp Act in 1766 was almost anti-climactic. But their success strengthened the radical political beliefs of Americans like John's cousin Samuel Adams who were soon plotting independence.

Jefferson had just begun to practice law in Albemarle (acquiring 68 clients his first year) and Adams had moved to Boston, when British Chancellor of the Exchequer Charles Townshend decided to try again to levy taxes on Americans. Townshend fastened on the distinction between external (okay) and internal (bad) taxation, proffered by Benjamin Franklin, a Pennsylvania agent in London. Franklin argued that Americans would accept a tax on exports to the colonies because it was an external tax not an internal tax, like the Stamp Act. Townshend and Franklin were wrong.

The so-called Townshend Acts tried to raise 40,000 pounds sterling annually by taxing paint, glass, and tea. This money would be used to pay colonial royal officials, thus making them independent of provincial assemblies. The colonies' loss of control of royal officials was reinforced by the creation of a new Board of Customs Commissioners and three new Admiralty Courts to prosecute smugglers and those who tried to avoid the taxes. Moreover, the customs officers would be armed with special search warrants, called writs of assistance, to search for and seize goods imported (smuggled) without paying the taxes.

The Townshend Acts touched off a firestorm of colonial opposition. In 1769 the Virginia House of Burgesses with Jefferson as a member sent a protesting petition to Parliament, arguing that the tax "imposed upon such of the British Exports, as are the necessaries of Life" is "a Tax internal to all Intents and Purposes." Jefferson helped draft the Virginia resolution. Massachusetts and Virginia were among the colonies to organize associations to boycott imported British goods.

Great Britain, of course, rejected the American petitions but in 1770 dropped all the taxes except that on tea, thus cooling the fires of rebellion.

Jefferson settled into what he later called "a state of insensibility to our situation." Adams did not.

With hard work and his newfound political connections, Adams became one of the most successful lawyers in Massachusetts. John's political principles led him to turn down a chance to become advocate general of the new Court of Admiralty. But when British troops fired on Boston citizens on March 5, 1770, Adams's sense of fair play nearly dragged him into a political quagmire.

Town toughs, sailors, and boys were harassing and taunting a lone British guard in front of the Custom House. His call for help brought a squad of British soldiers to the rescue. Taunts turned to stones, snowballs and ice chunks followed by gunfire from the British troops that killed five Americans.

No other lawyer was willing to defend the troops charged with murder and manslaughter. But Adams with his firm belief that no one in a free country should be denied the right of adequate counsel and perhaps seeing an opportunity to enhance his legal reputation accepted a request to defend them. If American radical leaders expected that one of their own lawyers might give the British soldiers a less spirited defense, they were wrong. If Conservatives believed that Adams would be best able to secure justice (read freedom) for the soldiers from an angry jury of Bostonians, they were right. The general populace simply heaped scorn on Adams for defending the hated British soldiers.

Adams was undeterred. In what many contemporaries and historians have called "a virtuoso performance" Adams first gained an acquittal for Captain Thomas Preston who was charged with giving the order to fire and thus "murdering "Americans.

In the second trial for the enlisted men, Adams argued that the fault lay with the British law allowing British troops to be quartered in private houses and angering the residents to the point of mob action instead of keeping the peace. The "motley rabble of saucy boys, Negroes and mulattoes, Irish teagues and outlandish jacktars" were the real killers of these men. Adams continued. "Soldiers quartered in a populous town will always occasion two mobs where they prevent one. They are wretched conservators of peace."

This was truly a "virtuoso performance" that resulted in the acquittal of six soldiers and the conviction of two for manslaughter. Their punishment of branded thumbs was minor.

For Adams it was indeed a triumph. On the one hand, Adams proved that in America even the hated British soldiers received equal and fair treatment in the courts of law. On the other, Adams blamed British laws and oppressive government actions for creating a situation that aroused popular anger and mob action. Adams's stature as a lawyer and patriot leapt forward. He would later conclude that his defense of the troops was "one of the most gallant, generous, manly and disinterested actions of my whole life, and one of the best pieces of service I ever rendered my country." He did not need to add "and myself."

The Boston Massacre produced no noticeable impact on Jefferson -- just an urban mob behaving badly. Indeed, most Americans seemed to drawback from the violent course of revolution hinted at by the Boston confrontation. Adams enjoyed a period of relative calm, prosperity and newfound acclaim.

During the respite in colonial turmoil Jefferson's legal practice flourished with more than five hundred cases on his books and £175 per annum in his coffers. Jefferson courted and wed the widow Martha Wayles Skelton bringing his bride and new domestic delights to Monticello Mountain in January 1772.

But the imaginative minds of the British government in London were about to propose what seemed to them to be an innocuous plan to raise taxes and aid the loyal friends of the government. It would prove to be anything but innocuous—more like obnoxious and inflammatory.

With the British East India Company in financial difficulty because Dutch tea undercut their sales even in Britain and smuggled tea ruled the trade in America, Parliament passed the Tea Act of 1773. This act kept the three pence per pound tax on tea, but provided a full rebate for East Indian tea imported in England and allowed the company for the first time to sell directly to the colonies where the full tax would be collected. Lord North was warned by many responsible Britons that Americans would not accept the taxed tea, but he insisted that the tax was necessary to support British officials in the colonies and make them independent of the provincial assemblies.

The colonists would have received cheaper tea under the Tea Act, but the Americans led by radical groups calling themselves Sons of Liberty began an opposition campaign as 600,000 pounds of tea headed to America. Opponents emphasized the principle of no taxation without representation, the threat of "slavery" and tyranny by parliament, and the tea monopoly imposed by the British Act, which undercut local merchants and smugglers.

Provincial assemblies including Massachusetts and Virginia became more alarmed at British oppression as a new royal proclamation authorized sending Americans accused of violating commercial and tax regulations to England for trial. Assemblies in many colonies including Massachusetts and Virginia created Committees of Correspondence to protest threats to Americans' "ancient legal and constitutional rights." In his autobiography, Jefferson asserted his central role in Virginia's establishing a Committee of Correspondence to "produce a unity of action" and to call for an inter-colonial "meeting of deputies from every colony" to chart a common course.

As England pushed its plans to curtail American judicial, political, and commercial liberties, eleven of the thirteen colonies ultimately established committees for inter-colonial communication. The fire was being laid. All it would take is a spark to touch off the conflagration. Parliament set about creating a fistful of sparklers.

By December of 1773 the consignees of the tea in Charleston, New York and Philadelphia had been forced to resign and the tea had been sent back to England. Only in Boston did the consignees, two of whom were the sons of Governor Thomas Hutchinson, stand their ground and the governor refused to allow the ships to leave without paying the taxes. On December 16 Sons of Liberty, backed by a large crowd of supporters, dumped nearly 90,000 pounds of tea from 342 chests into Boston harbor. The resulting furor in London propelled the mother country and her American colonies down the road to revolution.

Adams was living in Boston at the time of the Tea Party, and even though he applauded the action he was not a participant. Writing in his diary on December 17, Adams reveled in "the most Magnificent Movement of all." Adams continued. "This Destruction of the Tea is so bold, so daring, so firm, intrepid and inflexible, and it must have so important Consequences, and so lasting, that I cant but consider it as an Epocha in History." With Governor Hutchinson accusing the participants of "High Treason," Adams wondered, "What Measures will the Ministry take, in Consequence of this?" He did not have to wonder for very long.

Jefferson, a new family man, watched events from Monticello. Adams feared that political events would ruin his flourishing legal practice.

The Boston Tea Party aroused great anger in London. Parliament and the King's harsh reaction was a series of laws known in America as The Intolerable

Acts. This series of five acts closed the port of Boston until restitution was made, limited town meetings to one per year, allowed the transfer of royal officials to Great Britain for trial on crimes committed in America, allowed governors to forcibly quarter British troops in private residences, and enlarged the boundaries of Quebec while providing greater religious freedom to Catholics.

Rather than intimidate the Americans and quell their rebellious spirit, The Intolerable Acts set the angry Americans and Britons on converging roads that led inexorably to Concord and Lexington.

Adams reportedly told a visiting Englishman that there was no more justice in England for Americans than there was in hell. To Abigail on May 12, 1774, he wrote: "We live, my dear Soul, in an Age of Tryal. What will be the Consequence I know not. The Town of Boston, for ought I can see, must suffer Martyrdom: It must expire: And our principal Consolation is, that it dies in a noble Cause." With the closure of Boston, he faced "no prospect of business" for the near future. But Adams was in high Spirits believing that this was "the last Effort of Lord North's Despair."

In Virginia Jefferson echoed Adams's refrain and intransigence.

In his *A Summary View of the Rights of British America* Jefferson would justify the destruction of the tea at Boston, blaming the British government for creating a situation primed for potential violence. He saved his harshest condemnation for the British acts that "were now devoted to ruin" the ill-fated colony of Massachusetts. All of the inhabitants of Boston "were involved in one indiscriminate ruin, by a new executive power, unheard of till then, that of a British Parliament. A property value of many millions of money, was sacrificed to revenge, not repay, the loss of a few thousands. This is administering justice with a heavy hand indeed!" Jefferson then asked the key question. "And when is this tempest to be arrested in its course?" The answer would be written in the blood of Britons and Americans.

In May 1774 Jefferson was among the disbanded burgesses who met in the Apollo Room of Raleigh Tavern to draft a call for deputies to meet "in Congress" to direct "measures required by the general interest." About this time Jefferson drafted a Declaration of Rights, modeled on the Albemarle County Resolves, which Jefferson had also written. Jefferson declared the primacy of "natural and legal rights" and of the laws adapted by their own legislature. "That no other Legislature whatever may rightfully exercise authority over them; and that these privileges they hold as the common rights of mankind, confirmed by the political constitutions they have respectively assumed, and also by several chapters of compact from the crown." Two years later, another Virginia burgess, George Mason, would draft the famous Virginia Declaration of Rights, which Jefferson would use as an antecedent document in writing the Declaration of Independence.

Adams was one of five men chosen by the Massachusetts legislature to attend this meeting of delegates in Philadelphia. Adams was ecstatic. He was about to leap onto a national stage providing opportunities beyond his wildest imaginings. The quest for fame and fortune was about to ride the rising tide of revolution.

On the eve of the meeting of the first Continental Congress in September 1774, Jefferson sat down to write an informational and inspirational essay addressed to King George. Although Jefferson later asserted he had written it as instructions to the Virginia delegates traveling to Philadelphia, there can be little doubt judging from the format and the wording that he hoped for its publication. Because illness prevented his trip to the Virginia capital, two manuscript copies of Jefferson's *Summary View of the Rights of British America* arrived in the hands of his slave, Jupiter. Peyton Randolph quickly saw to its publication in Clementia Rind's *Virginia Gazette.*

Jefferson boldly asserted that Americans had the same rights as British citizens in England even though they had emigrated from England to America. They had come as conquerors not as slaves, said Jefferson. Although Jefferson stated, "It is neither our wish nor our interest to separate" from Great Britain, his implication was clear. And his references to "our own territories" skated dangerously near treason. Taxation without representation was out. "Still less let it be proposed that our properties within our own territories shall be taxed or regulated by any power on earth but our own. The God who gave us life gave us liberty at the same time; the hand of force may destroy, but cannot disjoin them."

However, Jefferson's *Summary View* went beyond the standard condemnation of the British to an innovative contention that the American colonies had already become an independent nation. Jefferson asserted that "the British parliament has no right to exercise authority over us" because Americans had established "new societies" by the act of immigration, just as the Saxons and Danes had established a new society centuries before in England.

He argued that "our ancestors, before their emigration to America, were the free inhabitants of the British dominion in Europe, and possessed a right which nature has given to all men, of departing from the country in which chance, not choice, has placed them, of going in quest of new habitations, and of there establishing new societies, under such laws and regulations as to them shall seem most likely to promote public happiness."

But an oppressive British government had violated their natural rights, denied them the fruits of laws passed by their legislatures, heaped illegal taxes upon them, banned American manufactures, and prevented free trade. Many of these charges were familiar to American revolutionaries, including Adams, and appeared in many pamphlets.

One of the charges stood out for its boldness, especially coming from an aristocratic Virginia planter and slaveholder. It is one thing for a New Englander like James Otis, or a Pennsylvanian like Benjamin Rush or a Briton like Thomas Paine to denounce slavery, but a Virginia planter!

Jefferson called for an end to domestic slavery and he condemned the British government's negation of a Virginia law prohibiting the foreign importation of slaves. "The abolition of domestic slavery is the great object in those colonies, where it was unhappily introduced in their infant state. But previous to the enfranchisement of the slaves we have, it is necessary to exclude all further importations from Africa; yet our repeated attempts to effect this by prohibitions, and by imposing duties which might amount to a prohibition, have been hitherto defeated by his majesty's negative: Thus preferring the immediate advantages of a few African [changed to "British" by Jefferson on his personal copy] corsairs to the lasting interest of the American states, and to the rights of human nature, deeply wounded by this infamous practice."

Jefferson had been a delegate to the Virginia House of Burgesses in 1769 when it tried to ban the importation of slaves from Africa as part of the Non-Importation Agreement in protest of the Townshend Acts and to allow unfettered manumission of slaves (A measure actually proposed by Richard Bland and roundly denounced by fellow burgesses.), and he was a delegate in the Virginia Assembly in 1778 when it did ban the importation of African slaves.

Gerard W. Gawalt

When this charge appeared in Jefferson's draft of the Declaration of Independence, along with many more acceptable charges against the "abuse of power" by the British monarch, Congress was forced to confront the apparent paradox of slaveholders seeking to cast off the chains of political bondage while keeping those of personal bondage tightly fastened.

Jefferson showed his gifted word usage when he concluded "single acts of tyranny may be ascribed to the accidental opinion of a day; but a series of oppressions, begun at a distinguished period, and pursued unalterably through every change of ministers, too plainly prove a deliberate and systematical plan of reducing us to slavery."

Jefferson's essay was an immediate sensation and vaulted the author into the revolutionary spotlight. Two years later, Adams would remember the skilled writing and fiery language of the *Summary View* and urge Jefferson to undertake drafting America's Declaration of Independence.

Jefferson returned to Monticello before reaching Williamsburg. Meanwhile Adams was traveling to Philadelphia for the meeting of the First Continental Congress. Adams's diary notes read more like a tourist than a revolutionary delegate as Adams made his first trip out of New England.

Adams settled in at the boarding house of Mrs. Sarah Yard. The "stone House opposite City Tavern" remained Adams's "headquarters" in Philadelphia until 1777. Dr. Benjamin Rush, who would become an intimate of Adams and Jefferson, described his first encounter with Adams just outside Philadelphia. "This gentleman's dress and manners were at that time plain, and his conversation cold and reserved. He asked me many questions relative to the state of public opinion upon politicks, and the characters of the most active citizens on both sides of the controversy."

Forty-eight delegates were present on September 5 when they gathered in Carpenter's Hall, a brick Georgian building owned by the carpenters' guild. The delegates' infighting over a voting procedure set the tone for Congress. The large states wanted a proportional vote based on population, while the small states demanded each state have one vote. After days of wrangling (an argument that would last until 1787) John Adams and the Massachusetts delegation accepted the small states demand and thus opened the road to some action by the Continental Congress.

Adams and the other Massachusetts delegates pushed for a strong stand against "these Grievances, which threaten Destruction to the Lives, Liberty, and Property, of his Majesty's Subjects in North America." Adams grew frustrated with the "nibbling and quibbling" of "These great Witts, these subtle Criticks, these refined Genius's" in Congress. "These wise Statesmen, are so fond of shewing their Parts and Powers, as to make this Consultations very tedius," complained Adams.

In the end, they had to settle for a petition to the King for a redress of grievances, a Declaration of Rights and a Continental Association of non-importation, non-consumption and non-exportation to Great Britain. Congress agreed to meet again in Philadelphia on May 10, 1775. After an "Evening together at the City Tavern," Adams did a little more sightseeing before departing on October 28 not knowing how many more days he would spend in "the elegant, the hospitable, and polite City of Phyladelphia."

# Revolutionary Paths Cross

*"The truth is, the authority of parliament was never generally acknowledged in America."*
JOHN ADAMS, NOVANGLUS ESSAY NUMBER FOUR, 1775

*"I know not what course others may take but as for me-give me liberty or give me death."*
PATRICK HENRY, MARCH 23, 1775

*"But by the god that made me I will cease to exist before I yield to a connection on such terms as the British parliament propose."*
THOMAS JEFFERSON TO JOHN RANDOLPH, NOVEMBER 29, 1775

NEITHER ADAMS NOR Jefferson fought as soldiers on the battlefields of the Revolution. Their battlefields were the legislative chambers and the courts of Europe. Yet both were essential to the revolutionary cause by creating the legislative, constitutional, and ideological sinews for success. As early as 1774 they were linked together on a list of proscribed Americans reportedly prepared for the British Parliament but never acted on. Before learning his own name was to be added to the list, Jefferson would ask his old professor William Small in a May 7, 1775 letter. "Can it be believed that a grateful people will suffer those to be consigned to execution, whose sole crime has been to the developing and asserting of their rights?"

Although military conflict had not yet broken out, tensions were running very high. Jefferson was at the Virginia Convention in St. John's Church in Richmond on March 23, when fellow delegate Patrick Henry called for

Gerard W. Gawalt

preparing for military action. "Gentlemen may cry Peace, Peace—but there is no peace. The War is actually begun!" declared Henry. Jefferson must have trembled with fear and excitement when Henry reached his peroration. "I know not what course others may take but as for me-give me liberty or give me death!"

Jefferson 's assignment was less inspiring. He was one of the committee appointed to prepare plans for putting the militia "into a posture of defense."

Throughout the colonies British soldiers and governing officials faced off against American revolutionaries with tensions growing every day. British General Thomas Gage in Boston received orders "that force was to be met with force." He was to seize rebel military supplies and "principal actors and abettors in the Provincial Congress whose proceedings appear in every light to be Acts of treason and rebellion."

Then Gage sent the Earl of Percy and hundreds of soldiers to seize arms and ammunition being stored in the Massachusetts towns of Concord and Lexington. To this day no one knows for certain who fired the first shot on Lexington Common. Within minutes it was immaterial who fired first because dead and wounded fell on both sides. Within hours swarms of Massachusetts militiamen joined the fight. British reinforcements rushed out from Boston. By day's end the thoroughly defeated and nearly destroyed British force was barely rescued by reinforcements from Boston. The revolution of the mind had become a war of revolution.

After spending a good part of the winter of 1774-1775 writing a series of sixteen essays over the pseudonym Novanglus, Adams was at home in Braintree preparing to leave for the Continental Congress in Philadelphia when word of the fighting at Lexington and Concord reached him. A week later Adams left Braintree in a hired sulky for Philadelphia. No contemporary comment of John has survived. But Abigail in a May 2, 1775, letter to Mercy Otis Warren no doubt summed up the family reaction. "What a scene has opened upon us." Abigail continued. "Such a scene as we never before Experienced, and could scarcely form an Idea of. If we look back we are amazed at what is past, if we look forward we must shudder at the view."

Before word of fighting at Concord and Lexington reached Virginia, Royal Marines seized the colonial stores of powder in Williamsburg. When the local militia rushed to Williamsburg threatening the seat of royal authority, Governor

Dunmore threw brimstone on the fire of revolution by declaring that he would "declare freedom to the slaves, and reduce the city of Williamsburg to ashes" if the rebels continue to "insult" the government. When Patrick Henry led militia reinforcements to Williamsburg on May 3, Dunmore fled the capital.

Jefferson attending the Virginia Convention wrote to his former college professor William Small on May 7, 1775 about the fight at Concord and Lexington. "This accident has cut off our last hope of reconciliation, and a phrensy of revenge seems to have seized all ranks of people."

Adams was in Congress on June 15 and Jefferson was on his way to Philadelphia when George Washington was chosen as commander-in-chief of America's armed forces despite the opposition of some delegates, such as Roger Sherman, Edmund Pendleton and Robert Treat Paine. They argued that the New England troops before Boston already had a capable general, Artemas Ward, and that New England troops would not willingly be led by a Virginian.

Adams believed strongly that, on the contrary, the American rebellion needed unification and a Virginian leading American troops in New England was just the ticket. Adams happily described Washington to Elbridge Gerry on June 18, just days after Washington's June 16 acceptance of the command. Washington is "A Gentleman of one of the first Fortunes, upon the Continent, leaving his delicious Retirement, his Family and Friends, Sacrificing his Ease, and hazarding all in the Cause of his Country. His views are noble and disinterested. He declared when he accepted the mighty Trust, that he would lay before Us an Exact account of his Expences, and not accept a shilling for Pay." Would that the adulation would last.

War was joined and the partnership of Adams and Jefferson was soon to begin. By the time Jefferson reached Philadelphia on June 21, Washington had been appointed commander in chief of America's armed forces, the bloody battle of Bunker (Breed's) Hill had been fought, and Adams had been hard at work in Congress for more than a month.

The forces of the American Revolution brought John and Tom together for the first time at the Continental Congress in Philadelphia in that summer of 1775. But they were not strangers to each other's thoughts. Adams no doubt had read Jefferson's *A Summary View* and Jefferson was no doubt familiar with Adams's fiery *Novanglus Essays*. Late in life John recalled appreciating Jefferson's writing style after reading *A Summary View*.

Shortly after Jefferson first attended Congress on June 21, Samuel Ward, a Rhode Island delegate, offered this view of him in a June 22, 1775, letter to Henry Ward. "Yesterday the famous Mr. Jefferson a Delegate from Virginia in the Room of Mr. Randolph arrived, I have not been in Company with him yet, he looks like a very sensible, spirited, fine Fellow and by the Pamphlet which he wrote last summer he certainly is one."

John and Tom's immediate reactions are not known, even though they worked together on congressional committees. Adams was almost certainly impressed by Jefferson's arrival at Congress in a phaeton pulled by four horses with two liveried slaves completing the traveling outfit.

Adams does not mention Jefferson in his family correspondence or his diary until October 25, 1775, when he reported that New York delegate James Duane remarked that "Jefferson is the greatest Rubber of Dust that he has met with, that he has learned French, Italian, Spanish, and wants to learn German."

Decades later, Adams commented on Jefferson's first year in Congress in his autobiography: "Mr. Jefferson had been now about a Year a Member of Congress, but had attended his Duty in the House but a very small part of the time and when there had never spoken in public: and during the whole time I sat with him in Congress, I never heard him utter three sentences together."

Jefferson left no contemporary comment of Adams that historians have found. In fact, Adams is absent from Jefferson's letters or notes until the debates over the Declaration of Independence. Jefferson later recalled in a February 14, 1783, letter to James Madison that Adams "had a sound head on substantial points."

On a personal level, all that can be said is that they shared a Philadelphia barber, John Byrne.

Fear and excitement permeated Philadelphia during July. Jefferson and Adams helped draft the revolutionary and treasonous document or declaration "Setting Forth the Causes and Necessity of Their Taking Up Arms." Jefferson was one of the primary authors with John Dickinson. Two drafts of the declaration still sit in Jefferson's papers at the Library of Congress revealing the careful choice of phraseology and extensive editing required as a still divided Congress moved toward all-out war and independence.

Jefferson cast his draft along the theme of the innocent Americans assaulted by the aggressive Britons—of innocent virtue versus entrenched, aggressive corruption. Jefferson was repeating and embellishing the views of Henry St. John Bolingbroke, Thomas Gordon, James Burgh, and other British Whigs.

Adams was a vocal supporter of rebellion in the congressional debates. Adams was also a chief worrier, expressing his mingled fear and pride in a July 6, 1775, letter to William Tudor, a former law student of Adams and soon to be Judge Advocate General of the American Army. "We have Spent this whole Day in debating Paragraph by Paragraph, a Manifesto as some call it, or a Declaration of the Causes and Necessity of our taking up Arms." Adams continued. "It has Some Mercury in it, and is pretty frank, plain, and clear. If Lord North don't compliment every Mothers Son of us, with a Bill of Attainder, in Exchange for it, I shall think it owing to Fear." Just the day before Jefferson had written George Gilmer. "As our enemies have found we can reason like men, so now let us show them we can fight like men also." They would need to.

Congress followed up its justification for war with a petition to King George III once again asking for his help in ending the oppressive actions against his colonies in America. The "Olive Branch Petition," followed the 1774 Address to the King into a back closet at Whitehall and into the dustbin of history.

Both men were aware of the dangers to themselves and their cause as they voted to raise an army of 27,000 men for the defense of the American colonies and authorized the invasion of Canada.

Jefferson headed south for home, family and the Virginia Convention on August 1, just before Congress adjourned until September 5. The next day Adams headed north for home and hearth.

Jefferson found peace and tranquility and a loving wife at Monticello. Not even former Governor Dunmore's depredations on Virginia's coastal towns aroused Jefferson. Edmund Randolph complained to Jefferson on August 31 of "the Supineness of Virginia, amidst the Robberies, and other Violations of private Property, said to have been committed by Lord Dunmore."

Jefferson took time to write to former Virginia Attorney General John Randolph trying to convince Britons of America's desire to find a peaceable solution. "I hope the returning wisdom of Great Britain will e'er long put an end to this unnatural contest. There may be people to whose tempers and dispositions Contention may be pleasing, and who may therefore wish a continuance of confusion. But to me it is of all states, but one, the most horrid. My first wish is a restoration of our just rights; my second a return of the happy period when, consistently with duty, I may withdraw myself totally from the public stage." Jefferson added. "Looking forward with fondness towards a reconciliation with Great Britain, I cannot help hoping you may be able to contribute towards expediting this good work." But the "unnatural contest" went on.

Jefferson was appointed a Lieutenant and Commander in Chief of the Militia of Albemarle County, before his return to Philadelphia on September 30. Jefferson would not lead them into battle.

Adams found chaos, contending armies around Boston and a loving wife in Braintree.

Both men would return to Philadelphia and the Continental Congress in the fall.

Adams spent considerable time at Washington's headquarters in Cambridge. Charles Lee gave Adams a guided tour of the American positions.

Washington struggled to bring order to a myriad of military units from many colonies. Men and entire units came and went on their own schedules. Camp sanitation was non-existent. Let's just say Cambridge residents did not have to fertilize their gardens for years. The supply service was chaotic and all the troops were short of arms, ammunition and winter clothes. All of the men had varying lengths of service and regulations governing their units and the choice of their officers.

Washington set about to establish discipline, reform the officer corps, erect defenses and ensure that the troops were properly fed and trained. He was careful to frequently consult with the Massachusetts legislature at Watertown. The president of that body and a friend of Adams, James Warren, wrote, "I pity our poor general, who has a greater burden on his shoulders and more difficulties to struggle with than I think should fall to the share of so good a man."

The British forces were blocked in Boston and after the battle of Bunker Hill they knew they could only leave by water.

Washington had made a favorable impression on New Englanders. John's wife Abigail was quite impressed by Washington, telling John "The half was not told me." No doubt Adams offered Washington some advice on the independent minds of the New England militia units.

Adams also spent about nine days in Watertown serving on the Massachusetts Council to which the House of Representatives had elected him on July 21. Among the useful information he brought from Philadelphia was that Congress had entered into a secret agreement with Bermuda to supply gunpowder to America in exchange for agricultural products.

Adams enjoyed his stay at home telling his good friend Mercy Otis Warren on August 26 how much he enjoyed his solitary rambles over his farm and the "conversation of the amiable Portia"[Abigail]. Two days later, just before a virulent "Distemper" struck the Adams household, he left Braintree for Watertown where he spent three days before leaving for Philadelphia with his cousin Samuel Adams.

By September 12 after an "agreeable Journey," Adams was back in Philadelphia. Jefferson did not return until September 30. Washington still sat in Cambridge, and Benedict Arnold led a small army into Canada by way of the Kennebec River.

Adams and the other radicals in Congress received gifts from King George. First, a proclamation declaring the colonies to be in a state of rebellion and its rebels to be guilty of "traitorous designs." Then he refused to even receive the Olive Branch Petition. Then in his annual speech to Parliament, King George declared that the ultimate aim of the Americans was independence. You can almost hear John and his cousin Samuel exclaiming—Thank you George.

How much interaction occurred between Adams and Jefferson is not known. However, Adams's first mention of Jefferson in his daily diary was on October 25 when he recorded that New York delegate James Duane thought Jefferson was "the greatest rubber off of dust" that he had ever met and with great exaggeration reported he spoke French, Italian, Spanish and German.

The American and British governments spent the fall of 1775 marshaling their forces, developing a strategy, and trying to publicly justify their actions. Adams and Jefferson were in the midst of the chaos as the Continental Congress struggled to organize military forces, raise money and supplies while trying to court hesitant Americans and foreign governments to support their revolution.

Congress was deeply divided into radicals, like Adams and Jefferson, who saw independence as the correct path forward for the American provinces, and reconciliationists or conservatives, led by men like Robert Morris and John Dickinson, who saw reunion with Great Britain as the correct path to peace.

As both sides gathered military strength, the radicals rallied around General Washington's suggestion to invade Canada. Supporters of a Canadian invasion, including Adams, believed that lightly defended Canada would fall easily to American arms. Canadians, particularly French colonists, would leap at the opportunity to shed the British yoke and join the American invasion forces.

Adams even wondered to his friend James Warren in an October 8 letter what to do after victory in Canada. "What is to be done with it? A Government will be necessary for the Inhabitants of Canada, as for those of the Massachusetts Bay? And what Form of Government, shall it be? Shall the Canadians choose an House of Representatives, a Council and a Governor? It will not do to govern them by Martial Law, and make our General Governor. This will be disrelished by them as much as their new Parliamentary Constitution or their old French Government."

Adams might as well have been speaking about Massachusetts and Congress, when he concluded. "This appears to me as serious a Problem as any We shall have to solve."

Jefferson too was overly optimistic telling John Randolph on November 29. "In a short time we have reason to hope the delegates of Canada will join us in Congress and complete the American Union as far as we wish to have it completed."

Success marked the first months. Fort Chambly fell, as did St. John's and Montreal to General Richard Montgomery. Only the capture of Quebec City by Arnold and Montgomery remained to complete the conquest. This didn't happened as the two-pronged American invasion broke on the fortress walls of Quebec City.

Meanwhile, Lord Dunmore's depredations on the Virginia coast and his proclamation calling on slaves to gain their freedom by joining his forces had "raised our country into a perfect phrensy."

Jefferson spoke for many Americans when he exclaimed his frustration with the British government on November 29. "Believe me Dear Sir there is not in the British empire a man who more cordially loves a Union with Gr. Britain than I do. But by the god that made me I will cease to exist before I yield to a connection on such terms as the British parliament propose and in this I think I speak the sentiments of America."

Adams created a crisis for himself by accepting an appointment as Chief Justice of the Massachusetts Superior Court of Judicature. At the time of his appointment in November 1775, he told the Council. "I dare not refuse to undertake this Duty." To Abigail he revealed his fears that senior members of the Massachusetts bar might be jealous of his appointment. And "The Confusions and Distractions of the Times, will encumber that Office with embarrassments, expose it to dangers and Slanders, which it never knew before," he told Abigail on November 18. Although he never took his seat on the bench, he did not resign until 1777 leaving himself open to the same charge of plural office holding that he had leveled against British Governor Thomas Hutchinson.

Congress was busy creating committees to purchase supplies, deal with Canada, oversee a navy, and to meet with Washington and the New England executives. Congress also recommended colonies establish new governments. In foreign affairs they appointed a Committee of Secret Correspondence and urged the acquisition of European arms and ammunition.

Adams and Jefferson served on committees with distinction, but as far as historians know the interaction of these two men remained superficial.

Adams was by far the most active in Congress, but both complained of being overwhelmed with committee assignments.

Adams still had time to begin outlining plans for new state and national governments. As can be seen in a November 15 letter to Richard Henry Lee in which he presented a sketch of government, Adams had already propounded the moderate plan for a balanced government of legislative, executive and judicial branches that would later be made public in his pamphlet, *Thoughts on Government.*

Jefferson set aside a full day for personal correspondence, but then complained that none of his friends or family were writing to him. He did warn his wife "to keep yourselves at a distance from the Alarms of Ld. Dunmore."

Adams did not have the same problems. While Jefferson wrote fewer than ten letters, Adams wrote more than seventy-five in the same period and maintained a daily diary. John was just a bundle of energy.

Both men left for home before the American defeat at Quebec City was known—Adams on December 8 and Jefferson on December 28.

While both men were at home they learned of the American disaster at Quebec City.

More importantly a pamphlet by a little known essayist, Thomas Paine, was sweeping the nation. *Common Sense* published on January 9, 1776, took the American provinces by storm and was destined to become the most influential piece of writing during the American Revolution after the Declaration of Independence. Paine, an impoverished recent English immigrant, had begun his pamphlet career in America the previous year by calling for an end to slavery.

In *Common Sense,* Paine mocked monarchy as evil and absurd. Americans should separate themselves from the brute George III. The war will be short and victorious asserted Paine. What are we waiting for, he asked. "Why is it that we hesitate?"

"The sun never shined on a cause of greater worth," shouted Paine. "For God's sake, let us come to a final separation." Paine reached a peroration: "The birthday of a new world is at hand."

Radicals from New Hampshire to Georgia were in ecstasy.

Momentum for independence had been building for months thanks to the work of radicals and the intransigence of the British. Now Paine's pamphlet by the tens of thousands brought the idea before hundreds of thousands of Americans in a form that aroused American patriotism among commoners as well as the political elites.

Everyone, that is except Adams. Adams first came across the pamphlet in New York and sent a copy to Abigail with this glowing recommendation. "I sent you from New York a Pamphlet intituled Common Sense, written in Vindication of Doctrines which there is a Reason to expect that the further Encroachments of Tyranny and Depredations of Oppression, will soon make the common faith."

But upon closer reading Adams became alarmed by Paine's arguments that the war would be short and that America should be solely governed by a popularly elected unicameral legislature. Paine's ideas of democratizing government simply scared Adams. Adams gave Abigail a more nuanced evaluation of *Common Sense* in a March 19, 1776, letter. "You ask, what is thought of Common Sense. Sensible Men think there are some Whims, some Sophisms, some artful Addresses to superstitious Notions, some keen attempts upon the

Passions, in this Pamphlet. But all agree there is a great deal of good sense, delivered in a clear, simple, concise and nervous Style." And generally approved are "his sentiments of the Abilities of America, and of the Difficulty of a Reconciliation with G.B."

On the other hand, "His Notions and Plans of Continental Government are not much applauded. Indeed this Writer has a better Hand at pulling down than building."

Adams was flattered that "it has been very generally propagated through the Continent that I wrote this Pamphlet. But altho I could not have written any Thing in so manly and striking a style, I flatter myself I should have made a more respectable Figure as an Architect, if I had undertaken such a Work. This Writer seems to have very inadequate Ideas of what is proper and necessary to be done, in order to form Constitutions for single Colonies, as well as a great Model of Union for the whole."

His thoughts had not yet evolved to his later evaluation of *Common Sense* as "a poor, ignorant, malicious, short-sighted, crapulous mass," but they were on the way.

Adams immediately began planning a rebuttal. In a long letter written the same day to North Carolina delegate John Penn, he argued against a "Single Assembly" and outlined his plans for a balanced government with an executive, two-house legislature, and an independent judiciary. At a request from Penn and William Hooper in late March Adams enlarged his ideas into a pamphlet manuscript. Adams felt so strongly he sent copies to George Wythe of Virginia and Jonathan Dickinson Sergeant of New Jersey.

Richard Henry Lee of Virginia then took the copy in the hands of Wythe and had it published in Philadelphia by John Dunlap. Adams's pamphlet, *Thoughts on Government: Applicable to the Present State of the American Colonies In a Letter from a Gentleman to his Friend* did not make the splash of *Common Sense* but it became famous as an antidote to proposals of radical democratic republican government and established Adams as the foremost spokesman for a balanced, some would say conservative, structure of government.

Adams saw this moment as the greatest opportunity for Americans to establish a new republican government. "It has been the Will of Heaven, that We should be thrown into Existence at a Period, when the greatest Philosophers and Lawgivers of Antiquity would have wished to have lived," asserted Adams in his original letter to Penn. "A Period, when a Coincidence of Circumstances, without Example, has afforded to thirteen Colonies at once an opportunity, of beginning government anew from the Foundation and building as they choose. How few of the human Race, have ever had an opportunity of choosing a System of Government for themselves and their Children? How few have ever had any Thing more of Choice in government, than in Climate? These Colonies have now their Election and it is much to be wish'd that it may not prove to be like a Prise in the Hands of a Man who has no Heart to improve it." Adams and Jefferson were two people ready for the challenge.

Thomas Nelson sent Jefferson a copy of *Common Sense* on February 4. Although Jefferson did not comment in writing on Paine's pamphlet, he must have heartily approved because in 1784 he urged Madison to seek a gift of 2000 guineas "or an inheritance of 100 guineas a year" for "Payne the author of Common Sense."

John Adams and a coterie of radical revolutionaries took every opportunity to push their cause. When Adams returned to Congress in February he brought a lengthy "to do" list including a Confederation, and alliance with France and Spain, a "new government to be assumed in every Colony," minting money, raising an army, issuing letters of marque to privateers, and accumulating supplies. It culminated in a "Declaration of Independency, Declaration of War with the Nation." The list was long, and the times were desperate.

Then came an apparent game changer. The British army and navy abandoned Boston on March 17. Adams was among those ecstatic Americans who celebrated a great triumph.

But for Adams joy was tempered by reality. "I give you Joy of Boston and Charlestown, once more the Habitations of Americans," exulted John to Abigail on March 29. But added. "We are taking Precautions to defend every Place that is in Danger---The Carolinas, Virginia, N. York, Canada."

To James Warren, he wrote the same day. "My Mind has been constantly engaged with Plans and Schemes for the Fortification of the Islands and Channells in Boston Harbour." Adams need not have worried. The British warriors would never return to Boston.

Adams guessed the British would sail to Canada to oust the Americans. Washington marched his army to New York.

Jefferson was still in Virginia as Adams and Congress worried about sending ambassadors abroad, bringing Canada into the American union, approving letters of marque for privateers, opening America's ports for trade to all nations "not under the dominion" of the King of Great Britain, ending the importation of slaves and finally on May 10 recommending that the colonies "adopt such government as shall, in the opinion of the representatives of the people, best conduce to the happiness and safety of their constituents."

In the midst of this overwhelming workload, Adams was urged by Abigail to "remember the ladies" in the process of making new laws. Adams jokingly responded. "Your letter was the first intimation that another tribe more numerous and powerful than all the rest were grown discontented. This is rather too coarse a compliment but you are so saucy, I won't blot it out." Abigail was not amused, replying on May 7. "I can not say that I think you very generous to the Ladies, for whilst you are proclaiming peace and good will to Men, Emancipating all Nations, you insist upon retaining an Absolute power over Wives."

On March 31, Jefferson suffered the shock of the death of his mother, Jane, just fifty-five years of age. As a militia officer he spent some time collecting money and supplies for Virginia's troops, but his time was mostly his own. Jefferson intended to return to Congress in early April but his mother's death and a "malady" including severe migraines delayed him. Then on May 7, he turned his horse northeastward toward Philadelphia and a return to the business of revolution and creating a new government.

On May 15, Jefferson was back in Congress. "I am here in the same uneasy anxious state in which I was the last fall without Mrs. Jefferson who could not come with me," Jefferson complained on May 16 to Thomas Nelson, a fellow Virginian and a non-attending delegate to Congress.

And he was ready to return home with the hope of drafting a constitution for Virginia. Jefferson desperately wanted to be in Williamsburg at the Virginia Convention working with George Mason on the writing of a new constitution.

This hope would lead him to prepare three drafts of a Virginia constitution during his time in Congress. Parts were conveyed to Edmund Pendleton, president of the Virginia Convention. George Wythe, a delegate and mentor to Jefferson carried a draft with him when he left Congress on June 13 for the convention. Jefferson's "train of abuses" would appear in a preamble to the

Virginia Constitution when it was adopted on June 29, the day after Jefferson had submitted the Declaration of Independence to Congress.

Jefferson seized on a Congressional resolution urging the states to create new governments. "Should our Convention propose to establish now a form of government perhaps it might be agreeable to recall for a short time their delegates," Jefferson suggested to Nelson. "It is a work of the most interesting nature and such as every individual would wish to have his voice in. In truth it is the whole object of the present controversy; for should a bad government be instituted for us in future it had been as well to have accepted at first the bad one offered to us from beyond the water without risk and expence of contest."

Jefferson and Adams were poised for action just as the grand scene of declaring independence and creating American republics began to unfold. Did they suspect they would be directors?

# Defining Moment

*"We hold these truths to be self-evident: that all men are created equal; that they are endowed by their Creator with certain unalienable Rights; that among these are Life, Liberty, and the pursuit of Happiness; that to secure these rights, Governments are instituted among Men, deriving their just powers from the consent of the governed; That whenever any Form of Government becomes destructive of these ends, it is the Right of the People to alter or to abolish it, and to institute new Government, laying its foundation on such principles and organizing its powers in such form, as to them seem most likely to effect their Safety and Happiness."*
DECLARATION OF INDEPENDENCE, JULY 4, 1776.

THE DRAFTING AND adoption of the Declaration of Independence has become the defining moment of the American Revolution. Jefferson and Adams were the two people most responsible for preparing this daring declaration.

Congress had barely finished conferring with Washington on plans for the coming campaign, when Richard Henry Lee, acting on instructions adopted on May 15 by the Virginia Convention, rose in Congress on June 7 to introduce resolutions respecting independence, foreign alliances and a confederation government. The Virginia resolutions minced no words. Congress was called on "to declare that these United colonies are & of right ought to be free and independent States, that they are absolved from all allegiance to the British Crown, and that all political connection between them and the State of Great Britain is, and ought to be totally dissolved. That it is expedient forthwith to take the most effectual measures for forming foreign Allegiances. That a plan of confederation be prepared and transmitted to the respective Colonies for their consideration and approbation."

Gerard W. Gawalt

Beset by divisions in Congress and the country, a vote on independence was postponed "to this day three weeks." But an aggressive nucleus pushed Congress forward toward independence even though events were not favorable for the American cause. The war was not going well. The army in Canada was in full retreat. British fleets and armies were hovering around Charleston and headed for New York. Native Americans were attacking the American frontiers from New England to Georgia. Loyalists were forming their own military units. Nevertheless Congress appointed a five-man committee (Jefferson, Adams, Franklin, Roger Sherman and Robert Livingston) to "prepare a Declaration" of independence for its consideration.

Adams may have been secretly relieved that he would not be solely responsible for drafting the Declaration because of the workload he was shouldering in Congress.

Adams was nearly overwhelmed with committee work. His work as the head of the newly established Continental Board of War and Ordnance was particularly onerous. In anticipation of a long war, Congress established the Board of War and Ordnance in June 1776. Adams chaired a committee of Sherman, Benjamin Harrison, James Wilson and Edward Rutledge.

Then on June 12 Adams was also named to the committee "to prepare a plan of treaties to be proposed to foreign powers." One might say Adams's plate was overflowing.

Adams complained with more than just a tinge of pride about his workload in a June 26 letter to Abigail. "The Congress have been pleased to give me more Business than I am qualified for, and more than I fear, I can go through, with safety to my Health. They have established a Board of War and Ordnance and made me President of it, an Honour to which I never aspired, a Trust to which I feel my self vastly unequal. But I am determined to do as well as I can and make Industry supply, in some degree the Place of Abilities and Experience. The Board meets every Morning and every Evening. This, with Constant Attendance in Congress, will so entirely engross my Time, that I fear, I shall not be able to write you, so often as I have." You can almost hear Adams saying. Thank God, I fobbed off writing the Declaration of Independence on that young Virginian so I can do the real work.

Unfortunately Adams did not keep a first hand account of Congress's run up to the Declaration. Fortunately Jefferson did and his story is best told in his own words.

"Friday June 7. 1776. The Delegates from Virginia moved in obedience to instructions from their constituents that the congress should declare that these United colonies are & of right ought to be free & independant states, that they are absolved from all allegiance to the British crown, and that all political connection between them and the state of Great Britain is & ought to be totally dissolved; that measures should be immediately taken for procuring the assistance of foreign powers, and a Confederation be formed to bind the colonies more closely together.

"The house being obliged to attend at that time to some other business, the proposition was referred to the next day when the members were ordered to attend punctually at ten o'clock.

"Saturday June 8. They proceeded to take it into consideration and referred it to a committee of the whole, into which they immediately resolved themselves, and passed that day & Monday the 10$^{th}$ in debating the subject.

"It was argued by Wilson, Robert R. Livingston, E. Rutledge, Dickinson and others.

"That tho' they were friends to the measures themselves, and saw the impossibility that we should ever again be united with Gr Britain, yet they were against adopting them at this time.

"That the conduct we had formerly observed was wise & proper now, of deferring to take any capital step till the voice of the people drove us into it:

"That they were our power, & without them our declaration could not be carried into effect:

"That the people of the middle colonies (Maryland, Delaware, Pennsylva., the Jersies & N. York) were not yet ripe for bidding adieu to British connection but that they were fast ripening & in a short time would join in the general voice of America:

"That the resolution entered into by this house on the 15$^{th}$ of May for suppressing the exercise of all powers derived from the crown, had shewn, by the ferment into which it had thrown these middle colonies, that they had not yet accommodated their minds to a separation from the mother country:

"That some of them had expressly forbidden their delegates to consent to such a declaration, and others had given no instructions, & consequently no powers to give such consent:

"That if the delegates of any particular colony had no power to declare such colony independent, certain they were the others could not declare it for them; the colonies being as yet perfectly independent of each other:

"That the assembly of Pennsylvania was now sitting above stairs, their convention would sit within a few days, the convention of New York was now sitting, & those of the Jersies & Delaware counties would meet on the Monday following & it was probable these bodies would take up the question of Independence & would declare to their delegates the voice of their state:

"That if such a declaration should now be agreed to, these delegates must retire & possibly their colonies might secede from the Union:

"That such a secession would weaken us more than could be compensated by any foreign alliance.

"That in the event of such a division, foreign powers would either refuse to join themselves to our fortunes, or having us so much in their power as that desperate declaration would place us, they would insist on terms proportionably more hard & prejudicial:

"That we had little reason to expect an alliance with those to whom alone as yet we had cast our eyes:

"That France and Spain had reason to be jealous of that rising power which would one day certainly strip them of all their American possessions:

"That it was more likely they should form a connection with the British court, who, if they should find themselves unable otherwise to extricate themselves from their difficulties, would agree to a partition of our territories restoring Canada to France, & the Floridas to Spain, to accomplish for themselves a recovery of these colonies:

"That it would not be long before we should receive certain information of the disposition of the French court, from the agent whom we had sent to Paris for that purpose:

"That if this disposition should be favorable, by waiting the event of the present campaign, which we all hoped would be successful, we should have reason to expect an alliance on better terms:

"That this would in fact work no delay of any effectual aid from such ally, as, from the advance of the season & distance of our situation, it was impossible we could receive any assistance during this campaign:

"That it was prudent to fix among ourselves the terms on which we would form an alliance, before we declared we would form one at all events:

"And that if these were agreed on & our Declaration of Independence ready by the time our Ambassadour should be prepared to sail, it would be as well, as to go into that Declaration at this day.

"On the other side it was urged by J. Adams, Lee, Wythe and others That no gentleman had argued against the policy or the right of separation from Britain, nor had supposed it possible we should ever renew our connection that they had only opposed it's being now declared:

"That the question was not whether, by a declaration of independence, we should make ourselves what we are not; but whether we should declare a fact which already exists:

"That as to the people or parliament of England, we had always been independent of them, their restraints on our trade deriving efficacy from our acquiescence only & not from any rights they possessed of imposing them, & that so far our connection had been federal only, & was now dissolved by the commencement of hostilities:

"That as to the king, we had been bound to him by allegiance, but that this bond was now dissolved by his assent to the late act of parliament, by which he declares us out of his protection, and by his levying war on us, a fact which had long ago proved us out of his protection; it being a certain position in law that allegiance & protection are reciprocal, the one ceasing when the other is withdrawn:

"That James the IId never declared the people of England out of his protection yet his actions proved it & the parliament declared it:

"no delegates then can be denied, or ever want, a power of declaring an existent truth:

"That the delegates from Delaware counties having declared their constituents ready to join, there are only two colonies Pennsylvania & Maryland whose delegates are absolutely tied up, and that these had by their instructions only reserved a right of confirming or rejecting the measure:

"That the instructions from Pennsylvania might be accounted for from the times in which they were drawn, near a twelvemonth ago, since which the state of affairs has totally changed:

"That within that time it had become apparent that Britain was determined to accept nothing less than a carte blanche, and that the king's answer to the Lord Mayor, Aldermen & common council of London, which had come to hand four days ago, must have satisfied every one of this point:

"That the people wait for us to lead the way:

"That *they* are in favour of the measure, tho' the instructions given by some of their *representatives* are not:

"That the voice of the representatives is not always consonant with the voice of the people, and that this is remarkeably the case in these middle colonies:

"That the effect of the resolution of the 15<sup>th</sup> of May has proved this, which, raising the murmurs of some in the colonies of Pennsylvania & Maryland, called forth the opposing voice of the freer part of the people, & proved them to be the majority, even in these colonies:

"That the backwardness of these two colonies might be ascribed partly to the influence of proprietary power & connections, & partly to their having not yet been attacked by the enemy:

"That these causes were not likely to be soon removed, as there seemed no probability that the enemy would make either of these the seat of this summer's war:

"That it would be vain to wait either weeks or months for perfect unanimity, since it was impossible that all men should ever become of one sentiment on any question:

"That the conduct of some colonies from the beginning of this contest, had given reason to suspect it was their settled policy to keep in the rear of the confederacy, that their particular prospect might be better even in the worst event:

"That therefore it was necessary for those colonies who had thrown themselves forward & hazarded all from the beginning, to come forward now also, and put all again to their own hazard:

"That the history of the Dutch revolution, of whom three states only confederated at first proved that a secession of some colonies would not be so dangerous as some apprehended:

John Adams and Thomas Jefferson

"That a declaration of Independence alone could render it consistent with European delicacy for European powers to treat with us, or even to receive an Ambassador from us:

"That till this they would not receive our vessels into their ports, nor acknowlege the adjudications of our courts of Admiralty to be legitimate, in cases of capture of British vessels:

"That tho' France & Spain may be jealous of our rising power, they must think it will be much more formidable with the addition of Great Britain; and will therefore see it their interest to prevent a coalition; but should they refuse, we shall be but where we are; whereas without trying we shall never know whether they will aid us or not:

"That the present campaign may be unsuccessful, & therefore we had better propose an alliance while our affairs wear a hopeful aspect:

"That to wait the event of this campaign will certainly work delay, because during this summer France may assist us effectually by cutting off those supplies of provisions from England & Ireland on which the enemy's armies here are to depend; or by setting in motion the great power they have collected in the West Indies, & calling our enemy to the defence of the possessions they have there:

"That it would be idle to lose time in settling the terms of alliance, till we had first determined we would enter into alliance:

"That it is necessary to lose no time in opening a trade for our people, who will want clothes, and will want money too for the paiment of taxes:

"And that the only misfortune is that we did not enter into alliance with France six months sooner, as besides opening their ports for the vent of our last year's produce, they might have marched an army into Germany and prevented the petty princes there from selling their unhappy subjects to subdue us.

"It appearing in the course of these debates that the colonies of N. York, New Jersey, Pennsylvania, Delaware, Maryland & South Carolina were not yet matured for falling from the parent stem, but that they were fast advancing to that state, it was thought most prudent to wait a while for them, and to postpone the final decision to July 1. But that this might occasion as little delay as possible, a committee was appointed to prepare a declaration of independence. The Commee. were J. Adams, Dr. Franklin, Roger Sherman, Robert R. Livingston & myself. Committees were also appointed at the same time to prepare a plan of confederation for the colonies, and to state the terms proper to be proposed for foreign alliance. The committee for drawing the Declaration of Independence desired me to do it. it was accordingly done and being approved by them, I reported it to the house on Friday the 28$^{th}$ of June when it was read and ordered to lie on the table."

But Jefferson's notes are not perfect, nor are they complete. So we must delve further into the story. At one point in this frustrating process, Adams told Marylander Samuel Chase on June 14. "But of all the Animals on Earth, that ever fell in my Way, your Trimmers, your double tongued and double minded Men, your disguised Folk, I detest more. The Devil I think has a better Title to those by half, than he has to those who err openly, and are bare faced Villains." Adams told Chase he would welcome his attendance at Congress. "But Mr Chase never was nor will be more welcome than, if he should come next Monday or Tuesday fortnight, with the Voice of Maryland in Favour of Independence and a foreign Alliance."

What is clear is that Jefferson and Adams were two members of the five-man committee appointed to draft a Declaration of Independence. The choice of Jefferson to write the initial draft is a story of several versions.

Unfortunately, the committee kept no minutes, or the minutes Adams later said the committee had kept have not survived. Adams, while minister to France in 1779, recorded in his diary a succinct conversation with Francois Chevalier de Marbois, which supports Jefferson's contention that he was the only member of the committee appointed to draft the declaration: "Whom, said the Chevalier, made the Declaration of Independence? Mr. Jefferson of Virginia, said I, was the Draughtsman." Adams pointed out that the five-person committee "appointed Mr. Jefferson a subcommittee to draw it up."

In his autobiography written decades later Adams wrote a more vibrant account of Jefferson's selection. "It will naturally be enquired, how it happened that he was appointed on a Committee of such importance. There were more reasons than one. Mr. Jefferson had the Reputation of a masterly Pen. He had been chosen a Delegate in Virginia, in consequence of a very handsome public Paper, which he had written for the House of Burgesses, which had given him the Character of a fine Writer.

"Another reason was that Mr. Richard Henry Lee was not beloved by the most of his Colleagues from Virginia and Mr. Jefferson was sett up to rival and supplant him."

Adams continued. "The Committee had several meetings, in which were proposed the Articles of which the Declaration was to consist, and minutes made of them. The Committee then appointed Mr. Jefferson and me, to draw them up in form, and cloath them in a proper Dress. The Sub Committee met, and considered the Minutes, making such Observations on them as then occurred: when Mr. Jefferson desired me to take them to my Lodgings and make the Draught. This I declined and gave several reasons for declining. 1. That he was a Virginian and I a Massachusettensian. 2. That he was a southern Man and I a northern one. 3. That I had been so obnoxious for my early and constant Zeal in promoting the Measure, that any draught of mine, would undergo a more severe Scrutiny and criticism in Congress, than one of his composition. 4thly and lastly and that would be reason enough if there were no other, I had a great Opinion of the Elegance of his pen and none at all of my own. I therefore insisted that no hesitation should be made on his part. He accordingly took the Minutes and in a day or two produced to me his Draught." Adams then added a few words and sentences before making a copy, which now rests in the Massachusetts Historical Society.

What seems to be the most reasonable explanation is that Jefferson was elected to the committee because Richard Henry Lee, like Jefferson, wanted to return to Virginia to help write the state's new constitution. Jefferson received the most votes for the committee, thanks to some lobbying by Adams, and under the prevailing rules of Congress was designated the chairperson. Because he was the chairperson and because he had a known gift and flair for writing, he was given the task of translating ideas into words.

"This was the object of the Declaration of Independence," Jefferson later recalled in a May 8, 1825 letter to Henry Lee. "Not to find out new principles, or new arguments, never before thought of, not merely to say things which had never been said before; but to place before mankind the common sense of the subject; in terms so plain and firm as to command their assent, and to justify ourselves in the independent stand we are compelled to take, neither aiming at originality of principle or sentiment, nor yet copied from any particular and previous writing, it was intended to be an expression of american mind, and to give to that expression the proper tone and spirit called for by the occasion. All its authority rests then on the harmonizing sentiments of the day, whether expressed in conversation, in letters, printed essays, or in the elementary books of public right, as Aristotle, Cicero, Locke, Sidney, &c."

Jefferson certainly did that.

Before the committee could meet for the first time, one of the most influential documents in the writing of the Declaration of Independence appeared in public print. The Virginia Declaration of Rights as drafted by George Mason and Thomas Ludwell Lee was published in the June 12 issue of the *Pennsylvania Gazette*. It is even possible that Jefferson brought a copy of Mason's early draft with him to Philadelphia or one was sent to him by Mason, Lee, or Edmund Pendleton, the convention president.

After the committee organized itself, discussed the Declaration, and assigned the task of writing it, Jefferson settled into his room at the home of brick mason Jacob Graff at the southwest corner of Market and Seventh Streets with his Windsor chair and portable writing desk made by Benjamin Randolph.

Of the surviving drafts or fragments of drafts of the Declaration, Jefferson wrote all but the one in Adams's handwriting.

No one now knows what documents, books, or pamphlets Jefferson had in his room when he sat down to write. He surely had access to Mason's Virginia Declaration of Rights, his own drafts for a Virginia constitution, his own *A Summary View of the Rights of British America*, his own draft of *The Causes and Necessity for Taking up Arms*, and Thomas Paine's *Common Sense*. The books of the Library Company of Philadelphia were also readily available.

Many of Jefferson's ideas and even phrases can be found in the works of John Locke, Algernon Sidney and Henry Home, Lord Kames.

But whether Jefferson relied on his detailed knowledge of these works or whether he turned to them in the drafting process is not known.

However, Adams, in an August 6, 1822, letter to Timothy Pickering, referred to Jefferson's ideas as "commonplace" and the phrases as "hackney'd"—surely not the level of work that would require reference materials. And Jefferson himself later claimed that he turned "to neither book nor pamphlet" while writing it. Jefferson was undoubtedly so familiar with the common radical Whig writings of the day, with Mason's Declaration of Rights, and certainly with his own writings that he may have dashed off the first composition draft without recourse to secondary sources. But the Declaration of Independence has more than its roots in some of these antecedent documents.

Jefferson sought to demonstrate in precise detail that George III was a tyrant unfit to rule the Americans or any free people. He did so by declaring that the denial of certain "unalienable rights" by a ruler justified an act of revolution. To prove the tyrannical nature of George III, Jefferson listed a long series of charges and indictments—"a long train of abuses" --against the king that justified the assertion of natural rights. If the people had a right to revolution, they had a right to institute new governments based on the authority of the people. Congress, acting as the people's representative, could and must end American allegiance to the British Crown to preserve the rights of life, liberty, and the pursuit of happiness. But it was Jefferson's assertion that "all men are created equal" that has resounded through the centuries.

These were not ideas new to Jefferson or the other American revolutionaries, but the expression and form that Jefferson was about to present was a unique, elegant and powerful declaration of natural and revolutionary rights.

Adams first saw Jefferson's draft immediately after Franklin made some notations on June 21. Adams made a copy that is the earliest surviving unedited draft.

Before Jefferson submitted the document to Congress on June 28 the committee made forty-seven changes. Adams made two minor corrections and Franklin made four. Who suggested the others is anyone's guess.

On June 28 the committee submitted its draft to Congress. Jefferson's notes provide us with a clear contemporary account of what happened next.

"On Monday the 1st of July the house resolved itself into a commee. of the whole & resumed the consideration of the original motion made by the delegates of Virginia, which being again debated through the day, was carried in the affirmative by the votes of N. Hampshire, Connecticut, Massachusets, Rhode Island, N. Jersey, Maryland, Virginia, N. Carolina, & Georgia. S. Carolina and Pennsylvania voted against it. Delaware having but two members present they were divided: the delegates for New York declared they were for it themselves, & were assured their constituents were for it, but that their instructions having been drawn near a twelve-month before, when reconciliation was still the general object, they were enjoined by them to do nothing which should impede that object. They therefore thought themselves not justifiable in voting on either side, and asked leave to withdraw from the question, which was given them. The Commee. rose & reported their resolution to the house. Mr. Rutlege of S. Carolina then requested the determination might be put off to the next day, as he believed his collegues, tho' they disapproved of the resolution, would then join in it for the sake of unanimity. The ultimate question whether the house would agree to the resolution of the committee was accordingly postponed to the next day, when it was again moved and S. Carolina concurred in voting for it. In the mean time a third member had come post from the Delaware counties and turned the vote of that colony in favour of the resolution. Members of a different sentiment attending that morning from Pennsylvania also, their vote was changed, so that the whole 12 colonies, who were authorized to vote at all, gave their voices for it; and within a few days the convention of N. York approved of it and thus supplied the void occasioned by the withdrawing of their delegates from the vote."

Independence having been voted Adams wrote a triumphant letter to Abigail on July 3. It took Adams seven paragraphs before he got to the important point. "Yesterday the greatest Question was decided, which ever was debated in America, and a greater perhaps, never was or will be decided among Men." Adams continued: "You will see in a few days a Declaration setting forth the Causes, which have impell'd Us to this mighty Revolution, and the Reasons which will justify it, in the Sight of God and Man."

In a second letter that same day to Abigail, Adams added. "The Second Day of July 1776, will be the most memorable Epocha, in the History of America. I am apt to believe that it will be celebrated, by succeeding Generations, as the great anniversary Festival. It ought to be commemorated as the Day of Deliverance by solemn acts of devotion to God Almighty. It ought to be solemnized with pomp and parade, with shows, games, sports, guns, bells, bonfires, and illuminations from one end of this continent to the other from this time forward forever more."

As we now know Adams was wrong. July 4, the day the Declaration of Independence was approved and signed, is our national holiday. Jefferson wrote no letters until July 8, but he did continue his journal and the actual approval of the Declaration. Again Jefferson's notes lead us on.

"Congress proceeded the same day to consider the declaration of Independance, which had been reported & laid on the table the Friday preceding, and on Monday referred to a comee. of the whole. The pusillanimous idea that we had friends in England worth keeping terms with, still haunted the minds of many. For this reason those passages which conveyed censures on the people of England were struck out, lest they should give them offence. The clause too, reprobating the enslaving the inhabitants of Africa, was struck out in complaisance to South Carolina & Georgia, who had never attempted to restrain the importation of slaves, and who on the contrary still wished to continue it. Our Northern brethren also I believe felt a little tender under those censures; for tho' their people have very few slaves themselves yet they had been pretty considerable carriers of them to others. The debates having taken up the greater parts of the 2d, 3d & 4th days of July were, in the evening of the last closed. The declaration was reported by the commee., agreed to by the house, and signed by every member present except Mr. Dickinson."

At the risk of being Talmudic it is necessary to point out that the Declaration of Independence was actually finally approved in the morning of the fourth and that only Hancock signed the Declaration on that day. Members of Congress began to sign the clean scripted copy of the Declaration on August 2 and continued even after Congress had fled Philadelphia for Baltimore in December 1776. Not until January 18, 1777, did Congress authorize the printing of the Declaration with the names of all the signers "to have the same put upon the record." In other words, there would be no turning back for those patriot/traitors who signed the Declaration.

We do know that Jefferson's draft received "severe Criticism" and that Adams carried the heaviest burden of defending the document as presented to Congress. Jefferson later described Adams as "the colossus of independence" for his defense of the document in Congress.

What emerged from Congress was essentially Jefferson's and the committee's draft, but in a shorter, simpler form.

Two critical paragraphs were totally removed from the Declaration. Gone were the paragraphs denouncing the British people for supporting the monarch in his oppression of America and denouncing the king for continuing to allow the enslavement of Africans and the continued importation of African slaves by negating provincial laws forbidding the foreign importation of slaves.

Then there was the replacement of Jefferson's final gothic paragraph, with words from the Virginia resolution calling for independence.

Most of the thirty-nine changes made in Congress were meritorious verbal corrections that only served to tighten the language and focus the view of the reader.

Those who want a detailed analysis of the drafting of the Declaration can consult Gerard W. Gawalt's revised edition of Julian Boyd's *The Declaration of Independence. The Evolution of the Text.*

Jefferson became so visibly upset during the Congressional editing, that Franklin tried to calm his colleague with a story about a Philadelphia hatter, John Thompson, who wrote a complicated sign extolling the virtues of the best and cheapest hats in town. As his friends saw and critiqued John's advertisement the elaborate plan was whittled down to a mere sign in the shape of a hat with John Thompson printed on it. Jefferson was not amused.

The Declaration of Independence, like liberty and freedom, was not easily or individually achieved. The completed document was clearly the product of a committee of five and then the entire Congress. Some historians quip that it was the only document improved by a committee of Congress.

The adoption of the Declaration by a "unanimous" Congress came in the morning of July 4. Reportedly Jefferson and Secretary John Thomson took a corrected copy of the Declaration to the printer, John Dunlop, who produced the first printed copies of the Declaration.

Colonel John Nixon first publicly read the Declaration of Independence on July 6 in Philadelphia. That same day Congressional President Hancock began sending copies of the Declaration to General Washington and various state leaders and assemblies with these words. "The Congress, for some Time past, have had their Attention occupied by one of the most interesting and important Subjects, that could possibly come before them, or any other Assembly of Men." Now, Hancock continued, "fully convinced that our Affairs may take a more favourable Turn, the Congress have judged it necessary to dissolve the Connection between Great Britain and the American Colonies, and to declare them free & independent States."

Spontaneous celebrations broke out as copies of the Declaration radiated out along the post roads from Philadelphia even as a great British fleet and army appeared in New York harbor.

After the Declaration was read to the Continental Army in New York on July 9, the soldiers drank an extra toast of rum, rushed down to the Bowling Green and tore down a statue of King George Third within sight of British warships. The lead and brass from the statue later made its way to Connecticut where it was melted down for bullets and cannons for the American army.

Having sent his triumphant exultations to Abigail on July 3, Adams was a little more restrained in a July 5 letter to an old family friend, Mary Palmer. "I will inclose to you a Declaration, in which all America is remarkably united. It compleats a Revolution, which will make a good Figure in the History of Mankind, as any that has preceeded it."

Boston celebrated the Declaration of Independence on July 18 and fortunately Abigail was recovered enough from her smallpox inoculation to attend.

John thought briefly of returning home to help his family through their ordeal, but he asked for no relief from Congress. Instead telling Abigail on July 16. "I cannot leave this Place, without more injury to the public now, than I ever could at any other Time, being in the Midst of scenes of Business, which must not stop for any Thing."

Jefferson's first known letter written after the event is more narcissistic concentrating on the changes made to his draft and his desire to return to Virginia to work on that state's constitution. "I enclose you a copy of the declaration of independence agreed to by the House, and also, as originally framed," Jefferson told Richard Henry Lee in a July 8 letter. "You will judge whether it is better or worse for the Critics." Lee expressed the sincere wish in a July 21 letter that "for the honor of Congress, as for that of the States, that the Manuscript had not been mangled as it is. It is wonderful, and passing pitiful, that the rage of change should be so unhappily applied. However the *Thing* is in its nature so good, that no Cookery can spoil the Dish for the palates of Freemen."

Gerard W. Gawalt

# Forming A Confederation

*"How few of the human race have ever enjoyed an oppor-*
*tunity of making an election of government."*
JOHN ADAMS, *THOUGHTS ON GOVERNMENT*, 1776

*"A great and necessary work, but I fear almost desperate."*
THOMAS JEFFERSON TO JOHN ADAMS, MAY 16, 1777

ONCE INDEPENDENCE WAS declared, Congress turned to the writing of a constitution for the new nation. Jefferson was a member of the committee that began
composing the Articles of Confederation on July 12. That both Adams and
Jefferson took notes signifies the importance both men attached to writing the
Articles of Confederation. Adams was an eager participant in Congressional
debates and Jefferson took notes on at least two of his speeches. Jefferson also
joined in the debates.

Jefferson kept notes on only "the two articles of Confederation respecting
taxes and voting. I took minutes of the heads of the arguments. On the first I
threw all into one mass, without ascribing to the speakers their respective arguments; pretty much in the manner of Hume's summary digests of the reasoning's in parliament for and against a measure. On the last, I stated the heads of
arguments used by each speaker." The debates summarized in Jefferson's notes
took place on July 30, 31 and August 1, 1776 as Congress sat in a committee
of the whole and thirty thousand British troops confronted Washington's much
smaller Continental army at New York.

Unfortunately, Jefferson did not record any participation on his part. But
Adams did. No doubt Jefferson agreed with the complaints voiced by delegates

from those states that wanted proportional representation rather than a single vote for each state and taxation based on the value of land not population.

One of those speakers he did note was John Adams. Delegates from states with large numbers of slaves did not want to count them in establishing financial quotas due from states to pay into a common treasury to defray costs of "war & other expenses that shall be incurred for the common defense, or general welfare."

Adams took to the floor. According to Jefferson's notes, "Mr. John Adams observed that the numbers of people were taken by this article as an index of the wealth of the state & not as subjects of taxation. That as to this matter it was of no consequence by what name you called your people, whether by freemen or slaves." Those laborers "add as much wealth" whether they are 500 slaves or 500 freemen, said Adams.

Adams argued, again according to Jefferson, that the conditions of New England fishermen were "as abject as that of slaves." Still it was the number of people that was important. "That a slave may indeed from the custom of speech be more properly called the wealth of his master; than the free labourer might be called the wealth of his employer; but as to the state both were equally it's wealth, and should therefore equally add to the quota of it's tax."

The states temporarily rejected the proposed amendment to count only "white inhabitants," but the issue was not dead. Ultimately the Articles of Confederation would assess a quota to each state in "proportion to the value of all land within each state, granted or surveyed for any person."

Congress then turned its attention to Article XVII that assigned one vote to each state "in determining questions."

The large states and the small states quickly divided into two camps. Representing a large state, Adams "advocated the voting in proportion to numbers." Adams turned quickly to the perceived inequities. "It has been objected that a proportional vote will endanger the smaller states. We answer that an equal vote will endanger the larger." Their geographic separation, "their difference of produce, of interests, & of manners" will prevent the larger states from combining "for the oppression of the smaller," argued Adams. He argued that individuals might have to submit individually to "the common mass."

Unfortunately, Adams did not record his own thoughts in his notes of debates on the Confederation for July 30. But the fact that both Jefferson and

Adams took notes on the debates in Congress over questions of assigned revenue quotas and the mode of voting in Congress underscores their importance to the two men and to Congress.

Again Adams's arguments failed, and the Articles of Confederation assigned each state one vote regardless of size, population or wealth.

Jefferson later recalled that he privately put forth to Adams a plan to break the deadlock between large and small states. "It was that any proposition might be negatived by the representatives of a majority of the people of the United States, or of a majority of the colonies of America. The former secures the larger the latter the smaller colonies."

Ultimately, the government under the Articles of Confederation would flounder because of the failure of Congress to solve these issues in a manner satisfactorily to the nation's leaders and to the pragmatic operation of a national government.

Jefferson strongly criticized the draft articles in a July 16 letter to Richard Henry Lee. The confederation plan "is in every interesting point the reverse of what our country [i.e. Virginia] would wish. You can never be absent at a time so interesting to your country. I make no doubt it will be long in it's passage through the Committee so that you may be here in time to attack it in the house from Alpha to Omega." I guess he didn't like it.

Jefferson, as the representative of a landed state, was particularly concerned about the regulation of the sale of lands and the control of state boundaries. On July 25, according to Adams's notes, Jefferson rose to speak. Jefferson "Moves an Amendment that all Purchases of Lands, not within the Boundaries of any Colony shall be made by Congress." No doubt with the Proclamation of 1763 in mind, he also wanted security that Congress "will not curtail the present Settlements of states." Jefferson added, "I have no doubt, that the Colonies will limit themselves."

On the same day, Jefferson also joined the debate over when Congress would meet.

On August 2 Jefferson again rose to protest any limitations on Virginia's claims to the Pacific Ocean. "I protest vs. the Right of Congress to decide, upon the Right of Virginia."

Perhaps, Adams's later recollection that Jefferson seldom spoke in Congress was somewhat exaggerated.

Adams, like Jefferson was worried about his family but did not seem ready to go home when he told Isaac Smith that he could not "in honor and duty to the public stir from this place." There was work to do and "We are in hourly expectation of some important event at New York." There was and it was not going to be pretty.

However, by July 26 he was asking James Warren for relief. "My health has lasted much longer, than I expected but at last it fails. The Increasing Heat of the Weather added to incessant application to Business, without any Intermissions of Exercise, has relaxed me to such a degree that a few Weeks more would totally incapacitate me for any Thing. I must therefore return home." Adams would stay until October 12.

By the end of July Jefferson too was more than ready to return to Virginia pleading with Richard Henry Lee for a replacement. "The minutiae of the Confederation" were too much. "For god's sake, for your country's sake, and for my sake, come. I receive by every post such accounts of the state of Mrs. Jefferson's health, that it will be impossible for me to disappoint her expectation of seeing me at the time I have promised, which supposed my leaving here on the 11th of next month."

Jefferson got so antsy to return that he prepared a Congressional resolution to require the states to replace one-half of the Congressional delegation at each annual election and to prohibit delegates from serving more than two years. There is no evidence in the Congressional journals that he ever formally submitted his proposal to Congress.

Congress concluded its three-week debate on the Confederation on August 8 with a host of unresolved questions. On August 20 the Articles of Confederation were printed in anticipation of a debate in the Committee of the Whole.

Meanwhile, Adams was still busy on the committee to prepare a plan to secure foreign alliances. The committee finally submitted its plan on July 18 when it was printed for the consideration of the members.

On August 27 Congress ordered Adams and the committee to prepare instructions to ministers abroad.

Jefferson told Lee on July 29 that it "will come on when we shall have got through the Confederation." Debate began on August 22 the day after British troops landed on Long Island to confront the Americans on Brooklyn Heights and debate continued until September 17 as Washington's army retreated north to White Plains.

Jefferson would have to wait until September 3 for his departure, not to return to Congress until late in 1783. But poor health or not, Jefferson's wife, Martha, was pregnant soon after his arrival in Monticello.

Two days later Adams told his wife Abigail that "our Affairs having taken a Turn at Long Island and New York, so much to our disadvantage, I cannot see my Way clear, to return home so soon as I intended. I shall wait here, until I see some more decisive event."

What Adams did not say was that on September 3 Congress had received a written proposal through the newly paroled General John Sullivan from British Admiral Lord Richard Howe calling for a peace conference on Staten Island. Adams promptly opposed the idea calling Howe's conference a "decoy duck" to expose their newly announced Declaration of Independence to ridicule.

Four days of debate followed. Adams recalled in his autobiography that he was convinced Howe was up to "Machiavellian maneuvers." Jefferson was on his way to Monticello.

Perhaps because of his staunch opposition to conferring with Howe Adams was chosen on September 6 along with Franklin and Edward Rutledge to form the committee to beard the lion's den and confront Howe. On the day of their departure from Philadelphia Congress revised the wording of Continental commissions, replacing "United Colonies" with "United States."

Adams assured his cousin Samuel that the meeting with Howe would lead nowhere. To James Warren he confided on September 8 that Congress had voted that "they can not send Members to talk with" Howe "in their private Capacities but will send a Committee of their Body as Representatives of the free and independent States of America." So concluded Adams "I presume his Lordship cannot see Us, and I hope he will not, but if he should the whole will terminate in nothing."

Leaving the arrangements to Franklin, the committee set off on September 9 and arrived at Staten Island on September 11. The meeting unfolded much as Adams had predicted. Howe announced he could only meet with them as private citizens and informed them that if Congress gave up the idea of independence the British government had authorized him to make peace and issue pardons.

Adams, who unknowingly was on Howe's list of unpardonable patriots to be hung, staunchly responded. "Your Lordship may consider me in what light you please, and indeed, I should be willing to consider myself, for a few moments, in any character which would be agreeable to your Lordship, except that of a British subject."

After three or four hours of jab and counter jab, the sparring ceased when it became clear Howe could only offer pardons if America abandoned independence. At last Howe apologized for the committee having had "the trouble of coming so far to so little purpose."

On September 14, John gave his own lengthy account of the meeting to his cousin Samuel. "The whole affair of the Commission appears to me, at it ever did, to be a Bubble, an Ambuscade, a mere insidious Manœuvre, calculated only to decoy and deceive, and it is so gross, that they must have a wretched opinion of our Generalship to Suppose we can fall into it." Adams ended the meeting by observing, "that all the Colonies had gone completely through a Revolution. That they had taken all authority from the officers of the Crown, and had appointed officers of their own, which his Lordship might easily conceive had cost great Struggles, and that they could not easily go back; and that Americans had too much understanding not to know that after such a declaration as they had made, the Government of G.B. never would have any Confidence in them, or could govern them again but by force of Arms." Lord Howe had just been verbally slapped in the face. Only war would settle the duel.

No doubt Adams would have smiled had he been able to read the conclusion of Ambrose Searle, one of Howe's staff. "They met, they talked, they parted and now nothing remains but to fight it out against a set of the most determined hypocrites and demagogues, compiled of the refuse of the colonies, that ever were permitted by Providence to be the scourge of a country."

And so Adams and the committee returned to Philadelphia and the British armed forces returned to attacking Washington's forces on Manhattan.

Once the committee was back in Philadelphia, Congress moved quickly to adopt a new plan for the Continental Army and a new set of Articles of War. Adams was key in the drawing up of both plans.

Then on September 17 Congress finally adopted its plan for foreign treaties and ministers after Adams lobbied hard to remove all "articles of entangling alliance." The same day it received the report of the committee appointed to confer with Lord Howe. Adams was a busy man.

Jefferson, during the same time span, had reached Monticello and decided to move his "ailing" wife, Martha, and their children to Williamsburg for the meeting of the state assembly.

Proving the adage that you should never leave a meeting lest you be appointed to an unpleasant or simply unwanted task, the Continental Congress appointed Jefferson a minister to France along with Franklin and Silas Deane of Connecticut on September 26, 1776.

Richard Henry Lee urged Jefferson on September 27 to accept his appointment, arguing that "great abilities and unshaken virtue" are "necessary for the execution of what the safety of America does so capitally rest upon." Lee pushed hard. "In my judgement, the most eminent services that the greatest of her sons can do America will not more essentially serve her and honor themselves, than a successful negotiation with France."

At work in Williamsburg on establishing the new Virginia government, Jefferson was reluctant to leave his wife, family, and the government of his own state. After some days of consideration, Jefferson rejected the opportunity because "circumstances peculiar in the situation of my family, such as neither permit me to leave nor to carry it, compel me to ask leave to decline." When Adams in turn was faced with the opportunity to replace the corrupt Deane as one of America's three ministers to France, he did not hesitate.

For the next three years Jefferson would see the war as a series of distant events, which seldom intruded into his conscious life. Every year he spent months in the Virginia capital and he saw himself as a central character in the revolution. Others were not so generous.

As the American army retreated before General Howe and Jefferson settled into life in Williamsburg, Adams was becoming irritated with General Washington's assigning blame for his defeats to "the New England Troops as Cowards running away perpetually." Adams complained to Henry Knox, a fellow New Englander and commander of Washington's artillery corps, in a September 29 letter. "I must say that your *amiable* General gives too much occasion for these Reports by his Letters, in which he <is eternally throwing some slur or other upon> often mentions things to the Disadvantage of some Part of New England, but <never one Word> Seldom any Thing of the Kind about any other Part of the Continent." The words in angle brackets had been crossed out in Adams's draft letter.

The problem Adams told Daniel Hitchcock on October 1 is that "Your Army, Sir, give me leave to say, has been ill managed, in two most Essential Points." They are untrained in military discipline and need to be introduced to "military ardour," asserted Adams. "Our inevitable Destruction will be the consequence if these Faults are not amended," he predicted. Adams criticism of Washington would reach a pinnacle over the next year of military defeats.

Years later Adams told Benjamin Rush in a March 19, 1812, letter that Congress had taken steps to protect Washington's public image by preventing the public disclosure of his errors. Faith in the commander had to be maintained.

Adams, like Jefferson before him, was tired and frustrated by the constant work and stress in Philadelphia. Adams had postponed his return home to deal with Lord Howe's peace offer and the selection of foreign ministers. Now he would wait no longer. When the Massachusetts government declined to replace him as a delegate, Adams sought and received a "leave of Absence" from Congress. The journals of Congress did not record a vote on a leave of absence for Adams, but he departed for home on October 13.

Jefferson remained in Williamsburg where he tried hard to modernize Virginia laws by ending primogeniture and entail, providing for freedom of religion, disestablishing the church in Virginia, reforming the courts, and establishing a system of gradual emancipation for slaves. Only the first gained any traction.

Adams and Jefferson remained at home through the fall. Both men enjoyed their return and both couples spent the winter in a pregnant state. Washington retreated to Pennsylvania and Congress retreated to Baltimore. Then suddenly on the day after Christmas Washington struck the Hessian forces at Trenton, New Jersey. The amazing victory was followed just days later by another bold attack on General Howe's forces at Princeton, New Jersey. No doubt Adams and Jefferson were among the American patriots who took heart from these striking victories. Some might say revolution saving victories.

By mid-January 1777 Washington had settled into winter quarters at Morristown, New Jersey and Adams was preparing to rejoin Congress in Baltimore. Abigail confided to her friend Mercy Otis Warren. "I had it in my heart to dissuade him from going and I know I could have prevailed, but our public affairs at the time wore so gloomy an aspect that I thought if ever his assistance was wanted, it must be at such a time."

Adams plunged off into the winter taking his seat in Congress on February 4 just days after Congress ordered the distribution of authenticated copies of the Declaration of Independence containing the names of all the signers, including Adams and Jefferson.

Just days later on February 10 Adams apparently gave up hope of returning to his home and his judgeship and sent his resignation as chief justice of the Massachusetts Superior Court of Judicature to the Massachusetts Council. Adams had held on for nearly two years to the hope that he would be able to give up his seat in Congress. No such luck.

By spring Jefferson was safely tucked away at Monticello where his wife gave birth to a short-lived and unnamed son on May 28. Congress was back in Philadelphia and all were awaiting the outcome of the new military campaigns. May also saw the beginning of a new stage in the relationship of Adams and Jefferson.

Jefferson and Adams began an episodic but lifelong correspondence in May 1777, when the former was a delegate to the Virginia Assembly in Williamsburg and Adams was still laboring as a delegate to the Continental Congress in Philadelphia. Their first letters were marked by the intellectual heft that characterized their entire correspondence. Despite the demands of the war, both men focused on the future of an independent United States. On May 16 Jefferson urged Adams to see that the Articles of Confederation still being drafted included measures that would enable the large states and the small states to equally negative legislative acts. Jefferson wrote: "I learn from our delegates that the Confederation is again on the carpet. A great and necessary work, but I fear almost desperate. The point of representation is what most alarms me, as I fear the great and small colonies are bitterly determined not to cede. Will you be so good as to recollect the proposition I formerly made you in private and try if you can work it into some good to save our union? It was that any proposition might be negatived by the representatives of a majority of the people of the United States, or of a majority of the colonies of America. The former secures the larger the latter the smaller colonies."

Gerard W. Gawalt

Responding to a debate that would continue through an unknown future federal constitutional convention, Adams assured his friend he would try to take care of it.

"The great Work of Confederation, draggs heavily on, but I don't despair of it. The great and Small States must be brought as near together as possible: and I am not without Hopes, that this may de done, to the tolerable Satisfaction of both. Your Suggestion, Sir, that any Proposition may be negatived by the Representatives of a Majority of the People, or of a Majority of the States, shall be attended to," wrote Adams in a May 26 reply. It was not.

Adams urged Jefferson to return to Congress. "We want your Industry and Abilities here extreamly. Financiers, We want more than Soldiers. The Worst Enemy We have now is Poverty, real Poverty in the Shape of exuberant Wealth." Adams pleaded with Jefferson to come help solve the problem of rampant inflation. "Pray come and help Us."

Even Jefferson's Virginia colleague, Richard Henry Lee, chided Jefferson for being "in your retirement."

In response on August 21, Jefferson suggested sending Philip Mazzei as a special agent to the Duke of Tuscany to ask for gold, which could then "be applied to reduce the quantity of circulating paper." Probably leading Adams to ask himself --Why didn't I think of that ever so practical idea?

Jefferson feared British forces were about to attack Virginia. "What upon earth can Howe mean by the manoeuvre he is now practicing?" Wouldn't he be better occupying Philadelphia, asked Jefferson? Yes he would, as Adams soon found out.

Adams no doubt received this letter, just as Lord Howe's army was rolling over Washington's forces at Brandywine Creek and rolling through southeast Pennsylvania into Philadelphia as Adams was preparing to flee.

Even as the British army pushed forward and Congress fled from Philadelphia to Lancaster and then York, Pennsylvania, Adams reported on October 24 to James Warren that Congress was still at work "upon Confederation, and have nearly completed it." Adams stayed in Congress until the Articles of Confederation were virtually completed. Two days after Adams left Congress on November 11, Gerry reported, "this Evening finished the Confederacy." In early November the Articles of Confederation were printed and distributed to the states for ratification. Adams was back in Massachusetts when Jefferson on December 17 wrote to inform him that Virginia had given "our approbation of the Confederacy."

No one knew it would be four years before they would be ratified by enough states to take effect.

Both men, who had worked on the Articles of Confederation since 1776, were no doubt disappointed that the Articles continued to allow only voting by states. With the genius of hindsight we know it was an issue that would continue to bedevil the American government and would dominate debates in the 1787 Federal Constitutional Convention in Philadelphia.

America's search for a workable plan of national government was a slow, difficult process and would last more than a decade. Compromise, cooperation and creativity were required as the Americans moved from being colonials in a patriarchal monarchy to citizen-leaders in a representative republic.

Most of the process took place in the midst of a long, revolutionary war. Not only were these "the times that try men's souls," in the words of Thomas Paine, they were also the times that tested Americans' intellects and practical political skills in creating a strong, national republican government.

The Atlantic Ocean and diverging interpretations of American culture and the form of government necessary for the success of the American republican experiment would soon separate Adams and Jefferson. During the final five years of the American Revolution Jefferson and Adams each wrote one perfunctory letter to the other. They never saw each other and no doubt seldom thought of each other from late 1777 (One unanswered letter from Adams on June 29, 1780, excepted.) until Jefferson's arrival in France as minister to France in 1784.

But back to the reality of the here and now of the Revolution. In the fall of 1777 Washington and the main Continental Army had been beaten at Brandywine Creek and Germantown and Congress had fled to York, Pennsylvania.

This sparked the only time Washington's leadership was seriously challenged and Adams did not have Washington's back.

Adams earlier had complained to his diary on September 21, 1777 as Congress lighted in Lancaster about Washington's tactics and a "very injudicious maneuver" that Adams believed led to his defeat at Brandywine. "Oh,

Heaven grant us one great soul!" We had been "out-generaled" yet again, and Adams wished for "one great Soul! One leading mind" to "extricate the best cause from that ruin which seems to await it."

Shortly, thereafter General Horatio Gates's northern army not only defeated the British at Saratoga, New York, but General Burgoyne surrendered his entire army on October 17.

Did Adams wonder whether General Gates who had won a tremendous victory over the British forces at Saratoga was that "One active Capacity" or "one great Soul" who "would bring order out of this Confusion and save this Country."

Writing to Abigail on October 26, 1777, Adams could not have been more delighted that General Gates and not General Washington had achieved the American victory at Saratoga. "Congress will appoint a Thanksgiving, and one Cause of it ought to be that the Glory of turning the tide of Arms, is not immediately due to the Commander in Chief nor to southern Troops. If it had been, Idolatry, and Adulation would have been unbounded, so excessive as to endanger our Liberties for what I know."

Washington will still get his due without fear of a Cromwell or a Caesar, asserted Adams. "Now We can allow a certain Citizen to be wise, virtuous, and good, without thinking him a Deity or a saviour."

His cousin Samuel Adams, along with James Lovell, Thomas Mifflin, Benjamin Rush and Richard Henry Lee, were outspoken critics of Washington in Congress. Adams's friend, Benjamin Rush, wrote this stabbing remark. "The northern army has shown us what Americans are capable of doing with a GENERAL at their head." Speaking of Washington's army, Rush reportedly added. "A Gates, a Lee or a Conway would in a few weeks render them an irresistible body of men." Rush told Adams in an October 21, 1777, letter, that not only had Gates achieved a victory that saved Pennsylvania and New York, but his army was much better disciplined than "General Washington's imitation of an army" which was "an unformed mob."

John Adams, meanwhile, took a backhanded slap at Washington. "I am sick of Fabian systems in all quarters."

Decades later in his autobiography, Adams would complain that Virginia delegate Benjamin Harrison was behind the "Calumnies that were written or otherwise insinuated into the Minds of the Army that I was an Enemy to

Washington, in favour of an annual Election of a General, against Enlisting Troops during the War &c. &c. all utterly false and groundless."

Clearly, in the aftermath of Gates' victory at Saratoga and Washington's defeats at Brandywine and Germantown, there was dissatisfaction with the commander-in-chief. John, however, had returned to Massachusetts and already decided to go to France, when matters reached a climax in Congress.

Irish born General Thomas Conway fueled the fire by writing a letter to Gates calling Washington "a weak General" with "bad Councellors." The letter went the eighteenth century version of viral.

Copies of the letter were everywhere. Military aides to all the generals threatened duels. Washington was at Valley Forge, when Generals Gates and Conway appeared before Congress on January 19, 1778. Faced with the opportunity and the need to directly challenge Washington's leadership, they backed down. Efforts to "reform" the army through the Board of War misfired.

Washington's leadership was never again seriously challenged.

But as Virginia Assembly leader Benjamin Harrison, wrote on February 19, 1778. "The General is fully inform'd of all these Cabals, they prey on his Constitution, sink his Spirits, and will in the end I fear prove fatal to him, if this should be the case excuse me for once more repeating it, America, will lose perhaps her only prop. He well knows bad consequences would follow his resignation, or he would not leave it in the powers of the wicked and designing, thus to insult him, with a few words more I shall finish this painful Subject, *Be Ware of your Board of War.*"

Ultimately Conway was promoted but soon resigned. Gates was removed from a command position and along with Thomas Mifflin was assigned to the newly formed Board of War. Washington emerged more secure as commander-in-chief than ever.

The crisis was over, but the fallout would continue. When Adams was appointed a minister to France in 1777, General Knox journeyed to Braintree to sound out Adams on his "relation to General Washington," Adams recorded in his autobiography. "I answered with the Utmost Frankness, that I thought him a perfectly honest Man, with an amiable and excellent heart, and the most important Character at that time among Us, for he was the Center of our Union. He asked the question, he said, because, as I was going to Europe it was of importance that the General's Character should be supported in other

Countries. I replied that he might be perfectly at his ease on the Subject for he might depend upon it, that both from principle and Affection, public and private I should do my Utmost to support his Character at all times and in all places, unless something should happen very greatly to alter my Opinion of him, and this I have done from that time to this. I mention this incident, because that insolent Blasphemer of things sacred and transcendent Libeller of all that is good Tom Paine has more than once asserted in Print, the scandalous lye, that I was one of a Faction in the fall of the Year 1777, against General Washington. It is indeed a disgrace to the moral Character and the Understanding of this Age, that this worthless fellow should be believed in any thing. But Impudence and Malice will always find Admirers."

Indeed, when Adams was in France in 1778 French leaders asked Adams "whether there was any foundation for the Reports which the Ministry had spread in England, of a Dispute between Congress and Gen. Washington. A Letter they say has been printed, from an officer in Phila. to that Purpose." Adams did not record his response in his diary, but in his autobiography he noted this sharp denial. "My answer was that no such dispute existed when I left Congress in November, that I heard of no such Thing after I left it, before my Embarkation in February, that I had not information of it, since my Arrival in France, and that so far from giving any Credit to the report, I believed it to be impossible."

We shall see there even would be a near disastrous effect for Adams on the election for vice-president in 1788.

Neither Jefferson nor his acolyte Madison was in Congress for the Conway Cabal, but the dispute extended to the Virginia Assembly where both men held seats. Richard Henry Lee and Patrick Henry were focal points of the debate. George Mason, author of the Virginia Declaration of Rights, the Virginia Constitution, and a friend of Washington, was forced to come to Washington's defense. According to Mason, "he was convinced from the whole of his conversations with Lee, Harrison and other members of Congress, that a Faction in Congress against you [Washington] had never existed."

No doubt Madison and Jefferson were not as convinced as Mason, and they undoubtedly heard reports or rumors of Adams's criticism of Washington's generalship and his hostility to the "idolatry" of Washington.

At the time Jefferson had nothing to say in writing about the opposition to Washington's command or much to say at all about the war.

Washington's aide, Alexander Hamilton, and Virginians, such as Madison, would forever accuse Adams of being hostile to General Washington. But all that was in the future. Now Adams had a decision to make.

Adams had "Sett off from York Town" and left Congress on November 11 after Congress fled westward from Philadelphia to Lancaster before settling in York, Pennsylvania. Adams arrived in Braintree on November 27.

In his autobiography, Adams claimed that "When I asked leave of Congress to make a visit to my constituents and my family in November, 1777, it was my intention to decline the next election, and return to my practice at the bar." His return to private life would be cut short by an offer he could not refuse.

As the American army under General Washington settled in for a winter of misery at the confluence of Valley Creek and the Schuylkill River just northwest of Philadelphia, Adams and Jefferson planned winters of comfort while "snug in their beds."

# Expanding Horizons

*"I should have wanted no motives or arguments to induce me to accept of this momentous trust, if I could be sure that the public would be benefited by it."*
JOHN ADAMS TO JAMES LOVELL, DECEMBER 24, 1777

*"All my plans of comfort and happiness reversed by a single event and nothing answering in prospect before me but the gloom unbrightened with one cheerful expectation."*
THOMAS JEFFERSON TO ELIZABETH EPPES, OCTOBER 3, 1782

PREVIOUSLY ALERTED BY Massachusetts delegate Elbridge Gerry, Adams would not have been surprised when official news of his November appointment as minister to France reached him in Braintree in December.

Former colleagues in Congress James Lovell and Daniel Roberdeau sent letters before the end of November urging Adams to accept and make "the great sacrifice." Not knowing French was no objection argued Lovell, "you may perfectly master the grammar on your voyage and gain much of the Speech too by having a genteel French man for a fellow passenger."

However, when the official news arrived Adams was away arguing a court case in Portsmouth, New Hampshire. Abigail was home, opened the letters, and was infuriated about this latest attempt to "rob me of all my happiness."

When Adams returned from New Hampshire on December 22, he had already made up his mind "after much Agitation of Mind and a thousand reveries." All that remained were the necessary obligatory spousal consultations and personal ministrations. The next day Adams wrote his letter of acceptance to Congressional President Henry Laurens.

Gerard W. Gawalt

To his friend and colleague, Lovell, Adams wrote on December 24, 1777, that despite the attraction of remaining home and making money "I should have wanted no motives or arguments to induce me to accept of this momentous trust, if I could be sure that the public would be benefited by it." Despite the injuries to himself and his family Adams was determined "to persevere in public life, and to engage in a new scæne, for which I fear I am, very ill qualified."

Abigail wanted to join John in the trip to France, but "I could not prevail upon him to consent," she told John's old law clerk, John Thaxter, on February 15, 1778. "I resign my own personal felicity and look for my satisfaction in the Consciousness of having discharged my duty to the publick." And so their long separation was renewed.

While Adams prepared to leave for France, Washington's army settled into Valley Forge, and Jefferson went to Monticello with a pregnant Martha.

Adams and his son John Quincy left Massachusetts in mid-February on a stormy and dangerous voyage to France. Adding to the excitement of the voyage, his ship, the frigate Boston, engaged an armed British merchantman Martha in a very brief firefight (one shot from the Martha) before the Martha struck her colors. Adams stood on deck, musket in hand, ready to join the fray. It would be John's only military confrontation of the war. Adams recounted the event in his diary for March 14, 1778. "We spied a sail, and gave her chase, we soon came up with her; but as we had borne directly down upon her, she had not seen our broadside, and knew not our force. She was a letter of marque, with fourteen guns, eight nines, and six sixes. She fired upon us, and one of her shot went through our mizzen yard. I happened to be upon the quarter deck, and in the direction from the ship to the yard, so that the ball went directly over my head. We upon this, turned our broadside, which the instant she saw, she struck." To paraphrase many battle survivors, joy is hearing the bullets whine and living to tell the story.

On March 30, while British troops still occupied the American cities of New York and Philadelphia, Adams reached Bordeaux to begin a decade of Foreign Service trying to wrest favorable treaties and loans from reluctant European countries. Over dinner on a French warship in Bordeaux harbor Adams learned that his mission had already been accomplished. France had agreed to an alliance with the United States on February 7.

Adams joined the "glittering clatter" of Paris on April 8 where he entered the seemingly endless tumultuous life in the diplomatic capital of Europe. The first person Adams went to see in Paris was Benjamin Franklin. Old colleagues from the Continental Congress, Adams and Franklin might be expected to work harmoniously together. They would not.

Adams and Franklin quickly came to a mutual dislike. On the one hand Adams soon became distrustful of the French Foreign Minister Charles Gravier, Comte de Vergennes. On the other hand, Franklin believed it was his job to mollify the French and by any means keep them engaged in the war. Adams quickly came to believe that the French were duping them and would abandon them if they saw an advantage. Moreover, Adams concluded that the French wanted to limit the size and strength of the United States thus keeping them dependent on France. Adams believed Franklin supported France to the detriment of the United States.

Some historians, such as James Grant, have concluded that Adams "loathed" Franklin. Certainly he did not trust his "servility" and "Selfishness."

Certainly, he thought he was lazy and came to believe that he too much favored the French in lifestyle and diplomacy.

"In truth Congress and their Ministers have been plaid upon like Children, trifled with, imposed upon, deceived. Franklin's Servility and insidious faithless Selfishness is the true and only Cause why this Game has succeeded. He has aided Vergennes with all his Weight, and his great Reputation, in both Worlds, has supported this ignominious system and blasted every Man and every Effort to shake it off. I only had a little Success against him," claimed Adams.

The thin-skinned Adams rankled when Parisians asked him if he was the "fameux Adams." John reported in his diary on February 11, 1779, that he valiantly tried to convince them he was not his cousin, the "fameux Adams" or "cette un homme célèbre."

Jefferson, on the other hand, was lionized as the author of the Declaration of Independence. No doubt Adams, who had served on the five-man committee to draft the Declaration, felt a twinge of resentment on every occasion.

Unfortunately when Adams first arrived he understood very few words of French. As a result an interpreter always filtered his ideas and those of the person with whom he was conversing. Adams worked assiduously on learning

French and within months was at least capable of carrying on a conversation. Soon he believed he understood and spoke French better than Franklin.

Adams attempted to throw himself into the Parisian whirl, attending the ballet, the opera and unnumbered dinners and receptions. In letters to Abigail he praised "the richness, the magnificence, and splendor" of aristocratic France.

And the women! "To tell you the truth," Adams admitted to Abigail on April 25, 1778, "I admire the ladies here. Don't be jealous. They are handsome, and very well educated. Their Accomplishments are exceedingly brilliant. And their Knowledge of Letters and Arts, exceeds that of the English Ladies, I believe." Franklin had even more privileges, teased Adams. "My venerable Colleague enjoys a Priviledge here, that is much to be envyd. Being seventy years of Age, the Ladies not only allow him to <kiss> embrace them as often as he pleases, but they are perpetually embracing him."

But don't be jealous while you weed the garden, raise the children, do the laundry and swill the pigs. Think of how I am suffering by being wined and dined in the fine houses of France on behalf of the United States.

Jefferson too would become enamored of French society and French women when he arrived in France nearly a decade later.

Adams tried mightily to understand his fellow American ministers, Franklin, Arthur Lee and Ralph Izard. They in turn continued to distrust each other and persisted with their bitter infighting while trying to win Adams to their point of view. He found Franklin fat, lazy, careless with money, and far too trusting of the French. He found few records of past financial and diplomatic activity. Adams and Lee tried to arrange the mission's finances without any effect.

Adams came to believe that many of Franklin's acquaintances, such as William Alexander, Edward Bancroft and David Hartley, were spies. And he was right, but Franklin didn't seem to care. In fact, British and French spies surrounded them, noting their thoughts and reading their mail.

Although Adams was inclined to denigrate his own contributions to American diplomacy, the British agent Alexander gave him high marks. "His knowledge of England and its constitution is a matter of real amazement to me. The most trite and common things as well as the more nice relative either to customs, manners, arts, policy, or constitution are equally known to him."

Perhaps, Alexander, a Scot, forgot that America had really once been part of Great Britain.

"He has, I believe, a keen temper which if he can command thoroughly, will be a great merit. His understanding lies, I think, rather in seeing large things largely than correctly." Alexander decided that "in the conduct of affairs he may perhaps be able to take so comprehensive a view as to render invention and expedient unnecessary, but were they to become necessary, I think he would fail in these—and I am not clear as to the first, or whether much of his reputation may not arise from a very firm and decisive tone suited to the times, with a clear and perspicuous elocution."

What was probably most disappointing to Alexander was "he is an enthusiast however with regard to everything in this country but the constitution and can conceive no country superiour to it" and his "discretion." The latter was something totally lacking in Franklin and Lee. Franklin assured Adams that he was not worried about spies or discretion because he had no information worth hiding. Adams disliked and distrusted the other two spies, Hartley and Bancroft, despite Franklin's nonchalance. In his autobiography Adams recorded his lack of confidence in Hartley and his belief that Bancroft was corrupt.

Adams realized the importance of French support for the American Revolution, but he didn't know what he was supposed to do in France. He was soon writing to Samuel Adams on May 21 that he and Lee were superfluous. Franklin could do the job himself. "In having three Commissioners at this Court. One in the character of Envoy is enough." Additionally, the frugal Adams added you would save money.

He became bored and labored valiantly at the only thing he could really grasp-the administrative paperwork of the mission. "Our Affairs in this Kingdom, I find in a State of Confusion and darkness, that surprizes me," John told the "fameux Adams." "Prodigious Sums of money have been expended and large Sums are yet due. But there are no books of Account, or any Documents, from which I have been able to learn what the United States have received as an Equivalent."

Unfortunately, neither Lee nor Franklin was the slightest bit interested and Adams "found that the business of our commission would never be done unless I did it."

"My two Colleagues would agree in nothing," Adams noted in his diary for May 27. "The Life of Dr. Franklin was a Scene of continual discipation. I could never obtain the favour of his Company in a Morning before Breakfast which would have been the most convenient time to read over the Letters and papers, deliberate on their contents, and decide upon the Substance of the answers." Both Lee and Adams believed the only records Franklin kept were those of the dinner invitations.

"I should have been happy to have done all the Business or rather all the Drudgery, if I could have been favoured with a few moments in a day to receive his Advice concerning the manner in which it ought to be done." But according to Adams "this condescention was not attainable. All that could be had was his Signature, after it was done, and this it is true he very rarely refused though he sometimes delayed."

No wonder Adams who admired hard work and dedication to duty, could not understand Franklin's approach to diplomacy. But the French loved Franklin's attention to society and they loved his celebrity. After all Adams was not the "fameux Adams."

Adams and his colleagues urged more French participation in the war; even after a French fleet under Count D'Estaing was nearly destroyed by a hurricane during a failed attempt to force the British from Newport, Rhode Island in August 1778.

In May of 1778, John had written to his cousin Samuel recommending the appointment of a single minister to France. For one thing Adams argued the expense of maintaining three ministers in France was not justified. With three ministers there were bound to be conflicts and jealousies, said John. John wanted some of the ministers recalled or sent to other courts to negotiate commercial treaties. In short, John claimed. "The Inconveniencies arising from the Multiplicity of Ministers and the Complications of Businesses are infinite."

By the end of the year Congress, too, had come to the conclusion that only one minister plenipotentiary was needed in Paris and that would be Franklin. When the Congressional orders arrived in February 1779, Lee was dispatched to Madrid as American minister; Franklin was to remain in Paris and Adams? Well, he was unmentioned in the dispatch.

Samuel informed John in an October 25, 1778, letter "that Dr. Franklin is appointed Minister Plenipotentiary at Versailes. It is not yet determined how you will be disposd of; but as Congress entertain great expectations from your Services, you may depend upon Employment being alloted for you somewhere." Congress did not make any appointment but sometimes silence speaks volumes.

Adams received the news on February 11, and his former colleagues Lovell and Gerry in an October 28, 1778, letter conveyed the information that he had no specific assignment, but "in the mean Time we hope you will exercise your whole extensive Abilities on the Subject of our Finance."

Although Congressional delegate Henry Laurens's October 4, 1779, letter, which Adams received "with great Pleasure, was meant to convince Adams to accept a new appointment as a peace commissioner, his words speak to Adams's treatment by Congress in 1778. "I perceived it extremely difficult to compose a palatable address, of blended gratulation & condolence to an exaustorated fellow-Citizen who had served well of his Country & who at the same time stood in the most awkward situation that an honest susceptible mind can be reduced to—sent, without his own desire & probably inconsistently with his Interest & inclination, on an ambassy beyond the Atlantic—kept unemployed--& in the course of a few Months virtually dismissed without censure or applause."

Adams informed Congress he assumed that there was no further need for his services in France. To Abigail he wrote on February 13, 1779. "I have received Intelligence much more agreeable, than that of a removal to Holland, I mean that of being reduced to a private Citizen. I shall therefore soon present before you your own good man."

Personally offended and disgusted, Adams swore in a bitter and angry February 25 letter to James Warren never to be toyed with in the future. "I have the Honour to be reduced to a private Citizen and if I could remain there without an eternal Clamour, no Consideration in the World should induce me ever again to rise out of it. But you know the Noise—the Lyes—the slanders—the stupid Groans and Lamentations, that would be raised at such a Resolution. However let them groan and hiss and curse as they will, I will never be again with my own Consent the sport of wise Men nor Fools."

Jefferson too was coming under fire from his fellow Virginian and the commander of America's armed forces. While sitting in winter quarters at Middlebrook, New Jersey, while awaiting the arrival of a French fleet or a

British move from New York, Washington launched into a verbal diatribe on the absence of the "ablest Men" from Congress in a March 27, 1779, letter to his friend and neighbor George Mason. "I have beheld no day since the commencement of hostilities that I have thought her liberties in such eminent danger as at present.

"It is a fact too notorious to be concealed that C [ongress] is rent by party—that much business of a trifling nature & personal concernment withdraws their attention from matters of great national moment at this critical period."

Then came Washington's scream of anger at Jefferson and others. "No man who wishes well to the liberties of his Country & desires to see its rights established, can avoid crying out where are our Men of abilities? Why do they not come forth to save their Country? Let this Voice my dear Sir call upon you—Jefferson & others—to not from a mistaken opinion that we are about to set down under our own Vine and our own fig tree. Let our hitherto noble struggle end in ignominy—believe me when I tell you there is danger of it."

Even though Jefferson and Adams were not aware of Washington's challenge, Adams at least stood ready to re-enter the fray. Jefferson was among those Americans whom Washington accused of believing the French alliance meant the war was nearly won and no effort on their part was needed. Jefferson served in the Virginia assembly, but spent nine months of each year at Monticello—even entertaining captured British officers and seeking better food supplies for them. No wonder critics accused him of sitting out the war in comfort. Edmund Pendleton joined Washington in chiding him for wanting a "happy quietus from the Public" life.

Adams left Paris on March 8, 1779 and four days later was in Nantes prepared to embark for home on the American frigate Alliance, but it was months before he could actually leave France. Delay followed delay until June 17 when Adams finally departed on the French frigate Le Sensible with the French minister to the United States, Chevalier de la Luzerne.

Jefferson, meanwhile, remained in Virginia concentrating on promoting domestic reforms in Williamsburg and domestic felicity at Monticello. He submitted his widely acclaimed bill for religious freedom and his plan "for the greater diffusion of knowledge." While neither proposal was adopted by the Virginia legislature in 1779, Jefferson has received accolades for more than two hundred years for the effort.

Jefferson unsuccessfully sought election as Speaker of the House as a way of furthering his reforms. Then he turned to the governorship in the hope of strengthening his cause even though the governor had no veto power and could only act with the approval of the Council of State. Still he acknowledged to friends it "would be wrong to decline" the governorship.

The Virginia legislature elected Jefferson governor on June 1, 1779. Just before Adams landed in the United States, Jefferson defeated his friend John Page on a run-off ballot sixty-seven to sixty-one. Jefferson's gubernatorial experience began well enough in the "palace" in Williamsburg, but it ended in full flight from British dragoons with the sound of British hunting horns in his ears and a vote of reprimand from the Virginia legislature.

On the home front, while Adams was separated by thousands of miles from the comforts of Abigail, Jefferson 's wife gave birth to a daughter Mary on August 1, 1778, and became impregnated with a daughter Lucy Elizabeth in 1779.

The governorship eliminated much of Jefferson's Monticello time for nearly two years. He complained that the duties of the governorship were "so excessive."

Weeks before he became governor the British had attacked and sacked Portsmouth and Gosport. Fortunately, the British forces left on their on, and didn't return for a year and a half.

As a governor in wartime, Jefferson was responsible for raising troops and supplies for the Continental Army as well as the Virginia militia. He led extensive preparations to guard against another British invasion, but refused to call up the militia worried about the cost and local opposition to military service. Jefferson planned a Virginia attack on Detroit as a follow up to George Rogers Clark's victories in the Illinois country. But he gave it up "for want of men, want of money and difficulty of procuring provisions." It was a sensible judgment under any circumstances.

Adams landed in Braintree on August 2, 1779, much to the surprise and delight of his wife and family. Still the war was not far away. British troops raided in Connecticut and a British force still held Newport, R.I. Adams like Jefferson had reason to feel surrounded.

While Jefferson was beginning to learn the ropes as Virginia's governor, Adams was chosen a delegate to the convention to prepare a new constitution for Massachusetts. Jefferson had dearly wanted to help write the Virginia constitution, preparing two drafts of a state constitution while in Philadelphia as a delegate to Congress in the summer of 1776.

Now Adams had his chance. He embraced it. For three months he labored in his home office preparing a draft "Constitution or Form of Government for the Commonwealth of Massachusetts." By the end of October he had printed copies ready for the consideration of the convention, which was to meet in the spring of 1780.

Adams's draft included an opening statement sounding a lot like the Declaration of Independence followed by a Declaration of Rights based on George Mason's Virginia Declaration of Rights. Adams's guarantee of "freedom of speaking" was one of the few casualties to convention corrections.

Adams's basic plan for a republican government was evident. There would be a balanced government with two houses of the legislature, an independently elected governor with veto power, and an independent judiciary with Supreme Court judges appointed for life. The state government was to be responsible for the education and training of "the body of the people."

In all, it was a tour de force. And the constitution became a model for many other states and even the national convention of 1787. It remains the oldest functioning written constitution in the world.

Adams was justifiably proud. From Amsterdam he told the Brit Edmund Jenings on September 23, 1780. "I take vast satisfaction in the general approbation of the Massachusetts Constitution." But Adams could not avoid a caveat that revealed his hubris and sometimes gave ammunition to his critics. "If the people are as wise and honest in the choice of their ruler, as they have been in framing a government, they will be happy, and I shall die content with the prospect for my children."

Before the draft constitution could be adopted or rejected, Adams was on his way back to France. This time he was American minister plenipotentiary to negotiate treaties of peace and commerce with Great Britain. On September 27 Congress had appointed Adams American "minister plenipotentiary for negotiating a treaty of peace and a treaty of commerce with Great Britain."

Having been once again alerted by Elbridge Gerry and James Lovell, Adams already knew of his appointment when President Samuel Huntington's October 20, 1779, letter of official notification reached Adams in early

November. Huntington urged Adams to "engage your Immediate Attention & induce you to undertake the Service, and Embark for France without loss of time."

Supporters wrote to Adams asking him to forgive Congress for its treatment of him and "once more be induced to quit the *Rank* of a Citizen to become a Servant of the Publick." Lovell wrote to inform him his salary would be 2500 pounds sterling.

Gerry wrote from Philadelphia on September 29 to apologize for "the Embarrassments, Difficulties & Delays" attending to the treatment and final selection of Adams. "I flatter myself that You will not hesitate a Moment, at accepting the highest office of Honor & Trust, under the United States when elected by the Voice of eleven states." Lovell too apologized "for the appearances of Injustice done you by an Assembly, 9/10ths of which profess, and probably have, Esteem for you."

This new post required a man of his judgment, knowledge and negotiating skill. Adams was the only man nominated as minister to negotiate peace with Great Britain. How could he refuse the ringing endorsement of the entire nation?

Buoyed by assurances of Congressional support from Laurens, Lovell and Gerry, Adams wasted little time in consultation before sending a positive response.

Abigail who had by this time undoubtedly learned to fear letters from Congress was "disconsolate."

Adams was more than happy to be back in the game.

When the French warship Le Sensible was refitted and left Boston on November 15, Adams was on it with his two sons, Charles and John Quincy.

After another dangerous crossing with everyone including Adams fearing for his or her life, he reached Spain on December 8. An arduous trip on mules took Adams to France in mid-January. Adams was back on the hunting grounds, but he would find the prey still elusive.

While Adams was writing the Massachusetts constitution and sailing to France, Jefferson was grappling with the problems of governing Virginia and helping to fight the war under a federal system that required states to raise troops, supplies and monies. President Huntington wrote to him urging him to restrain Virginia settlers from encroaching on Delaware Indian tribal lands

across the Ohio. Jefferson unsuccessfully tried to have Congress supply ten thousand barrels of wheat flour to feed the British prisoners of war who were being held in Charlottesville. Jefferson, who happily entertained the British officers at Monticello, had to tell them that Congress thought "Indian Flour is equally wholesome" unless "the Commander of the British forces will supply them with Wheat flour."

Adams was on the ground, but he still found little to do. Vergennes even refused the publication of Adams's appointment. "It is the part of prudence to conceal your eventual character and, above all, to take the necessary precautions that the object of your commission remain unknown to the Court of London," Vergennes told Adams.

Fat chance that would happen with all the British spies in Paris.

Adams would have preferred the "bolder plan" of direct communication with the British. Vergennes was not about to give up control of America's contact with Britain. As Adams colorfully put it, Vergennes means, "to keep his hand under our chin to prevent us from drowning, but not to lift our heads out of water." Adams would remain acutely aware of French intentions to "Keep us weak. Make us feel our obligations. Impress our minds with a sense of gratitude."

When the time came to negotiate with the British, Adams was prepared to stand fast for American interests.

With no means of contacting the British, Adams spent his time writing endless articles for newspapers in France and England and almost daily letters to Congress. By August he had penned ninety-five letters to Congress without a reply. You can almost hear the president of Congress saying: "Not another one. Doesn't Adams have anything to do? Doesn't Adams know we are trying to win a war?"

Congress had talked about sending a minister to Holland to secure a treaty and a foreign loan, but had not done so until 1779 when Henry Laurens was appointed. Laurens went to Holland and returned home early in 1780. On his return trip in late 1780 he was captured by the British, charged with treason and imprisoned in the Tower of London where he stayed until exchanged for Lord Cornwallis in late 1781.

In Paris Adams was tired of doing nothing in the grand city, and in July 1780 he headed north with his two sons to try to negotiate a treaty and secure a loan. He had no authority. He was on his own.

Vergennes, of course, was opposed. But Adams was beyond the point of caring. By the time Francis Dana arrived in Paris on September 16 with authority from Congress to seek a loan pending the arrival of Laurens, Adams was already in full operation in Amsterdam.

Working with Charles W. Dumas, a Dutch radical and friend of Franklin, Adams literally inundated the Dutch with letters, documents, and papers trying to convince them to recognize the independence of the United States and loan them a large sum of money.

But the American surrender at Charleston in May 1780, another British victory at Camden in August 1780 and Arnold's treason in September 1780 cooled any ardor the Dutch had to either recognize American independence or make a loan. No one would even meet with Adams. He was again, all alone.

Adams's refusal to bow to French interests landed him in hot water. Vergennes told the French minister at Philadelphia that Adams's actions in Holland were embarrassing. Adams said Vergennes "has a rigidity, an arrogance, and an obstinacy that will cause him to foment a thousand unfortunate incidents." Ten years later Vergennes would have been yelling "Off with his head."

While Adams was in Europe struggling to find money and supplies to support the war effort, Jefferson, even though he was governor of Virginia, spent a great deal of time at home at Monticello entertaining the British prisoners quartered in Charlottesville. British and Hessian officers found dinners, wines, music, good company and "politeness and generosity" at Monticello.

On May 1 the Virginia legislature had reconvened in Richmond. Jefferson had urged the Virginia government to move the capital from Williamsburg because he thought the upland city of Richmond would be healthier and safer from British depredations and located in the center of the state. No one mentioned it was also closer to Monticello. On December 24, 1779, the Virginia legislature adjourned at Williamsburg for the last time.

In late 1780 and early 1781 the Confederation Congress belatedly took steps to try to strengthen the national government. Congress sought states' approval for a national impost duty. Executive offices of war, finance, marine and foreign affairs were created and a national bank established.

At the same time a French army was assembling in Rhode Island. Still the main Continental Army sat idle outside New York, while British forces moved on from their conquests in Georgia and South Carolina.

Adams tried to break out of the stalemate and diplomatic malaise in Europe. Jefferson tried to avoid an onslaught of British forces in Virginia.

When Continental forces surrendered at Charleston on May 10, 1780, Jefferson sensed that Virginia would be the next target. He was right.

"We are threatened with a formidable attack from the northward on our Ohio settlements and from the southern indians on our frontiers convenient to them, our eastern country is exposed to invasion from the British army in Carolina," explained Jefferson to William Preston on June 15, 1780. Jefferson begged Washington to move south to defend Virginia or at a minimum dispatch troops from the northern army.

Then the American army cut and ran at Camden, South Carolina, with its commander Horatio Gates, the hero of Saratoga, far outpacing the troops. The man once trumpeted as a replacement of Washington was now in disgrace. The way was open to Virginia.

The British soon arrived under the command of Benedict Arnold. As the new year opened British forces reinvaded coastal Virginia, while Jefferson hesitated to commit the full forces of Virginia. By the time Jefferson called out the militia, Arnold was in Richmond and Jefferson had fled to Tuckahoe Plantation. Jefferson watched as the British sacked Richmond and then sailed back to Portsmouth. In retaliation Jefferson made a fanciful plan to capture and hang Arnold in a "public spectacle."

By the spring of 1781 Adams was situated in Holland in a "House on the Keysers Gragt" which Adams declared must be "decent enough for any Character in Europe to dine on with a Republican Citizen." There he continued to barrage the Dutch officials with memorials and letters. He decided to break diplomatic protocol and go directly to The Hague to present his latest memorial.

The French minister to The Hague urged Adams to wait for Vergennes to approve. Adams refused. He marched forth to present a copy to the president of the States-General and then covered the country in a blizzard of copies of his memorial. In informing the president of Congress of his actions, Adams correctly guessed that they would deliberate and consider and deliberate.

Adams's rodeo excursion to Holland was the final straw for Vergennes.

France lobbied successfully to have Adams removed as America's sole peace negotiator. In Congress Madison and John Witherspoon joined those who wanted a negotiator willing to be more pliant to French dictates. Franklin continually reported Vergennes's displeasure with Adams. A congressional committee was appointed in 1781 to investigate the "conduct of Mr. Adams." Jefferson's acolyte Madison was heavy involved in the denigration of Adams and the subservience of American interests to France. Perhaps, Madison sincerely believed Adams lacked the necessary diplomatic skills. Perhaps Madison was maneuvering to replace Adams with his neighbor and friend, Jefferson. Whatever his aim; there is little if any mention of Adams in Madison's written conversations with Jefferson until 1783. But what was said in private conversation remains private.

The French minister to the United States, La Luzerne, urged the appointment of a minister who would "receive his directions from the Comte de Vergennes" and "take no step without the approbation of his Majesty."

Congress acted on June 15, 1781, just as the American war was about to take a dramatic turn. Adams would become part of a five-man committee to negotiate peace. Laurens, John Jay, Franklin, and Jefferson would join Adams.

Two weeks later on July 16 Madison, seconded by John Mathews of South Carolina, successfully moved in secret session to strip Adams of his commission to negotiate a treaty of commerce with Great Britain. Madison later explained this action in a March 16, 1784, letter to Jefferson. The revocation "was however effected with much difficulty, and some members of the minority even contested the validity of the proceeding. My own opinion then was and still is that the proceeding was equally valid and expedient. The circumstances which had given birth to the commission had given place to others totally different; not a single step had been taken under the commission which could affect the honour or faith of the U.S. and it surely can never be said that either the letter or spirit of the Confederation requires the same majority to decline as to engage in foreign treaties. The safest method of guarding against the execution of those great powers after the circumstances which dictated them have changed is to limit their duration, trusting to renewals as they expire, if the original reasons continue."

Adams attributed this action to the machinations of Marbois, who wanted "the Power of the Commission for Peace" put "into the hands of Dr. Franklin. To this End the Choice was made to fall upon him, and four other Gentlemen [including Jefferson] who could not attend." Adams continued. "But their

Policy did not stop here. I had still a Parchment, to make a Treaty of Commerce with G. Britain, and an Instruction annexed to it, which would be a powerfull Motive with G.B. to acknowledge our Right to the Fisheries. This Commission and these Instructions were to be and were revoked."

Adams's critics, like Madison and Witherspoon (Madison's teacher at Princeton), were ecstatic. Adams's supporters, like Lovell and Thomas Rodney of Delaware were angry and depressed. Rodney expressed their frustration in a letter to his brother Caesar, a signer of the Declaration of Independence. Giving France control over American independence was "too Abject and Humiliating," complained Rodney, and "I think it must convince even the French Court that we are reduced to a weak and abject state and that we have lost all that spirit and dignity which once appeared in the proceedings of Congress."

Jefferson declined his appointment as minister to negotiate peace just as British forces settled in at Yorktown.

France was to be the final decider in the negotiations of peace. Fortunately for America, neither Adams nor Jay agreed. Adams remained at his self-appointed post in Amsterdam plugging away.

Much later on January 12, 1783, Adams recounted in his diary a conversation with Benjamin Vaughan, Lord Shelburne's confidential observer at the peace talks that reflected his matured interpretation of Congress's actions. France had been "artfully negotiating with Congress" for my removal. "They could not get me removed or recalled." France wanted him removed because he was "unalterable for Independence, our Alliance, Fisheries and Boundaries. But it was known also to be a fixed Principle with me, to hurt G. Britain no farther than should be necessary to secure our Independence, Alliance and other Rights." Adams noted that Vaughan agreed to pass this "new information" on to Lord Shelburne.

Abigail was furious at the Congressional action. In a July 20, 1781, letter to Gerry, she unleashed her anger. "The plan which appears to be adopted both at Home and abroad is a servile Adulation and complaisance to the Court of our Allies." She blamed "intrigues and malicious aspersions on her husband particularly from Franklin "who has shown himself to be Enimical" to Adams.

While Congress was relieving Adams of his duties, Jefferson was in full flight from a British force commanded by Colonel Tarleton. Having left

Richmond and with his governorship technically ended on June 1, Jefferson prepared to flee Monticello for his Bedford County land when word reached him the British were in Charlottesville.

Jefferson and his family made their getaway from Monticello stopping in Amherst County. While there Jefferson decided to return to Monticello where he saw little damage. But at his Elk Hill plantation on the James, the British had ransacked his house, looted his supplies and animals. And "carried off" at least eleven slaves. In total twenty-three slaves took the opportunity to flee Jefferson's plantations. Many died of disease at Yorktown and in the West Indies, but others gained their liberty.

On June 13 Jefferson returned to Hugh Rose's house in Amherst, gathered up his family, and moved on to his plantation in Bedford County. It was there that he received word the Virginia legislature on June 12 (almost the same day Congress was relieving Adams of his position) decided to launch a formal investigation into his behavior as governor. Succinctly, he was being charged by his critics with leaving Virginia defenseless and abandoning his post as commander of the state militia.

Jefferson challenged the man, George Nicholas, whom he blamed for the legislature's censure, in a July 28 letter. "As I suppose that this was done under the impression of some particular instance or instances of ill conduct, and that it could not be intended just to stab a reputation by a general suggestion under a bare expectation that facts might be afterwards hunted up to boulster it, I hope you will not think me improper in asking the favor of you to specify to me the unfortunate passages in my conduct which you mean to adduce against me, that I may be enabled to prepare to yield obedience to the house while the facts are fresh in my memory and witnesses and documents are in existence."

While settling his family and preparing his public defense, he received word on July 9 of his appointment to the American peace commission in Paris in a June 15 letter from Samuel Huntington. By early August he had decided he could not go to France, even though he was mortified by this missed opportunity, telling La Fayette in an August 4 letter: this office "I cannot avail myself of has given me more mortification than almost any occurrence of my life. I lose an opportunity, the only one I ever had and perhaps ever shall have of combining public service with private gratification, of seeing countries whose improvements in science, in arts, and in civilization it has been my fortune to admire at a distance but never see and at the same time of lending further aid to a cause which has been handed on from it's first origination to its present stage by every effort of which my poor faculties were capable." But he could not leave his family in Bedford and he had to disprove the charges of misconduct.

To newly elected president Thomas McKean, Jefferson excused his delayed response to a fall from his horse. Jefferson formally declined the appointment because of "the existence of circumstances, which take from me the right of accepting so desireable an office." He had an "indispensable obligation" to remain within Virginia until the end of the year. Unmentioned were the legislature's call for an investigation of Jefferson's actions as governor.

Jefferson had remained for five weeks in his small house at Poplar Forest writing his defense and drafting his answers to a series of questions posed in 1780 by the Marquis de Barbé-Marbois, secretary to the French legation. These responses would become famous as Jefferson's *Notes on the State of Virginia*.

In the meantime American forces without the aid of Jefferson were gathering in Virginia and headed toward a showdown with the British. As the British retreated toward Yorktown in late July, Jefferson felt safe enough to leave Poplar Forest for Monticello.

In late August Adams learned of his new commission from Franklin. The edge of his sarcastic response was probably not lost on Franklin. "Our dear country will go fast asleep in full assurance of having news of peace by winter, if not by the first vessel. Alas! What a disappointment they will meet. I believe I had better go home and wake up our countrymen out of their reveries about peace. Congress have done very well to join others in the commission for peace who have some faculties for it. My talent, if I have one, lies in making war."

Adams too fought through his second rejection by Congress. Too proud and too stubborn to give in after Congress had reduced his role from sole peace negotiator to one of a five-man committee, Adams stayed on in Europe determined to do his best for the United States.

To Franklin and Jay, Adams wrote that fall of 1781 that he welcomed the additional peace commissioners. On November 28, he told Jay it "takes off my mind a load which if I had ever at anytime expected I should be called to sustain alone, would have been too heavy for my focus."

But to his friend and confidante, Francis Dana, then minister to Russia, Adams unburdened himself in a December 14, 1781, letter. "But I will consent upon these terms to be diminished down to the Size of a Lilliputian, or of an Animalcule in Pepper Water. There is no prospect for peace, wrote Adams, and therefore I "may be the more indifferent." Adams pointed out he could not be envious of Franklin, because his own name came before Franklin on the commission.

Despite his own issues, Adams expressed concern for Jefferson in an October 5, 1781, letter to Franklin. "Have you any Information concerning Mr. Jefferson, whether he has accepted the Trust? Whether he has Embarked? Or proposes to embark. I saw a paragraph in a Maryland paper, which expressed an apprehension that the was taken Prisoner by a Party of Horse in Virginia."

Seven days later, Franklin dismissed Adams's concerns for Jefferson's safety or his arrival in France. After expressing doubts of Jefferson's capture, Franklin brushed aside any anticipation of a Jefferson arrival in Paris. "From his original Unwillingness to leave America when he was sent hither, I think his Coming doubtful." On that matter Franklin was absolutely right.

Adams was recovering from a "nervous fever" in Amsterdam and Jefferson was back at Monticello trying to preserve his reputation when Lord Cornwallis surrendered his British army to George Washington on October 17.

Many thought the war would soon be over. They would be wrong. The killing would continue until preliminary articles of peace reached the United States in 1783.

In December 1781 Jefferson returned to the Virginia Assembly to defend his honor. No one in the Assembly rose to challenge him but he took his day in the public forum. In the end, even though everyone acknowledged his defense of Virginia in the face of Arnold and Cornwallis was a disaster, the legislature apologized and thanked him for his service. But his failed efforts as a governor and his flight from Monticello would hover in the background just waiting for his critics to pull it forward time and time again.

On hearing the news of Yorktown, Adams immediately pressed the Dutch for a response to his April memorial. Even though he was even criticized by the newly appointed American Foreign Secretary, Robert R. Livingston, Adams refused to back down. He defended his memorial in a very long official letter to Livingston of February 21, 1782, as an "act of national bravery." In a sharp retort to Livingston's criticism, Adams countered the charge of vanity and rogue diplomacy. "The charge of vanity is the last resort of little wits and mercenary quacks, the vainest men alive, against men and measures that they can find no other objection to. I doubt not but letters have gone to America containing their weighty charge against me; but this charge, if supported only by the opinion of those who make it, may be brought against any man or thing." Adams concluded, "I have long since learned that a man may give offense and yet succeed. The very measures necessary for success may be pretended to give offence."

In early 1782, the Dutch moved ever closer to recognizing Adams as the minister from the United States. Adams wrote triumphantly to Abigail on March 22, 1782. "I should think I was going to be received, at the Hague in awfull Pomp in a few Weeks." Adams continued. "Some folks will think your husband a negotiator, but it is not he, it is General Washington at York Town who did the substance of the Work, the form only belongs to me."

Finally on April 22, 1782, William, Prince of Orange, received Adams at The Hague. Adams became the resident minister in the Netherlands, and in June the Dutch made a large loan to the United States, but the war continued.

In the spring of 1782 anger and fears still seized Jefferson's mind. On May 20 Jefferson told James Monroe that he feared that he "stood arraigned for treasons of the heart and not mere weakness of the head." Even the birth a new daughter, the second Lucy Elizabeth, provided little solace because his wife "has been ever since and still continues, very dangerously ill."

Martha would die on September 6, 1782, leaving Jefferson temporarily inconsolable and now the single parent head of a family of three young girls. He wrote his sister-in-law Elizabeth Eppes on October 3, 1782. "All my plans of comfort and happiness reversed by a single event and nothing answering in prospect before me but the gloom unbrightened with one cheerful expectation." The duties of a single parent offered "some temporary abstractions from wretchedness and nourishes a soothing reflection that if there is beyond the grave any concern for the things of this world here is one angel at least who views these attentions with pleasure and wishes continuance of them while she must pity the miseries to which they confine me."

But soon Jefferson was telling the Marquis de Chastellux on November 26 he was "a little emerging from that stupor of mind which had rendered me as dead to the world as she was whose loss occasioned it."

When in November 1782 Congress renewed its appointment of Jefferson as a peace commissioner, Jefferson readily accepted. He noted in his autobiography. "I had two months before that lost the cherished companion of my life, in whose affections, unabated on both sides, I had lived the last ten years in unchequered happiness. With the public interests, the state of my mind concurred in recommending the change of scene proposed, and I accepted the appointment, and left Monticello on the 19th of December 1782 for Philadelphia."

That fall Adams had received an urgent letter from Jay, who had arrived in Paris from Spain in June, with the news that the British negotiator Richard Oswald had been instructed to negotiate with "the United States." Independence was at hand, but Jay needed help to secure it.

Upon reaching Paris in October, Adams became infuriated with the information that the Americans were to do what the French instructed. Adams and Jay refused. Adams threatened to resign in a letter to Livingston, but before the threat could reach America independence and peace had been secured.

Adams informed Abigail on November 8, 1782, that Great Britain "has Shifted Suddenly about, and from persecuting Us with unrelenting Bowells [Blows?], has unconditionally and unequivocally acknowledged Us a Sovereign State and independant Nation." Adams pointedly took credit with the statement that Franklin "as usual would have taken the advice of [Vergennes] and treated without" a recognition of Independence but Jay and I refused to "speak or hear before we were put on an equal foot."

Franklin, however, agreed with Jay and Adams to "go on with these gentlemen in the business without consulting this Court."

In violation of the Congressional instruction and the wishes of their ally, the American ministers began formal negotiations with the British on October 30. Adams was just forty-seven. The United States was six.

In just a month a preliminary treaty was drafted and signed by the Americans and the British negotiators. Despite the continued opposition of Vergennes to the agreed upon boundaries and American rights to Newfoundland fisheries, the Americans had their way. Adams, Jay, Franklin, and Laurens could not know that Great Britain and the United States would be haggling over the implementation of entire sections of the treaty for decades.

Shortly after the signing of the preliminary treaty in the fall of 1782, Jay went on an excursion to Normandy and Laurens went to Bath. Adams stayed in Paris and signed the Declarations for Suspension of Arms and Cessation of Hostilities between the United States and Great Britain on January 20. John told Abigail on January 22, 1783, "I want an Excursion too."

Just three weeks after his nomination to the peace commission in November 1782, Jefferson and his daughter Martha (Patsy) left Monticello prepared to sail from Baltimore. Delayed by ice, Jefferson settled in Philadelphia where he met Elizabeth House Trist, the married daughter of his landlady, and began a life long friendship with young Eliza, who was married to a former British officer, Nicholas Trist.

Jefferson read the correspondence of Jay, Franklin and Adams. No doubt seeing the long acerbic letters of his old colleague John. Jefferson modestly told Jay. "Had I joined you at a more early period I am sure I should not have added to the strength of the commission and, coming in at the eleventh hour, I can propose no more than to avoid doing mischief."

No mischief need be avoided, because Jefferson never sailed for France. News of the preliminary treaty of peace reached Philadelphia, his mission was suspended in March, and on April 12 Jefferson left for Monticello. Still, he told his friend Madison in a May 7, 1783, letter. "Should the call be made on me, which was sometimes the subject of our conversation," he would be ready to go. One month later he was elected a delegate to the Confederation Congress. His seven-year absence from the national stage was about to end.

Congress did not accept Adams's December 4, 1782, proffered resignation. Despite Arthur Lee's April 23 assurance to Abigail "you may rely upon it, that leave will be given as he requests." Adams, Franklin and Jay triumphantly signed the definitive treaty of peace in Paris on September 3, 1783.

Adams swore to Abigail on December 28 that he would embark as soon as Congress accepted his resignation. "You may depend upon a good domestic husband for the remainder of my life, if it is the will of Heaven that I should once more meet you." And he could have added, "The Check is in the mail."

Laurens and Jay came home, but Adams remained in Europe.

On June 10 Jefferson was nominated to replace Livingston as Secretary of Foreign Affairs, but according to Madison's notes his name was withdrawn after "being told he would not accept."

On the recommendation of Dr. James Jay, Adams took the waters at Bath for his health.

John told Abigail on June 19, that he would like "to take a Short Tour to London before my Return for the Sake of taking a look at the Country, and Seeing some personages there." It was not until October 1783 that Adams and Jay went to London and to Bath. From London John wrote several letters to Abigail urging her come to "England France or Holland." "My Life is Sweetened with the Hope of Embracing You in Europe," Adams cooed.

In London Adams met with some of England's leaders, including the Duke of Portland, Charles James Fox, and Edmund Burke. If Adams were thrilled he provided no details to Abigail. It was John Quincy Adams who provided a detailed description of the trip in an April 18, 1784, letter to Elizabeth Cranch. They toured London, its palaces and museums, before moving on to Oxford and Bath.

Jefferson reported their poor reception in England in a February 29, 1784, letter to Edmund Pendleton. "Mr Adams and Mr Jay have some how or other got themselves over to London. Their reception was not a kind one by any means and they must have [been chagrined?] at this faux pas, as their friends here have been." Jefferson did not indicate where he got his information, but undoubtedly there was a report to Congress where Jefferson represented Virginia.

Adams's trip was cut short by word that Congress' bills of exchange were being protested in Holland. Adams set out from London on January 2 to try to secure another Dutch loan. Despite dire predictions of failure and American bankruptcy, Adams was able to negotiate a second Dutch loan for two million guilders on March 9.

Adams stayed in The Hague until early in 1784, eagerly awaiting the arrival of Abigail. "When Madam comes I shall take her to Paris and shew her that fine City, there perhaps I may stay," Adams exulted to Richard Cranch in an April 3, 1784, letter.

Even then he planned "in the month of May 1785" to "embark for Boston. This is my Plan, but Plans are easily dashed." He was so right.

Gerard W. Gawalt

# Together In Paris

---

*"He hates Franklin, he hates Jay, he hates the French, he hates the English. To whom will he adhere."*
THOMAS JEFFERSON TO JAMES MADISON, FEBRUARY 14, 1783

*"My new partner is an old friend," wrote Adams, "whose character I studied nine or ten years ago, and which I do not perceive to be altered. The same Industry, Integrity, and Talents remain without diminution."*
JOHN ADAMS TO ARTHUR LEE, JANUARY 31, 1785

HISTORIANS HAVE GENERALLY traced the Adams-Jefferson rivalry to the politics of the 1790's. But this is not true.

Jefferson's dislike and distrust of Adams began before the Revolution was even over.

During the time he spent in Philadelphia in late 1782 and early 1783, Jefferson immersed himself in the correspondence of Adams, Franklin and the other American diplomats. After reading literally hundreds of carping and complaining letters in the diplomatic files, Jefferson formed a new opinion of Adams and it wasn't good.

Madison, no doubt, had a strong influence on Jefferson's views of Adams. We have already seen how the Virginians resented Adams's criticism of General Washington. As a Virginia delegate to Congress from 1780, Madison was involved in all the diplomatic decisions made by Congress.

Although he had no personal knowledge of Adams, Madison readily condemned his correspondence with Congress in a February 11, 1783, encoded letter to Jefferson. His letters were "not remarkable for any thing unless it be a full display of his vanity, his prejudice against the French Court & his venom against Doctr. Franklin."

Upon hearing from his friend and acolyte Madison, that Adams might be named American minister to work with the other American ministers in Paris; Jefferson condemned Adams while supporting his appointment as a leaven on the commission in a February 14, 1783, letter to Madison.

"He hates Franklin, he hates Jay, he hates the French, he hates the English. To whom will he adhere? His vanity is a lineament in his character, which had entirely escaped me. His want of taste I had observed. Notwithstanding all this he has a sound head on substantial points, and I think He has integrity. I am glad therefore that he is of the commission and expect he will be useful in it. His dislike of all parties, and all men, by balancing prejudices, may give the same fair play to his reason as would a general benevolence of temper. At any rate honesty may be expected even from poisonous weeds." But to compare him to a "poisonous weed"! Ouch!

While Adams remained in Europe, Jefferson was elected to the Confederation Congress, which was meeting in Annapolis. Jefferson must have been ready to immerse himself in the French culture if the opportunity arose, because he brought a French cook with him to Annapolis.

Jefferson also continued to immerse himself in America's foreign affairs. For example, Jefferson chaired committees of Congress that in December 1783 were assigned the consideration of the September 3 definitive treaty, joint letters from the commissioners, and more than thirty-five letters from Adams, Franklin, Laurens, Dana, Charles Dumas and Thomas Barclay. As Jefferson told Edmund Pendleton on December 16, the American commissioners believed that European powers would not sign favorable commercial treaties with the United States unless Britain did. And Britain would not until America had a government that could "be brought to act as one united nation" that could retaliate against unfavorable commercial actions by other nations.

Reports abounded, even in Europe that Jefferson would be coming to France. Adams reported on such rumors in a July 19, 1784, letter to Thomas Barclay, adding a humorous comment. Franklin "writes me, that Mr Jefferson is talked of to succeed him. Is he to die? To resign? Or be displaced." Adams would not have to wait long to find out.

Jefferson soon had his chance to join Adams, because on May 7, 1784, Congress received word that Jay was on his way home. At the urging of the southern states, Congress then named Jefferson a minister plenipotentiary to collaborate with Adams and Franklin in signing treaties of commerce with virtually any European nation that was willing. All three were also authorized to negotiate treaties of amity with the "Barbary Powers." This action was "ardently solicited by the mercantile part of America & warmly espoused by a large majority of Congress," according to the Virginia delegates May 13 letter to the Virginia Governor Benjamin Harrison.

The Virginia delegates agreed, because "It was an object with us, in order to render the Commission, as agreeable as possible to the southern States to have Mr. Jefferson placed in the room of Mr. Jay." They argued that "want of information "of the former commissioners "with respect to the true Commercial Interests of the Southern States, must have remain'd an insurmountable obstacle with us. To the commission of such extensive Powers of clogging our Commerce to a Delegation wholly from Northern States."

"We flatter ourselves" that any objection from the Virginia legislature "will have been remov'd by the appointment of Mr. Jefferson—and that the present European Commission will be as satisfactory to the State of Virginia as it appears to be to Congress."

After months of frustration in an increasingly divided and ineffective Congress, Jefferson was ecstatic. The next day he wrote Madison in high-sounding phrases omitting any reference to the sectional interest that led to his appointment. "I am now to take my leave of the justlings of the states and to repair to a field where the divisions are fewer but on a larger scale. Congress yesterday joined me to Mr. Adams & Dr. Franklin on the foreign commercial negotiations. I shall pursue there the line I have pursued here, convinced that it can never be the interest of any party to do what is unjust, or to ask what is unequal."

Adams's old friend, Arthur Lee, assured Adams on May 11 that "The arrangement of our foreign affairs which makes Mr Jay Secretary here, & joins Mr Jefferson with you, must I think be pleasing to you, as they both have friendship for you & are men of ability."

Upon hearing of Jefferson's appointment, Adams optimistically wrote to his old friend James Warren on August 27, 1784 that the appointment "gives me pleasure.

He is an old Friend with whom I have often had occasion to labour at many a knotty Problem, and in whose Abilities and Steadiness I have always found great Cause to confide."

Jefferson and Abigail almost sailed to Europe on the same ship in the summer of 1784. Abigail must have been very surprised on June 19 when Jefferson arrived at the house where she was awaiting her departure. Abigail told John that Jefferson had urged her to cancel her passage from Boston and sail with him from New York, but the ever practical and careful Abigail insisted "my passage was paid on board capt Lyde, The Season of the year was best I could wish for and I had no desire to take such a journey in the Heat of summer." Abigail, her daughter Nabby, two servants and a cow sailed the next day on the *Active*.

Jefferson too informed Adams that he had "hopes of having the pleasure of attending Mrs. Adams to Paris" but he arrived in Boston to find she had already booked passage and he was unable "to alter her measures." On July 5 Jefferson, his daughter Martha, and his slave James, sailed from Boston on the *Ceres*. By August 10 Jefferson had settled into the "Hôtel d'Orleans rue Petits Augustus." Jefferson would remain there until October when he moved to a house on the Cul-de-sac Taitbout belonging to François Guireared de Talairac.

The opportunity for friendship would have to wait. Unbeknownst to Abigail she would become the lynchpin in the Adams-Jefferson friendship.

"With respect to our joint agency," Jefferson wrote on June 19, "our instructions are more special than those formerly sent."

John hurrying from Amsterdam met Abigail in London on August 7 and the next day they left for Paris. Their separation had been four long eventful years. The joys of their reunion must remain with the ages. As Abigail told her sister Mary, "you know my dear sister that poets and painters wisely draw a veil over those scenes which surpass the pen of one or the pencil of the other; we were indeed a very happy family once more met together after a separation of four years."

The Adams family, as noted in Adams's diary for August 17, 1784, settled in Auteuil "at the House of the Comte de Rouault near the Bois de Boulogne, elevated above the River Seine and the low Grounds, and distant from the putrid Streets of Paris."

Arthur Lee, who had already told Adams in a January 14, 1784, letter that Adams "stood fairest for the Embassy to St. James," wrote to warn Adams of his new partner. Jefferson was vain, affected, and of mediocre intelligence, and should not be confided in, said Lee. If Adams had seen some of the letters exchanged by Madison and Jefferson, he would not have defended Jefferson in his January 31, 1785, reply to Lee. "My new partner is an old friend," wrote Adams, "whose character I studied nine or ten years ago, and which I do not perceive to be altered. The same Industry, Integrity, and Talents remain without diminution." Adams concluded "I am very happy with him but whether We Shall be able to accomplish any Thing here, I know not, any thing I mean which may make it worth while to keep Us together. But if Congress order Us to Separate there will be the Same good Understanding and Correspondence between Us."

The same feelings were shared by Abigail and John's son, John Quincy, who, to judge from his diary, spent as much time at Jefferson's house as his own.

To his friend Elbridge Gerry, Adams happily wrote. "Jefferson is an excellent hand. You could not have sent a better." Had Adams known that Jefferson was chosen to represent the southern states in order to offset Adams, he might have concluded differently. "He appears to me to be infected with no party passions or national prejudices, or any partialities, but for his own country," John mistakenly added. Perhaps, John's happier less paranoid outlook was due to his wife's companionship.

Abigail happily told Jefferson in a June 6, 1785, letter from London that she was glad her husband had someone he could work with in such "perfect freedom and unreserve; and whose place he had no reason to expect supplied in the Land to which he is destined." Jefferson was "one of the choice ones of the earth," Abigail told Mary Smith Cranch in May 1785. "I shall really regret to leave Mr. Jefferson." As David McCullough put it so well. Abigail "was charmed by his perfect manners, his manifold interests and breadth of reading, and though she did not say it in so many words, by the attention he paid to her." Jefferson could charm the ladies, and Abigail succumbed in France.

Had John and Abigail known what Jefferson had written to Madison or that Jefferson had been happily feasting and entertaining Hessian officers at Monticello from 1779 to 1781, while Adams worked desperately to secure loans in Holland, Abigail struggled to raise a family and run a farm without her husband and Americans fought and died from Penobscot Bay to the Georgia-Florida border, they might not have had such a favorable view of their "old friend."

Charming, sensitive to others' interests, omnivorously curious, unencumbered by a spouse, and bearing the fame of the author of the Declaration of Independence, Jefferson was an immediate hit in the intellectual salon culture of Paris. Women and men cultivated his friendship and Jefferson responded in kind.

The five years Jefferson spent in Paris were some of the most vibrant of Jefferson's life. Parisian salon culture was at its revolutionary, flirtatious height, and Jefferson was introduced to artistic and intellectual ideas that would affect him for the rest of his life.

Jefferson affected a distain for French manners, French women and the decadence of the French court in letters to America. Famously writing to Anne Willing Bingham on February 7, 1787. "Tell me truly & honestly, whether you do not find the tranquil pleasures of America preferable to the empty bustle of Paris. For to what does that bustle tend? At eleven o'clock it is day chez Madame. The curtains are drawn. Propped on bolsters & pillows, her head scratched into a little order, the bulletins of the sick are read, & the billets of the well. She writes to some of her acquaintance & receives visits of others. If the morning is not very thronged, she is able to get out & hobble round the cage of the Palais royal: but she must hobble quickly, for the Coeffeur's turn is come; & a tremendous turn it is! Happy, if he does not make her arrive when dinner is half over! The torpitude of digestion a little passed, she flutters half an hour thro' the streets by way of paying visits, & then to the Spectacles. These finished, another half hour is devoted to dodging in & out of doors of her very sincere friends, & away to supper. After supper cards; & after cards bed, to rise at noon the next day, & to tread, like a mill-horse, the same trodden circle once again. Thus the days of life are consumed, one by one, without an object beyond the present moment. Ever flying from the ennui of that, yet carrying it with us; eternally in pursuit of happiness which keeps eternally before us."

Not to mention the air "filled with political debates into which both sexes enter with equal eagerness," as he told Madame de Bréhan on May 9, 1788. Comparing French women and American women "is a comparison of

Amazons and Angels," Jefferson told Anne Bingham in a May 11, 1788, letter. "Paris is now become a furnace of Politics. All the world is now politically mad. Men, women, children talk nothing else; & you know that naturally they talk much, loud & warm. Society is spoilt by it, at least for those who, like myself, are but lookers on. You too have had your political fever. But our good ladies I trust have been too wise to wrinkle their foreheads with politics."

However, Jefferson fawned over French women in salons, at endless dinners and receptions. The intellectual planter fell in completely with a fast cosmopolitan set, and though he occasionally denounced the "empty Parisian bustle" and longed for the solitude of Monticello, it is clear that he enjoyed most aspects of the diplomatic lifestyle.

Report and official letter writing were excepted for Jefferson. It was here that Adams excelled and truly reveled in the tasks, turning out hundreds of letters and official memoranda. Jefferson believed himself burdened as the paperwork "crouded in" on him.

Unlike Adams and Franklin who lived outside the city in the more bucolic suburbs, Jefferson lived in the middle of the city-on the rue des Petits-Augustins and the Cul-de-Sac Taibout. As David McCullough wrote. "He relished all that Paris offered in the way of luxurious shopping, architecture, painting, music, theater, the finest food, the best wine, and the most cultivated society in his experience—never mind what he may have written about cities or the expenses he incurred."

Both men frequently attended the theatre, attended uncounted receptions and dinners. It was after all their job. Here Jefferson excelled, and Adams preferred the quiet of his family and his study.

Adams normally dined at two. Then went to work with Jefferson and Franklin at Passy. By five o'clock teatime, Adams was back home. Then he usually read or helped John Quincy with his studies. According to young Abigail, her father went to bed promptly at ten. "We see but little company, and visit much less," complained an obviously bored and disappointed Nabby.

Jefferson certainly went the extra-mile to immerse himself in Parisian culture and the life style of the rich and famous. Jefferson may have preached frugality in personal life and government, but he certainly did not practice it.

Jefferson purchased over 2000 books and sixty-three paintings; acquired an expensive carriage for 15,000 francs (the equivalent of six years' wages for the average Frenchman); remodeled his house; furnished his house with expensive new furniture and drapes; hired six additional servants and a French butler; and filled his wine cellar with expensive wines (at one point buying 200 bottles of Bordeaux.). His slave James was trained as a French chef. His daughters Patsy and Polly went to the expensive private convent school, the Abbaye Royale de Panthemont.

According to Abigail Adams, Jefferson spent so much money that he had to turn to Adams to secure a personal loan from Dutch bankers as an advance on his salary, which like many other loans he failed to repay.

Meanwhile, Abigail was planning to use the 2000 pounds sterling Adams "was able to save" from his salary to purchase another farm in Braintree. Abigail complained to Cotton Tufts on January 3, 1785, that Adams had purchased a new carriage from England, but had worn out the wheels making "ten different journeys" between Holland and France from 1780 to 1784.

In the homes of Madame de Corny and other saloniéres, Jefferson met some of the leading lights of the Parisian intellectual scene. Henry Adams once wrote that Jefferson never seemed more satisfied than "in the liberal literary, and scientific air of Paris."

Jefferson acquired a bevy of friends in France--most of them women. Adams acquired none. Many of them became friends and correspondents for life. Madame de Tessé, Madame de Corny, Maria Cosway, the Comtesse d"Houdetot, Marie le la Rochefoucauld d'Enville, Angelica Schuyler Church, Lucy Ludwell Paradise, and the Baroness de Staël were just a few of the ladies to fall under Jefferson's spell or vice versa.

Of the many flirtatious friendships with married women that Jefferson pursued in Paris, his relationship with Maria Cosway burned brightest and lasted the longest. Like a summer love, the romantic attachment flared for a few glorious weeks. Despite his well-known condemnations of French society, Jefferson became a Francophile through and through.

Each man received 2500 pounds sterling for his annual salary. Most men would have been overwhelmed with joy to receive that much money in the eighteenth century. But then they were not American ministers in a foreign country.

Not that both men didn't constantly complain to Congress and their friends that their salaries and allowed expenses were simply not enough. Both men, but particularly Jefferson, wanted Congress to reimburse them for their expenses in purchasing their "outfit" to establish their household.

Jefferson told his friend Monroe in an encoded letter of June 15, 1785, that for his furniture, clothes, and carriage "I have been obliged to anticipate my salary from which however, I shall never be able to repay it. I find that by a rigid economy bordering however on meanness I can save perhaps five hundred livres a month in the summer at least. The residue goes for expences so much of course and of necessity that I cannot avoid them without abandoning all respect to my public character." Jefferson wanted Monroe, who was a delegate to Congress to seek more funds. "I will pray you to touch this string, which I know to be a tender one with Congress, with the utmost delicacy. I'd rather be ruined in my fortune, than in their esteem."

Secretary of Foreign Affairs Jay agreed with Adams that his salary was not enough for a diplomat in London in an August 3, 1785, letter. "I have long been of Opinion that your Salary is not equal to what the Expenses of a Minister ought to be." But added Jay. "There are Men in all States who make a Merit of saving Money in small Matters, without sufficiently attending to the Consequences of it."

It was not simply that Adams relied on Abigail to direct his business affairs, although she certainly was a strong influence. Adams was just frugal. He was a thrifty Yankee. Jefferson was a spendthrift. Jefferson kept detailed records without ever following a personal budget. When Jefferson was paid $25,000. per year as president, he still managed to spend more. Adams accumulated enough savings to purchase an expensive piece of property back in Braintree. Jefferson accumulated enough debt to send him into a lifelong spiral of splurge spending and chronic indebtedness that ended only with his death and the forced sale of Monticello, its contents, and his slaves.

Both men were bolstered by the presence of family members. John had his beloved Abigail, his daughter Nabby, and his son John Quincy. John was doubly satisfied about his daughter, believing that her presence in France enriched her life and prevented her from continuing a parentally disapproved marriage to a young lawyer, Royall Tyler. He would be right.

Thomas's daughter Martha (Patsy) was a delight for her father. But as a single parent in a foreign country, he decided to send his daughter to a boarding school. There she flourished and matured. Unfortunately, Jefferson's youngest daughter died of whooping cough shortly after her second birthday. The "greatly affected" Jefferson determined to bring his only other surviving daughter, Mary, to France. The decision began an entirely new and notable but not noble chapter in Jefferson's life.

The presence of their families brought Jefferson and Adams closer together. At times it is difficult to tell which Adams Thomas was closest to—John or Abigail.

If Adams recognized Jefferson's adulation for all things French, he did not seem concerned. He assured Henry Knox on December 15, 1785. "You can scarcely have heard a character too high of my friend and colleague, Mr. Jefferson, either in point of power or virtues." Adams added "I have found him uniformly the same wise and Prudent Man and Steady Patriot." One can't help wondering what Adams might have thought had he read this effusive praise in the next decade.

After his February 14, 1783, critical outburst to Madison on Adams, Jefferson for years kept his opinions of Adams out of his letters. Abigail was urged by Jefferson to ignore his critics in London. "The squibs against Mr. Adams are such as I expected from the polished, mild tempered, truth speaking people he is sent to. It would be ill policy to attempt to answer or refute them."

In 1785 all was well with his new best friend in Adams's mind.

The happy tandem of Adams and Jefferson was to be short-lived.

By December 1784 Congress had determined to send a minister to reside at the Court of St. James and on February 24, Adams was appointed. James Monroe had forewarned Jefferson of the pending appointment of a minister to England and his own advancement to replace Franklin as minister to France in a December 14 letter. Congress might want Jefferson to go to Spain to negotiate a loan (A post unsuccessfully offered to Madison.), but because Franklin may leave Paris "you should not leave the court in case of that appointment." Monroe told Madison on the same day, "I think there will be little difficulty in obtaining it for Mr. Jefferson, for the opinion of all the members seem to concur in the propriety of it." Jefferson's friend Madison told Monroe on April 13, 1785, that he supported Adams' appointment to London because New England "will always have one of the principal appointments" and this "has removed all obstacles to the establishment of Mr. Jefferson at the Court of France."

It was years before a deadlocked Congress could agree on a replacement for Adams at The Hague. Not that they didn't need Dutch loans, but sectional divisions prevented the election of any of a number of nominees.

Adams would have by far the trickier job. His instructions were to obtain a commercial treaty, get the British out of the American Northwest outposts, achieve the recovery of runaway American slaves, end restrictions on British trade, and settle the pre-war debts owed to British merchants. What could be simpler?

Just as well to get new assignments, for the old had produced little results. As Adams wrote back home. "Public life is like a long journey, in which we have immense tracks of waste countries to pass through for a very few grand and beautiful prospects. At present, I scarcely see a possibility of doing anything for the public worth the expense of maintaining me in Europe."

What did Adams and Jefferson accomplish in the two years after the signing of the definitive treaty? Really, not very much. One commercial treaty with Prussia was the only solid product and that was not signed until September 10, 1785 long after Adams had gone to London.

# To London To London To
# See The Bad King

*"I had the Honour on the first of this Month to be intro-
duced by his Lordship to his Majesty, in his Closet with all the
Ceremonies and Formalities, practiced on such occasions."*
JOHN ADAMS TO THOMAS JEFFERSON, JUNE 3, 1785

*"The quantity of animal food"* eaten in England *"renders their character insusceptible of Civilization."*
THOMAS JEFFERSON TO GEORGE WYTHE, AUGUST 13, 1786

*"This People cannot look me in the Face, there is con-
scious Guilt and Shame in their Countenance."*
JOHN ADAMS DIARY, MARCH 30, 1786

UPON LEARNING OF his February 24th appointment to be America's first minister to London from an Elbridge Gerry letter delivered by Jefferson on April 26,
1785, Adams assured his friend Richard Cranch the next day that he looked
forward to the challenge though "I shall part with Mr. Jefferson with great
Regret." Without knowing the full implications of his remarks, Adams asserted
that the British have "less cause to fear from me, than some others, because, I
confess that although I would contend for my Country's Rights against them,
as much as any Man, yet my System of politics is not so hostile to them, nor
so subservient to the Views of some of their Enemies as some others." Adams
may have included Jefferson as well as Franklin among "some others."

Gerard W. Gawalt

Adams's pride at his appointment was no doubt tempered by Gerry's information that his appointment had come after protracted debates. After nominations on January 31, Adams, Robert Livingston of New York and John Rutledge of South Carolina were the major contenders. Not only was Adams a New Englander but also, it was charged (as we have seen by Jefferson and Madison), that he was vain even crazy. Monroe anticipated "difficulty of obtaining a vote for any person."

James McHenry, a delegate from Maryland, noted that a former American minister in Europe, Ralph Izard, thought Adams was "some times a madman." But then Izard reportedly said "Doctr. Franklin is destitute of every principle of moral rectitude" and that Adams "says that Doctr. Franklin just does what the court of France bids him." Just one big happy family.

After learning of his appointment, Adams unburdened himself in a long letter to Gerry on May 2, 1785. He was proud of having labored for the good of the country, while other men simply collected material goods. "If at times I have betrayed in word or writing such a sentiment, I have only to say in excuse for it that I am not a hypocrite, nor a cunning man, nor at all times wise, and that although I may be more cautious for the future, I will never be so merely to obtain the reputation of a cunning politician, a character I neither admire nor esteem." Having decided he may have said too much yet again, Adams simply filed the letter.

Adams became minister to London when suspicion of Great Britain dominated Americans' views of foreign affairs. Izard complained to Jefferson on June 10, 1785. "The backwardness which you mention of Great Britain toward America is very astonishing. It seems to be a continuation of the same Bad Policy which has already brought them into so much trouble, and which I think will bring them into more." Jay wrote to Jefferson on July 13, 1785, that they were anxious to hear from Adams "to learn with certainty the Intentions of that Court with Respect to those Posts" on the frontier.

Secretary of Foreign Affairs Jay warned. "We have intelligence (which though not entirely authentic as believed by many) that the British are enticing our people to settle lands within our lines under their government and protection by gratuitous supplies of provisions, implements of husbandry etc." Great Britain still refused to turn over several frontier forts to America, supported Indian attacks on Americans, and openly solicited Vermonters to secede from the United States and join Canada. Izard, now a member of Congress, charged Great Britain with urging the Barbary States to attack the United States. "It is said that Great Britain has encouraged the piratical states to attack our vessels. If this could be proved, I should prefer a war against her, rather than against Algiers." Washington wondered in a December 5, 1784, letter to Henry Knox how long it would be before America would become "the sport of European politics, & the victims of our own folly."

Adams and family left Auteuil by carriage on May 20, traveling to Calais where they took a boat to London arriving on May 26. Abigail reported to Jefferson "we journeyed slowly and sometimes silently." Adams, on the other hand, told Jefferson their journey was easy and they read his newly published *Notes on the State of Virginia.* "It is our meditation all Day long. I cannot say much about it, but I think it will do its Author and his Country great Honour. The Passages upon slavery, are worth Diamonds. They will have more effect than Volumes written by mere Philosophers."

Jefferson missed his companions of the past year, telling Adams-- "The departure of your family has left me in the dumps. My afternoons hang heavily on me." Judging from the excited conversational correspondence of Abigail and Jefferson (Abigail would write 20 letters and Thomas 18 while the Adams family was in London.), compared to the business like letters between John and Thomas, (John would write 61 letters and Thomas 68.) one could conclude it was Abigail's presence that Thomas missed. Nevertheless, his depression would not last long in gay Paris.

Adams found London dirty and disgusting. While still in a hotel, Adams wrote Jefferson on June 7, regretting the loss of "my fine walks and pure Air at Auteuil" and condemning living conditions in London. "The Smoke and Damp of this City is ominous to me. London boasts of its Trottoir, but there is a space between it and the Houses through which all the Air from Kitchens, Cellars, Stables and Servants Appartements ascends into the Street and pours directly on the Passenger on Foot. Such Whiffs and puffs assault you every few Steps and are enough to breed the Plague if they do not Suffocate you on the Spot."

Within days Abigail had found a suitable house "in the North East angle of Grosvenor Square" at Number 8. The elegant townhouse had ample room for the Adams family members, their possessions, and their eight servants.

Abigail was happy it was on "one of the pleasantest squares in London." But she mourned her garden in Paris. John would only admit to Richard Cranch on August 22, 1785, that the house was "in as good an Air as this fat greasy Metropolis can afford." Take that George III.

Still, Adams, no doubt, would be pleased that the American embassy now sits just on the other side of Grosvenor Square.

Whether inspired by the Adams's new mansion or simply the desire for a large home, Jefferson moved into a new house. The Hôtel de Langeac stood at the corner of the Champs-Élysées and the rue de Berri. He described it to Abigail. "I have at length procured a house in a situation much more pleasing to me than my present. It is at the grille des Champs Elysees, but within the city. It suits in every circumstance but the price, being dearer than the one I am now in. It has a clever garden in it," Jefferson assured Abigail on September 4, 1785.

The British greeted Adams with derision. Newspapers printed mocking headlines. "An ambassador from America! Good heavens what a sound!" exclaimed the *London Public Advertiser*.

Abigail complained about the incivility so much that Jefferson speculated on September 25, 1785, that their pugnacious attitude was due to their diets. "The quantity of animal food" eaten in England "renders their character insusceptible of civilization." In brief, the British were caught in a web of inequality dominated by aristocratic "nobility, wealth and pomp," Jefferson speculated in a letter of August 13, 1786, to his old mentor George Wythe. The demonstrated inhospitality of the British did not subside over time. The cause of their hostility was their own embarrassment, Adams explained to his diary on March 30, 1786 after attending the French Ambassador's Ball. "But there is an Auwkward Timidity, in General," when talking to Britons. "This People cannot look me in the Face, there is conscious Guilt and Shame in their Countenance."

Within a few weeks, June 1 to be precise, Adams had his eagerly antici-pated formal audience with King George III, the sometimes crazy but always royal ruler of Great Britain.

Adams had intended to merely present his credentials, but he was told that the custom of making a speech is settled and "indispensable."

Nervous as a student making his maiden presentation, Adams bowed three times before the King; then made a stilted formal speech introducing himself as "the minister plenipotentiary to your majesty," and then added a personal note. "I think myself more fortunate than all my fellow-citizens, in having the distinguished honor to be the first to stand in your Majesty's royal presence in a diplomatic character," Adams told Jay on June 2.

The normally loquacious King, as reported by Adams to Jay, spoke briefly with "more tremor than I had spoken with." Fortunately, he did not call Adams a traitor. George III received with "pleasure the assurance of the friendly dispositions of the United States" and told Adams "I am very glad that the choice has fallen upon you to be their minister." The King defended his actions during the war as doing "what I thought myself indispensably bound to do by the duty which I owed to my people." Admitting he was "the last to consent to separation," the King now claimed he "would be the first to meet the friendship of the United States as an independent power."

The King then remarked: "there is an opinion among some people that you are not the most attached of all your countrymen to the manners of France." To which Adams countered. "I must avow to your Majesty, I have no attachment but to my own country." Adams reported. "The King replied, as quick as lightening, 'an honest man will never have any other'." And on that note the climatic meeting ended.

Adams told Jay he thought the conversation would make his "residence less painful than I once expected, as so marked an attention from the King will silence many grumblers; but we can infer nothing from all this concerning the success of my meeting." Adams was certainly right.

To Jefferson, Adams reported on June 3 the reception "was treated by his Majesty with all the Respect, and the Person with all the Kindness, which could have been expected or reasonably desired, and with much more, I confess, than was in fact expected by me."

Interestingly, Adams did not provide Jefferson a copy of his exchange with King George until September asking Jefferson. "Have I compromised myself or the public in any thing?" Jefferson offered assurances to Adams in his September 22 reply. "I think therefore you by no means compromitted yourself or our country, nor expressed more than it would be our interest to encourage, if they were disposed to meet us. I am pleased however to see the answer of the King. It bears the marks of suddenness and surprise, and as he seems not to have had time for reflection we may suppose he was obliged to find his answer in the real sentiments of his heart, if that heart has any sentiment."

Not letting the Brits off the hook, Jefferson added. "I have no doubt however that it contains the real creed of an Englishman, and that the word which he has let escape is the true word of the ænigma." In other words, don't hold your breath for any commercial agreement with Great Britain.

In his June 22 reply to Adams's June 3 letter, Jefferson failed to comment on Adams's triumph instead concentrating on a request for London newspapers and a possible negotiation with the Barbary Powers.

One of the instructions for Adams and Jefferson was to negotiate peace treaties with the Barbary Powers or pirates.

Pirate ships and crews from the North African states of Tripoli, Tunis, Morocco, and Algiers were the scourge of the Mediterranean. Capturing merchant ships and holding their crews for ransom provided the rulers of these nations with wealth and naval power. In fact, the Roman Catholic Religious Order of Maturins had operated from France for centuries with the special mission of collecting and disbursing funds for the relief and ransom of prisoners of these ruthless, unconventional foes.

Before the United States obtained its independence in the American Revolution, American merchant ships and sailors had been protected from the ravages of the North African pirates by the naval and diplomatic power and cash of Great Britain. British naval power and the tribute or subsidies Britain paid to the piratical states protected American vessels and crews. During the American Revolution, the ships of the United States were protected by the 1778 alliance with France, which required the French nation to protect "American vessels and effects against all violence, insults, attacks, or depredations, on the part of the said Princes and States of Barbary or their subjects."

After the United States won its independence, it had to protect its own commerce against dangers such as the Barbary pirates. As early as 1784 Congress followed the tradition of the European shipping powers and appropriated $80,000 as tribute to the Barbary States, directing its ministers in Europe, Jefferson and Adams, to begin negotiations with them.

Trouble began the next year in July 1785 when Algerians captured two American ships and the Dey of Algiers held their twenty-one sailors for a ransom of nearly $60,000.

In the fall of 1785 Jefferson and Adams sent Thomas Barclay, American consul general in France, to Morocco, and John Lamb, merchant and consul in Spain to Algiers. Jefferson complained to Adams on September 19, 1785, that Lamb had brought "not even a recommendation" from Congress on how to proceed.

After Adams had established himself as the American minister in London, the ambassador from Tripoli approached Adams to begin negotiations for an annual subsidy.

Adams explained to Jefferson on February 17 and 21,1786, that he had already had three conferences with a Tripolitan Ambassador. In a humorous letter Adams described his meeting with the "Tripoline Ambassador." The two men sat down to smoke pipes that were "more than two Yards in length" and Adams "Smoaked in aweful Pomp, reciprocating Whiff for Whiff, with his Excellency, until Coffee was brought in. His Excellency took a cup, after I had taken one, and alternately Sipped at his Coffee and whiffed at his Tabacco, and I wished he would take a pinch in turn from his Snuff box for Variety; and I followed with Such Exactness and Solemnity that the two secretaries appeared in Raptures and the superiour of them who speaks a few Words of French cryed out in Extacy, Monsieur votes etes un Turk."

But the Barbary Pirates were not really a laughing matter to those American sailors who were being captured and held for ransom.

"What has been already done and expended will be absolutely thrown away and We shall be involved in a universal and horrible War with these Barbary States, which will continue for many Years, unless more is done immediately," wrote Adams.

Jefferson must come to London to complete the negotiations. Someone must go to Congress to secure more funds and then someone must go to Holland "to obtain the means, and then somebody perhaps to Algiers to make Use of them."

Jefferson eagerly accepted the invitation spending March and April in England with John and Abigail.

Jefferson arrived on March 14 and the two men began negotiations with Ambassador Abdrahaman. The Tripolitan immediately asked for 30,000 guineas to make peace and 3000 pounds sterling for himself. Obviously the sums were much too high. Compared to the Barbary demands, the $60,000 authorized by Congress was, as they reported to Jay, "but a drop in the bucket." The meeting ended, but not America's confrontation with the Barbary pirates.

By May it was clear Lamb and Barclay were equally unsuccessful. On May 23, 1786, in a letter to Jefferson, Adams acknowledged the failure, but argued that the pirates "must be beaten down as low as possible. We shall find at last the Terms very dear. The Algerines will never make Peace with us, until We have treaties finished with Constantinople, Tunis, Tripoli and Morocco. They always stand out the longest." Barclay and Lamb should withdraw, agreed both men, and Congress must decide whether to fight or talk.

Jefferson opposed the payment of tribute, arguing in letters to Adams and Monroe that paying ransom would only lead to further demands. War was preferable to paying tribute asserted Jefferson.

As Jefferson wrote to Adams on July 11, 1786: "I acknolege I very early thought it would be best to effect a peace thro- the medium of war." Peace through war-how many times in American history have we heard that cry?

"Paying tribute will merely invite more demands, and even if a coalition proves workable, the only solution is a strong navy that can reach the pirates," Jefferson argued in an August 18, 1786, letter to Monroe: "The states must see the rod; perhaps it must be felt by some one of them." Jefferson continued. "Every national citizen must wish to see an effective instrument of coercion, and should fear to see it on any other element than the water. A naval force can never endanger our liberties, nor occasion bloodshed; a land force would do both."

Jefferson reported to Adams on May 30, 1786, that Vergennes thought the only operating agents at Algiers were "money and fear." Adams responded that paying tribute was cheaper than war, but the real problem was Congress does not have revenue. "But for Gods Sake don't let us amuse our Countrymen with any further Projects of Sounding. We know all about it, as much ever we can know, until we have the Money to offer."

"From what I learn from the temper of my countrymen and their tenaciousness of their money," Jefferson added in a December 26, 1786, letter to Ezra Stiles, the president of Yale College, "It will be more easy to raise ships and men to fight these pirates into reason, than money to bribe them."

Jefferson, as he recorded in his autobiography, then "endeavored to form an association of the powers subject to habitual depredation from them. I accordingly prepared, and proposed to their ministers at Paris, for consultation with their governments articles of a special confederation."

Jefferson argued: "The object of the convention shall be to compel the piratical States to perpetual peace."

Jefferson prepared a detailed plan for the interested states. "Portugal, Naples, the two Sicillies, Venice, Malta, Denmark, and Sweden were favorably disposed to such an association," Jefferson remembered in his autobiography, but there were "apprehensions" that England and France would follow their own paths and "so it fell through."

Jefferson 's plan for an international coalition foundered on the shoals of indifference and a belief that it was cheaper to pay tribute than fight a war. The United States' relations with the Barbary States continued to revolve around negotiations for the ransom of American ships and sailors and the payment of annual tributes or gifts.

The United States was forced to pay tribute and ransoms, even though Jefferson, when secretary of state declared to Thomas Barclay, American consul to Morocco, in a May 13, 1791, letter of instruction for a new treaty with Morocco that it is "lastly our determination to prefer war in all cases to tribute in any form, and to any people whatever."

When Jefferson became president in 1801, he refused to accede to Tripoli's demands for an immediate payment of $225,000 and an annual payment of $25,000. The pasha of Tripoli then declared war on the United States and Jefferson dispatched a squadron of naval vessels to the Mediterranean.

But this was far in the future. Even further was the second war with Algiers in 1815 that finally put an end to all payments of tribute by the United States.

Only slightly more successful was Jefferson's introduction to George III.

Jefferson's autobiographical account of his meeting with George III was very realistic. "On my presentation, as usual to the King and Queen, at their levees, it was impossible for anything to be more ungracious, than their notice of Mr. Adams and myself. I saw at once that the ulcerations of mind in that quarter, left nothing to be expected on the subject of my attendance; and, on the first conference with the Marquis of Caermarthen, the Minister for foreign affairs, the distance and disinclination which he betrayed in his conversation, the vagueness and evasions of his answers to us, confirmed me in the belief of their aversion to have anything to do with us." Adams and Jefferson presented their proposals. According to Jefferson, Adams was not "despairing as much as I did."

Jefferson played the tourist in London-visiting the King's Library, touring the Tower of London, hitting the play circuit, the bookstalls and attending balls. Jefferson even managed to make some new friends, such as Lucy Ludwell Paradise.

Adams repeatedly visited Lord Carmarthen, the British foreign secretary, and even the Prime Minister, William Pitt. Adams would demand the British remove its troops from frontier forts and the British would reply the Americans must pay their pre-war debts. As Adams told Jefferson on January 19, 1786, Lord Carmarthen is always "labouring at an answer." No doubt the British thought the Americans either crazy or naïve for expecting the British to enter into a treaty of commercial reciprocity.

Jefferson was of course one of those Americans whose indebtedness to British merchants hung over their heads like the sword of Damocles. Jefferson had not only his own debt, but also a large debt his now deceased wife had inherited from her father, John Wayles. Jefferson later claimed the "debts had become hereditary from father to son, for many generations, so that the planters were a species of property, annexed to certain mercantile house in London." Jefferson and thousands of other Americans were in no hurry to pay.

When it became clear to both Jefferson and Adams, that they would not have a fruitful diplomatic meeting during Jefferson's visit, they decided to go on a tour of the English countryside.

Abigail watched John go off with mixed feelings. Her seemingly neutral comments to her sister Mary Cranch on April 6 reveal the frequency of the Adams's separations. "Mr Adams is gone to accompany mr Jefferson into the Country to some of the most celebrated Gardens. This is the first Tour he has made since I came abroad, during which time we have lived longer unseperated than we have ever done before since we were married." That is a true test of love and fidelity.

Adams and Jefferson set off from London and like thousands of other tourists headed for Wooburn Farm designed by Phillip Southcote in the 1730's. Wooburn Farm was not an ornamental garden but a celebrated attempt to integrate farming and horticultural planning and planting. Alexander Pope's garden at Twikenham, and the gardens at Chiswick, Hampton Court, Esther Place and Paintshill were also on the Adams-Jefferson tour.

Jefferson would later try to produce an integrated ornamental garden-- farmland, groves of trees, experimental vegetable plots and crop fields to produce a graduated vista in the English style. Unwilling to spent the money or time on an ornamental garden, Adams would stick with the small formal garden surrounded by vegetable gardens, fruit trees and fields.

Jefferson's short visit to London only served to increase his dislike of the British. His tepid reception by George III and his ministers was followed by simply bad experiences with rude and arrogant Brits who no doubt were not willing to let bygones be bygones. Jefferson later told Adams's son-in-law, William Smith, in a September 28, 1787, letter. "Of all nations on earth," the British "require to be treated with the most hauteur. They require to be kicked into common good manners."

Still Jefferson spent freely in London, as he seemed to do everywhere. Footwear, a rifle, brass-plated harness and stirrups, and scientific instruments were eagerly acquired. Jefferson later told his friend, Madame de Corny, that British "mechanics certainly excel all others in some lines" and "the splendor of their shops is "all that is worth seeing in London."

Jefferson and Adams engaged in eighteenth century picture taking for the well to do. Jefferson sat for a portrait by Mather Brown and then Adams and Jefferson exchanged copies of their portraits. This was the highpoint of their friendship.

Jefferson departed for France on April 26. Their diplomacy had been a failure. There was no treaty with Great Britain. No solution to the piracy problems.

Shortly after Jefferson's departure, Adams had to make a quick trip to Holland to obtain another loan for the near-bankrupt American Government. The deadlocked Congress could not agree on a minister to Holland, so Adams had to do double duty. The Confederation Congress' impotence led more and more American leaders to conclude it must receive a major overhaul or simply be replaced with a stronger national government.

Adams and Jefferson's personal lives frequently overlapped. When John was in Paris, John Quincy had spent time nearly everyday at Jefferson's home. Both families mourned the death of Jefferson's daughter Lucy. As parents of young women, Jefferson and Adams no doubt commiserated over the Adamses' tribulations with their daughter's unapproved engagement to Royall Tyler. And no doubt they all enjoyed a private toast when Nabby became engaged to John's secretary William Stephens Smith. After the wedding, John only offered this opinion to James Warren: "the young couple appear to be very happy."

In the aftermath of Nabby and William's marriage on June 12, Abigail even joked with Jefferson in a July 23 letter about a union of the two families. Perhaps, John Quincy and Martha would marry. "Now I have been thinking of an exchange with you Sir. Suppose you give me Miss Jefferson and in some future day take a son in lieu of her. I am for strengthening the federal union." Jefferson quickly responded in the same easy vein. "This proposition about the exchange of a son for my daughter puzzles me. I should be very glad to have your son, but I cannot part with my daughter. Thus you see I have such a habit of gaining in trade with you that I always expect it."

The next year Abigail would have a chance to help out one of Jefferson's daughters.

Shortly after Jefferson's return to France, he would meet one of the most enchanting women in his life--Maria Cosway.

It was Abigail who introduced John Trumbull to Jefferson in a July 23, 1786, letter. "Mr. Trumble will have the honour of delivering this to you. The knowledge you have of him and his own merit will ensure him a favourable reception." The young American painter introduced Jefferson to the beautiful, intriguing Italian born wife of an English portraitist, Richard Cosway.

The Cosways were in Paris to drum up business among the rich and well-born French, as well as British and American ex-patriots living there. The twenty-seven year old Maria may just have been simply trying to help out her husband by striking up a friendship with the famous and well-connected American—Thomas Jefferson. Certainly, Jefferson was no stranger to flirtation and the seduction of another man's wife. Betsy Walker springs to mind.

Jefferson however became deeply infatuated if not in love with the strikingly beautiful and no doubt enchanting young woman. If Jefferson were a teenager with a sudden crush on the school beauty, he could not have been more overwhelmed by this young society woman.

The attraction between the tall, soft-spoken Virginian and the vivacious, English-Italian was instant. Jefferson cancelled the rest of his engagements on the day of their first meeting, including a dinner with the Duchess d'Enville, who knew a little about affairs of the heart.

While Madison was in Annapolis planning for a national convention to revise or replace the Articles of Confederation, Jefferson embarked on a torrid love affair.

Thomas and Maria spent time together nearly everyday. Long walks, visits to museums, quiet talks in getaway spots and secluded gardens, and dinners together were the order of the day. Jefferson was clearly smitten with Maria, but we will never know if his love was consummated on anything more than an emotional and imaginative level.

On September 18, Jefferson injured his wrist while reportedly "showing off" by leaping a fence or some said trying to balance on the rails of a fence--all for his lady love during an outing in the Cours la Reine, a park near the Champs-Elysées. Jefferson told Adams's son-in-law, "It was one of those follies from which good cannot come, but ill may." Maria would leave France on October 8 but Jefferson's sore wrist and his attachment to Maria would last a lifetime. Like young lovers going off to college they promised to write. And surprisingly they did.

One of Jefferson's most famous letters is his "Head and Heart" letter to Maria of October 12, 1786. Some commentators have acclaimed it one of the greatest American love letters. Employing a common literary device, Jefferson imagines a spirited dialogue between his head and his heart to express his immense affection for Maria and his fears that his love will be unfulfilled. Jefferson produced a beautiful literary epistle tinged with passion and unacknowledged frustration.

Perhaps absence does make the heart grow fonder. Caught up in a long distance relationship Jefferson certainly pined for Maria even though they only saw each other again briefly a year later. When Maria chided Thomas in 1788 for his infrequent letters, Jefferson gave this meaningful reply. "I am incapable of forgetting or neglecting you my dear friend; and I am sure if the comparison could be fairly made of how much I think of you, or you of me, the former scale would greatly preponderate. Of this I have no right to complain, nor do I complain. You esteem me as much as I deserve. If I love you more, it is because you deserve more."

Later that year, Jefferson told Maria he was returning to the United States. For the first of many times Thomas invited Maria to journey to America where

142

"I should find excuses for being sometimes of your parties." Maria headed to Italy; leaving even Jefferson to sense there was no future physical romance in this relationship.

The two would never meet again before Jefferson sailed back to America, and for the next thirty years their relationship would be confined to the written page. Through their correspondence we can witness the flare of love, their painful separation, the gradual cooling of their romance, and the hardening of their durable friendship.

It is perhaps emblematic of the superficial relationship of Thomas with the Adams family, that he would never mention Maria or his exhilarating if brief time with her in his letters to Abigail. But then how do you tell a couple as straitlaced as the Adamses about an affair with a married woman. The closest he would come is his report of injuring his wrist in a December 21, 1786, letter. There would be no mention of how he injured his wrist while cavorting with young Maria. "An unfortunate dislocation of my right wrist has for three months deprived me of the honor of writing to you. I begin now to use my pen a little, but it is in great pain, and I have no other use of my hand."

And so back to diplomacy or the lack thereof.

Adams regularly communicated with Lord Carmarthen, pointing out that the Treaty of Paris required British troops to leave American territory "with all convenient speed." Lord Carmarthen regularly responded that Americans must pay their English creditors in full and in pounds sterling.

Although Jefferson was not a party to these talks, he certainly had a stake in their outcome. In 1774 Virginians alone owed British merchants £2.3 million. Through his deceased wife Jefferson had inherited additional debts to British factors. Jefferson's share of John Wayles's indebtedness to Farell and Jones in Bristol was nearly £4000 in 1774 and growing with interest each year. Jefferson sold slaves and land in an effort to pay off the debt, but it hung on for decades. For Jefferson, who never saw a luxury he could resist, the burden became increasingly heavy. By the time of his death he owed over one hundred thousand dollars-millions at today's rates. Indeed, he was one of those Americans complained about by Lord Carmarthen and defended by Adams.

Adams and Jefferson continued to consult each other through the public mail. But of course all had to be circumspect, because both the British and French governments were notorious for reading people's mail.

The Barbary pirates were always a hot topic. In January 1787 they signed a treaty with Morocco agreeing to pay protection money for sailors and ships.

The only commercial treaty negotiated by Adams and Jefferson was with Prussia and that was ratified in May of 1786. Both nations agreed to meet at The Hague for the signing. Jefferson was a no show; he was more interested in Maria Cosway. But John, accompanied by an eager Abigail, crossed the channel once again for the signing ceremony on August 8. Then came a five-week tour of the Netherlands, before a return to the chilly if not frigid diplomacy of London.

In the fall of 1786 delegates at the Annapolis Convention called to discuss inter-state commercial issues, called for a national convention to revise the Articles of Confederation. News of a growing rebellion of small farmers and debtors in Massachusetts began to intrude on the thoughts of Jefferson and Adams.

Back home the rebellion seemed to prove that the nationalists were right. Unless a new more powerful central government emerged, the United States might once again dissolve into civil war and rebellion.

Named after one of its leaders, Daniel Shays, the uprising closed courts in Massachusetts to end suits for debts, demanded an end to foreclosures, lower taxes, the abolition of lawyers, paper money and a legislature that was responsive to the needs of indebted farmers and artisans.

Adams reassured Jefferson in a letter of November 30, 1786. "Don't be alarmed at the late Turbulence in New England. The Massachusetts Assembly had, in its Zeal to get the better of their Debt, laid on a Tax, rather heavier than the People could bear; but all will be well, and this Commotion will terminate in additional Strength to Government." He was right.

Jefferson was "not alarmed at the humor shewn by your countrymen. On the contrary I like to see the people awake and alert."

Their calm did not last long.

The Amazon spirit had overtaken Abigail once again. She was not calm or forgiving. In a January 29, 1787, response to Jefferson's comments of December 21, 1786, Abigail lashed out at the rebels and those who would coddle them. "With regard to the Tumults in my Native State which you inquire about, I wish I could say that report had exaggerated them. It is too true Sir that they have been carried to so alarming a Height as to stop the Court of Justice in several Counties. Ignorant, wrestless desperadoes, without conscience or principals, have led a deluded multitude to follow their standard, under pretense of grievances which have no existence but in their immaginations." The state must "quell and suppress it. Instead of that laudible spirit which you approve, which makes a people watchfull over their Liberties and alert in the defence of them, these mobish insurgents are for sapping the foundation, and destroying the whole fabrick at once."

But Jefferson was not done. In a February 22 response to Abigail he defended the idea of rebellion and hoped the rebels were pardoned. "The spirit of resistance to government is so valuable on certain occasions, that I wish it to be always kept alive. It will often be exercised when wrong, but better so than not to be exercised at all. I like a little rebellion now and then. It is like a storm in the Atmosphere."

And Jefferson was not just trying to aggravate Abigail to judge from his response to Ezra Stiles: "The commotions which have taken place in America, as far as they are yet known to me, offer nothing threatening." Jefferson continued. "If the happiness of the mass of the people can be secured at the expense of a little tempest now and then, or even of a little blood, it will be a precious purchase." As Jefferson would famously quip. "The tree of liberty must be refreshed from time to time with the blood of patriots and tyrants."

Neither Adams was quite so diffident when it came to rebellion. Abigail expressed outrage in her letters. John expressed his beliefs in scholarly writing.

While Adams was receiving news of Shays's Rebellion and the growing plans for a constitutional convention, he began work on a series of essays, which became a three-volume book, *A Defence of Constitutions of the United States*. Worried about the status of government in America and the European perception of the United States, Adams decided to use his abundant free time to explain the virtues and limitations of republican government.

The radical French philosophers, such as Turgot, with their arguments for a democratically elected single legislative house that held all the power of government frightened Adams. He wrote to defend the balanced governments created by the constitution of the American states and by inference condemn the unbalanced government of the Confederation, which Adams asserted was "not a legislative, but a diplomatic assembly."

Adams used erudite references to ancient republics and Italian aristocracies to argue that a balanced government of executive, bicameral legislature and independent judiciary was the best form of government to preserve liberty and republican government.

Adams made a straightforward argument. "The people's rights and liberties, and the democratical mixture in a constitution, can never be preserved without a strong executive, or, in other words without separating the executive from the legislative power. If the executive power, or any considerable part of it, is left in the hand of an aristocratical or democratical assembly, it will corrupt the legislature as necessarily as rust corrupts iron, or as arsenic poisons the human body; and when the legislature is corrupted, the people are undone."

Adams saw merit in the balanced government of Great Britain with a monarchy, aristocratic House of Lords, an elected Parliament and an independent judiciary. He saw no room for a hereditary monarch or hereditary aristocracy in America, but his critics, including Jefferson, would soon label him a friend of monarchy.

Part of Adams's problem was that the three volumes were published over the course of more than a year. It wasn't until January of 1788 that his third volume was published and he barely had time to add a long paragraph on the new constitution.

Jefferson promptly agreed that a balanced distribution of powers was "the first principle of good government." But he disagreed with Adams's assessment that the Confederation Congress was a "diplomatic assembly." In the future, he would label Adams a "monocrat."

Thirty years later Adams would still be trying to explain his book to Jefferson.

Jefferson refrained from commenting on Adams's actions or personality for almost three years in France. In fact, Jefferson never mentioned Adams in all of his letters to Madison. Then with Madison's return to Congress Jefferson decided, "it will become of importance that you should form a just estimate of certain public characters." Adams was first on his list in an enciphered January 30, 1787, letter.

As a result of his close work with Adams in France and England, Jefferson altered his view of Adams, despite seeing "a degree of vanity" in him. "You Know the opinion, I formerly entertained of my friend Mr. Adams. Yourself

& the governor were the first who shook that opinion. I afterwards saw proofs which convicted him of a degree of vanity and of a blindness to it, of which no germ had appeared in Congress." Even knowing Madison had a low opinion of Adams, Jefferson could say. "A 7 months intimacy with him here and as many weeks in London have given me opportunities of studying him closely. He is vain, irritable and a bad calculator of the forced and probable effect of the motives which govern men," Jefferson temporized. But "this is all the ill which can possibly be said of him. He is as disinterested as the being which made him: he is profound in his views: and accurate in his judgment except where knowledge of the world is necessary to form a judgment. He is so amiable, that I pronounce you will love him if ever you become acquainted with him." That is one judgment of Jefferson's that proved to be wrong, wrong, wrong.

Jefferson concluded, "He would be, as he was, a great man in Congress." Like many Jeffersonian assessments, you can quote parts of his statement for totally opposite purposes.

By early 1787, Adams was willing to return home. He had fulfilled his dream of being America's first minister to Great Britain. By early 1787, Jefferson reported to Madison "Mr. Adams desires to be recalled."

Indeed, Jefferson wrote in a March 1, 1787, letter to Adams that if he left Europe, he would regret "the interruption of that intimate correspondence with you, which is one of the most agreeable Events of my Life."

What seems clear is that Adams considered Jefferson a true friend, while Jefferson still considered Adams a colleague subject to careful analysis and cautious trust.

And if he left, well "friendship" would move on too.

Jefferson, however, had no such plans to return to America and in fact embarked in the spring of 1787 on a long tour of southern France and northern Italy. The trip exposed Jefferson to more classical buildings that significantly influenced his own architectural visions. For example, the Maison Carrée at Nimes inspired Jefferson's designs for the Virginia state capitol in Richmond.

Jefferson was disappointed in his hopes that the mineral waters at Aix en Provence would help his injured wrist. But as he reported to Adams on July 1, the ports of southern France and northern Italy provided opportunities for American merchants to ship tobacco, whale oil, tar, turpentine and fish oils.

Jefferson returned to Paris just in time for the arrival of his daughter Mary from America.

Jefferson had alerted Abigail in December of 1786 that his "little daughter" Mary would be sailing in May for England. "She is about 8 years old, and will be in the care of her nurse, a black woman, to whom she is confided with safety." Jefferson knew he did not have to ask in advance to secure Abigail's help.

So Adams had both a professional and personal obligation, when young Mary (Polly) Jefferson and her maid, the slave Sally Hemings, were delivered to Adams's door at Grosvenor Square on June 26, 1787. It was Abigail, of course, not John, who took Mary under her wing. Abigail reported in two letters that Mary "is in fine Health and a Lovely little Girl" but was upset enough to cry when the ship captain left the "poor little girl" in the hands of "Strangers."

All of Abigail's maternal instincts fully emerged when Mary clung to first Captain Ramsay and then to her, crying that she didn't know her father.

She was not accompanied by an older nurse, but by her young slave companion, Sally Hemings, whom Abigail said is "quite a child." In her letter of June 26, Abigail added that "She is a Girl about 15 or 16" and "the Sister of the Servant [James] you have with you." Abigail clearly agreed with the ship captain that Sally would "be of so little Service that he better carry her back with him." Little did Abigail know what services Sally would be capable of rendering in the Jefferson household.

Abigail expected Jefferson to come to London to pick up his daughter. She even suggested that he bring Martha to "reconcile her little Sister to the thoughts of taking a journey." However, Jefferson sent his French butler, Petit, to carry out the chore. Writing to Abigail on July 1, Jefferson sent "a thousand thanks to you, My dear Madam, for your kind attention to my little daughter. Her distresses I am sure have been troublesome to you; but I know your goodness will forgive her, & forgive me too for having brought them on you." We do not know how John reacted to Jefferson's seemingly cavalier treatment of his daughter.

Abigail barely cloaked her anger in a letter written the day after Petit's July 5 arrival. "I am really loth to part with her, and she last evening upon Petit's arrival, was thrown into all her former distresses, and bursting into Tears, told me it would be as hard to leave me as it was her Aunt Epps."

Abigail also took a swipe at Jefferson's parenting skills as exemplified by placing his eldest daughter in a convent school. "I cannot but feel Sir, how many pleasures you must lose by committing her to a convent."

By July 16 Mary was in Paris. Jefferson happily wrote to thank Abigail, and to report. Mary "had totally forgotten her sister, but thought, on seeing me, that she recollected something of me."

To his sister, Mary Jefferson Bolling, Thomas reported the happy arrival of Polly and her placement "in the same convent with her sister," and she "will come to see me once or twice a week." Jefferson assured his sister "it is a house of education altogether" and "not a word is ever spoken to them on the subject of religion." Sometimes a little self-delusion is necessary for parenting.

# Creating A New Federal Government

*"Let us now inquire, whether the new constitution of the United States is or is not a monarchical republic, like that of Great Britain. The monarchical and the aristocratical power in our constitution, it is true, are not hereditary; but this makes no difference in the nature of the power, in the nature of the balance, or in the name of the species of government."*
JOHN ADAMS TO ROGER SHERMAN, JULY 18, 1789

*"I will now add what I do not like. First the omission of a bill of rights providing clearly and without the aid of sophisms for freedom of religion, freedom of the press, protection against standing armies, restriction against monopolies, the eternal and unremitting force of habeas corpus laws, and trials by jury in all matters of fact triable by the laws of the land and not by the law of Nations."*
THOMAS JEFFERSON TO JAMES MADISON, DECEMBER 20, 1787

IN THE SUMMER of 1787 Jefferson and Adams were both "impatient to hear what our federal convention is doing."

America's search for a plan of national government was a slow, difficult process. Compromise, cooperation and creativity were required as the Americans moved from being colonials in a patriarchal monarchy to citizen-leaders in a representative republic.

Most of this process took place in the midst of a long revolutionary war. Not only were those "the times that try men's souls," in the words of Thomas Paine, they were also the times that tested Americans' intellectual and practical political skills in creating a strong, national republican government.

Gerard W. Gawalt

Jefferson and Adams had both helped write the Articles of Confederation that governed the national government of the United States. The Continental Congress adopted the Articles of Confederation in 1777, but the states did not ratify them until 1781. The Articles created a loose confederation of sovereign states and a weak central government leaving most of the power with the state governments. The single legislative body elected the president and appointed the judiciary. Once peace removed the rationale of wartime necessity the weaknesses of the Articles became increasingly apparent.

The Confederation had no power to tax. It could not control commerce. The British refused to leave its forts within American territory. The national government could not successfully negotiate a way for westerners to ship their crops down the Mississippi River. Northerners feared a plot to establish a southern confederacy. Southerners feared a New England plot to control the nation by limiting western expansion. Some Americans, including a president of the Confederation (Nathaniel Gorham who admitted to being "monarchy inclined"), plotted to bring a European prince to America to lead an American monarchy. Most Americans recognized the weaknesses of the Confederation, which was without power, without money and without prestige.

Washington and his nationalist allies sought to remedy the problems with a strong national government. To secure this reform a national convention to revise or replace the Articles of Confederation was needed.

Jefferson and Adams were not part of the coterie of nationalists led by Washington, Madison, John Jay, Henry Knox and Alexander Hamilton who pushed for a strong national government.

Hardly had the ink dried on the definitive treaty of peace when Madison was drumming up support for a new constitution. He reported to Jefferson on a meeting with Virginia's George Mason conducted on his way home from Annapolis. "On the article of a convention for revising our form of government he was sound and ripe and I think would not decline a participation in the work," Madison wrote on December 10, 1783.

A month later on January 18, 1784, Washington summed up the problems with the government in a letter to Benjamin Harrison. "The disinclination of the individual states to yield competent powers to Congress for the Fœderal Government—their unreasonable jealousy of that body & of one another--&

that disposition which seems to pervade each, of being all-wise & all-powerful within itself, will, if there is not a change in the system be our downfall as a Nation."

Fresh from the battlefields, Washington worried to Harrison. "For my part, altho' I am returned to, & am now mingled with the class of private citizens, & like them must suffer all the evils of a Tyranny, or of too great an extension of fœderal powers; I have no fears arising from this source, in my mind, but I have many, & powerful ones indeed which predict the worst consequences from a half starved, limping Government, that appears to be always moving upon crutches, & tottering at every step."

Foreign powers would soon take advantage of the new republic if there were not a change, Washington warned Henry Knox on December 5, 1784. "Would to God our own Countrymen, who are entrusted with the management of the political machine, could view things by that large & extensive scale upon which it is measured by foreigners, & by the Statemen of Europe, who see what we might be, & predict what we shall come to. In fact, our fœderal Government is a name without substance: No State is longer bound by its edicts, than it suits *present* purposes, without looking to the consequences. How then can we fail in a little time, becoming the sport of European politics, & victims of our folly."

Jefferson and Adams were in Europe essentially marking time while Washington, Madison, Jay, and Hamilton were already plotting and planning a new federal constitution.

In fact, Jefferson watching France poised on the edge of bankruptcy and chaos told Washington that the problems of the Confederation government were "so light in comparison with those existing in every other government on earth, that our citizens may certainly be considered as in the happiest political situation that exists." Compared to the situation in Europe, political life in the United States was fine. Jefferson commented it was "like a comparison of heaven & hell."

Not that they didn't recognize the problem.

Jefferson's experience in France made him realize that the United States must present a united front. Congratulating Madison on Virginia's decision to let the Confederation Congress handle commercial regulations in a February 6, 1786, letter he concluded. "The politics of Europe render it indispensably necessary that with respect to everything external we be of one nation only, firmly hooped together."

Madison and Washington used regional commercial conferences in Alexandria and Annapolis to prepare the ground for a national convention. In September 1786 twelve men from five states meeting in Annapolis pondered the nation's prospects and called for a national convention to meet in Philadelphia in May 1787 to strengthen the Articles of Confederation. Change was in the wind and the breezes reached Europe.

There in late 1786 and early 1787, Adams wrote and published a work he hoped would influence any new federal constitution, counter radical French writers, and establish him as a constitutional authority. *A Defence of the Constitutions of the United States of America* made an immediate impact. Adams sent copies to Jefferson and to his friends in the United States.

It was a long, sometimes tedious argument for checks and balances in government. A line he had established in better and much shorter form in *Thoughts on Government* back in 1776. A bicameral legislature and an independent judiciary must balance a strong executive, wrote Adams.

What caused problems for Adams was his definition of a Republic. Great Britain with its monarch and parliament was a republic in Adams's view. Not that he advocated the British form of government for America. He opposed monarchy and a hereditary aristocracy for America, but he was not ready to condemn the British form of government. What he feared most was the French political philosophy of men like Turgot, and writers like Paine who criticized America's bicameral state legislatures and espoused democracy and government by a single legislative chamber.

Jefferson's praise was effusive. "I have read your book with infinite satisfaction and improvement. It will do great good in America," wrote Jefferson on February 23. His one quibble (carefully referenced to page 362) was important. Adams saw the legislative branch of the Confederation as "a diplomatic assembly." Jefferson saw the Confederation Congress as part executive, part judicial, and mostly legislative. Virginia courts had even decided, "the Confederation is part of the law of the land, and superior in authority to the ordinary laws, because it cannot be altered by the legislature of any one state." Therefore, "I doubt whether they are at all a diplomatic assembly," corrected Jefferson.

The first volume arrived in America by early June in time to influence the delegates in Congress, and certainly to influence the debates after the convention. Benjamin Rush, a former colleague and mutual friend of Adams and Jefferson, believed that Adams's book made such an impression that "there is little doubt of our adopting a vigorous and compounded federal legislature." Rush continued in his June 2, 1787, letter to Richard Price. "Our illustrious minister in this gift to his country has done us more service than if he had obtained alliances for us with all the nations in Europe."

Madison was not as uncritical of Adams's book. Taking time out from his work at the Federal Constitutional Convention, Madison wrote Jefferson on June 6, 1787, that Adams's book "has excited a good deal of attention." There were already multiple editions, and "It will probably be much read, particularly in the Eastern States, and contribute with other circumstances to revive the predilections of this Country for the British Constitution. Men of learning find nothing new in it. Men of taste many things to criticize. And men without either not a few things, which they will not understand." But continued Madison. "It will nevertheless be read, and praised, and become a powerful engine in forming the public opinion. The name & character of the Author, with the critical situation of our affairs, naturally account for such an effect. The book also has merit, and I wish many of the remarks in it, which are unfriendly to republicanism, may not receive fresh weight from the operations of our Governments."

Others too were not very complimentary. Adams's friend Cotton Tufts sent word to Adams that some people in Massachusetts claimed he advocated for monarchy and plotted with Nathaniel Gorham to put a foreign prince on an American throne. Tufts told his niece, Abigail, on September 20, 1787. "There are a few however, that seem to be disgusted with his Encomiums on the British Constitution and the Spirit which the Defence discovers against pure Democracy. There are some whom we may suppose to be fomentors of Faction under british Influence and perhaps employed to poison the Minds of People & sew Discord, who have endeavoured to insinuate into the Minds of some People, that Mr. A. was for Monarchy and his Plan to introduce one of the young Princes of England to take the Throne in America." Tufts added. "The ill nature of Great Britain towards the American Productions will continue until we have a national efficient Government."

On the other hand he told Adams on June 30, 1787. "You have the Thanks of the best judges & Patriots among us for yr. judicious & timely Publication, it has already passed through one impression at New York and is now reprintg. at Boston." And on September 30 added that Adams's book "has met with great Applause" and gone "through several Editions."

Another James Madison, the president of the College of William and Mary, found evidence in the book that Adams was "plotting" to establish a monarchy in America. In a June 11, 1787, letter to his cousin James Madison, delegate to the Federal Constitutional Convention, Bishop Madison asserted he has "what appears to be the secret Design of his Works." Madison couldn't believe he wrote this massive book just to refute Mr. Turgot who has few advocates in America. No! Adams thinks the "British System of Gov't beyond Comparison, the wisest & the best ever yet invented." Madison then concluded. "He must wish then to introduce a similar Gov't into America." Moreover, "His Executive (which he thinks sh[oud] be single) must be a King—the Senators-Lords." Adams, charged Madison, "seems insidiously attempting" to present a plan "to overthrow our Constitution or at least to sow the Seeds of discontent."

Madison continued by blaming Adams's long term as a foreign minister. "I fear his Optics have been too weak to withstand the glare of European Courts. There Air may have corrupted the plain Republican, & lest he should be farther Mortified, I think Congress w [oul] d do well, to give him as speedily as possible, the oppy. of breathing once more the purer American Air."

"Jefferson thanks his God, that the Days of Kings, Nobles & priests are almost past," exulted Madison. "Adams must trust in his, that they will be seen to rise in America with new Splendor; which sentiment is the most worthy of a Man of common Sense," advised Madison.

And so the die was cast. The Virginians would forever label Adams a monarchist and Jefferson would be the pure republican.

By early July Jefferson was "impatient to hear what our federal convention are doing," but as he told Abigail on July 10, he had "no news from America later than the 27th of April."

Adams and Jefferson were well aware of the Federal Constitutional Convention but they had little effect on the final product. Washington had written to Jefferson on May 30 soon after the Federal Constitutional Convention began informing him that he was president of the convention. Jefferson offered some advice in his response to Washington on August 14. "I remain in hopes of great & good effects from the decisions of the assembly over which you are presiding to make our states one as to all foreign concerns, preserve them several as to all merely domestic, to give to the federal head some peaceable mode of enforcing their just authority, to organize that head into Legislative, Executive and Judiciary departments are great disiderata in our federal constitution." By the time Washington received the letter the convention was over.

Adams wondered whether there was a need for a new constitution. "All the Perplexities, Confusions and Distresses in America arise not from defects in their Constitutions or Confederation, not from a want of Honour or Virtue, So much as from downright Ignorance of the Nature of Coin, Credit and Circulation," Adams complained to Jefferson on August 25.

On August 30, 1787, Jefferson reported to Adams that he had word from the United States as of July 19. The net of secrecy the convention had cast over its deliberations irked Jefferson. "Nothing had then transpired from the Federal convention. I am sorry they began their deliberations by so abominable a precedent as that of tying up the tongues of members," complained Jefferson. "Nothing can justify this example but the innocence of their intentions, and ignorance of the value of public discussions."

Despite the oath of secrecy that kept Jefferson and Adams, as well as most other people, in ignorance of the constitutional debates, Jefferson was sure all would be well. "I have no doubt that all their other measures will be good and wise. It is really an assembly of demigods." Jefferson added that Washington believed the convention would not end until October.

Adams was not concerned enough to reply.

When Jefferson and Adams finally saw the new federal constitution of 1787, they were like two men who go away on a long business trip only to discover that their spouse has replaced their house with a radically different structure while they have been gone. Sure they had been warned of renovation plans and even discussed the plans in a general way. But when they saw the final product they were shocked and "staggered."

They found fault with the new federal constitution early and often.

The government is the means of resolving conflict and contention within a society and the constitution is the vehicle for establishing that government. With this in mind the delegates to the Federal Constitutional Convention had labored long and hard to produce a Republican government balanced between the executive, judicial and legislative branches.

Both Adams and Jefferson had experience in drafting constitutions. Both had worked on the Articles of Confederation. Adams had drafted the Massachusetts Constitution and Jefferson had written two drafts for a Virginia Constitution.

Both men received copies of the final draft of the Federal Constitution. Both men were somewhat taken aback.

Jefferson admitted to a "want of facts" but was "contented to amuse, when we cannot inform."

Apparently the assembly of demi-gods had produced a totally new form of government. And it wasn't all to the satisfaction of Adams and Jefferson.

Adams questioned why there was no Declaration of Rights as a preamble. But he conceded in a November 10 letter to Jefferson that the document "seems to be admirably calculated to preserve the Union, to increase affection and to bring us all to the same mode of thinking."

Jefferson was staggered. "I confess there are things in it which staggered all my dispositions to subscribe to what such an assembly has proposed," Jefferson told Adams in a November 13 letter.

Jefferson wanted a Bill of Rights and term limits as a protection against a Cromwell or a would- be monarch. The president "may be reelected for life," wrote a shocked Jefferson. "Their President seems a bad edition of a Polish king. He may be reelected from 4 years to 4 years for life. Reason and experience prove to us that a chief magistrate, so continuable, is an officer for life. When one or two generations shall have proved that is an office for life, it becomes on every succession worthy of intrigue, of bribery, of force, and even of foreign interference." Jefferson continued. "I wish that at the end of the 4 years they had made him for ever ineligible a second time."

It was the fault of the press, Jefferson complained. Jefferson thought the Articles of Confederation had not been as unstable as the American and particularly the British press had described them. Unfortunately, "we have believed" these misrepresentations.

"Indeed I think all the good of this new constitution might have been couched in three or four new articles to be added to the good, old and venerable fabrick, which should have been preserved even as a religious relique," concluded Jefferson on November 13.

"We have had 13 states independent 11 years. There has been one rebellion. That comes to one rebellion in a century and a half for each state. What country before ever existed a century and a half without a rebellion? And what country can preserve its liberties if their rulers are not warned from time to time that their people preserve the spirit of resistance? Let them take arms. The remedy is to set them right as to facts, pardon and pacify them. What signify a few lives lost in a century or two. The tree of liberty must be refreshed from time to time with the blood of patriots and tyrants. It is its natural manure. Our Convention has been too much impressed by the insurrection in Massachusetts."

Then began the differing views of the dangers of the new constitution. Adams pointed out the key difference between himself and Jefferson when he said, "You are afraid of the one—and I, of the few."

"The Project of a new Constitution, has Objections against it, to which I find it difficult to reconcile my self, but I am so unfortunate as to differ somewhat from you in the Articles, according to your last kind Letter," wrote Adams on December 6.

"You are afraid of the one—I, of the few. We agree perfectly that the many should have a full fair and perfect Representation. You are Apprehensive of Monarchy; I, of Aristocracy. I would therefore have given more power to the President and less to the Senate," stated Adams.

"You are apprehensive the President when once chosen, will be chosen again and again as long as he lives. So much the better as it appears to me."

"You are apprehensive of foreign Interference, Intrigue, Influence. So am I." Then Adams turns Jefferson's argument on its head. "But as often as Elections happen, the danger of foreign Influence recurs. The less frequently they happen the less danger."

Adams seemed to have gotten little positive reinforcement from his experiences with local annual elections and town meetings and feared the democratic aspects of a Republican government. "Elections, my dear sir, Elections to offices which are great objects of Ambition, I look at with terror. Experiments of this kind have been so often tried, and so universally found productive of Horrors, that there is great Reason to dread them."

Yet both men were willing to put their doubts aside and join the new Federal Government.

Jefferson saw the addition of a Bill of Rights as a way to cement support for the new constitution among those who had previously opposed its adoption. "I am in hopes that the annexation of a bill of rights to the constitution will alone draw over so great a proportion of the minorities, as to leave little danger in the opposition of the residue," Jefferson told Washington in a December 4, 1788, letter. "And this annexation may be made by Congress and the assemblies, without calling a convention which might endanger the most valuable parts of the system."

Nationalists, like Washington, Hamilton, Madison, and indeed Jefferson and Adams, were deathly afraid of how a second convention might undermine the plans for a strong central government.

Washington endorsed this idea in his inaugural address and Madison made his own proposals for amendments in a June 8, 1789, speech to Congress.

Jefferson was enlarging the scope of the parts of the constitution that he liked and the alterations needed to improve the proposed Federal Constitution. On December 20, 1787, Jefferson wrote a now famous letter to Madison, which deserves to be quoted at some length. "I much like the general idea of framing a government which should go on of itself peaceably, without needing continual recurrence to the state legislatures. I like the organization of the government into Legislative, Judiciary and Executive. I like the power given the Legislature to levy taxes and for that reason solely approve of the greater house being chosen by the people directly. For tho' I think a house chosen by them will be very illy qualified to legislate for the Union, for foreign nations &c yet this evil does not weigh against the good of preserving inviolate the fundamental principle that the people are not to be taxed but by representatives chosen immediately by themselves. I am captivated by the compromise of the opposite claims of the great and little states, of the latter to equal, and the former to proportional influence. I am much pleased too with the substitution of the method of voting by persons, instead of that of voting by states: and I like the negative given to the Executive with a third of either house, though I should have liked it better had the Judiciary been associated for that purpose, or invested with a similar and separate power.

'I'hen to the parts that Jefferson did not like.

"I will now add what I do not like. First the omission of a bill of rights providing clearly and without the aid of sophisms for freedom of religion, freedom of the press, protection against standing armies, restriction against monopolies, the eternal and unremitting force of habeas corpus laws, and trials by jury in all matters of fact triable by the laws of the land and not by the law of Nations."

Then to "the second feature I dislike, and greatly dislike, is the abandonment in every instance of the necessity of rotation in office, and most importantly in the case of the President." All these points were often reiterated in the campaign for ratification.

But by May of 1788 Jefferson was ready to accept the constitution, telling the French minister to the United States Comte de Moustier. "There are indeed some faults which revolted me a good deal in the first moment: but we must be contented to travel on towards perfection, step by step."

Adams too was foursquare for accepting the new constitution and moving forward even in it did need a little tweaking. "I am much Mortified at the Mixture of Legislative and Executive Powers in the Senate, and wish for Some other Amendments," Adams told Cotton Tufts on January 23, 1788. "But I am clear for accepting the present Plan as it is and trying the Experiment. At a future Time Amendments may be make, but a new Convention at present, would not be likely to amend it."

Adams added a single paragraph on the new federal constitution to the third volume of his *Defence of Constitutions*, which he sent to Tufts for his distribution in January 1788.

Adams agreed that the Articles of Confederation needed to be replaced and praised the new constitution, but no doubt further antagonized Madison by asserting the need to amend "the Report" of the convention.

"The former confederation of the United States was formed upon the model and example of all the confederacies, ancient and modern, in which the federal council was only a diplomatic body. Even the Lycian, which is thought to have been the best, was no more. The magnitude of territory, the population, the wealth and commerce, and especially the rapid growth of the United States, have shown such a government to be inadequate to their wants; and the new system, which seems admirably calculated to unite their interests and affections, and bring them to an uniformity of principles and sentiments, is equally well combined to unite their wills and forces as a single nation."

And here comes the part that no doubt gave Madison and Washington heartburn.

"A result of accommodation cannot be supposed to reach the ideas of perfection of any one; but the conception of such an idea, and the deliberate union of so great and various a people in such a plan is, without all partiality or prejudice, if not the greatest exertion of human understanding, the greatest single effort of national deliberation that the world has ever seen. That if may be improved is not to be doubted, and provision is made for that purpose in the report itself. A people who could conceive, and can adopt it, we need not fear will be able to amend it, when by experience its inconveniencies and imperfections shall be seen and felt."

In late 1787 Adams was ready to leave London for America. Jefferson, on the other hand, was prepared to stay in France, but his personal life had taken a wrong turn when Maria Cosway returned to Paris in November 1787. Unfortunately, Jefferson and Maria were unable rekindle the fire of their first encounter, because Maria was unable or unwilling to break away from her husband and friends to meet alone with Jefferson. Maria acknowledged the reason for Jefferson's failure to visit often in Paris in a December 10 letter written after her return to London. "I suspected the reason" for your non-appearances "and would not reproach you since I know your Objection to Company."

Jefferson's sexual relationship with Sally Hemings may have started in the aftermath of his last frustrating encounter with Maria. Little imagination is required to envision Jefferson turning to the attractive young woman living in his house who probably bore a resemblance to his late wife and whose slave status put her in no position to turn down the advances of Jefferson. Perhaps, Sally seized the opportunity to deepen her personal relationship with Thomas. To those who say a fourteen or fifteen-year old Sally was far too young to interest a forty-four year old Jefferson—Madison had been engaged to fifteen-year old Kitty Floyd with Jefferson's blessing. Enough said. We can speculate, but we cannot know with any degree of certainty.

Just three-years later, Jefferson would caution his own daughter about the needs of an older man, when her father-in-law married Gabriella Harvie, a seventeen-year-old acquaintance of Martha. "All his amusements depending on society, he cannot live alone."

On the other side of the English Channel, Adams was preparing to depart. By December 10, 1787, Adams had learned that Congress had approved his dismissal. "And now as we say at Sea, huzza for the new world and farewell to the Old one." Adams wistfully told Jefferson in a December 25 letter "it would rejoice me in my soul to meet you before I embark for America."

Jefferson offered to meet Adams in Amsterdam "if you have to go there to take leave" as minister to Holland. "In so doing I shall gratify my wish to see you before you leave Europe, to confer with you on some subjects, and become acquainted with our money affairs at Amsterdam" added Jefferson.

But this meeting would not happen.

Instead Adams sent some information by letter on February 12, 1788, offering this consolation for having to negotiate and renegotiate the Dutch loans. "My dear Friend farewell. I pity you, in your Situation, dunned and teased as you will be, all your Philosophy will be wanting to support you. But be not discouraged, I have been constantly vexed with such terrible Complaints and frightened with such long Faces these ten years. Depend upon it, the Amsterdamers love Money too well, to execute their Threats. They expect to gain too much by American Credit to destroy it."

Yet, in the end Adams had to make a quick trip to The Hague in order to take formal leave. Abigail informed Jefferson, that John "would be delighted to meet you there. But time is so pressing after that he cannot flatter himself with that hope, nor be able to stay a day after he had completed his business."

Their last communication in Europe was a bill, which Adams sent Jefferson for his expenses at The Hague.

But Jefferson was busy sending information to Madison about Adams "to cast your eye over" but "not proper for me to state to Mr Jay" the Secretary of Foreign Affairs. Jefferson was crusading for more salary and expenses, and even though he admitted Adams was "of rigorous honesty," he suspected their accounts would be in deficit. "I suspect however, from an expression dropped in conversation, that they were not able" to make both ends meet "and that a deficit in their accounts appeared in their winding up." In short, because Jefferson was madly outspending his salary and allowed expenses, he was willing to implicate his "friend" in unbalanced accounts.

In Paris Jefferson had no intention of permanently returning to Virginia.

In Massachusetts and Virginia battle lines were being drawn over ratification of the proposed new federal constitution.

Neither man attended a state ratification convention. Historians, including Pauline Maier, have found little evidence that Adams was directly involved in the ratification process. In the New York Ratification Convention Hamilton cited Adams as one of America's patriots who supported the new constitution.

However, Jefferson was particularly, if indirectly, influential. His letters were used to both oppose and support ratification of the constitution.

In the Virginia Convention, Patrick Henry used Jefferson's February 7, 1788, letter to Richmond merchant Alexander Donald to oppose ratification. Henry argued that Jefferson stated that nine states should approve the constitution while four opposed it. Then the desired amendments, such as a Bill of Rights, could be passed at a second convention.

Jefferson's full statement was. "I wish with all my heart that the nine first Conventions may accept the Constitution, because this will assure to us the good it Contains, which I think is great & important. But I equally wish that the four latter conventions, whichever they may be, may refuse to Accede to it till a declaration of rights be annexed."

Not even Madison knew that by May Jefferson had changed his mind and now favored unfettered ratification of the new constitution.

Madison opposed the citation of outside authorities and argued that he knew that if Jefferson were a delegate to the convention he would vote for ratification. Edmund Pendleton then used the same letter of Jefferson to argue that Jefferson would vote to ratify because Jefferson believed no objections should be allowed to create "an incurable evil" by dividing the country.

In North Carolina opposition leader Willie Jones cited the same February 7, 1788, letter to Alexander Donald in which he hoped only nine states would ratify the Constitution so that the desired amendments to the constitution were adopted at a new convention. Jones wanted North Carolina to be one of the four not to ratify the proposed constitution. He was victorious. North Carolina ultimately rejected the Federal Constitution until amendments were proposed, approved by Congress and sent to the states in September 1789. Then they joined the union in November 1789.

---

Back in Europe, Jefferson urged Adams to continue his service to the country. "I am in hopes it will be only a change of service, from helping us here, to help us there. We have so few in our councils acquainted with foreign affairs, that your aid in that department, as well as others, will be invaluable," Jefferson wrote on February 20. Adams should have framed that endorsement for later use.

Abigail was already planning that her husband would hold an office under the new federal constitution. She told her son John on February 10, that she would not allow her husband to retire "and bury himself amongst His Books—and Live only for himself!" Rather she hoped "upon the establishment of a New Constitution-to see Him in some respectable and Usefull Office under it. The Americans in Europe say he will be Elected Vice President." One thing Abigail was sure of—"he would not I am well convinced be happy in Private Life."

By early 1788 the Adams family was packing. On March 30 after Adams made a quick trip to The Hague they were on the move and on June 17 Adams was in Boston.

Even before Adams could unpack his trunks, he was elected a delegate to the Confederation Congress by the Massachusetts legislature on June 6. Everyone including his daughter, Abigail Adams Smith, hoped "he will accept." "Independent of my wish that he should not retire from public business, I think his presence in Congress would do a great deal towards reforming the wrong sentiments and opinions that many are biased by," Abby told her mother on June 15. John never attended Congress.

One month later Samuel A. Otis, a member of the Confederation Congress, wrote from New York welcoming Adams, and assuring him that even though the New York convention had yet to act, and North Carolina and Rhode Island had not yet joined, "the experiment will soon be tried. Ten states had acceded. Congress feeling an obligation to call upon the people to elect their president."

Everyone knew Washington, a southerner, would be president. The only question was who would be the vice president and likely successor to Washington?

Most historians write as if Adams's election as vice-president was almost foreordained. Little is written about the months of planning, maneuvering and manipulating that preceded the selection of the electors and the counting of their votes in 1789.

Neither the Federalists nor the Anti-Federalists had any party apparatus to run a campaign. But have no doubts about it, there was a campaign.

The truth is that friends and supporters of several candidates, primarily Adams, John Hancock, John Jay and John Rutledge were quickly and somewhat quietly testing the waters. Even the candidates jumped into the large written conversation. Letters were written. Essays were printed. Candidates' private letters were circulated. Candidates, even Adams, wrote private letters they expected to be circulated to answer questions that had been raised about their policies or even their political loyalties.

By August Massachusetts leaders, such as Theodore Sedgwick, Benjamin Lincoln and Otis, were already speculating on which northern candidate, Hancock or Adams, would be the vice-president. Should Hancock decline, "Mr J. Adams will undoubtedly be the most generally voted for," speculated Sedgwick to Lincoln on August 15, 1788.

Hamilton was already involved in manipulating elections, and trying to denigrate Adams by portraying him as an opponent of Washington. His October 9, 1788, letter to Sedgwick, Massachusetts delegate to Congress and speaker of the Massachusetts House of Representatives, is worth quoting at length. "On the subject of Vice President, my ideas have concurred with yours, and I believe Mr. Adams will have the votes of this state. He will certainly, I think, be preferred to the other Gentleman (Hancock). Yet, *certainly* is perhaps too strong a word. I can conceive that the other, who is supposed to be a more pliable man, may command Antifoederal influence.

"The only hesitation in my mind with regard to Mr. Adams has arisen within a day or two; from a suggestion by a particular Gentleman that he is unfriendly in his sentiments to General Washington. Richard H. Lee who will probably, as rumour now runs, come from Virginia is also in this state. The Lees and Adams' have been in the habit of uniting; and hence may spring up a Cabal very embarrassing to the Executive and of course to the administration of the Government. Consider this. Sound the reality of it and let me hear from you."

Sedgwick was quick to defend, or at least excuse, Adams in an October 19 letter. "Mr. Adams was formerly infinitely more democratical than at present and possessing that jealousy which always accompanies such a character, he was averse to repose such unlimited confidence in the commander in chief as was then the disposition of Congress."

In a classic example of "what goes around, comes around," Adams's criticism of Washington after his defeat at the Battle of Brandywine in 1777 came back to bite him.

The debate of who should be vice-president swirled around Adams. With Washington, a Virginian, sure to be president, most calculations were that a man from Massachusetts, the most important northern state, should be vice president.

Benjamin Lincoln endorsed Adams in a September 24, 1788, letter to Washington. "few men can boast of equal abilities and information and of so many virtues, his foiables are few, I am happy in knowing his sentiments of your Excellency, there is no virtue in your character, which the most intimate of your friends have discovered but it seems to be known and acknowledged by him."

Others, like Jonathan Trumbull, Jr., tried to sidetrack the Adams candidacy by recommending him for "One, if not the first, of the Supreme fœderal Court."

Otis, who would soon be seeking Adams's support for an appointment as clerk of the Senate, told Sedgwick on October 13, that Hancock would prefer being governor because he was determined to "be second to no man." Otis then asserted. "And I think Mr. Adams abundantly the properest Candidate; health & that kind of experience necessary for the office, point to Adams in preference." Still he did not want to anger Hancock by formally endorsing Adams. He was afraid "the glare of popularity dazzles all eyes" and Hancock would "probably as usual prevail." Still he was working with New York and Pennsylvania delegates to secure the choice of Adams.

Madison remained adamantly opposed to Adams, castigating him in a sharply worded letter in cipher to Jefferson on October 17, 1788. Rutledge was the only southern candidate. The northern states had limited their choice for vice-president to Hancock and Adams. "Hancock is weak, ambitious, a courtier of popularity given to low intrigue and lately reunited by a factious friendship with S. Adams. J. Adams has made himself obnoxious to many particularly in the Southern States by the political principles avowed in his book.

Others recollecting his cabal during the war against General Washington, knowing his extravagant self importance and considering his preference of an unprofitable dignity to some place of emolument better adapted to private fortune as a proof of his having an eye to the presidency conclude that he would not be a cordial second to the general and that an impatient ambition might even intrigue for a premature advancement. The danger would be greater if particular factious characters as may be the case, should get into the public councils. Adams it appears, is not unaware of some of the obstacles to his wish: and thro a letter to Smith [most assuredly, Adams's son-in-law from New York] has thrown out popular sentiments as to the proposed president."

It is a good thing that Madison did not know what Adams would later say about Washington. "That Washington was not a scholar was certain. That he was too illiterate, unread, unlearned for his station and reputation is equally past repute." Ouch!! But he certainly did remember what Adams had said about Washington in the aftermath of the fall of Philadelphia in late 1777.

Jefferson made no mention of the vice-presidential contest in his March 15, 1789, reply to Adams preferring to concentrate on the prospect of adding a Declaration of Rights to the constitution. Jefferson claimed he was more afraid of the tyranny of the legislature than of the executive. "I know there are some among us who would now establish a monarchy. But they are inconsiderable in number and weight of character. The rising race are all republicans."

Within a few years both Jefferson and Madison would be openly associating Adams with those who wanted to establish a monarchy.

Adams's letter to his son-in-law William Smith, which has not been found, had the desired effect in New York, because by November 9, Hamilton had decided to relinquish his one scruple and had taken measures to support Adams he informed Sedgwick in a November 9 letter. "On the question between Mr. H [ancock] and Mr. A [dams] Mr. [Rufus] King will probably have informed you that I have upon the whole concluded that the latter ought to be supported. I had but one scruple; but after mature consideration I have relinquished it. Mr. A to a sound understanding has always appeared to me to add an ardent love for the public good; and as his further knowledge of the world seems to have corrected those jealousies which he is represented to have once been influenced by I trust nothing of the kind suggested in my former letter will disturb the harmony of the administration." Little did he know that the disharmony would come from a Virginian, Jefferson, who was not even mentioned for national office.

Abigail reported in a December 15 letter to John that Hamilton had shown their son-in-law Smith a letter from Madison supporting him that said: "We consider your Reasons conclusive. The Gentleman you have named will certainly have all our votes & interest for vice President."

Hamilton became so much an Adams supporter or a political opportunist that he briefly took John's son Charles as an apprentice in his law office.

Adams received another boost for the vice-presidency, when New York's William Duer learned Adams opposed calling a second constitutional convention and so reported to Madison on November 25. "You may remember some Conversation I once had with you on the Subject of Electing Mr. John Adams as Vice President. I have ascertained it in a Mode perfectly satisfactory, that this Gentleman if chosen, will be a strenuous Opposer against Calling a Convention" to amend the constitution.

By December 8 Madison was informing Jefferson. "General Washington will certainly be called to the Executive department. Mr. Adams, who is *pledged to support him* will probably be the vice president."

John Jay was also a supporter of Adams, according to Abigail. In a December 15, 1788, letter to her husband she reported that Jay had come to visit her at their daughter's house near New York City. When Abigail told Jay her husband was thinking of resuming his legal practice, "he replied with some warmth, that if your Countrymen permitted it, they would deserve to be brought to the Bar—that you must not think of retireing from public Life. You had received your portion of bitter things in politicks it was time you should have some of the sweets." No doubt thinking of the vice presidency Abigail pressed Jay to define "the sweets," but "he smild and said that he hoped for good things."

Madison was no doubt further disappointed, when Tench Coxe wrote on January 27, with the news that "The Office of V.P. seems destined for Mr. Adams who will have all Pennsa, Delaware & New England, probably Jersey." Madison probably gritted his teeth as Coxe continued. "Mr. Adams is esteemed by the people—has high ideas of Government—is a friend to property—will take the feelings of New England with him—and has been used to the forms of legislative & diplomatic business—he is a man of pure private Character, &

has knowledge & abilities beyond the proper duties of a V.P. which indeed are not very important." Coxe made it plain that to ensure Washington's election a few votes would not be cast for Adams.

Surprisingly, some people feared that Adams would receive more votes than Washington and become president. This fear apparently cost Adams some electoral votes in Connecticut. Or so Adams's son-in-law, William Smith, reported to Jefferson in a February 15, 1789, letter. Adams received "5 out of 7 of the electors of Connecticut. That he had not the whole there, originated from an apprehension, that if the state of Virginia should not vote for General Washington that Mr. A. would be President, which would not be consistant with the wish of the country and could only arise from the finesse of anti-fœderal Electors with a View to produce confusion and embarrass the operations of the Constitution." Jefferson made no reply.

Washington, himself, was silent on the vice-presidential contest until it had been decided. Then he confided to Henry Knox on January 1, 1789. "From different channels of information it seems probable to me (even before the receipt of your letter) that Mr John Adams would be chosen Vice President. He will doubtless make a very good one: and let whosoever may occupy the first seat, I shall be entirely satisfied with the arrangement for filling the second Office."

By March it was clear to Otis that Adams would be the new vice-president, "even admitting those not known should be lost to you."

Washington, of course, would "have the united voice of a free people," wrote Coxe on February 12, 1789, —"a transcendant honor infinitely beyond the proudest triumphs of ancient times."

# In Double Harness

*"The new government has my best Wishes and most fervent Prayers for its
Success and Prosperity: but whether I shall have any Thing more to do with
it, besides praying for it, depends on the future suffrages of Freemen."*
JOHN ADAMS TO THOMAS JEFFERSON, JANUARY 2, 1789

*"That you and I differ in our ideas of the best form of government is
well known to us both; but we have differed as friends should do."*
THOMAS JEFFERSON TO JOHN ADAMS, JULY 17, 1791

WITH ADAMS BACK in Massachusetts and Jefferson still in France, the men
maintained their written conversation. Jefferson reported on events in Europe.
France was beginning to experience the first rumbles of the revolution that
would ultimately devolve into chaos and bloody massacres. But on August 2,
1788, Jefferson could report to Adams. "The nation presses on sufficiently
upon the government to force reformations, without forcing them to draw the
sword. If they can keep the opposition always exactly at this point, all will end
well." It did not.

Jefferson kept reporting all European events, particularly the Russo-
Turkish war.

Then there was the situation in England. There "the lunacy of the king of
England will probably place the affairs of that country under a regency; and
as regencies are generally pacific, we may expect they will concur with this
country in an unwillingness to enter into war." Jefferson predicted the calling
of the meeting of the "states General" for next year seemed to avoid violence
and bloodshed. A bad prediction.

Jefferson did announce on December 5, 1788, that "the necessity of recon-
ducting my family to America and of placing my affairs there under permanent arrangements, has obliged me to ask Congress for a six months absence,
to wit from April to November next."

Jefferson hinted that he hoped Adams would be serving in the new government when he returned. "I hope therefore to have the pleasure of seeing you
there, and particularly that it will be at New York that I shall find you."

Adams kept Jefferson abreast of events leading up to the start of the
new federal government. "Our Fellow Citizens are in the midst of their
Elections for the new Government, which have hitherto in general run very
well," Adams assured Jefferson in a January 2, 1789, letter. "The new government has my best Wishes and most fervent Prayers for its Success and
Prosperity: but whether I shall have any Thing more to do with it, besides
praying for it, depends on the future suffrages of Freemen," modestly wrote
Adams.

By March 1, Adams could inform Jefferson that he might be vice-president
under the new federal constitution. "In four days the new Government is to be
erected. Washington appears to have an unanimous vote," said Adams, "and
there is probably a Plurality if not a Majority in favour of your Friend."

Still he cautioned the new government might have a rough beginning.
"It may be found easier to give Authority, than to yield Obediance," opined
Adams.

Jefferson congratulated Adams in a May 10 reply. "Though I have not
official information of your election to the Presidency of the Senate; yet I have
such information as renders it certain. Accept I pray you my sincere congratulations. No man on earth pays more cordial homage to your worth nor wishes
more fervently your happiness. Tho' I detest the appearance even of flattery,
I cannot always suppress the effusions of my heart." Would that the good will
would last!

Adams warned Jefferson that "you must expect the first Operations" of
the new government "will be slow." Everything must be established from new
government agencies to raising revenue and halting smuggling.

On March 4 Elbridge Gerry informed Adams that indeed he had received
"three or four times the number of votes of any other candidate." Yet it was
obvious from information provided by John Trumbull, that Hamilton was

already trying to undermine the stature of Adams by successfully maneuvering to decrease votes for him in Connecticut and New Jersey.

Receiving the second largest number of electoral votes made Adams the vice-president.

Adams received thirty-four votes out of sixty-nine possible votes. Washington, of course, received sixty-nine. Ten other men including Jay, Hancock, Clinton and Robert H. Harrison also received some votes.

Adams received official word of his election on April 9 from Sylvanus Bourne, a representative of the Senate. After an "elegant collation at this house" with a "numerous collection of gentlemen, he set off for New York on April 13 with a military escort "to attend him through the counties of Suffolk, Middlesex and Worcester." Despite the urging of her son-in-law William Smith, Abigail did not accompany John but joined him in New York in June.

Without any of the fanfare greeting President Washington, the President Pro Tem John Langdon introduced Adams to the Senate on April 21. There was no oath for the vice president. Wearing a plain suit made in the United States, Adams simply made a brief address praising the president, the Congress, the constitution, and the people of the United States. Adams apologized in advance for any actions "inconsistent with propriety." Little did he know how rancorous his relations would be with some of the members of the Senate!

Adams, in turn introduced Washington for his inauguration on April 30 in the new Federal Hall, formerly City Hall. Washington, dressed in a dark brown wool suit made in Connecticut and boasting a steel-hilted sword and silver shoe buckles, repeated the oath of office administered by New York Chancellor Robert R. Livingston as Adams and thousands of cheering Americans looked on.

Senator William Maclay reported in his diary that after Washington delivered his inaugural address in an "agitated and embarrassed" manner there was a "grand procession to St. Pauls Church where prayers were said by the Bishop."

Adams could report to Abigail on May 1 that the "President has received me with great Cordiality, of affection and Confidence, and everything has gone very agreeably."

Adams and Washington developed a good working relationship. Some might consider it a collegial friendship. They and their families socialized at formal and informal functions for eight years. Sometimes they went to the theatre. On November 24, 1789, Washington sent a ticket to Abigail for the comedy "The Toy; or a Trip to Hampton Court." That night Abigail but not John joined President and Mrs. Washington at the John Street Theatre.

Occasionally, they even made excursions together. On July 10, 1790, Washington noted in his diary. The president, vice-president and "his lady, Son & Miss Smith," along with members of the cabinet, including Jefferson, "visited the old position of Fort Washington and afterwards dined on a dinner provided by Mr. Mariner at the House lately of Colo. Roger Norris but confiscated and in the occupation of a common farmer."

Senator Maclay of Pennsylvania seemed to take an immediate dislike of Adams. After attending a dinner with Washington, Adams, several cabinet members and members of Congress, Maclay made this acerbic observation of Adams. Next to the President, wrote Maclay, "sat bonny Johnny Adams, ever and anon mantling his visage with the most unmeaning simper that ever dimpled the face of folly. Goddess of Nature, forgive me if I censure thee for that thou madest him not a tailor, so full of small attentions is he."

Washington almost immediately consulted Adams about the proper presidential public and social activities. Neither the subjects discussed nor Adams's answers are really pertinent to our present discussion. But it is important to note that the president did seek the vice president's advice as all members of the administration struggled to establish the forms and practices of the new government.

Adams was sucked into or leaped into a month long debate in the Senate over the proper title to use when addressing the president. In the House, where Madison wanted to keep everything "republican," they voted to simply say "George Washington, President of the United States."

Unfortunately, the vice president objected to a title as plain as "President" or even "Excellency." Adams suggested "His Highness the President of the United States,' leading Jefferson to comment this was "the most superlatively ridiculous thing I ever heard" and proved that Adams was "absolutely mad."

Adams took the lead in the month long discussion, lecturing and haranguing the Senate, and generally making himself obnoxious and looking quite aristocratic, not to mention pompous and ridiculous. Senators like Maclay of Pennsylvania and Ralph Izard of South Carolina mocked him. Izard jokingly called him "His Rotundity" --a sarcastic title that haunted Adams for the rest of his life. Maclay privately described him as "a monkey just put into breeches."

Madison reported to Jefferson on Adams's actions in a May 23/24 letter. "J. Adams espoused the cause of titles with great earnestness. His friend R.H. Lee tho elected as a republican enemy to an aristocratic constitution was a most zealous second. The projected title was—His Highness the President of the United States and Protector of Their Liberties."

To these aristocratic tendencies of Adams, Jefferson quoted Franklin in his July 29 reply to Madison. "The president's title as proposed by the Senate was the most superlatively ridiculous thing I ever heard of. It is proof the more of the justice of the character given by Doctr. Franklin of my friend [Adams]: always an honest man often a great one but sometimes absolutely mad. I wish he could have been here during the late scenes. If he could then have had one fibre of aristocracy left in his frame he would have been a proper subject for bedlam."

George Mason, a leading anti-federalist, according to Lund Washington reportedly condemned "the Pomp & parade that is going on at New York, and tells of a number of useless ceremonies that is now in fashion." Moreover, Mason believed "those Damned Monarchical fellows with the Vice President, & the Woman" [Abigail] would "ruin the Nation" if it wasn't for Washington. "Mason has seen some poem in which the Vice President is much Satarised & was so pleased at it, that he took two copys of it in his own handwriteg."

After endless debate the Senate on May 17 finally voted to use the title, "The President of the United States." But the damage was already done to Adams's reputation. Men, like Jefferson, Mason, Madison, and Maclay already thought Adams had not abandoned hopes for an American monarchy. They simply added his attempts to dignify the presidency with an exalted title to his public writings and concluded he was dangerous to the American Republic.

Adams was criticized for his emblazoned coach and driver. John Randolph, a young Virginia relative of Jefferson, was angered that the Massachusetts schoolteacher was acting like a lord in a Republic. Forty years later Randolph was still sputtering that Adams's coachman had "spurned" his brother for coming too close to "the scutcheon of the vice-regal carriage."

Adams further damaged his republican credentials in three letters to Senator Roger Sherman, a framer of the constitution and a strong advocate of decentralized power with sovereignty resting with the legislative branch. Writing from his New York home in Richmond Hill in July 1789, Adams argued that the only difference between the British monarchy and that American presidency was that the former was hereditary and the latter elected. "The monarchical and the aristocratical power in our constitution, it is true, are not hereditary; but this makes no difference in the nature of the power, in the nature of the balance, or in the name of the species of government."

Adams called the British government a "monarchical republic." As to the American presidency, Adams said. "I know of no first magistrate in any republican government, excepting England and Neuchatel [a Swiss canton], who possesses a constitutional dignity, authority, and power comparable to his." And Adams wondered why he was accused of being a monarchist?

Adams's efforts to secure an illustrious or respectful title for the new president also caused heartburn to Washington himself. On July 14, David Stuart, friend and family member, gave Washington his view from Abingdon, Virginia, of the disastrous debate over presidential titles. Adams is "not only unpopular to an extreme, but highly odious. As I consider it very unfortunate for the Government, that a person in the second office should be so unpopular, I have been much concerned at the clamor and abuse against him." Stuart continued. "The opponents of the government affect to smile at it, and consider it as a verification of their prophecies about the tendency of the government. Mr. Henry's description of it, that it squinted towards monarchy is in every mouth." Moreover, Adams is criticized for always traveling in his "carryage & six," while you are often seen walking from place to place.

Washington was quick to reply to Stuart on July 26, jesting that he never saw Adams "with more than *two* horses in his Carriage." On a more serious note, Washington commented. "But it is to be lamented that he, and some others, have stirred a question which has given rise to so much animadversions; and which I confess, has given me much uneasiness, lest it should be supposed by some (unacquainted with the facts) that the object they had in view was not displeasingly to me."

Critics of the new government had bigger fish to fry, particularly amending the constitution.

Almost immediately there were the demands to amend the new constitution. Most of the states had proposed amendments to the new constitution.

Adams was sure that "Amendments to the Constitution, will be expected, and no doubt discussed." Adams told Jefferson he must read the constitution and propose "Sentiments of Amendments" that he thought "necessary or usefull?"

Adams thought that the executive should be strengthened and he worried about the separation of power between the executive and the legislature. "That greatest and most necessary of all Amendments, the Seperation of the Executive Power, from the Legislative Seems to be better understood than it once was. Without this our Government is in danger of being a continual struggle between a Junto of Grandees, for the first Chair."

But still, Adams told Jefferson on March 1, "The Success of the new Plan will depend in the first Place upon a Revenue, to defray the Interest of the foreign and domestic debt. But how to get a Revenue? How to render Smuggling and Evasion Shameful?"

Clearly, Adams had no idea that Madison planned to divert attention from substantive amendments by throwing out a "Bill of Rights" like a Tub to a Whale.

With Jonathan Swift's "Tale of a Tub" no doubt in mind, Madison would propose a series of amendments on individual rights prohibiting Congress from violating a "Federal Bill of Rights." Thus the amendments would serve as a Tub to a Whale or a diversion so the ship, in this case the ship of state, could sail away from its anti-federalist opponents.

On June 8 Madison took to the floor of the House of Representatives to propose more than twenty amendments to the constitution. But unlike the later plan to add amendments as a supplement to the constitution, Madison proposed inserting the changes into the body of the constitution. Jefferson had suggested amendments be added as a supplement, but Madison had his own idea. Only later, when members of the Congress, such as Roger Sherman, suggested that Madison's plan would subject the entire constitution to a new process of ratification by the states did Madison switch his plans to the addition of supplemental amendments.

Still most of the proposed amendments avoided substantive changes to the constitution, and concentrated on individual rights.

Opposition leaders pounced.

George Mason told his son John In August 1789 that the Madisonian plan was "a Farce.' Mason accurately came to this conclusion. "Perhaps some milk & Water Propositions may be made by Congress to the State Legislatures byway of throwing out a Tub to the Whale; but of important & substantial Amendments, I have not the least hope."

Aedanus Burke of South Carolina took to the floor of the House to assert that the proposed amendments were "little better than whipsyllabub, frothy and full of wind" and they were "like a tub thrown out to a whale, to secure the freight of the ship and its peaceable voyage."

And they were right.

Jefferson and Adams had agreed in an exchange of letters in 1787 and early 1788 that a Bill of Rights would be beneficial.

Adams believed that a Declaration of Rights should have been a preamble to the new constitution. His own draft of the Massachusetts Constitution in 1780 had included such a Bill of Rights.

"What think you of a Declaration of Rights? Should not such a thing have preceded the model," Adams wrote to Jefferson.

Jefferson's first reaction to the constitution, he told Adams, was the confession that "there are things in it which stagger all my dispositions to subscribe to what such an assembly has proposed."

Jefferson, of course, had already told Madison on December 20, 1787, that the number one problem with the new constitution was that it lacked a bill of rights to protect "freedom of religion, freedom of the press, protection against standing armies, restrictions against monopolies, the eternal an unremitting force of the habeas corpus laws, and trials by jury."

During the debates in Congress during the summer of 1789 Adams said little publicly about the proposed amendments.

After seeing an early draft of the amendments sent by Madison, Jefferson told his friend on August 28. "I like it as far as it goes but I should have been for going further. Jefferson then offered a series of "alterations and additions" strengthening the rights of freedom of speech, trial by jury, habeas corpus, but lessening the terms of patents and monopolies.

"These restrictions I think are so guarded as to hinder evil only," said Jefferson. Ever the master of the backhanded compliment, Jefferson added "However if we do not have them now, I have so much confidence in my countrymen as to be satisfied that we shall have them as soon as the degeneracy of our government shall render them necessary." Degeneracy! Really!

At the same time as Congress debated amendments and tried to erect a new federal government, Jefferson was in France awaiting "my Congé" (Jefferson had taken to affectedly sprinkling French words into his written conversations.) as "there were great tumults in Paris." The next day, July 14, the Paris mobs stormed the Bastille. The revolution was on.

Jefferson witnessed foreign mercenaries battling Parisians. Mobs ransacked the house of the wealthy including Jefferson. Jefferson reported on July 16. "The tumults in Paris which took place on the change of the ministry, the slaughter of the people in the assault of the Bastille, the beheading the Governor and Lieutenant Governor of it excited in the king so much concern, that bursting from the shackles of his minister and advisers, he went yesterday morning to the states general."

To his long distance lady friend, Maria Cosway, Jefferson wrote on July 25. "In the mean time we have been here in the midst of tumult and violence. The cutting off heads is become so much as la mode, that one is apt to feel of a morning whether their own is on their shoulders."

One's misfortune is another's fortune. As Jefferson added to Maria, "My fortune has been singular, to see in the course of fourteen years two such revolutions as were never before seen."

In late July and August Jefferson helped his old friend Lafayette draft a Declaration of the Rights of Man and of the Citizen. Two amended copies still reside in the Jefferson papers at the Library of Congress.

The ever glib Jefferson assured Lafayette "that your revolution had got along with a steady pace: meeting indeed with occasional difficulties and dangers, but we are not to expect to be translated from despotism to liberty in a feather-bed."

On August 26, the National Assembly adopted the French Declaration of Rights. Jefferson had the distinction of helping to draft the documents central to the American and the French revolutions.

Lafayette gifted Washington the key to the Bastille, which still hangs on the wall of Mount Vernon.

The American "Bill of Rights" still confounded the legislative process in New York.

Determined to mollify the anti-Federalists while warding off calls for a second constitutional convention Madison moved on with his plan. Even though Adams was the presiding officer of the senate, there is no evidence he played a major role in their passage. Jefferson, who played a key role in writing the French Declaration of Rights, could only offer advice to Madison from France.

Twelve amendments to the constitution finally passed through Congress and were sent to the states in late September. The last ten are now called the Bill of Rights. The proposed second amendment is now the twenty-seventh that regulates Congressional pay. The proposed amendment to adjust the proportional ratio for representatives was defeated.

A second constitutional convention has never been called. Madison and Washington were victorious.

Jefferson's return would soon change the working relationships in the new government. Madison would drift from the nationalist orbit of Washington, Adams and Hamilton to the new Jeffersonian orbit.

Adams and Congress had spent months establishing the new Federal Government when Jefferson left Paris at the end of September 1789. Thomas planned a quick six month trip to Virginia to check on his estate and once again to settle his daughters with his sister-in-law Elizabeth Wayles Eppes in Virginia so that they could learn to become American rather than French ladies. Jefferson feared Martha's rebellious desire to become a Catholic nun. He wanted her settled i.e. married to an American and he needed to settle his crushing debts. Those pre-war debts to British merchants "tormented" him and were threatening to overwhelm him.

Jefferson left so quickly he failed to say goodbye to many of his French friends, such as Madame de Corny. In a November 25, 1789, letter Madame de Corny describes how she "cried tears at your absence" after discovering his departure. Like all of his friends, Madame de Corny wished for "his solemn promise" to return to France.

Jefferson assured his friend Maria in an October 14, 1789, letter that he looked forward to renewing their relationship when he returned in the spring. "We have left a turbulent scene, and I wish it may be tranquilized on my return, which I count will be in the month of April. under the present circumstances, aggravated as you will read them in the English papers, we cannot hope to see you in France. but a return to quiet & order may remove that bugbear, and the ensuing spring might give us a meeting at Paris with the first swallow." As lyrical as Jefferson's words were and as sincere his intention, Jefferson would never see his lady love again except in his mind.

At the same time Jefferson was crossing the Atlantic, Washington embarked on a tour of the New England states. New Englanders turned out by the thousands as he passed through more than fifty towns and gave unnumbered houses and taverns the opportunity to forever claim Washington slept or dined there.

Adams was front and center as Washington spoke to the crowds in Boston. On November 1 John gave a glowing account to Abigail, who had remained at Richmond Hill. "General Washington between Sam. Adams and John, The Fratum dulce Par, mounted up to view in the Stone Chapell and in Concert Hall to be sure was a Spectacle for the Town of Boston. The Remarks were very Shrewd. Behold three Men, Said one, who can make a Revolution when they please. There, Said another are the three genuine Pivots of Revolution. The first of these Observations is not I hope, so true as I fear the last is. Of all the Pictures that ever were or ever will be taken this ought to be done with the greatest Care, and preserved in the best Place."

From Boston John went to Braintree before returning to New York in late November just as Jefferson was arriving in Virginia.

While in Braintree, John began drafting a series of essays, which came to be known as Discourses on Davila. When the French Revolution broke out, Adams became fearful that an unbridled majority was as dangerous as an unrestricted monarchy. Adams correctly foresaw "terrible ravages" in France. His essays, built around a rough translation of Enrico Davila's sixteenth century history of French civil wars, were designed to show the efficacy and necessity of a balanced government. The essays began in the April 17, 1790, edition of the *Gazette of the United States* and continued for nearly a year. To Francophiles like Jefferson the essays were seen as an attack on French republicans and construed as a defense of the French monarchy.

Jefferson, his daughters, and slaves arrived at Norfolk on November 23. Then they traveled to Eppington, and on to Monticello. No sooner had Jefferson arrived for his six month "congé," than he saw newspaper stories and heard reports that he was to be offered the position of Secretary of State. Washington's letter soon arrived offering the position to Jefferson with stock praise. "In the selection of characters to fill the important offices of government in the United States, I was naturally led to contemplate the talents and disposition which I knew you to possess and entertain for the service of your country."

The Adamses were apparently very happy to have Jefferson appointed Secretary of State, if only because John Jay would not hold that position. Abigail trumpeted to her sister, Elizabeth Shaw, in a September 27, 1789, letter. "Mr. Jefferson is nominated for Secretary of state in the room of mr Jay who is made chief Justice thus we have the fairest prospect of settling down under our own vine in peace, provided the wrestless spirit of certain characters who foam & fret, are permitted only their hour upon the Stage and then shall no more be heard off or permitted to sow the seeds of discord amongst the real defenders of the Faith." Abigail would be sadly disappointed.

At first Jefferson offered an inconclusive answer to President Washington.

Madison urged Jefferson on January 24, 1790, to accept because "such an event will be more conducive to the general good and perhaps to the very objects you have in view in Europe, than your return to your former station."

Jefferson at first feared the administration of foreign affairs "and the whole domestic administration" (war and finance excepted) would be in one department. This he did not want to do.

Once Jefferson found out his oversight of domestic concerns would be limited, he told Washington he preferred to return to France, "but it is not for an individual to choose his post."

Washington praised Jefferson for his work in France, but insisted he had to decide. After further warnings from Madison that it would be political suicide not to accept the position, Jefferson accepted. Even though Washington "had left me at liberty to accept" the post of Secretary of State or return to France, I "saw plainly he preferred the former, and learnt from several quarters it would be more agreeable," Jefferson told William Short on March 12. "Consequently to have gone back would have exposed me to the danger of giving disgust, and I value no office enough for that."

Jefferson was back on the farm even after seeing gay Paris.

Jefferson and Adams would be reunited in New York, but the magic of friendship was gone. Maybe it was the shared sense of isolation and duty that kindled their friendship in France. Maybe it was the influence of Madison that ended it in New York.

Whatever the reasons their friendship was soon on the wane.

Vice President Adams was already well ensconced in New York, when Jefferson arrived on March 21st to become Secretary of State. Their friendship renewed, Adams and Jefferson settled in to strengthen the foundation of the American Republic.

John and Abigail had rented a house called Richmond Hill in what is now Greenwich Village. When Jefferson arrived he rented "an indifferent house" at 57 Maiden Lane in lower Manhattan. At least Abigail was happy, telling her sister Mary Cranch on April 3. "Mr. Jefferson is here and adds much to the social circle."

Men, such as Mason, who refused to accept the new federal constitution continually, contacted Jefferson. Mason reportedly told friends that they needed to keep the government out of the hands "of those Damned Monarchical fellows with the Vice President, & the Woman [Abigail] to ruin the Nation." Mason and others feared "by G—d that if the President was not an uncommon Man—we should soon have the Devil to pay." They did not fear the monarchists as "long as it pleased God to keep him at the Head." When Adams grabbed for the reins, there was hell to pay.

Not that they were opposed to an independent United States. They certainly were in favor of a republican government, but they emphasized STATES and certainly feared and opposed the concentration of power in the national government. They found Jefferson to be a sympathetic ear in a position of power. Jefferson and Madison became regular visitors at Mason's Gunston Hall on their way to and from the capital.

Even before Jefferson reached New York, Mason pounced on Jefferson in a March 16, 1790 letter. "I wished too, to have had some Conversation with you upon the Subject of our new Government; from which, unless some Material Amendments shall take place, I have always apprehended great Danger to the Rights & Liberty of our Country, and to that Cause, in Support of which I have so often had the Honour of acting in Concert with you, and other Patriots, & Friends to the Rights of Mankind, for which so much Blood & Treasure has been expended, I fear in vain!"

With their contrasting views of the role of government and the division of power within the structure of government, political pressures were bound to separate the two old acquaintances.

Gerard W. Gawalt

Jefferson quickly established a good working relationship with the president. After all the two men had known each other since their pre-war days in the Virginia House of Burgesses. His duties meant they were in frequent consultation. However, they did not enjoy social outings to dances, assemblies, or even Washington's "birth night" celebrations. Because Jefferson asserted he did not attend evening events. Even though he was careful to subscribe $12 to one of Washington's "birth night" celebrations, which he claimed not to have attended.

As we shall see they did not always see eye to eye. We shall see that Jefferson's posterity description of Washington did not always coincide with their actual experiences.

Much later Jefferson would say in a January 2, 1814, posterity letter to Dr. Walter Jones. "Perhaps the strongest feature in his character was prudence, never acting until every circumstance, every consideration was maturely weighed; refraining if he saw a doubt, but when once decided, going through with his purpose, whatever obstacles opposed." "His mind was great and powerful," Jefferson continued, but "slow in operation, being little aided by invention or imagination, but sure in conclusion." Washington kept his irritable temper under control, but "If ever, however, it broke its bonds, he was most tremendous in his wrath." For nearly four years, Jefferson, Adams and Hamilton would spar and vie to gain the favor of Washington and to influence the decisions of the president. Washington would watch, listen, manipulate, and try to prevent the growth of political factions, which he feared most of all.

In the first year of Jefferson's return from France, he had so little impact on Adams's life or conscious thought that Jefferson's name was never mentioned in all of the letters John and Abigail exchanged. Clearly, their warm friendship in Europe had cooled.

But they did find themselves of the same mind during the nation's first international crisis. In July of the previous year Spain had attacked and seized two British ships in Nootka Sound on Vancouver Island on the west coast of North America. Both England and Spain claimed the territory and competed for the fur trade of the Native Americans.

Britain threatened war with Spain over the "Nootka Sound Incident." The problem for the United States was that if war came the British would certainly attack the Spanish in Louisiana and Florida. If the British captured those two

Spanish colonies, the United States would again find itself surrounded by a hostile power-this time Great Britain rather than France.

President Washington asked his Cabinet and the vice-president for their opinions on what course to follow should Great Britain and Spain "come to the decision of arms."

Jefferson and Adams feared encirclement by Great Britain. Jefferson wanted to avoid war, because the outcome would be in doubt. Delay might allow for events to unfold in our favor. "War is full of chances which may relieve us from the necessity of interfering; and if necessary, still the later we interfere the better we shall be prepared," he argued. But he told Washington on August 27,1790 that to prevent encirclement "in my opinion we ought to make ourselves parties in the *general war* expected to take place, should this be the only means of preventing the calamity."

Adams agreed with Jefferson. "The consequences," said Adams in his own August 27 reply "on the general security and tranquility of the American confederation of having them in our rear, and on both our flanks, with their navy in front, are very obvious." Adams advocated "neutrality, as long as it may be practicable." Then they could negotiate even if Great Britain sent troops across American territory to reach the Spanish.

Fortunately, for the United States Spain caved to the British. The Americans were reminded that becoming entangled in European affairs was very dangerous and very hard to avoid.

In 1790 the critical domestic issues of the federal government were the permanent location of the federal capital, the funding of national debts, and the federal assumption of state revolutionary war debts. Hamilton wanted the federal government to assume the state debts to further tie the wealthy merchants and investors to the national government. Madison did not want the federal government to assume the state debts because he did not want to centralize power and Virginia had already paid its revolutionary war debts.

Southerners wanted the federal capital on the Potomac River, northerners preferred New York, and the middle states preferred Pennsylvania.

Debates over these two issues raged in New York throughout 1789 and 1790. At one point in September 1789, the House had agreed to locate the capital on the Susquehanna River in Pennsylvania. When the issue came to the Senate Adams played a prominent role. With the Senate divided between the Susquehanna, the Potomac or Germantown, Adams twice cast the tie-breaking vote for Germantown and the Northern Liberties of Philadelphia. Senator William Maclay who favored the Susquehanna location, accused Adams of grossly unfair conduct by openly speaking and voting against that location for the capital.

When debate resumed in 1790, feelings still ran very high.

Ultimately, Hamilton and Madison made a deal. In exchange for agreeing to the funding of federal debts and the federal assumption of debts the federal capital would go to the Potomac. Moving the capital from New York to Philadelphia for ten years while the new capital city was being built mollified Pennsylvanians.

Adams presided over the rambunctious debates in the Senate. At a critical moment he cast the tie-breaking vote to remove the capital from New York to Philadelphia and then to the Potomac.

Jefferson claimed credit for brokering the deal between Hamilton and Madison.

"On the considering the situation of things, I thought the first step towards some conciliation of views would be to bring Mr. Madison and Col. Hamilton to a friendly discussion," Jefferson reported. The danger was imminent. Jefferson concluded "that if everyone retains inflexibly" in his present opinion "There will be no bill passed at all for funding the public debts and," he argued "without funding there is an end of government."

Apparently upon the suggestion of Hamilton, Jefferson invited Hamilton and Madison to his house for dinner.

There they agreed that in exchange for Virginia's support or to be precise the absence of opposition to assumption, Hamilton would provide New York votes and help convince the Pennsylvanians to move the capital to Philadelphia for ten years and then onto a new federal district on the Potomac. Compromise prevailed.

But happiness with the compromise was short-lived. Only two years later on September 9, 1792, Jefferson was telling Washington that "I was duped into" the agreement "by the Secretary of the Treasury and made a tool for forwarding his schemes, not then sufficiently understood by me; and of all the errors of my political life, this has occasioned me the deepest regret."

By early 1790 Adams's great fear "of a Division of the Republic into two great parties, each arranged under its leader and converting measures in opposition" came to fruition. The "turbulent maneuvers," Adams told his son-in-law William Smith on May 20, 1790, "tie the hands and destroy the influence" of "right minded men." Division ruled. "How few aim at the good of the whole, without aiming too much at the prosperity of parts."

Leaders and political observers were already measuring Adams and Jefferson as successors to Washington. Adams and Jefferson had begun to circle like cocks in a barnyard.

A French diplomat in New York, Louis-Guillaume Otto, was an early prognosticator. "It appears certain at present" that Adams "will never be President and that he will have a very formidable competitor in Mr. Jefferson, who, with more talents and knowledge than he, has infinitely more the principles and manners of a republican." And so the fight was on.

When the government met in the fall of 1790 the Federal Capital had moved from New York to Philadelphia. The vice president rented Bush Hill, a large brick house, two miles west of Philadelphia with a view of the Schuylkill River. The house became such a money pit, that after a year the Adamses moved into a smaller house at the corner of Fourth and Arch Street and reduced their staff to a driver and cook.

The President and family moved into "the grandest house" in Philadelphia. Ironically the Robert Morris house had also been the headquarters of British General William Howe during the British occupation of Philadelphia.

Jefferson rented a house from Thomas Leiper at 274 Market Street for £250 per year and as was his wont promptly set about renovating and enlarging it with a library, garden house, and stable. Furniture, books, and other household goods soon arrived from France and Monticello. Ironically, it was through Leiper that Jefferson later channeled money to James Callender, anti-Federalist writer who excoriated Adams before turning on Jefferson.

Jefferson became convinced that Adams and Hamilton would like nothing more than to destroy the American Republic and erect a monarchy. Jefferson believed Hamilton was the greater evil because he favored a corrupt government, but Adams was not to be trusted. Reporting a meeting of the cabinet in April 1791, Jefferson made precisely these two points. After dinner conversation turned to the "British constitution, on which Mr. Adams observed, 'purge that

constitution of its corruption, and give to its popular branch equality of representation, and it would be the most perfect constitution ever devised by the wit
of man.' Hamilton paused and said, 'purge that constitution of its corruption,
and give its popular branch equality of representation, and it would become an
*impracticable* government: as it stands at present, with all its supposed defects, it
is the most perfect government which ever existed.' And this was assuredly the
exact line, which separated the political creeds of these two gentlemen. The one
was for two hereditary branches and an honest elective one; the other, for an
hereditary King, with a House of Lords and Commons corrupted to his will, and
standing between him and the people." And so the trouble boiled.

Hamilton's plan for a Bank of the United States, which would be funded by
federal deposits, was the linchpin of the Hamiltonian financial plan. Jefferson and
Hamilton both wrote long opinions on the constitutionality of a national bank.

Jefferson, backed by Madison, was naturally opposed. Jefferson, now a
strict constructionist, argued: "To take a single step beyond the boundaries
thus specifically drawn around the powers of Congress, is to take possession of
a boundless field of power, no longer susceptible of any definition." Jefferson
also rejected the argument that the bank could be established under the general phrase "to make all laws necessary and proper for carrying into execution
the enumerated powers." If one were to accept that argument, said Jefferson
"there is not one" power "which ingenuity may not torture" into this phrase.
"It would swallow up all the delegated powers and reduce the whole to one
power," concluded Jefferson.

Hamilton argued that the general welfare clause and the "necessary and
proper" clause of the constitution permitted a national bank or any other measure that would benefit the people of the United States. Placing limits on the
powers of the constitution "would at once arrest the motions of government,"
asserted Hamilton.

Jefferson was also correctly convinced that speculators would make enormous profits on the government debt and securities. Jefferson and Madison
urged Washington to veto the legislation, and their hopes rose when Washington
asked Madison to draft a veto message. But on February 25, 1791, the president signed it into law.

Abigail, who had assured Cotton Tufts, that it would pass, was eager
to purchase government securities. However, John, who professed never to

understand "coin and commerce", "held to his faith in land as true wealth," Abigail told Tufts.

Adams had his own plan.

More than twenty years later, Adams reminded Jefferson that he had once proposed to Jefferson that they unite behind "an Amendment to the Constitution prohibiting to the separate States the Power of creating Banks; but giving Congress Authority to establish one Bank, with a branch in each State; the whole limited to Ten Millions of dollars. Whether this Project was wise or unwise, I know not, for I had deliberated little on it then and have never thought it worth thinking much of since. But you spurned the Proposition from you with disdain."

Adams added in his November 15, 1813, letter that he considered the national banks "a system of national injustice."

"This System of Banks begotten, hatched and brooded by Duer, Robert and Gouverneur Morris, Hamilton and Washington, I have always considered as a System of national injustice. A Sacrifice of public and private Interest to a few Aristocratical Friends and Favourites. My scheme could have had no such Effect."

Jefferson professed not to remember Adams's proposal in his January 24, 1814, reply.

"I do not remember the conversation between us which you mention in yours of Nov. 15. on your proposition to vest in Congress the exclusive power of establishing banks. My opposition to it must have been grounded, not on taking the power from the states, but on leaving any vestige of it in existence, even in the hands of Congress; because it would only have been a change of the organ of abuse."

Perhaps because he was heavily in debts to banks, Jefferson asserted. "I have ever been the enemy of banks; not of those discounting cash; but of those foisting their own paper into circulation, and thus banishing our cash. My zeal against those institutions was so warm and open at the establishment of the bank of the U.S. that I was derided as a Maniac by the tribe of bank-mongers, who were seeking to filch from the public their swindling, and barren gains. But the errors of that day cannot be recalled. The evils they have engendered are now upon us, and the question is how we are to get out of them?"

But their near meeting of minds was not even a distant breeze.

Gerard W. Gawalt

President Washington embarked on his tour of southern states on March 24, 1791. The Washington party traveled down the eastern side of the states to Savannah, Georgia and then returned on the western route from Augusta, Georgia through the Carolinas to Virginia.

Unlike Adams who gloried in Washington's New England tour, Jefferson remained in Philadelphia during March and April. Then Jefferson and Madison left on their own northern tour during May and June under the fireworks produced by the growing dispute over Jefferson's endorsement of Thomas Paine's *The Rights of Man*.

From Philadelphia the duo set off for a political foray into the Federalist strongholds under the guise of a study of northern botanical plants and the Hessian fly. After studying the plants of New York City with political leaders, they set off up the Hudson River Valley and down through western New England. While in Connecticut, a Federalist stronghold, they shunned the gentry, according to Pierpont Edwards. That politics was high on the list of discussion at their stops in New York and Vermont is testified to by a June 13 report in Anthony Haswell's *Vermont Gazette*. "they not only ingratiated themselves deeply with the discerning, but obtained, unreservedly, the sentiments of the people, and secured themselves a fund of political knowledge, which cannot fail to render them more essentially serviceable to their country." Jefferson reported to Washington from Bennington on June 5, that the British still maintained a post on the Vermont side of Lake Champlain and this "exercise of power further within our jurisdiction became the subject of notice and clamour with our citizens in that quarter."

It seems unnecessary to say that Eastern Massachusetts and Adams's home in Quincy were not on the tour.

Jefferson complained about the weather in New England while extolling that of Virginia in a May 31 letter to his daughter Martha. "When we consider how much climate contributes to the happiness of our condition," he assured her, "we have reason to value highly the accident of birth in such an one as that of Virginia."

On a more political note Jefferson informed Monroe on June 17, that after their northern trip he and Madison agreed "the bulk of the people are for democracy, and if they are well inform'd the ruin" of attempts to "elevate the government above the people" will "infallibly follow."

What Adams thought of this Jefferson foray is lost to history.

Neither Adams nor Jefferson would follow the example of Washington by making a tour of the states when they became president.

The smoldering embers of conflict between Jefferson and Adams burst into flames when Jefferson endorsed the 1791 reprint of Paine's *The Rights of Man* with the hope that it would prove to be the antidote to "the political heresies that have sprung among us."

There was no doubt in any reader's mind that Jefferson was referring to Adams's *Defence of the Constitutions of Government of the United States* and his 1790 newspaper essays *Discourses on Davila*.

Jefferson tried to explain his behavior to Washington, but his letter only confirmed and then reinforced his condemnation of Adams. Jefferson explained that he never expected to be "mortified" by being exposed on the public stage. You know I have a "love of silence and quiet and my abhorrence of dispute." he told Washington. It was the fault of the printer, he claimed. But then he doubled down on his criticism of Adams in a backhanded apology. I did not mean to offend my "friend Mr. Adams for whom, as one of the most honest and disinterested men alive, I have cordial esteem" except for "his apostacy to hereditary monarchy." Wow!!

Jefferson and Adams said nothing to each other for three months while Adams was castigated in the press. Then an anonymous writer began defending Adams and attacking Jefferson and Paine over the name "Publicola." Jefferson and most of the reading public assumed the writer was John Adams, never suspecting that the real author was his twenty-four year old son John Quincy.

Finally, on July 17 Jefferson wrote a half-hearted defense of his actions to Adams with additional criticisms that only served to throw gasoline on the fire. Saying he had started to write "a dozen times" but had stopped, Jefferson launched into a lengthy explanation affixing the blame on John Beckley, the clerk of the House and a friend of Jefferson. Jefferson said he "was thunderstruck with seeing my note to the printer "come out at the head of the pamphlet." He explained, "I hoped it would not attract notice." So far so good.

Then came more trouble. "That you and I differ in our ideas of the best form of government is well known to us both; but we have differed as friends should do," explained Jefferson.

Adams's response was nearly consumed by the fire of his temper. The pamphlet with your endorsement "has sown the Seeds of more evils," than can ever be atoned for, a smoldering Adams wrote on July 29. Your action is considered an "open personal attack upon me, by countenancing the false interpretation of my Writings as favouring the Introduction of hereditary Monarchy and Aristocracy into this Country. The Question every where was, What Heresies are intended by the Secretary of State?"

"The answer in the Newspapers was," challenged Adams "The Vice Presidents notions of a Limited Monarchy, an hereditary Government of King and Lords, with only elective commons."

Adams went on to challenge Jefferson's statement that they differed in "Ideas of the best form of Government." "I know not what your Idea is of the best form of Government. You and I have never had a serious conversation together that I can recollect concerning the nature of Government."

Adams continued to deny that he supported any form of limited monarchy or aristocracy for the United States.

Then he indirectly accused Jefferson of "the daring Traits of Ambition and Intrigue, and those unbridled Rivalries which have already appeared."

Adams ended with a pro forma acceptance of Jefferson's statement as "most pure and the most friendly." Fifteen years of friendship was "still dear to my heart," offered Adams.

Jefferson responded on August 30. First he tried to diminish the public effect of his letter. Then he said "no person saw with more uneasiness than I did this unjustifiable assault." He insisted he had referred only to what "I had heard in common conversation" and not to Adams's writings. Jefferson continued. "Thus I hope, my dear Sir, that you will see me to have been as innocent in effect as I was in intention."

Jefferson then declared. "The business is now over, and I hope it's effects are over, and that our friendship will never be suffered" to be torn down by "the use others may think proper to make of our names."

But of course the political and intellectual battle between Adams and Jefferson was not over. It had hardly begun.

John Adams and Thomas Jefferson

# Diverging Paths

*"I am really astonished at the blind Spirit of Party which has Seized on the whole soul of this Jefferson: There is not a Jacobin in France more devoted to Faction."*
JOHN ADAMS TO ABIGAIL ADAMS, DECEMBER 28, 1793

*"Jefferson went off yesterday and a good Riddance of bad ware. He has talents I know, and integrity I believe; but his mind is now poisoned with passion, prejudice, and faction."*
JOHN ADAMS TO ABIGAIL ADAMS, JANUARY 6, 1794

*"Judging from this of the rest of the Union, it is evident to me that the people are not in a condition either to approve or disapprove of their government, nor consequently influence it."*
THOMAS JEFFERSON TO JAMES MADISON, FEBRUARY 15, 1794

ADAMS WAS AGAIN a candidate for vice-president but Jefferson was not much of a factor in the election of 1792. Adams had his doubts, telling Abigail. "An Election is a Lottery." They hoped they had the winning ticket.

Adams and Jefferson realized that any past friendship was quickly being smothered by differing political philosophies and outright partisan politics.

Even though electors had two votes to cast everyone knew Washington would receive half of the votes thereby being unanimously re-elected president.

Jefferson urged Washington to run again to unify the country. In a May 23, 1792, letter he told Washington "North and South will hang together, if they have you to hang on." Meanwhile Washington was being warned that

Jefferson was "a serpent" in "your Bosom" who "is now endeavouring to sting you to death."

Jefferson was telling Washington that "internal dissentions" have taken place within the government and were having disagreeable effects on the working of the government. Jefferson confessed to being partly responsible. "To no one have they given deeper concern than myself: to no one equal mortification at being part of them."

Mostly though he blamed Hamilton. "The Secretary of the treasury, by his cabals with members of the legislature, & by high-toned declamation on other occasions, has forced down his own system," cried Jefferson.

Jefferson found it necessary to declare to Washington in the same very lengthy letter it was not he who was known "as an enemy to the republic, nor an intriguer against it, nor a waster of it's revenue, nor prostitutor of it to the purposes of corruption." Clearly, Washington should understand that Hamilton was all of these and more.

Still national elections loomed.

Washington's Secretary Tobias Lear had his hand tightly on the political pulse of the nation. Lear assured Washington that everyone wanted him to run for re-election and that Adams was certain to be re-elected vice president. Not everyone was that certain that Adams would be vice-president.

Even Lear, a supposed Washington loyalist, told Jefferson in February 1792, that he was becoming disenchanted with the president. Lear told Jefferson he had the "utmost confidence" that the Republican opposition to the Federalists would prevail. Moreover, he reportedly informed Jefferson that he was personally upset when people tried to convince Washington that his opponents were "a small faction that would soon be silenced."

The Democratic-Republicans or Anti-Federalists made Adams their primary target.

New York's George Clinton was their candidate. Adams thought he knew why. It was not personal or party it was sectional—New York versus New England. Adams told his son John Quincy so in a December 9, 1792 letter. "There is a general Interest taken in my reelection in such a number of States as affects me. The Utmost Efforts of my Enemies have undoubtedly been exerted, and what success they may have had in Virginia and the States to the southward of it, is uncertain. New York it is expected will show their vain

Spite against New England. It is not Antifederalism Against Federalism, nor Democracy against Aristocracy. This is all pretext. It is N York vs N England."

John insisted to his family and friends that although he was considered the favorite, there was strong opposition to his re-election. Writing Abigail on November 24, 1792, Adams said even though his friends told him "that an unanimous Vote will be for me in New England," he feared an electoral disaster.

Jefferson, of course, had a different view of the election. He knew that the Republicans were throwing their weight behind Clinton.

His friend and relative Thomas Boylston told Adams in a November 2 letter. "'Tis said to be your *happy fate* to be the most obnoxious character in the United States to a certain party, (whose hatred & opposition is the glory of every honest man) who for a long time have considered you as the first barrier to be removed in order to the success of their designs." These concerns would have been confirmed, if Adams had had access to Jefferson's correspondence.

There was a much broader issue than simply the office of vice-president. Jefferson tried to explain this to the American Minister to Great Britain, Thomas Pinckney, on December 3. The Federalists "endeavored with as little success to conjure up the ghost of anti-federalism, and to have it believed that this and republicanism were the same, and that both were Jacobinism. But those who felt themselves republicans and federalists too, were little moved by this artifice; so that the result of the election has been promising. The occasion of electing a Vice president has been seised on as a proper one for expressing the public sense on the doctrines of the Monocrats. There will be a strong vote against Mr Adams, but the strength of personal worth and his services will I think prevail over the demerit of his political creed."

From Presidential Elector Archibald Stuart in Richmond Jefferson received word in a December 6 missive that they were "unanimous in our wishes to Remove Mr. A from the V. Presidency."

Abigail already saw the attacks on her husband. She complained to her daughter, Abigail Adams Smith that the Jeffersonians portray Adams "as a man who by his Conduct and his writings was endeavouring to introduce a Government of Kings Lords & commons."

Adams recounted to Abigail several stories of Virginians spreading false rumors. "These Anecdotes show the real Genius of this enlightened Age,"

John sarcastically remarked. A relative of President Washington was telling people "the VP was always in opposition to the President, and that all opposition which was ever made to him in Senate originated with the V.P."

Judge Cushing related another story. While dining in Richmond on December 5, 1792, with Patrick Henry, Arthur Lee and others, Henry harangued against Adams's writings, prompting Arthur Lee to stand up and defend Adams's book as "the work of the greatest Genius that had ever written in this Country." Not surprisingly, John praised Lee for "his Independence and his personal Friendship."

"There is no end of the Fictions and Falsehoods which were propagated and not contradicted in those remote States," Adams commented to Abigail on January 8, 1793.

Adams saw the grasp that party spirit, affection for France, and hatred for Great Britain had on Jefferson. On December 28 he told Abigail. "I am really astonished at the blind Spirit of Party which has Seized on the whole soul of this Jefferson: There is not a Jacobin in France more devoted to Faction."

And Adams was sure he knew why. Jefferson was caught between the vice grips of "Debt by his French Dinners and Splendid Living" and his old family debts to British merchants. "I wish somebody would pay his Debt of seven Thousand Pounds to Britain and the Debts of all his Country men," John told Abigail on February 3, 1793, "and then I believe his Passions would subside, his Reason return, and the whole Man and his whole State become good Friends of the Union and its Govt."

When Adams as presiding officer of the Senate received the "votes from Kentucky" on January 8, 1793, they were "said to be all for Mr. Jefferson." Adams immediately leaped into panic mode. On January 9 he told his absent wife. We should "prepare our minds, as well as we can our Circumstances" for defeat. Still he hoped, no, really planned on victory.

In reality, Adams had some cause to be worried. Clinton was a formidable opponent, but as Adams had noted, he was not a national candidate. When the electoral votes were finally cast on December 5 and then publicly counted by Adams himself on February 13, Washington was unanimously reelected with 132 votes. Adams received 77 votes to retain his job. His main opponent, Clinton, did very well in New York, Pennsylvania and Virginia garnering 50 votes. In fact as Adams had predicted New York cast twelve votes for Clinton.

Jefferson received only the four votes from Kentucky, while his future running mate Aaron Burr received one vote.

In the aftermath of the election, Jefferson contemplated retiring from his post as Secretary of State. Perhaps Jefferson saw "no future beneficial course" in the Federal Government. Perhaps he was simply tired of public life after nearly two decades of service that often kept him away from home and family. Some of his friends urged him to stay. Jefferson's personal lawyer, Archibald Stuart suggested in a December 6, 1792, letter that the Federalists attacked him and Madison "to disgust you with public life."

"Should you retire at This Moment I fear by some it may be Ascribed to that cause," challenged Stuart. Could Jefferson stand up to the political attacks and vilifications?

Could Jefferson and Adams remain "upon terms" of friendship, as Adams told Abigail he thought they still did.

Meanwhile, the French Revolution continued to spiral out of control. Adams hoped that American rejoicing at French military victories was "not intended as Approbation of all the Jacobinic Councils." Despite the slaughter in the streets, Adams told his wife on February 3, 1793, that his hands were clean. "If I had not washed my hands of all this Blood, by warning them against it, I should feel some of it upon my soul."

Jefferson had no such fears or qualms of conscience. Even after his friends in Paris wrote to tell him of the cold-blooded killings of their friends and relatives, Jefferson held firm.

The man who had said "the tree of liberty must be refreshed from time to time with the blood of patriots," was unmoved by the deaths of a few friends. "The liberty of the whole earth was depending on the issue of the contest," Jefferson told William Short on January 3, 1793. "And was ever such a prize won with so little innocent blood? My own affections have been deeply wounded by some of the martyrs of this cause, but rather than it should have failed I would have seen half the earth desolated; were there but an Adam and an Eve left in every country, and left free, it would be better than as it now is."

France was not only in the throes of revolution, but it was also at war. Shortly after the execution of Louis XVI, Great Britain joined the long list of France's enemies on February 1, 1793, placing the United States between a rock and a hard place. Federalists and Republicans too chose their sides.

Onto this fevered stage strode Citizen Edmund Genet, the newly appointed envoy from France, determined to pull, push, or drag the United States into war with Great Britain.

Republicans deliriously welcomed Genet all along his triumphal journey from Charleston, South Carolina to Philadelphia.

Adams informed Abigail that Genet had changed little since they had met while Adams was in France. "He appears a Youth totally destitute of all Experience in popular Government popular Assemblies or Conventions of any kind." Adams added he was "wholly ignorant of the Law of Nature & Nations."

In short, Adams could not figure out why Genet was representing France in the United States. "A declaratory Style a flitting fluttering Imagination an Ardour in his Temper, and a Civil Deportment are all the Accomplishments & Qualifications I can find in him, for his place."

Washington brought the question of the reception of Citizen Genet before his cabinet. The debates on February 25 over whether to officially receive Genet had been "lengthy considerations of doubt and difficulty," according to Jefferson. When Washington left Philadelphia for Mount Vernon, he told Jefferson that Genet "should unquestionably be received, but he thought not with too much warmth or cordiality so only as to be satisfactory to him." Jefferson blamed this hesitancy on Washington making "a small sacrifice to the opinion of Hamilton."

President Washington seeing the danger of being dragged into a war that threatened the very existence of the United States issued a proclamation of neutrality on April 22.

Adams was not influential in the decision, although he certainly believed that the United States should "avoid as much as possible entangling ourselves" with European "ways and politics."

Citizen Genet enraptured Jefferson and other Francophiles when he reached Philadelphia on May 16. Hundreds, perhaps thousands, held a torchlight reception. Jefferson estimated the crowd at 1000, Genet at 6000, and years later Adams said there were 10,000 rioters threatening "to drag Washington out of his house." Jefferson expected the enthusiastic welcome to turn the administration from its path of neutrality.

Jefferson was certainly consulted about the neutrality proclamation and found it pro-English. At a November 18, 1793, cabinet meeting, Jefferson and

Edmund Randolph, the Attorney General, opposed the President's right "to declare any thing future on the qu[estion] shall there or shall there not be war?" Washington argued that he was not trying to prevent Congress from declaring war, but only preserving peace until their next session. He then wisely called for a dinner break.

Republicans thought that Washington had no constitutional right to decide matters of war and peace without the approval of Congress. Jefferson noted that in a May 23 meeting Washington had told him that he feared the "danger of anarchy being introduced" rather than the threat of "a few individuals" trying to overthrow the republic in favor of monarchy. He added, "he despised all their attacks on him personally."

Ironically, Jefferson was receiving inside information on Washington from the president's own private secretary, Tobias Lear. Again and again Jefferson noted information he had received during private conversations with Lear. In April 1793 Lear was informing Jefferson that Washington "was not in the way of getting full information" from his aides and cabinet members. On July 18, while Washington was at Mount Vernon, Lear and Jefferson tried to determine the identity of a particularly nasty anti-federalist essayist, Veritas, whom the Republicans suspected of being a Federalist trying to turn Washington against them. According to Jefferson, Lear "said that lately one of the loudest pretended friends to the government, damned it, and said it was good for nothing, that it could support itself, and it was time to put it down and set up a better."

Political parties or factions were so well formed by 1792, that Jefferson's acolyte, Madison, coined the phrase Republican Party for those who opposed the Federalists. For those historians and political scientists who still believe there were no political parties in 1792, I recommend Madison's essay, "A Candid State of Politics," in the September 22, 1792, issue of the *National Gazette.*

Jefferson believed that the Hamiltonians were secretly writing many of the hostile essays to make Washington believe that the leaders of the Republican Party "were his enemies and so throw him entirely into the scale of the monocrats." The Clerk of the House Beckley told Jefferson on July 18, the Federalists were "writing in the character of the most exaggerated democrats, and incorporating with it a great deal of abuse on the President."

Washington and Adams bridled at the increasing attacks on Washington and the administration in the press. Newspapers tended to support one faction

198

or the other. To offset the Federalist papers, Jefferson and Madison helped start and supported a newspaper edited by Phillipe Freneau. In 1792 Jefferson had denied to Washington that "I never did myself or any other, directly or indirectly, say a syllable, nor attempt any kind of influence" over Freneau's newspaper.

Now Washington and Adams wanted the radical newspaperman Freneau removed from his post as translating clerk in Jefferson's State Department. Washington, Jefferson reported on May 23, "was evidently sore and warm and I took his intention to be that I should interpose in some way with Freneau, perhaps withdraw his appointment of translating clerk in my office, but I will not do it: his paper has saved our constitution which was galloping fast into monarchy."

"All the old spirit of 1776 is rekindling," because the English are attacking American shipping interests exulted Jefferson. The people would soon warm up "the cold caution" of the administration, Jefferson wrote Monroe on May 5. "In the mean time H [amilton] is panick struck if we refuse our breach to every kick which G. Brit [ain] may chuse to give it." Hamilton is for proclaiming neutrality, which "would invite and merit habitual insults," Jefferson asserted. .

In the midst of this partisan battling Genet and the Republicans over-played their hand. Genet insulted Washington by appealing to the people over his head. More importantly Genet continued to issue French letters of marque to privateers in direct violation of the Neutrality Proclamation.

Jefferson defended Genet and grudgingly supported the Neutrality Proclamation. Only when he was elected president would he utter his own famous declaration of neutrality in his first inaugural address. "Peace, commerce and honest friendship with all nations, entangling alliances with none."

By August Washington and his administration had had enough of Genet. On August 3, the cabinet voted to ask the French government to recall Genet whose enthusiasm had destroyed his support. "We have decided unanimously to require the recall of Genet," noted Jefferson.

Even Jefferson came to believe that Genet was dangerous for their party if not their country, telling Madison in an encoded message on August 3 "he will sink the republican interest if they do not abandon him."

In France thousands of men, women and children were being guillotined, stoned, shot and even drowned in the name of the Revolution. While yellow fever again ravaged Philadelphia killing hundreds and driving thousands from the city.

Adams returned to his farm, which was now in the newly incorporated town of Quincy. Jefferson returned to his plantation.

In France the parties in power changed again. When they recalled Genet, they also sent an arrest warrant. Knowing that if he returned to France he would be guillotined, Genet begged Washington for asylum. Only Hamilton's support for the request, gained Washington's approval. Genet moved to New York and married Cornelia Clinton, daughter of George Clinton, who had challenged Adams for the vice-presidency in 1792.

By the end of 1793 the public had grown tired of public political paroxysms and so had Jefferson. Having threatened to resign at the end of 1792 and been coaxed to stay, he would not be denied in 1793. On New Year's Eve he tendered his resignation to Washington, who accepted it the next day "with sincere regret." Washington assured Jefferson "that the opinion which I had formed of your integrity and talents" had "been confirmed by the fullest experience; and that both have been eminently displayed in the discharge of your duties."

Adams thoughts ran more toward "good riddance" and "Don't let the door hit your backside on the way out."

To his wife and confidant Adams was honest and bitterly biting. "I am told Mr Jefferson is to resign tomorrow," Adams informed Abigail on December 26. "I have so long been in an habit of thinking well of his Abilities and general good dispositions, that I cannot but feel some regret at this Event: but his Want of Candour, his obstinate Prejudices both of Aversion and Attachment: his Real Partiality in Spite of all his Pretensions and his low notions about many Things have so nearly reconciled me to it, that I will not weep." And finally came the ultimate insult. "I know he is indolent, and his soul is poisoned with Ambition."

The depths of Adams's dislike and distrust of Jefferson can be seen in his January 2, 1794, letter to his son Charles.

"Mr Jefferson is going to Monticello to Spend his Days in Retirement, in Rural Amusements and Philosophical Meditations—Untill the President dies or resigns, when I suppose he is to be invited from his Conversations with Egeria in the Groves, to take the Reins of the State, and conduct it forty Years in Piety and Peace. Amen."

Still Adams recognized Jefferson's talents and the need for a balanced presidential cabinet. "I cannot say that I am pleased with his Resignation. He might have worn off his sharp Points and become a wiser Minister than he has been sometimes. His abilities are good-his Pen is very good—and for what I know the other Ministers might be better for being Watched by him."

To his eldest son, John Quincy, Adams compared Jefferson to Oliver Cromwell. "Jefferson thinks he shall by this step get a Reputation of an humble, modest, meek Man, wholly without Ambition or Vanity. He may have deceived himself into this Belief. But if a Prospect opens, The World will see and he will feel, that he is as ambitious as Oliver Cromwell though no soldier." Little did Adams know the twist of fate that time and the constitution would reveal to him?

Jefferson spent the next few days settling his affairs and left for Virginia on January 5.

After Jefferson departed, Adams had no kind words for the man he had once considered his friend, but now the feeling had not been reciprocated. "Jefferson went off yesterday and a good Riddance of bad ware," Adams wrote to Abigail on January 6, 1794. "He has talents I know, and integrity I believe; but his mind is now poisoned with passion, prejudice, and faction." OUCH!

When Jefferson resigned as Secretary of State he avowed in many letters that his departure from politics was permanent. On February 4, 1794, Jefferson wrote to Horatio Gates. "My private business can never call me elsewhere, and certainly politics will not, which I have ever hated both in theory and practice." He might as well have added I can give up wine and women too. Wisely he did not.

Within weeks of his retirement, his isolation began to wear on him, he confided to Madison in a February 15, 1794, letter. "I could not have supposed, when at Philadelphia, that so little of what was passing there could be known even at Kentucky, as is the case here."

His experience did bring on an epiphany concerning the average American. "Judging from this of the rest of the Union, it is evident to me that the people are not in a condition either to approve or disapprove of their government, nor consequently influence it." No doubt Jefferson concluded it was necessary for the informed to rule the ill-informed people.

Jefferson remained in his self-imposed exile at Monticello for four years. This social exile Jefferson later admitted to his daughter Mary was a mistake. "We should continue to mix with the world & to keep pace with it as it goes," Jefferson wrote on March 3, 1802. "I can speak from experience on this subject. From 1793 to 1797 I remained closely at home, saw none but those who came there, and at length became very sensible of the ill effect it had upon my own mind, and of it's direct & irresistible tendency to render me unfit for society, & uneasy when necessarily engaged in it. I felt enough of the effect of withdrawing from the world then, to see that it led to an antisocial & misanthropic state of mind, which severely punishes him who gives into it: and it will be a lesson I shall never forget as to myself."

After Jefferson resigned as Secretary of State on December 31, 1793, Adams and Jefferson occasionally exchanged brief, almost pro forma letters. On April 4, 1794, Adams congratulated Jefferson "on the charming Opening of the Spring" and, I suspect disingenuously wished "I was enjoying of it as you are upon a Plantation."

Jefferson assured Adams on April 25, 1794, that my only regret was "that my retirement has been postponed four years too long." Jefferson added: "I return to farming with an ardour which I scarcely knew in my youth, and which has got the better entirely of my love of study."

Jefferson tried to devote himself to plantation management and the destruction and reconstruction of his house. Telling George Wythe in an April 15, 1795, letter, "I live on my horse from early breakfast to a late dinner, and very often after that till dark."

Adams, on the other hand, remained at the center of action as vice-president. Even though he told Jefferson in a November 21, 1794, letter. "I have spent my Summer So deliciously in farming that I return to the Old Story of Politicks with great Reluctance." He couldn't help but add. "Virginia I hope will send Us Some good Senators, We grow very thin.," wrote Adams, "But this is not a time for Changes." Jefferson could not have disagreed more. Jefferson did not reply until February 6, 1795, disingenuously assuring Adams "I have found so much tranquility of mind in a total abstraction from every thing political."

Just days later Jefferson received another of his regular multi-page letters from Madison detailing the state of politics throughout the nation.

Jefferson kept in close contact with the other leaders of the growing Republican or Jeffersonian-Republican party. When Washington verbally attacked the Democratic-Republican Societies in his annual address to Congress, and after Washington led a federal military force against frontiersmen who refused to pay the federal excise tax on whiskey, Jefferson was quick to voice his anger in a December 28, 1794, letter to Madison. "The denunciation of the democratic societies is one of the extraordinary acts of boldness of which we have so many from the faction of Monocrats. It is wonderful indeed that the President should have permitted himself to be the organ of such an attack on the freedom of discussion, the freedom of writing, printing and publishing."

Jefferson believed the excise tax on whiskey was "an infernal one" and unconstitutional. So too was the use of federal troops without a Congressional declaration of war. Jefferson urged Madison to "hold on then, my dear friend, that we may not shipwreck" while "the Augean herd over your heads are slowly purging off their impurities."

Adams was back in Massachusetts as the crisis called the Whiskey Rebellion built in intensity. By the time Adams returned to Philadelphia for the December session of Congress, the rebels were on the run and the Federalists were enjoying the afterglow of the unfettered demonstration of Federal power.

Adams crowed in a November 8, 1794, letter to Abigail, "All Submission, in the Whiskey Counties. But a Force will be kept there to ensure their Obedience for some necessary time. Antifœderalism, Jacobinism and Rebellion are drooping their heads, very much discouraged."

And just two weeks later in a November 23 letter to Abigail, Adams saw the crushing of the Whiskey Rebellion as a warning to anti-federalists (read Jeffersonian Republicans) and the British. "An Army of 15,000 militia so easily raised from 4 states only to go upon such as Enterprize, ought to be a terrible Phænomenon to antifœderal Citizens as well as to insolent Britains."

At the same time British seizures of American neutral ships and sailors, as well as their refusal to settle wartime debts and evacuate British forts on American soil along the Ohio River brought demands for retribution against Britain.

Instead Washington on April 15, 1794, nominated Chief Justice John Jay, a leading Federalist, to negotiate a treaty to resolve the several issues with Great

Britain. Even before Jay was formally nominated by Washington it proved to become yet another point of division between Federalists and the rising Jeffersonian Republicans.

Adams believed that opposition to Jay was an effort to undercut Jay's future candidacy for the presidency. "If Jay Should Succeed, it will recommend him to the Choice of the People for President as soon as a Vacancy shall happen. This will weaken the hopes of the Southern States for Jefferson. This I believe to be the Secret Motive of the opposition to him," Adams argued in an April 19, 1794, letter to Abigail.

Still Adams had modest hopes that the Jay mission would preserve peace, telling Jefferson on May 11, 1794. "The President has sent Mr. Jay to try if he can find any Way to reconcile our honour with Peace. I have no great Faith in any very brilliant Success: but hope he may have enough to keep Us out of a War."

Another war, Adams, claimed would raise our indebtedness and "raise up a many headed and many bellied Monster of an Army to tyrannize over Us, totally disadjust our present Government, and accelerate the Advent of Monarchy and Aristocracy by at least fifty Years." Adams then added a little dig to Jefferson and Madison. "Those who dread Monarchy and Aristocracy and at the same time Advocate War are the most inconsistent of all Men."

Jefferson did not reply.

Nevertheless Jay was confirmed by the Senate on April 19th, and rushed off to Great Britain. The Anglo-American Commercial Treaty of 1794/95 (known as Jay's Treaty) called for the withdrawal of British forces from forts along the Ohio River, authorized limited trading with British colonies, and the arbitration of mutual debt claims and boundary issues.

Although signed in England in November 1794, Jay's Treaty remained a continual point of contention. Some historians argue that the treaty dispute gave birth to the Republican Party. Madison, William Branch Giles, and Jefferson led the opposition to the treaty. Demonstrations against the treaty were organized and led by Democratic-Republican Clubs. Jay was burned in effigy and threats were even made to impeach Washington.

Adams delayed his return home in the winter of 1794-95, telling Abigail in a February 2 letter. "The Expectation of a Treaty, hourly to arrive will not allow me to leave my Chair till the fourth of March. I shall be charged with deserting the President, forsaking the secretary of State, betraying my friend Jay, abandoning my Post and Sacrificing my Country to a weak Attachment to a woman and a fondness for my farm, if I quit at this moment."

The contents of the treaty were kept secret for months. Not until August 14, 1795, did the Senate approve the treaty and not until May 6, 1796, did Washington finally sign the treaty.

As anger against the treaty with Great Britain built to a crescendo in 1795, Jefferson became more invested in the opposition to a treaty that Jefferson believed signified the Washington administration's overly submissive behavior to their former enemy, Great Britain, and overly confrontational behavior towards their former ally, France.

Jefferson railed to his son-in-law, Thomas Mann Randolph in an August 11, 1795, letter. "From North to South this monument of folly or venality is universally execrated. The chamber of commerce of New York, made up of English merchants, is the only body which has yet expressed a sentiment approving it."

By October Jefferson was drafting his own political list of pros and cons in response to a July 30, 1795, letter from Christoph Daniel Ebeling, noted German scholar, who was collecting newspapers and other sources of information for a general history of the United States.

Jefferson acknowledged the existence of the two parties one "Anti-Republican" and the other "The Republican part of our Union." The former consisted of "old refugees and torries," most merchants, "speculators," office holders, and "nervous persons," wrote Jefferson. His own Republican Party, he argued, consisted of "the entire body of landholders" and "the body of laborers." Since Republicans outnumbered Federalist by "500 to one," all that was needed was an organization to communicate with them to excite them to "crush the machinations against their government."

Jefferson obviously saw victory in the near future.

When his successor as Secretary of State, Edmund Randolph, was forced to resign on August 19, 1795, under a cloud after Jean Antoine Joseph Fauchet, the French minister to the United States, informed his government that Randolph had revealed secret information and solicited a bribe, Jefferson could not restrain himself. Writing to Madison on November 26, 1795, Jefferson condemned the administration. Jefferson agreed with Randolph's assertion that "the President, tho' an honest man himself, may be circumvented by snares and artifices, and is in fact surrounded by men who wish to clothe the Executive with more than constitutional powers. This when public, will make a great impression. It is not only a truth, but a truth leveled to every capacity, and will justify to themselves the most zealous votaries, for ceasing to repose the unlimited confidence they have done in the measures which have been pursued."

In the aftermath of Randolph's resignation, Jefferson and Madison were said to be involved in his conspiracy. In his dispatch Fauchet had included Jefferson, Madison, Monroe and Randolph in a small group of "honest" men defending the constitution. Pierce Butler warned Madison on August 21, 1795, "There is a vile underhanded game playing, with a View of injuring unspotted Characters." Even in his defense, Randolph implicated Jefferson in his attacks on the president, by denying the British minister George Hammond's accusation that he was part of a conspiracy "to destroy the popularity of the President, and to thrust Mr. Jefferson into his chair."

Jefferson even went so far as to make notes on and to annotate his copy of *A Vindication of Mr. Randolph's Resignation*. Something he seldom did. Charges of his alleged involvement elicited no comment from Jefferson.

Adams told Abigail on December 24, 1795, that he was glad Randolph was gone. He "was a Serpent that might have Stung if his Invention, Cunning and Courage had been adequate." In Adams's view, relayed in a January 7, 1796, letter to Abigail, Washington "appears great in Randolph's Vindication." Adams then took a backhanded slap at Jefferson and the "southern faction." "Happy is the Country to be rid of Randolph." But cabinet members had to be appointed from different sections of the country and "in the Southern Part of the Union false Politicks have struck their roots so deep that it is very difficult to find Gentlemen who are willing to accept of public Trusts and at the same time capable of discharging them."

No sooner was the Randolph scandal been put to rest, than word of Washington's retirement began to circulate in the capital. Adams confided to his wife. "In perfect Secrecy between you & me, I must tell you that I now believe the P[resident] will retire. The Consequence to me is very Serious and I am not able as yet to see what my Duty will demand of me. I Shall take my Resolutions with cool deliberation, I shall watch the Course of Event with more critical Attention than I have done for sometime, and what Providence shall point out to be my Duty I shall pursue with Patience, and Decision. It is no light thing to resolve upon Retirement."

Adams believed that Washington had been driven from office by the incompetence of his cabinet officers and everyone's believe that Washington listened only to Hamilton. Certainly Jefferson nodded in agreement when Adams told Jefferson in a July 3, 1813 letter. "The Truth is, Hamiltons Influence over him was so well known, that no Man fit for the Office of State or War would accept either. He was driven to the Necessity of appointing such as would accept. And this necessity was, in my Opinion the real Cause of his retirement from office: for you may depend upon it, that retirement was not voluntary."

Adams said he wouldn't run if he had "a want of Abilities or of public Confidence." But of course in his mind he certainly had abilities and public support. But "I ought not to serve in my present Place under another especially if that other should entertain sentiments so opposite to mine as to endanger the Peace of the Nation."

With ironic prescience, Adams began his campaign for "a higher Station" with this cautionary line to Abigail. "It will be a dangerous Crisis in public affairs if the President and Vice President should be in opposite Boxes."

Even when the presidential campaign in 1796 was underway, Jefferson wrote to Adams on February 28 professing to "hate" politics while backhanding Adams. "The morals of the people" must be the basis of the American government, Jefferson told Adams. We must turn from the corrupt government of Great Britain. "I am sure," wrote Jefferson, "from the honesty of your heart, you join me in detestation of the corruption of the English government, and that no man on earth is more incapable than yourself of seeing that copied among us, willingly."

No doubt a man as paranoid as Adams flamed with anger when he read the word "willingly" and the implication he might be duped.

Jefferson continued. "I have been among those who have feared the design to introduce it here, and it has been a strong reason with me for wishing there was an ocean of fire between that island and us." Jefferson then closed with a dismissive "But away politics."

Much later after he had successfully been elected president, Jefferson confided to his daughter Polly in a March 3, 1802 letter that the period 1793-1797 when he was out of office had an "ill effect" on "my mind, and its direct and irresistible tendency to render me unfit for society." Jefferson continued. "I felt enough of the effect of withdrawing from the world then, to see that it led to an antisocial and misanthropic state of mind." And he vowed that "I shall never forget" the lesson."

# Two Scorpions In A Bottle

*"You know what is before you, the whips and scorpions, the Thorns*
*without Roses, the dangers anxieties and weight of Empire."*
ABIGAIL ADAMS TO JOHN ADAMS, FEBRUARY 20, 1796

*"The whole system is utterly repugnant to my Judgment and Wishes."*
JOHN ADAMS TO ABIGAIL ADAMS, DECEMBER 16, 1796

*"Be silent till we see what turn the new administration will take."*
THOMAS JEFFERSON TO ARCHIBALD STUART, JANUARY 4, 1797

*"A little patience and we shall see the reign of witches pass over, their spells dissolve,*
*and the people recovering their true sight, restore their government to it's true principles."*
THOMAS JEFFERSON TO JOHN TAYLOR, JUNE 4, 1798

ADAMS AND JEFFERSON both expected Washington to retire in 1797. Both men pretended publicly that they were not candidates for the presidency and assured one and all that they would rather be shoveling dung on their farms than wading through the political swamps of Philadelphia. No one took them at their word.

The presidential campaign to succeed Washington began at least two years before the election. Both men revealed their true intentions only to one person. Adams confided his inner thoughts and ambitions to Abigail. Having no wife, Jefferson consulted with Madison.

At first Jefferson half-heartedly suggested that Madison seek the highest office. Then in an April 27, 1795, letter to Madison he denied that he hoped to succeed Washington saying, "The Little spice of ambition, which I had in my younger days, has long since evaporated." But then in true Jeffersonian style, he opened the door to his candidacy by saying that "my sole object" is to prevent "any division or loss of votes, which might be fatal to the Southern interest." In other words, if Madison and other Republicans feared a victory by a northern federalist candidate, such as Adams, he would be willing to accept the burden.

Madison, Giles and other supporters of a Jefferson candidacy needed no more than this sliver of encouragement to press for Jefferson's election.

By the beginning of 1796 it was clear that the coming presidential election was between Adams and Jefferson. Both publicly remained aloof from the contest that was waged in the press and in person by surrogates.

Only to Abigail could John confide that he was the heir apparent to Washington in a January 20, 1796, letter. "I am heir apparent, you know and a Succession is soon to take Place." Adams added, "All these hints must be Secrets. It is not a subject of Conversation as yet."

Almost simultaneously in a January 21 letter Abigail was almost ordering John not to accept the vice-presidency again if Jay or Jefferson were president. "I would be Second under no man but Washington." She disingenuously added, "My Ambition leads me not to be first in Rome."

Washington's retirement might have been a public secret, but John and Abigail could not stay away from the subject of his successor. Adams posited a scenario in a February 15 letter that would have Jefferson or Jay elected president. This did not frighten him, John told Abigail. "If jay or even Jefferson and one or the other it certainly will be, if the Succession should be passed over, should be the Man, the Government will go on as well as ever. Jefferson could not stir a step in any other system than that which is [begun]. Jay would not wish it."

The contest will be between Jefferson, Jay and myself, predicted Adams. "If Jefferson and Jay are President and Vice President, as is not improbable, the other retires without Noise, Cries or Tears to his farm." If he won and Jefferson or Jay were to be vice-president, Adams guaranteed Abigail that eight years would be the "utmost Limit of time that I will ever continue in public Life at any rate." So Abigail "Be of good Courage therefore and tremble not," reassured John.

Always the realist, Abigail correctly foresaw the difficulties if John was elected president. First and foremost it will be impossible to find another vice-president "without intrigue, without party Spirit, with an honest mind and a judicious Head." Abigail warned him on February 20. "You know what is before you, the whips and scorpions, the Thorns without Roses, the dangers anxieties and weight of Empire."

Despite his obvious candidacy, Jefferson disingenuously wrote to Washington on June 19, 1796, claiming that despite reports to the contrary he was not "still engaged in the bustle of politics, and in turbulence and intrigue against the government." He blamed Henry Lee who spoke "the slander of an intriguer, dirtily, employed in sifting the conversations of my table, where alone he could hear me, and seeking to atone for his sins against you by sins against another."

No political novice, Washington returned his own backhanded compliment in a July 6 response. "It would not be frank, candid or friendly to conceal that your conduct has been represented as derogating from that opinion I had conceived you entertained of me." Washington went on to express his disbelief that political parties would form and to the length they would go in denigrating him with "the grossest and most insidious misrepresentations" in so "indecent terms as could scarcely be applied to a Nero; a notorious defaulter; or even a common pickpocket."

Jefferson believed that the Federalist victories in domestic and foreign affairs were due solely to the prestige of Washington. In a July 10, 1796, letter to James Monroe, minister to France and an acolyte of Jefferson, he urged patience. "The Anglomen have in the end got their treaty through, and so far have triumphed over the cause of republicanism. Yet it has been to them a dear bought victory. It has given the most radical shock to their party."

"They see that nothing can support them but the Colossus of the President's merits with the people, and the moment he retires, that his successor, if a Monocrat, will be overborne by the republican sense of his constituents, if a republican, he will of course give fair play to that sense, and lead things into the channel of harmony between the governors and governed. In the meantime, patience," Jefferson concluded.

At the same time Republicans were telling Jefferson he would be the next president. William Cocke of Tennessee wrote in an August 17, 1796, letter to

Jefferson "the people of this State, of every description, express a wish that you should be the next President of the United States."

Jefferson in an October 21 response said he was not arrogant enough to refuse the job if elected. "I would rather be thought worthy of it than to be appointed to it." His supporters loved his modesty and public lack of ambition.

The signal for the start of the public part of the presidential campaign was the publication of President Washington's Farewell Address on September 19, 1796. Even without a formal nominating process, it was widely assumed that Adams and Jefferson were the leading candidates.

The race was on. First man to seventy electoral votes wins.

However, before the Twelfth Amendment to the Constitution was certified as ratified by Secretary of State Madison on September 25, 1804, electors simply voted for two people. The person who received the most electoral votes became president. The person who polled the next highest number of electoral votes became vice-president. The popular vote when it occurred was uncounted and unappreciated except in those instances where voters directly elected the presidential electors.

All were aware, but were unworried that the campaign could result in the election of Adams and Jefferson to the two positions.

In the states, both parties maneuvered to control the selection of favorable electors. Because states chose their own method of selecting electors manipulation was widespread. Legislatures elected some. Some were popularly elected by districts and others were elected on a statewide basis.

Jefferson later claimed to "sincerely wish to be the second on that vote rather than the first." He admitted in his November 28, 1796, letter to Thomas Mann Randolph, "few will believe" my preference for the vice-presidency. And he was right. Nor would they believe his statement "Ambition is long since dead in my mind."

Jefferson and his supporters regularly labeled Adams as a monarchist and the Federalist Party as the "British Party" or the "Anglican, monarchical and aristocratical party."

Adams refused to personally participate in the election campaign, referring to partisan electioneering as the "cankerworm" of republics. He remained on his farm. Judging by his diary, his main interests were fertilizing, plowing and planting his fields and harvesting his crops. Not until November 23 did he leave Quincy for Philadelphia, where the political cauldrons were boiling over with heated rhetoric, political reports and unfounded rumors.

In a December 5 letter to John Quincy, he said. "I look upon this Event as the throw of a Die, a mere Chance, a miserable, meager Tryumph to either Party." I doubt anyone believed this sentiment. Not even John.

He feared that the Republicans and the Democratic Republican Societies would usher in a period like the massacres and bloody excesses of the French Revolution. The best and brightest should be naturally chosen to lead by the general populace. Still he was quick to charge that Jefferson was "poisoned by Ambition" and supported by Republican "Demons."

The Democratic Republican Societies were a particular concern to Adams.

At first, he took them lightly, joking to his son John Quincy in a December 14, 1793, letter. "How does your Democratical Society proceed in Boston? There ought to be another Society instituted according to my Principles, under the Title of the Aristocratical Society: and a third under that of The Monarchical Society and no Resolution ought to have Validity, until it has been considered & approved by all three."

But soon he took them more seriously. He blamed foreigners, especially French immigrants, and Jefferson for their success in fomenting support for France and opposition to the Federalists. Adams predicted in a November 26, 1794, letter to Abigail that James Callender, a British radical and an the author of a nasty political pamphlet, "will soon be a Member of the Democratical society, as I foresee. This Country is to be the Asylum of all the discontented, turbulent, profligate and Desperate from all parts of Europe and Democratical societies are to raise them to fame, Popularity, Station & Power."

Even worse, "Jefferson it seems is to give the first Passport to Incendiaries. Malignity seemed to have Seized upon that Mans mind as deeply as upon Paines & Callenders." Adams's anger was further stoked by the knowledge that Jefferson was paying subsidies to radical writers including Callender and Freneau. In the future Callender would continue to be subsidized by Jefferson and continue to attack Adams, until jailed under the Sedition Act in the Adams administration.

Both men feared being exposed to "the Butt of Party Malevolence."

But neither shied away from the contest. And Adams concluded in a February 15, 1796, letter to Abigail that the presidency held no "ill forebodings or faint Misgivings." Jefferson simply let Madison and men like Aaron Burr and John J. Beckley, the clerk of the House of Representatives, run his campaign.

Neither man made a public speech nor wrote a public letter on behalf of their own candidacy. Neither did former South Carolina governor and diplomat Thomas Pinckney who was widely considered to be a dark-horse presidential candidate as well as a Federalist vice-presidential candidate. Aaron Burr, however, openly campaigned as Jefferson's vice-presidential running mate.

But remember each of the 138 electors in sixteen states voted for two people without distinction. The person with the most votes became president and the second most votes became vice-president.

The newspapers, however, were filled with essays extolling the virtues and criticizing the faults of both men. Local and state party organizations marched and countermarched. Supporters and even national leaders wrote anonymous letters to the press.

Adams was accused of being a monarchist who was plotting to overturn the republican government in favor of a hereditary leader and an aristocratical legislature. Adams's *A Defence of the Constitutions of Government of the United States* was cited as proof. Pennsylvania Republicans led by Beckley distributed broadsides screeching, "Thomas Jefferson is a firm REPUBLICAN—John Adams is an avowed MONARCHIST." Among the more printable labels for Adams was the "Duke of Braintree" or "His Rotundity."

Federalists called Jefferson an atheist or at best irreligious, a coward, a Jacobin, and a slave monger. He was mocked as the Genius of Monticello. One of the kinder cuts on Jefferson was that he was "a weak, wavering, indecisive character." Federalists in Virginia were busily charging Jefferson with cowardice for fleeing Richmond and then Monticello with the British hot on his trail in 1781. Federalists voiced the fear that Jefferson's election would bring the French Revolution to America and endanger Christianity.

Hamilton was busy trying to limit the votes for Adams in hopes that Pinckney might be elected. Abigail began referring to Hamilton as Cassius, Caesar's avowed political enemy. The Adams family agreed that Hamilton was "as great a Hypocrite as any in the U.S. His intrigues in the election I despise." While Burr was maneuvering to lessen Jefferson's votes in hopes that he might seize the gold ring and become president.

Republicans had their Freneau, Callender and Bache. Federalists had men like William Cobbett, an English soldier turned pamphleteer. Under the pseudonym Peter Porcupine Cobbett began writing pro-English and anti-republican articles. Cobbett described Jefferson as a deist, "a Frenchman in politics and morality" and "a man as much qualified to be president as I am to be an Archbishop." If the Republicans won, Jefferson would be wielding the guillotine in downtown Philadelphia, if one could believe Cobbett.

The verbal vituperation became so strident, that Adams told his son John Quincy in a November 11, 1796, letter "Poor Jefferson is tormented as much as" I am.

Still as paranoid as Adams was, he could not help but fear he would somehow be robbed of the prize.

I am afraid Pinckney will be "smuggled in" to the presidency, Adams confided to Abigail in a December 1, 1796 letter.

A week later on December 7 John was full of self-doubt but put on a strong face to Abigail. "If the Southern States are as unanimous as the Northern are Supposed to be I shall be left out. But it is Said there will be 3 in Virginia & one in Carolina against Jefferson. In Pensilvania the Rebells in the West and the corrupt Mob of Philadelphia aided by frightened Quakers gave a Majority of from 20 to 100 against the great Agricultural Counties of Lancaster, York and Cumberland."

"It really Seems to me as if I wished to be left out. Let me See! Do I know my own heart? I am not sure. However all that I seem to dread, is a foolish, mortifying, humiliating Residence here, for two tedious months after I shall be known to be Skimmed, as my Wallmen Speak."

"I can pronounce Thomas Jefferson to be chosen P [resident] of US with firmness and a good grace. That I don't fear. But here alone abed, by my fireside, nobody to speak to, pouring upon my disgrace and future prospects—this is ugly." John added, "The 16 of Feb. will come and then I take my Leave, forever. Then for Frugality and Independence. Poverty and Patriotism. Love and a Carrot bed."

Strangely, Adams did not mention the ten to thirteen extra votes Jefferson and Pinckney would receive because the southern states received additional congressmen from the three-fifths rule in the constitution that counted three-fifths of the slaves in assigning proportional representation in the House of

Representatives. Thereby, also giving those states the same number of additional presidential electors.

People assumed that Jefferson would receive one vote from most if not all Republicans electors. And Federalists believed Adams would receive one vote from every Federalist elector in New England and that Pinckney would receive a vote from every southern Federalist. For all the candidates then the key question was what would each elector do with his second vote.

Adams feared a Pinckney not a Jefferson victory. Because of the electoral system Adams could foresee southerners casting votes for Jefferson and Pinckney and not Jefferson and Adams. Everything came down to North Carolina and Virginia deciding if "J.A. had better be P [resident] than Pinckney." "The whole system is utterly repugnant to my Judgment and Wishes," John told Abigail on December 16.

Adams was disgusted at the prospect of a Pinckney victory. "Pinckney has no pretentions" to any electoral votes "more than Dr. Jarvis." It would be better for the "French influence" to prevail. "For either Jefferson or Hamilton had better Pretentions and would have made better Presidents than Pinckney."

Jefferson, like a Sphinx or that Uncle Remus hero Tar Baby just sat at Monticello and said nothing except to Madison.

Madison warned Jefferson in a December 5 letter, he would most likely be the vice-president. Hamilton, according to Madison, was intriguing to elect Pinckney in place of Adams because he is "too headstrong to be a fit puppet for the intrigues behind the skreen."

This evoked a December 17 reply from Jefferson authorizing Madison in case of a tie "fully to solicit on my behalf that Mr Adams may be preferred. He has always been my senior from the commencement of our public life, and the expression of the public will being equal, this circumstance ought to give him the preference." Jefferson told Madison "there is nothing I so anxiously hope, as that my name may come out either second or third."

Jefferson closed with this peroration. "Let there come to the helm who think they can steer clear of the difficulties. I have no confidence in myself for the undertaking."

No wonder Jefferson was so angry in 1801 when the Federalists refused to support him over Burr.

On December 19 Madison wrote to Jefferson advising him that he would finish second to Adams and that "you must prepare yourself therefore to be summoned to the place Mr Adams now fills."

Jefferson should come to Philadelphia to be sworn in as vice-president for the good of the country and because of the "valuable" influence he would have on the new administration.

Madison gave valuable personal and political advice in a partially encoded letter to protect it from spying eyes. Hamilton and Washington are described in harsh terms. (The italicized words were in cipher and decoded by Jefferson.) "On the whole it seems *essential* that you should not refuse the station which is likely to be your lot. There is reason to believe also that your neighbourhood to Adams *may have a valuable effect on his councils* particularly in *relation to our external system.* You know that *his feelings* will not *enslave him to the* example of *his predecessor.* It is certain that his *censures of our paper system* and the intrigues at *New York for setting P [inckney] above him* have fixed an *enmity with the British faction.* Nor should it pass for nothing, that the true *interests of new England* particularly requires reconciliation with France as the road to her commerce. *Add to the whole that he is said to speak of you now in friendly terms* and will no doubt be *soothed by your acceptance of a place subordinate to him.* It must be confessed however that all these calculations are qualified by *his political principles and prejudices.* But they add weight to the *obligation from which you must* not withdraw yourself."

Jefferson replied on January 1, 1797, "no arguments were wanted to reconcile me to a relinquishment of the first office or acquiescence under the second."

However, if lightening should strike, he should accept the presidency "to put our vessel on her republican tack before she should be thrown too much to leeward of her true principles."

Still, as the bitter 1796 campaign came to a close, Jefferson expressed hope that Adams would steer the republican ship in the right direction and protect the nation from a Hamilton presidency. "If Mr Adams can be induced to administer the government in it's true principles, and to relinquish his bias to an English constitution, it is to be Considered whether it would not be on the whole of the public good to come to a good understanding with him as to his future elections. He is perhaps the only sure barrier against Hamilton's getting in."

He also enclosed a letter to Adams full of friendship and reconciliation or if you are a cynic a very disingenuous letter. In any event for reasons we shall soon see, the letter was never sent to Adams.

In this December 28, 1796, letter Jefferson vowed that he was happy in Adams's victory. Despite the antagonisms of the campaign Jefferson offered, "I trust with confidence that less of it has been felt by ourselves personally." Adams had won and Jefferson said "I have never one single moment expected a different issue: and tho' I know I shall not be believed, yet it is not the less true that I have never wished it." Jefferson announced, "I have no ambition to govern men. It is a painful and thankless office."

Even though they would serve as president and vice-president for four years, they would not exchange another letter until Adams had been defeated for reelection in 1801.

Jefferson sent his letter to Madison with the request that he forward it to Adams unless Madison found it "ineligible in your opinion." Madison never delivered the letter explaining in his January 15, 1797, letter that those "delicate trusts" deserved further consideration, so he did "suspend the delivery of the letter." Madison argued that the letter might be misinterpreted and lead Adams to suspect that you encouraged his "pseudo-friends of N.Y." Adams might suspect that the letter is merely a cover for your ill will towards his administration. And finally Madison put forth the clinching argument that the efforts of his supporters might be "Depreciated" by your comments and your compliments of Adams may prove "real embarrassments from giving written possession to him, of the degree of compliment and confidence which your personal delicacy and friendship have suggested." The chasm was growing deeper. Personal friendship, superficial as it had become, could not be allowed to interfere with politics.

Nevertheless, it is worth quoting at even greater length from this December 28,1796, letter for the insight provided into Jefferson's political and personal thoughts on the eve of his defeat.

"Our latest intelligence from Philadelphia at present is of the 16th inst. but tho' at that date your election to the first magistracy seems not to be have been known as a fact, yet with me it has never been doubted. I knew it impossible you should lose a vote North of the Delaware, and even if that of Pensylvania should be against you in the mass, yet that you would get enough South of that to place your succession out of danger. I have never one single moment expected a different issue: and tho' I know I shall not be believed; yet it is not the less true that I have never wished it. My neighbors, as my compurgators, could aver that fact, because they see my occupations and my attachment to them. Indeed it is possible that you may be cheated of your succession by a trick worthy the subtlety of your arch-friend [Hamilton] of New York, who has been able to make of your real friends tools to defeat their and your just wishes. Most probably he will be disappointed as to you; and my inclinations place me out of his reach. I leave to others the sublime delights of riding in the storm, better pleased with sound sleep, and a warm birth below, with the society of neighbors, friends and fellow laborers of the earth, than of spies and sycophants. No one then will congratulate you with purer disinterestedness than myself. The share indeed which I may have had in the late vote, I shall still value highly, as evidence of the share I have in the esteem of my fellow citizens.

Jefferson ended with good wishes. "That your administration may be filled with glory and happiness to yourself and advantage to us is the sincere wish of one who tho', in the course of our voyage thro' life, various little incidents have happened or been contrived to separate us, retains still for you the solid esteem of the moments when we were working for our independence."

Jefferson later told Madison in a January 30, 1797, letter that he was glad Madison had refused to send the letter to Adams but he wished Adams to know that he was no "less sensible of the rectitude of his heart.' Adams needs to "be convinced of these truths" because it "is important to our mutual satisfaction, and perhaps to the harmony and good of the public service." So, he told Madison, he had written a January 22 [27] letter to John Langdon "in which I have said exactly the things which will be grateful to Mr. A. and no more." Jefferson asked Langdon for to believe in his "candor." Jefferson denied the rumors that he would not accept the office of vice-president. "Least of all could I have any feelings which would revolt at taking a station secondary to Mr Adams. I have been secondary to him in every situation in which we ever acted together in public life for twenty years past. A contrary position would have been the novelty, and his right of revolting at it." Jefferson told Madison he was sure Langdon would show Adams the letter. Perhaps he did.

Adams was still angered by the vicious tone of the election. Even though most historians depict the election of 1800 as the most vicious in American history, the election of 1796 set the nasty bar very high. Even when Adams knew he had won the election, his anger boiled out in a vituperative letter on January 9, 1797, to Abigail that was a harbinger of Adams's course of action during his presidency.

"Our H [ouse] of R [epresentatives] boasts that We are the most enlightened People in the World: but We behave like the most ignorant Babies, in a thousand Instances. We have been destroying all Terror of Crimes and are becoming the Victim of them. We have been destroying all Attachment and Obligation to Country and are Sold in Consequences by Traitors. We have been opening our Arms wide to all Foreigners and placing them on a footing with Natives; and Now foreigners are dictating to Us if not betraying us." Alien and Sedition Acts here we come.

Then, knowing the party disloyalty of Hamilton, Adams slammed his fellow Federalist Party leader. "Hamilton I know to be a proud Spirited, conceited, aspiring Mortal always pretending to Morality, with as debauched Morals as old Franklin who is more his Model than any one I know. As great an Hypocrite as any in the U.S. His intrigues in the Election I despise. That he has Talents I admit but I dread none of them. I shall take no notice of his Puppy hood but retain the same Opinion of him I always had and maintain the Same Conduct towards him I always did, that is keeping him at a distance." The first presidential term of Adams was seemingly doomed to a rough and rocky road.

The electoral vote was so close. As late as January 8, 1797, Madison calculated the votes as 71 for Adams and 68 for Jefferson. Indeed it would have been closer if Federalist Leven Powell of Virginia had not cast that state's sole vote for Adams. Then, a disputed election result in Vermont with its four electors threatened to produce a political and constitutional crisis. Vermont was one of seven states where the electors were chosen by the state legislature. Newspapers speculated that if the Vermont election, which was based on a legislative resolve and not a law, were excluded, the election would go to the House of Representatives because no man would receive a majority of half of the votes cast.

To his lasting credit, Jefferson urged Madison to avoid a conflict over Vermont's votes even though he knew Adams and Pinckney were recipients of Vermont's eight votes. "Surely in so great a case, substance and not form should prevail. I cannot suppose that the Vermont constitution has been strict in requiring particular forms of expressing the legislative will. As far as my disclaimer may have any effect, I pray you to declare it on every occasion foreseen or not foreseen by me, in favor of the choice of the people substantially expressed, and to prevent the phænomenon of a Pseudo-president at so early a day." Good thing Jefferson could not see four years into the future.

The nation and the federal government were still so new that the procedures for counting the electoral votes and announcing the new president and vice-president still had to be negotiated between the House and Senate.

When the electoral votes were opened and counted by Adams on February 8 in the Senate, Adams received a bare majority of 71 votes. Jefferson received 68 votes. Pinckney received 59 votes. Burr received 30 votes. Nine other men received the remainder of the 276 votes cast.

John and Thomas's election would "serve as a bond of union between the States," Abigail told her sister Elizabeth Peabody, in a February 10, 1797, letter. "I have long known mr Jefferson and have ever entertained a Friendship for him; he is a man of understanding and of probity." Abigail continued: "between him and mr Adams there has ever Subsisted harmony. Tho they have not accorded always in Sentiment, they have dissented without warmth, or ill will, like gentlemen and mr Jefferson I have not a doubt will support the president, nor do I fear any unpleasant Conduct from him at the Head of the Senate."

Jefferson was already in Georgetown on his way to Philadelphia when he received Timothy Pickering's official notification of his election as vice-president.

The sky was fair on March 4, Adams, Jefferson and Washington gathered in Congress Hall for the first transfer of power under the new Federal Constitution. Jeffersonian Republicans did not rebel; they attended the ceremonies. Most realized the importance of this symbolic ceremony. Most realized that this would be the last time the three greatest founders of the nation would be seen together. Most regretted Washington's return to private life.

Abigail was not on hand to witness her husband's inauguration.

"A solemn scene it was indeed," reported John to Abigail in his letter the next day. Washington looked relaxed and happy. "Me thought I heard him think. 'Ay! I am fairly out and you are fairly in!' See which of us will be the happiest."

Robert Goodloe Harper, a Federalist congressman from South Carolina, recorded thoughts that must have been in the minds of many as they viewed the swearing in of presidential and vice-presidential rivals "and to see the two distinguished citizens who lately were rival candidates for the highest office cheerfully submit to the decision of the majority, and unite cordially in serving their country each in the post which their country had assigned them!" Harper contintuned. "These circumstances form the highest encomium on republican government, and on the character of our country." Harper could not restrain himself from adding this not so subtle slap at the anti-federalists in his March 13, 1797, letter: "and they furnish additional grounds for the pleasing confidence, that our constitution will disappoint, by its durability and happy effects, the predictions of its enemies, and the fears of its friends."

President Pro Tem of the Senate William Bingham, whose wife Anne had been so admired by Jefferson in France, administered the oath of office to Jefferson in the Senate. Jefferson, in turn, then administered the oath of office to eight new senators, and gave a short address to the Senate, which was meeting in a special one-day session.

Jefferson declared "zealous" attachment to the constitution and promised "diligent attention" as presiding officer of the Senate and paid tribute to Adams, "the eminent character which has preceded me here, whose talents and integrity have been known and revered by me thro' a long course of years."

Alluding to the hollow nature of the office of vice president, Jefferson said. "I suppose these declarations are not pertinent to the occasion of entering into an office whose primary business is merely to preside over the forms of this house, and no one more sincerely prays that no accident may call me to the higher and more important functions which the constitution eventually devolves on this office."

Jefferson then walked to the House Chamber for the inauguration of Adams.

At noon Chief Justice Oliver Ellsworth administered the oath of office as president of the United States to Adams.

Adams, dressed in a suit of grey broadcloth without fancy buttons or new buckles, stepped forward to give his only inaugural address. Adams later told Abigail that he planned "to say some things as an appeal to posterity." But his address of 2308 words contained no posterity phrases or surprise policy announcements.

Most importantly Adams promised "neutrality and impartiality among the belligerent powers of Europe." On the domestic front, he promised to uphold "a free republican government" and show impartiality among the states and sections of the country while "preserving our Constitution."

With the Republican accusations of monarchist in mind, Adams asserted "Nor have I ever entertained a thought of promoting any alteration" to our new constitution and "I have repeatedly laid myself under the most serious obligations to support the Constitution."

Memories of the Genet and Fauchet affairs hovered in Adams's memory, as he warned against the ability of foreign powers to influence elections. And he promised "to maintain peace and inviolable faith with all nations, and that system of neutrality and impartiality among the belligerent powers of Europe which has been adopted by this Government and so solemnly sanctioned by both Houses of Congress and applauded by the legislatures of the States and the public opinion." He assured his listeners that his "residence of seven years" in France made him a friend to that country.

To those who feared his New England heritage would cause him to make decisions detrimental to the southern and western states he stated he would act "without preference or regard to a northern or southern, an eastern or western position." The "interest, honor, and happiness of all the States in the Union" would be his sole goal.

Unfortunately for Adams's historical reputation the most notable aspect of the inaugural address was that it contained a 737- word sentence, which still reigns as the longest sentence in any presidential inaugural address.

Fortunately for Adams both Federalist and Republican newspapers extolled "the most august and sublime" ceremony and Adams's "incorruptible integrity" and "Republican plainness."

Ever the cynic, Adams told Abigail that he believed Republican publisher Benjamin Franklin Bache was only trying to diminish his chances for success by creating "coolness between me and Mr. Washington."

Jefferson was willing to adopt a wait and see attitude toward his old colleague. Even to his supporters, such as Archibald Stuart in a January 4, 1797, letter, Jefferson urged Republicans "to be silent till we see what turn the new administration will take." Adams, he was sure, "is detached from Hamilton, and there is a possibility he may swerve from his politics in a greater or less degree."

No matter his public demeanor toward Jefferson, Adams harbored an inner distrust of Jefferson the politician and public man. In a letter to their mutual friend Benjamin Rush, Adams accused Jefferson of multiple duplicities. Jefferson "has honored and salaried almost every villain he could find who had been an enemy to me." "Jefferson has succeeded, and multitudes are made to believe that he is pure benevolence," Adams commented. Then acidly added: "But you and I know him to be an intriguer."

Adams, Jefferson and Washington dined together on March 6, just before the former president left for Mount Vernon. One of the advantages of his present office, Jefferson told William Strickland on March 12, 1797, before he left Philadelphia, was that while it will "keep me here during the winter months" it will "permit me to pass my summers in my farms." The next day Jefferson left Philadelphia arriving at Monticello on March 20.

Adams remained in Philadelphia until late July when he finally headed north for Peacefield.

What was the relationship of Adams and Jefferson during the four years of John Adams's presidency?

Evidence is hard to come by. Adams and Jefferson exchanged no letters between April 6, 1796, and February 20, 1801.

One should ask what was the precedent. What about Adams and Washington? Well, they were never real friends, but yes they and their wives did go on outings together, make joint ventures to plays, and meet at many social events. And they did communicate during their two terms. As noted before a conciliatory letter of December 28, 1796, from Jefferson to Adams was never mailed upon the recommendation of Madison. Neither man kept a diary during this period. Neither man's autobiography extends to this period.

Jefferson, however, did accumulate a book of notes, which he labeled his Anas. Many of these notes and letters were contemporary documents and give insight into Jefferson's actions or inactions.

Jefferson recalled in it that Adams had planned a bi-partisan political and diplomatic effort including the appointment of Madison as minister to France and the inclusion of Jefferson in his cabinet. But after their March 6 dinner with Washington, Adams told Jefferson the Federalist leaders had disapproved of his unitary government. Jefferson in turn informed Adams that Madison would not accept an appointment as envoy to France.

The two then went their separate ways-literally and politically. Adams hopes to be a reconciliationist ended early. Jefferson recalled, "He immediately said that on consultation some objections to that nomination had been raised which he had not contemplated." Adams "was going on with excuses which evidently embarrassed him, when we came to 5th Street where our roads separated, his being down Market Street, mine off along 5th, and we took leave; and he never after that said one word to me on the subject or ever consulted me as to any measures of the government."

"The opinion I formed at the time on this transaction was that Mr. A. in the first moments of enthusiasm of the occasion (his inauguration) forgot party sentiments, and as he never acted on any system, but was always governed by the feeling of the moment, he thought for a moment to steer impartially between the parties; that Monday the 6th of Mar. being the first time he had met his cabinet, on expressing ideas of this kind he had been at once diverted from them, and returned to firm former party views."

Adams's recollection was somewhat different. Adams claimed in an April 6 letter to Gerry he indeed did not ask Madison but Jefferson if he would accept an appointment as special envoy to France. "He as frankly refused, as I expected he would. Indeed, I made a great stretch in proposing it, to accommodate to the feelings, views, and prejudices of a party. I would not do it again, because upon more mature reflection, I am decidedly convinced of the impropriety of it." The vice-president held too high a rank to be sent as an ambassador, concluded Adams. President Adams later recalled that they "consulted very little together" after that meeting.

They did not correspond and they did not formally consult each other. Was there a less formal communication? Did they meet at presidential levees or private balls and entertainments?

Not according to Jefferson. He told Thomas Willing, a wealthy Philadelphian, on February 23, 1798. "He had not been at a ball these twenty years, nor for a long time permitted himself to go to any entertainment of the evening, from motives of attention to health. On these grounds he excused to Genl Washington when living in the city his not going to his birth nights, to

Mrs. Washington not attending her evenings, to Mrs. Adams the same, and to all his friends who have been so good to invite him to tea & card parties, the declining to go to them. It is an indulgence which his age and habits will he hopes obtain and continue to him." But as we shall see contrary to Jefferson's letter, they did occasionally meet and converse at dinners and other social occasions.

In fact, according to Edward Coles, friend and later private secretary to President Madison, Jefferson told him that he "regularly called on the President, and had his visits as Vice President returned, and from time to time dined with the President." Adams told Coles in 1811 that he "concurred" with his account.

Part of Jefferson's problem was that he had no spouse to leaven his spirit by making social connections with the wives of other leaders. One could certainly suggest that Adams and Jefferson might have talked more often if their wives were socially friendly. Jefferson and Adams were both veterans of the French salons. Parlor politics was certainly not new or unusual.

Certainly, the men made little effort or initiated few opportunities to converse or communicate in any way except through third parties. Clearly both men chose party loyalty and their vision of the future of the United States over personal friendship or loyalty. Washington's warning about the "baneful effects of the spirit of party" was quickly ignored.

Like the absence of the barking dog in the Sherlock Holmes tale, the silence of the protagonists speaks volumes.

Jefferson understood that whoever followed Washington would have an impossible task. If things went well, Washington would get the credit for having set the plans in motion. If things went badly, it would be the fault of his successor. In a January 8, 1797, letter to Madison, Jefferson laid out the crux of the matter. "The President is fortunate to get off just as the bubble is bursting, leaving others to hold the bag. Yet, as his departure will mark the moment when the difficulties begin to work, you will see, that they will be ascribed to the new administration, and that he will have his usual good fortune of reaping credit from the good acts of others, and leaving to them that of his errors."

Adams made his first mistake by offering a foreign post to Madison, which was quickly rejected and then suggesting that Jefferson might wish to return to France as a special emissary. He made his second, and some might say fatal mistake for his administration, by keeping all of Washington's cabinet. Timothy Pickering, as high and inflexible a Federalist as could be found, would remain Secretary of State. Young Oliver Wolcott, Jr., a Federalist from Connecticut who threatened to resign if Madison were appointed a commissioner to France stayed on as Secretary of the Treasury. Federalists James McHenry of Maryland and Charles Lee of Virginia kept their posts as Secretary of War and Attorney General.

The problems for Adams were multiple. They were all highly partisan Federalists with no wish to pursue a bi-partisan program at any level, never mind in regards to France and Great Britain. They had all been appointed by Washington and had no personal loyalty to Adams. Wolcott and perhaps others in the cabinet had secretly backed Pinckney for president in 1796. Although younger than the President, they all assumed the role of seniors advising a junior member of the administration. They all held an allegiance, if not their positions, to Hamilton, Adams's leading critic. In short, Adams faced opponents both within his own party and from the Jeffersonian Republicans.

No wonder Jefferson cautioned the Republicans to be patient, while the Federalist House of Cards collapsed from within.

Adams's decisions were further complicated by the growing number of immigrants from the boiling cauldron of revolutionary France and Sainte Domingue (Haiti). Alternative waves of radical republicans and monarchists made their way to America as the political wheel spun in France propelling the guillotine up and down.

More wealthy French slaveholders fled to the United States when slaves and patriotic creoles revolted in the French colony of Sainte Domingue.

Meanwhile, Great Britain still sent America the refuse of her courts and welfare system. And hopeful redemptioners and emigrants continued to find their way to America.

On the one hand these refugees infused power into the pro-French and anti-Federalist Democratic-Republican Clubs. On the other hand they provided support for those extreme Federalists who still supported hopes for a monarchy in the United States.

Jefferson often spoke about his dislike and fear of monarchy and the threat that it might raise its ugly head in America. Since less than twenty years had passed since at least one-third of the population had sworn allegiance to the crown and many loyalists had fought to retain the monarchy, this was not a hollow threat or an unfounded fear.

"The evils of monarchy are beyond remedy," wrote Jefferson in an August 4, 1787 letter to David Ramsay. "If any of our countrymen wish for a king, give them Aesop's fable of the frogs." Then "if this does not cure them, send them to Europe: they will go back good republicans." In other words beware of the consequences of your actions before you take them.

Yet rumors of a monarchical conspiracy continued to percolate in the United States even reaching Congress and the ears of the vice-president.

Jefferson, himself, heard the reports of a conspiracy in the 1780's to raise Washington to royalty or to bring a European prince to do the job. Former president of the Confederation Congress and signer of the federal constitution Nathaniel Gorham and Secretary of War McHenry were said to have been involved in the plan.

On January 5, 1798, Jefferson's housemates in Philadelphia, Congressmen Thomas Skinner of Massachusetts and Abraham Baldwin of Georgia told him a "very extensive combination had taken place in N.York & the Eastern states among that description of people who were partly monarchical in principle or frightened with Shays's rebellion & the impotence of the old Congress. Delegates in different places had actually had consultations on the subject of seizing on the powers of a government and establishing them by force, and corresponded with one another, and had sent a deputy to Genl. Washington to solicit his cooperation."

Although Washington had refused to cooperate and the Federal Constitution had replaced the old confederation government with the new Federal Republic, led by Hamilton they had tried to propose an aristocratical government and when that failed they had tried to undermine the convention. Republicans still harbored fears that the monarchists still hovered hoping for an opportunity to seize the federal government.

Jefferson feared Adams's view that a monarch and a republic's president were equal as executives he did fear Adams's ideas on the necessary power of an aristocracy. But he did fear that the men surrounding Adams and those hovering in the background, like Hamilton and Pickering, were perfectly capable of destroying the work of the revolution and ending America's freedoms.

In Jefferson's mind (as recorded in his *Anas*) the difference between Adams and Hamilton when it came to their support of aristocratical government was that Adams "was for two hereditary branches and an honest elective one; the other, for an hereditary King, with a House of Lords and Commons corrupted to his will, and standing between him and the people."

"Mr. Adams," wrote Jefferson, "had originally been a republican. The glare of royalty and nobility, during his mission to England, had made him believe their fascination a necessary ingredient in government." "Upon his return to the United States," Adams "was taken up by the monarchical federalists" and led to "believe that the general disposition of our citizens was favourable to monarchy."

Hamilton was an outright monarchist, Tench Coxe reported to Jefferson. Coxe said in a December 27, 1797, conversation with Jefferson, that Hamilton stated. "I avow myself a monarchist; I have no objection to a trial being made of this thing of a republic, but."

This fear can be seen in the Republicans constant characterization of Federalists as monarchists or monocrats. To readers over two centuries later, this seems more political ploy than realistic fear, but in the minds of too many Jeffersonian Republicans the fate of the national republic was at stake.

Jon Meacham, a recent biographer of Jefferson, caught the fever of the time. "The perpetual threat of conflict—first with one European power, then with another—infused American politics with a sense of constant crisis. Both Federalists and Republicans believed the fate of the United States could turn on the confrontation of the hour. In the broad public discourse, driven by partisan editors publishing partisan newspapers, there seemed no middle ground, only extremes of opinion or of outcome."

Unfortunately for Adams, the new administration's first crisis involved France-always a flash point for Republicans and Federalists. Within days of his inauguration, Adams learned that France had rejected and expelled the American emissary Charles Cotesworth Pinckney. Pinckney was sent packing to Amsterdam, while the French Directory launched an undeclared war on American shipping. Seizures skyrocketed and so did demands for American action.

Adams hoped Jefferson would provide the kind of support he i.e. Adams had given Washington. He was wrong.

Gerard W. Gawalt

230

In an effort to garner support for another attempt to seek a peaceful solution to French hostilities, Adams called for a special session of Congress on May 15 "to consult and determine on such measures as their wisdom shall be deemed meet for the safety and welfare of the United States."

Pickering, Wolcott and McHenry in turn consulted their éminence grise, Hamilton. They were no doubt surprised when Hamilton supported Adams's plan to send a new bi-partisan commission to France while vastly enlarging the navy and army to prove to France and the Federalists that this administration had a backbone and would fight to protect American interests.

Jefferson assured his political friends in New England there were no misunderstandings between the president and himself. He told Elbridge Gerry, a leading Massachusetts political leader who considered himself a centrist that is a man of no party, in a May 13, 1797, letter. "Though not a word having this tendency has ever been hazarded to me by any one, yet I consider as a certainty that nothing will be left untried to alienate him from me. These machinations will proceed from the Hamiltonians by whom he is surrounded, and who are only a little less hostile to him than to me."

Not only did he harbor no ill will towards Adams, said Jefferson, but also he could not possibly influence the executive councils because "I consider my office as constitutionally confined to legislative functions, and that I could not take any part whatever in executive consultations, even were it proposed."

In fact, Jefferson told his friend, Edward Rutledge, that he was too old to enjoy the passionate politics being practiced in Philadelphia. He preferred a course of neutrality and balance in foreign affairs akin to the plan being offered by the president. But he feared they would not see this plan take root, because, as he told Rutledge in a June 24, 1797, letter. "The passions are too high at present, to be cooled in our day. You and I have formerly seen warm debates and high political passions. But gentlemen of different politics would then speak to each other, and separate the business of the Senate from that of society. It is not so now. Men who have been intimate all their lives, cross the streets to avoid meeting, and turn their heads another way, lest they should be obliged to touch their hats."

In a few days Jefferson planned to escape the political passions of the capital for the countryside of Virginia. Where "my farm, my family, my books & my building give me more pleasure than any public office would, and especially one which would keep me constantly from them," he explained in a letter to the Comte de Volney on January 8, 1797.

Jefferson insisted to Volney that he had no wish to govern others and he would prefer the office of vice-president. "I value the late vote highly; but it is only an index of the place I hold in the esteem of my fellow-citizens."

Adams could not be so sanguine nor could he so easily escape the passions of politics and the dangers of diplomacy.

When the special session of Congress met, Adams told them that despite France having "inflicted a wound in the American breast" he would send another special mission to France. "While we are endeavoring to adjust all our differences with France by amicable negotiations, with the progress of the war in Europe, the depredations on our commerce, the personal injuries to our citizens, and the general complexion of our affairs, render it my duty to recommend to your consideration of effectual measures of defence."

Adams presented a series of proposed actions, including sending a three-man commission to France and enlarging the army, but excluding the raising of a 25,000-man army.

The Hamiltonian Federalists immediately claimed he was doing too little. The Republicans, led by Jefferson now that Madison was busy with his new wife, howled that Adams was leading the country into war.

Jefferson sat back pulling the Republican strings; soliciting money for Republican mouthpieces, like Bache and Callender; cajoling Republicans into writing opposition essays; gathering information on Federalists in quiet dinner parties.

Once Jefferson was an outspoken cheerleader for the French Revolution. Now with American blood rising in anger against the French, Jefferson urged neutrality, telling Gerry in a June 21, 1797, letter: "if we engage in a war during our present passions and our present weakness, our union runs the greatest risk of not coming out of that war in the shape in which it enters it."

Just when you thought things couldn't get worse, an intemperate letter criticizing Washington and Adams as "apostates" to the Revolution that Jefferson had written to his Italian friend Phillip Mazzei on April 24, 1796, was published first by Noah Webster in the *New York Minerva*. "The aspect of our politics has wonderfully changed since you left us. In place of that noble love of liberty and republican government which carried us triumphantly thro' the war, an Anglican, monarchical & aristocratical party has sprung up, whose avowed object is to draw over us the substance, as they have already done the forms, of the British government." Jefferson claimed, "the main body of our citizens remain true to their republican principles." Their opponents are "all timid men who prefer the calm of despotism to the boisterous sea of liberty," charged Jefferson. "It would give you a fever were I to name you the Apostates who have gone over to these heresies; men who were Samsons in the field, and Solomons in the council, but who have had their heads shorn by the harlot England," he concluded. Double ouch!!

Enough, you might think. But no there was still more. Against the forces of evil, Jefferson asserted, "we are likely to preserve the liberty we have obtained by unremitting labors and Perils" but only if we "awake and snap the Lilliputian Cords with which they have entangled us during the first sleep which succeeded our labors." This from a man who professed to be distanced from politics.

The reactions were intense and long lasting.

Federalists accused Jefferson of near treason. Adams denounced Jefferson in private as a man whose mind was "eaten to a honeycomb with ambition, yet weak, confused, uninformed, and ignorant."

Adams was castigated and excoriated by the Republican press. "His rotundity" was acting like "a man divested of his senses," screamed Bache and Callender. France's envoy to the United States, Phillipe Letombe reported on June 7, 1797, that Jefferson still was "penetrated with gratitude to France." Reportedly Jefferson condemned the president as "Vain, irritable, stubborn, endowed with excessive self-love, and still suffering pique at the preference accorded Franklin over him in Paris." Jefferson predicted that in four years the country would have a new president.

Abigail's idea that having a president and vice president of different parties could strengthen the country if they both aimed at "the good of their country" died a fiery death.

Adams pressed on, naming Charles Cotesworth Pinckney, John Marshall and Gerry as special envoys to go to France and negotiate a settlement with France.

Facing stiff Republican opposition, Adams could only get minimal support for a larger navy, enhanced coastal defenses, and authority to call up 80,000 militiamen.

After the departure of the three envoys to France in the summer of 1797, America awaited the result. Members of Congress abandoned the special session in July. Adams returned to his farm. Jefferson returned to his plantations. John Quincy Adams married Louisa Catherine Johnson in London.

Jefferson and Adams no doubt both silently enjoyed the diminishment of Hamilton when John Beckley and Callender publicized his 1791-1792 affair with Maria Reynolds. Hamilton had an adulterous relationship with Maria, the wife of a swindling employee of the Treasury Department, James Reynolds. The Reynolds duo blackmailed Hamilton even while the "improper connection" continued and Reynolds went to jail for a swindle. Reynolds then complained to Congress, who sent a three-man delegation, including Jefferson's acolyte James Monroe to investigate. Hamilton copped to the affair, claimed he was a victim of blackmail and denied any malfeasance of office. The members of Congress promised silence, but the Clerk of the House Beckley leaked the material to Callender, who promptly broadcast the news to the nation.

Adams, Jefferson and the nation were still awaiting news from France. Jefferson later recalled that old friends would "cross the street to avoid meeting and turn their heads another way, lest they should be obliged to touch their hats."

Tempers flared in the streets, the boardinghouses, and the halls of Congress. After Congress had reconvened, a Federalist Roger Griswold of Connecticut and a Republican Matthew Lyons of Vermont exchanged spittle and blows on the floor of Congress, after Griswold accused Lyons of being a coward during the Revolution.

In the midst of this high tension, Jefferson and Adams attended a large dinner on February 15, 1798. Unable to converse during the dinner, they met briefly afterward. Fortunately for us, Jefferson jotted down some notes on his conversation with the president.

After some light banter about Hamilton's "bank paper" being responsible for high prices, they settled into a talk on the constitution. According to Jefferson's memory, Adams "said that no republic could ever last which had not a Senate and a Senate deeply and strongly rooted, strong enough to bear up against all popular storms and passions." Adams believed the Senate had done well because the senators were chosen by the state legislatures, he feared that they might become popularly elected. Then Adams continued. "That as to trusting to a popular assembly for the preserv [atio] n of our liberties it was the merest chimera imaginable." Jefferson added no comment of his own. Nor did he think he needed to.

Finally, on March 4 the official dispatches arrived from America's envoys in France. Nothing had gone right. After a brief meeting with the French Foreign Minister Talleyrand, the envoys received several visits from underlings, labeled X, Y and Z by the Americans. They demanded a bribe of $250,000 to sweeten the hands of Talleyrand and an American "loan" of ten million dollars to compensate France for Adams's insulting comments about France in his address to Congress in May 1797.

The American envoys refused these terms. Pinckney reportedly cried "No! No! Not a six pence."

In short, the French government had refused to meet with the American envoys without a sweetener and the Directory declared that all neutral ships could no longer trade with France and all British goods even in neutral bottoms were subject to seizure.

Rumors of war swirled through Philadelphia as state department employees spent eight days decoding the messages. Finally on March 19 Adams informed Congress only that the mission had failed, more military preparations were needed, but Adams still hoped for a negotiated settlement.

Jefferson was beside himself. Adams had given "an insane message" to Congress, he told Madison and Monroe on March 21. Delay was the Republican's best hope. "As to do nothing, & to gain time, is every thing with us, I propose that Congress should go home to consult their constituents before acting rashly." Jefferson expected people would tell their congressmen to seek peace not war. Jefferson argued that the constitution required the legislature to declare war and they were evenly divided so were unlikely to act. Moreover, Jefferson coolly calculated that this would allow the hoped for successful results of France's invasion of England to become known in America. Jefferson even suspected that the New England federalists had "in contemplation a separation of the union."

Republicans, led in the House by a Swiss immigrant Albert Gallatin since Madison had retired from Congress, demanded the release of the full text of the dispatches. Charging that Adams was withholding information that would exonerate the French government, they were sorely surprised when they got their wishes.

The day after the House by a sixty-five to twenty-seven vote demanded the release of the documents, Adams complied. Anger boiled over in Congress even among many Republicans at the gall and effrontery of the French. Gallatin fought to keep the documents from being published, but the Senate ordered their printing and so they entered the public domain and touched off widespread anger against France.

Speakers and writers by the hundreds condemned France and praised America's envoys for standing firm and refusing to bend to the greedy Gallic officials. Patriotism soared. The Republican cries that this was a crisis manufactured by the Chief Executive went unheard or unheeded.

War against France was demanded. Congress approved money for coastal defenses and armaments. An army of ten thousand men and letters of marque for privateers were authorized for the defense of the nation.

President Adams was being hailed as a hero throughout most of the country for standing up to the French, particularly after the XYZ affair. Even retired President Washington supported Adams, telling his dinner guests on June 13, as reported by Polish aristocrat Julian Niemcewicz. "They censure Mr. Adams for haste in deeds and excessive boldness in words; from the moment that I left the administration, I have not written a word to Mr. Adams, nor yet received a word from him except the dispatches which we have seen in the papers." But "with all this I am certain, as a reasonable and honest person, as a good American, that he cannot do other than he does. I, in his place, perhaps would be less vehement in expression, but I would prepare myself steadily and boldly in the same fashion."

Jefferson was unmoved. He was not ready to support Adams or to heed the calls for disunion from some of his supporters.

Conflict was normal. Disunion would lead nowhere. If the union was reduced to Virginia and North Carolina divisions would soon occur, argued Jefferson. "A little patience and we shall see the reign of witches pass over, their spells dissolve, and the people recovering their true sight, restore their government to it's true principles," wrote Jefferson to John Taylor on June 4. "If the game runs sometimes against us at home, we must have patience, till luck turns, & then we shall have an opportunity of winning back the *principles* we have lost."

He enjoined his daughter Martha in a May 17, 1798, letter to enjoy her peace and quiet, because "you should know the rancorous passions which tear every breast here, even of the sex which should be a stranger to them. Politics and party hatreds destroy the happiness of every being here. They seem like salamanders, to consider fire as their element." He later claimed that the XYZ affair was a "dish cooked up by Marshall," a Federalist, and that quondam Jeffersonian Gerry's public letters had cleared the French government.

Adams spent his days working feverishly to prepare the nation for the struggle and to respond to all his new admirers. To all he cautioned preparedness, proffered his thanks, and occasionally urged them "to arms, especially by sea." Abigail worried to her sister Mary in the summer of 1798 that he was working too hard and smoking too many cigars. If the French thought Adams would bend they would be sadly disappointed. "Poor wretches, I suppose they want him to cringe, but he is made of oak instead of willow. He may be torn up by the roots, or break, but he will never bend."

Adams did not ask Congress to declare war in the summer of 1798, although the Federalist majority would certainly have done it if asked. Instead, Adams promised not to send another envoy to France unless he was assured that France would properly received him. Meanwhile, Gerry, whom Federalists considered the lone Republican in the commission, had remained in France to "prevent war."

Without Adams's request, Congress passed a series of four harsh laws that have come to be known simply as the Alien and Sedition Acts. Fearing the thousands of French and Irish immigrants who had been swarming to the United States as wartime Britain and France cracked down on any and all opposition, Congress struck out at these "enemy agents."

One act extended the required period of residence needed to qualify for citizenship from five to fourteen years. Another granted the President authority to expel any foreigner he considered "dangerous." Both these acts proved rather harmless. Most of the French nobles returned home. The "Wild Scotch Irish" settled down. There were no mass deportations. In fact, not a single "alien" was expelled by the Adams administration, contrary to Jefferson's and the Republicans' fears.

The Sedition Act was the most onerous and most dangerous. The act declared that making "false, scandalous, and malicious" statements against government officials or attempting to "excite" people against the United States or "to stir up sedition" were crimes. Many Americans opposed a federal sedition law arguing that it violated the constitution and also unconstitutionally infringed on the rights of states to regulate free speech through slander laws.

Even Adams fell victim to the belief that although this was a clear violation of the First Amendment, wartime conditions justified this action. In practice, the law was used to curb and curtail outspoken Republican critics of the President and his administration. Particularly targeted were newspaper editors.

Adams said nothing to support or oppose the measure. His wife was an outspoken supporter of the need to use the act to curb "the most wicked and base, violent and culminating abuse." Abigail saw victory. "Let the vipers cease to hiss. They will be destroyed with their own poison," angrily remarked Abigail to her sister Mary on July 9,1798.

Jefferson went home.

Congress continued on its rant passing a direct tax to support the military, abrogating the Franco-American treaty of 1778, and appointing George Washington commander in chief of the new American armed forces. The undeclared war or as historians like to call it the Quasi-War with France was on.

Jefferson urged delaying tactics to Madison on June 21. He suggested having Congress go home. Perhaps this would withdraw "the fire from the boiling pot."

Jefferson returned to Monticello where he continued to pull strings behind the scenes and urge people to write in opposition. Jefferson said he would "never put a sentence into any newspaper." Telling Samuel Smith on August 22, 1798, that he has "religiously adhered to the resolution throughout his life." It would be impossible to answer the calumnies of those "warring" against the principles of the people, argued Jefferson. To answer any of the writings of men like "Porcupine & Fenno" whose believers "cover me with implacable hatred" would simply bring on more verbal attacks.

"We have chosen war," said Jefferson. "Whether the choice may be a popular one in the other States I know not." But he had no doubts that the other states would join Virginia in opposing war with France.

238

Adams returned to Peacefield in August. He went about his normal routines of reading and directing his farm operations, even occasionally pulling on his boots to wade and fork in the muck and mire of the farmyard and fields.

His enjoyment was severely curtailed by worries over the war or Half War as he called it with France. And Abigail was stricken with ill health, remaining bed-ridden for eleven weeks. Even an extended visit by his daughter Abigail could not lift his spirits in this "most gloomy summer." Abigail's "destiny is still very precarious, and mine in consequence of it," he confided to Washington in an October 9, 1798, letter.

Meanwhile the naval construction continued unabated. Infantrymen and dragoons continued to be recruited and trained. Adams appointed Washington commander in chief of America's armed forces, but the old general desperately wanted to avoid active service. His plan was to have Hamilton named second in command and to let him do all the busy work of organizing an army. Then if France actually invaded the United States, Washington could take active command.

Adams objected to Hamilton's appointment. Writing to his Secretary of the Treasury, Oliver Wolcott, on September 24, 1798, Adams refused to accept Hamilton as second in command, saying he respected his talents, but "his character—I leave."

By the end of the month, Adams gave in and notified Secretary of War James McHenry, that Washington would have the final say on his officers. Adams's letter crossed in the mail with one from Washington demanding final say on his officers or he would resign. Hamilton became inspector general with the rank of major general.

Fortunately for Adams, Gerry arrived from France that same day with the news that the French wanted peace. Joined with similar opinions from Marshall and his son John Quincy, Gerry's report convinced Adams that France would seriously entertain a new peace commission.

Adams decided to send a new envoy to France and to limit the size of the army. To his Secretary of State Pickering, he stated his plans for a new envoy and asked for suggestions. To his Secretary of War McHenry, he indicated he would not ask Congress for the funds to enlarge the army saying, "At present there is no more prospect of seeing a French army here than there is in heaven." And his critics said Adams had no sense of humor.

Adams set off for Philadelphia in high spirits on November 12. The next day he wrote Abigail that the British destruction of the French fleet in Egypt had ended any threat of a French invasion of the United States.

In Philadelphia Adams met with his cabinet. Despite the beliefs of McHenry and Pickering that war with France was just over the horizon, the cabinet agreed that asking Congress for a declaration of war would be "inexpedient." Adams made it plain that "while we do not fear ...war, we shall give no room to infer that we abandon the desire of peace."

Adams addressed the Congress on December 7 stressing both his preparations for war and his hopes for peace with France. His speech was written by his hawkish cabinet, so it would be "left with France" to assure the United States that any envoy would be seriously and properly received.

The president's address to Congress would be a beacon to the country, Abigail told William Shaw in a December 23, letter. She thought that in "this eventful period, when nothing but darkness is visible on our political horizon; The Speech of the president has appeard like a Star emerging from the Storm-threatening clouds and patriotic fears of true Americans have subsided."

The Republicans did not see things in quite the same light. Neither did the radical Federalists. His foes and nominal friends castigated Adams. Both had anticipated a declaration of war. But Congress was not in a warlike mood.

Hamilton still planned and plotted with Adams's cabinet members to use the American army. Perhaps an invasion of Spanish Florida? Perhaps the capture of New Orleans?

Abigail warned John that Hamilton wanted to "become a second Bonaparte." Much later, Adams would remember he thought Hamilton was "stark mad."

Gerry would report after a March 29, 1799, meeting that Adams "thought Hamilton and a party were endeavoring to get an army on foot to give Hamilton the command of it, and thus to proclaim a regal government and place Hamilton as the head of it." Jefferson would certainly have agreed with Adams on that note-if he had only known. Moreover, Jefferson believed Hamilton intended to use the army to suppress all internal opposition. Both men believed the other conspired to carry out a counter-revolution.

Washington met with Hamilton to appoint officers for the paper army, and then left Philadelphia for Mount Vernon.

Adams then embarked on a controversial use of the American Navy.

Adams planned to use the American fleet in conjunction with and in support of the new "black republic" of Haiti led by Toussaint L'Ouverture. Adams ordered the Caribbean squadron to protect American merchants and Haitian privateers. Adams went so far as to dine with L'Overture's representative.

Adams risked a political backlash because many Americans were opposed to the use of American force and influence to encourage a slave revolution.

Jefferson was torn between his support for another republic in the Americas, and his fear that support for the "cannibal republic" would encourage southern slave revolts.

When he became president, Jefferson refused to recognize the independence of Haiti.

Despite what Hamilton called "the feebleness and pusillanimity" of Jefferson's later policies toward Haiti, Jefferson was able to acquire Louisiana for the United States after Napoleon's armies failed to subdue the Haitian rebels.

Meanwhile in Albemarle, Jefferson resolved to avoid using the public mail in order to give his enemies no new information to use in their "slanders." "I shall trust the post offices with nothing confidential, persuaded that during the ensuing twelvemonth they will lend their inquisitorial aid to furnish matter for new slanders," Jefferson wrote Madison on November 22.

Well after Adams had addressed Congress, Jefferson made his arrival in Philadelphia on December 29. He had not been politically inactive during his six-month absence. Jefferson advised Madison. "Firmness on our part, but passive firmness, is the true course."

Adams and Jefferson did not consult. In fact, they seldom spoke even in passing.

Jefferson already saw the Alien and Sedition Laws "as merely an experiment on the American mind to see how far it will bear an avowed violation of the constitution. if this goes down we shall immediately see attempted another act of Congress declaring that the President shall continue in office during life, reserving to another occasion the transfer of the succession to his heirs, and the establishment of the Senate for life." Or so he said in an October 11, 1798, letter to Stevens Thomson Mason, a Jeffersonian Republican senator and nephew of George Mason. Adams and his followers were like Cromwell and his Oliverian followers seeking to overturn the constitution by force and chicanery, according to Jefferson. After authorizing a $50 payment to his mouthpiece, Callender, Jefferson argued "I have no doubt" others "may be playing the game for the restoration of his most gracious Majesty George the Third."

This might be dismissed merely as Jeffersonian paranoia, but nothing was firmly established in 1798 except that the American Republic was still a lonely experiment.

Thoroughly angered by the Alien and Sedition Acts and fearful that they might be used to oppress all political opposition, Jefferson helped draft the Virginia and Kentucky Resolutions, which asserted a state legislature's right to declare a federal law unconstitutional. In Jefferson's draft of the Kentucky resolutions, Jefferson bluntly resolved that the Sedition Act "which does abridge the freedom of the press, is not law, but is altogether void & of no force." Furthermore, that "every state has a natural right, in cases not within the compact to nullify of their own authority all assumptions of power by others within their limits." And that these acts "unless arrested at the threshold, necessarily drive these states into revolution & blood & will furnish new calumnies against republican government."

Jefferson's doctrine of nullification would later be frequently invoked to justify support for states' rights and opposition to the Federal government ultimately leading to civil war.

Unlike Adams who consistently favored a strong central government, Jefferson shifted to suit his personal and political desires. Even though he was the holder of the second highest office in the national government, he felt comfortable in arguing for the power of a state to defy the government if it met his current political need or political philosophy. In this case, the defeat of Federalist measures.

Even his prime supporter in Kentucky, John Breckinridge pointed out in a December 13, 1799, letter that the Kentucky Senate had almost refused to adopt Jefferson's nullification language. "There was considerable division, particularly on that Sentence, which declares 'a Nullification of those acts by the States, to be the rightful remedy'."

In his reply of January 29, 1800, Jefferson only responded. "I was glad to see the subject taken up, and done with so much temper, firmness and propriety."

Gerard W. Gawalt

No one mentioned that the Sedition Act was due to expire in 1801.

Even Jefferson realized he may have gone too far, telling Madison he thought they should "leave the matter in such a train that we may not be committed absolutely to push the matter to extremities, and yet may be free to push as far as events will render prudent."

Despite Jefferson's greatest fears and Secretary of State Pickering's highest hopes, Adams showed little enthusiasm for using the Alien and Sedition Acts against Republicans. The president signed only three orders for the deportation of aliens, and these Frenchmen had already fled the country.

Seventeen court actions were brought under the Sedition Act. Fourteen men were fined or imprisoned. One was Callender, the vicious critic of Adams and his administration who was in the pay of Jefferson. He was sent to jail for his writing in *The Prospect Before Us.* After Jefferson released him in 1801, he became angry when Jefferson refused to appoint him postmaster of Richmond. In revenge Callender then published the first account of Jefferson's relationship with Sally Hemings before drowning in a rain puddle on a dirt road in Richmond.

The Virginia and Kentucky Resolutions brought little support for the Republicans and Jefferson's authorship was kept secret from the public until after his death. Even a large minority in the Virginia legislature opposed the passage of the Virginia Resolutions and published a protest statement, *The Awful Crisis which has arrived.*

Jefferson began to fear that the Federal Army would be used to crush the Republicans if the Federalists came to believe they were disunionists. He warned Republicans in a February 14, letter to Edmund Pendleton, to use only constitutional means of protest lest "the ill-designing may produce insurrection. Nothing could be so fatal. Anything like force would check the progress of the public opinion & rally them around the errors of the government. This is not the kind of opposition the American people will permit. But keep away all show of force, and they will bear down the evil propensities of the government, by the constitutional means of election & petition."

Jefferson found it necessary to declare his support for the Constitution in a January 26, 1799, letter, which he no doubt hoped Gerry would publicize. "I do then with sincere zeal wish an inviolable preservation of our present federal constitution, according to the true sense in which it was adopted by the states, that in which it was advocated by it's friends, & not that which it's enemies apprehended, who therefore became it's enemies: and I am opposed to the monarchising it's features by the forms of it's administration, with a view to conciliate a first transition to a President & Senate for life, & from that to a hereditary tenure of these offices, & thus worm out of the elective principle. I am for preserving to the states the powers not yielded by them to the Union, & to the legislature of the Union it's constitutional share in the division of powers: and I am not for transferring all the powers of the states to the general government, & all those of that government to the Executive branch."

Jefferson went on to admit he was "a well wisher to the success of the French revolution, and still wish it may end in the establishment of a free & well ordered republic but I have not been insensible under the atrocious depredations they have committed on our commerce."

Jefferson declared, "the first object of my heart is my own country."

Jefferson urged his supporters to proceed with caution in an August 23, 1799, letter to Madison. "That the Principles already advanced by the Virginia & Kentuckey are not to be yielded in silence, I presume we all agree." Jefferson continued. "Make a firm protestation against the principle & the precedent; and a reservation of the rights resulting to us from these palpable violations of the constitutional compact by the Federal government." Moreover, he urged Republicans to "Express in affectionate & conciliatory language our warm attachment to union with our sister-states, and to the instrument & principles, by which we are united; that we are willing to sacrifice to this every thing except those rights of self government the securing of which was the object of that compact."

In the winter of 1799, Jefferson had been aghast at the prospect of Adams's proposed recognition and aid to "the rebellious negroes under Toussaint. "We may expect therefore black crews" and "missionaries" in the states. Slave uprisings must be anticipated. "If this combustion can be introduced among us under any veil whatever, we have to fear it."

The realization of Jefferson's worst fears was not far in the future. A slave revolt led by Gabriel Prosser rocked Virginia less than a year later in September 1800. Jefferson's friend and political supporter Governor James Monroe quickly contained and then squelched the threatened slave insurrection. No one doubted its effect on the southern psyche.

Gerard W. Gawalt

Jefferson, as was his style, sought to enlist supporters to publicly fight his battle. In a January 29, 1799, letter to Edmund Pendleton, a Virginia legislator and former president of the Virginia Ratification Convention in 1788, Jefferson asserted that a "recapitulation is now wanting of the whole affair." "Nobody in America can do it so well as yourself," Jefferson continued. And then it "may yet be printed in hand bills, of which we could print and disperse ten or twelve thousand copies" to be distributed "by members of Congress when they return home." This would arouse the people's "republican spirit."

Still, he feared that Adams was raising "a Presidential army, or Presidential militia," that Hamilton and the Federalists intended to use "on the Constitution." In Jefferson's mind, the Republicans were now the sole defenders of the Federal Constitution.

Adams too was rethinking his options. First, Gerry had returned from France telling one and all, including Adams in a private conference, of France's desire for peace. France had already taken concrete steps to lessen tensions, including a renunciation of demands for loans and reparations. Moreover, Gerry argued France had not declared war and had repeatedly pressed him for new negotiations.

Then in January Adams's son Thomas arrived from Europe bearing news from his son John Quincy, the American ambassador to Prussia, that France was serious about negotiating peace.

Adams wasted no time in nominating Williams Vans Murray, the current minister to The Hague, as minister plenipotentiary to the French government. On February 18, Jefferson read Adams's message asking the Senate to "advise and consent to his appointment" and promised "effectual care shall be taken in his instructions that he shall not go to France without direct and unequivocal assurances from the French government" that he "shall be received in character," and he would meet with "a minister of equal rank, title and powers "who can discuss and conclude all controversies between the two Republics by a new treaty."

The Federalists were "thunderstruck," according to Secretary of State Pickering.

Jefferson was flummoxed. This "event of event" mortified the Federalists, according to the vice president. "Never did a party shew a stronger mortification & consequently that war had been their object." Adams had done this "hoping that his friends in the Senate would take on their own shoulders the odium of rejecting it," he opined to Madison. "But they did not chuse it. the Hamiltonians would not, & the others could not," wrote Jefferson on February 26.

Adams was unmoved by Federalist efforts to side track the nomination, or to name someone more suitable to their point of view. In the meanwhile, the American frigate Constellation captured the French frigate, L'Insurgent, setting nerves afire and bringing all out war closer and closer.

Adams wanted to pursue a two-pronged struggle--seeking peace while bringing the naval war to France by sending American frigates to cruise on the French coast. His message was clear. Negotiate peace or face a protracted naval war with a rising power.

Adams would not waver despite his weak position. On March 29, 1799, he told Attorney General Charles Lee. "If anyone entertains the idea, that, because I am President of three votes only, I am in the power of a party, they shall find that I am no more so than the Constitution forces on me." If they demand measures "that I cannot adopt," I will resign "but I will try my own strength at resistance first."

In April, nearly a month after Jefferson had departed for Virginia, Adams then left for home where he remained until September. In Braintree he received a letter from Talleyrand promising that he was ready to respectfully receive an American envoy. Adams hurriedly wrote to Pickering directing him to instruct William Vans Murray to go to France.

Adams had had long years of experience with the French. "Still," he told Pickering on August 6, 1799, "they shall find, as long as I am in office, candor, integrity, and, as far as there can be any confidence and safety, a pacific and friendly disposition. If the spirit of exterminating vengeance ever arises, it shall be conjured up by them, not me." Then in a statement demonstrating his cabinet's lack of support, Adams directed Pickering. "In this spirit I shall pursue the negotiation, and I expect the cooperation of the heads of departments." Talk about wishful thinking or self-delusion.

Secretary of the Navy Benjamin Stoddert warned Adams on September 13 "that artful and designing men" sought to take advantage of his absence from Philadelphia. Not only were they seeking to disrupt the peace efforts, but also they sought to "make your next election less honorable than it would be otherwise."

On October 16 while still enroute to the capital and despite the continued warnings of some cabinet officers, mainly Pickering, Wolcott, and McHenry, Adams ordered the American commission to France.

The die was cast. Adams was wagering the future of the nation and his presidency on negotiations.

Just as domestic politics and foreign affairs were reaching toward potentially violent crescendos, a near national disaster struck. On a cold, wet, December day with snow and hail mixing in a blustery wind, Washington went for his usual ride around his Mount Vernon plantations. Early the next morning, December 13, he was deathly sick of a throat infection-perhaps strep perhaps not. His doctors bled and blistered him to no avail. Stoic to the end, Washington died on December 14.

The nation had lost its father figure and the man who had led the nation through a long revolutionary war and the sometimes bitter and contentious establishment of a national republican government. The man who had feared factions and tried to alleviate the worst of political partisanship was gone.

Eulogies and paeans of praise flowed from virtually every mouth and pen from Georgia to New Hampshire. On December 26 a long procession made its way through Philadelphia to the German Lutheran Church in commemoration of the fallen hero. Sermons were preached and essays written.

"I felt on his death, with my countrymen, that 'verily a great man hath fallen this day in Israel'," Jefferson recalled in a January 2, 1814, letter to Walter Jones.

In a special address to Congress, Adams bemoaned the loss of the nation's "most esteemed, beloved, and admired citizen." Adams could not avoid a telling personal note. "I feel myself alone, bereaved of my last brother."

To Martha, the president offered "condolence" and "profound respect" for General Washington and tendered a request that Washington be buried in the federal district. A request Martha turned down.

Abigail Adams summed up the national sense of loss in a February 4, 1800, letter to Elizabeth Shaw. "There is not any part of the united States where the knowledge of the death of Washington has been heard but with sorrow lamentation and mourning. The virtues, which embalm his memory, add dignity to the Character of the Hero and Statesman and the gratitude of his Country, has been upon this occasion commensurate with his past Services.

In some instances, the orator and Eulogists have forgotten that he was a Man!" Still Abigail continued. "Washington's fame stood not in need of any such exaggeration. Truth is the brightest diadem with which his memory can be Crowned, and the only Eulogy which will render his fame immortal."

Jefferson did not speak at or even attend any of the events commemorating Washington's death. Many years later Jefferson's secretary, William A. Burwell, noted in his journal. "Mr. J [efferson] often spoke of G. Wtn. [Washington], attributed the alienation of his affection to the artifices of H [amilton] & his party to whom he was peculiarly obnoxious from his Known hostility to G. Wtn." Jefferson "believed him a man of remarkable strong Judgement capable of deciding accurately when the whole evidence upon the Subject was presented to his mind." Burwell added that Jefferson "mentiond G.W. was a man of strong passions, but never the less able to divest himself of them so far as to do *Justice* to his enemies." Apparently Jefferson did not have the same skill.

Perhaps, Jefferson saw a partisan gain by not attending. Perhaps, he still believed in his distaining words to Mazzei. Perhaps, he was just lazy. Perhaps, he was jealous. He had come to see Washington as the head of the despised Federalists rather than a national leader and personal friend to be respected.

His man Freneau mocked Washington and the Federalists in his *National Gazette*. "He was no god, ye faltering knaves," squawked the Republican spokesman.

Still, Jefferson may have voiced his true feelings in a February 25, 1800, letter to the Reverend William Miller. Washington's eulogies bordered "on impiety," they "revolt us by their extravagance" and they "would have revolted" even "the great man" Washington.

There was still a political race to be run—both sides firmly convinced that the fate of the Republic depended on their victory.

More than a year later, while awaiting his electoral fate in the Congress, he did go to visit Martha at Mount Vernon on January 3, 1801. Perhaps, he was sincere. Perhaps, he just hoped to mellow his partisan image.

Gerard W. Gawalt

# Republican Battle

*"How mighty a power is the spirit of party! How decisive and unanimous it is!"*
JOHN ADAMS TO ELBRIDGE GERRY, DECEMBER 30, 1800

*"However, the storm is over and we are in port. The ship was not rigged*
*for the service she was put on. We will shew the smoothness of her*
*motions on her republican tack. I hope we shall once more see harmony*
*restored among our citizens, & an entire oblivion of past feuds."*
THOMAS JEFFERSON TO SAMUEL ADAMS, MARCH 29, 1801

THE ELECTION OF 1800 was unique. Not only did the parties correctly believe that the future of the republic could well be decided by the contest, but for the first time (They could not know it would be the only time.) the sitting president and the sitting vice-president were running against each other. The stakes were high, tension mounted, and tempers flared.

One thing was certain. Neither Jefferson nor Adams would openly campaign. Neither would they publicly state that they were seeking the office of the presidency. As in the previous two elections both candidates left it to surrogates and supporters to make their cases to the public.

The election of 1800 had really begun in 1797, as soon as Adams was inaugurated. By the middle of 1799 it was in full swing and the spokesmen in full cry.

The political vituperation in the election of 1800 made the public and private rants in 1796 seemed like a child's prayer. Even the moderate Republican candidate for Massachusetts's governorship in 1800 Gerry described his opponents in a June 13, 1800, letter to John Wendell as "anti-revolutionists, feudalists, monarchists, counter-revolutionaries, war advocates, & office seekers in the State, together with their dupes, dependants, & connections." Eight days later Gerry told Elliot that the Federalists were part of an international conspiracy of "Monarchs and Despots, professedly leagued to annihilate republicanism." He blamed his loss of the governorship on "anti-revolutionists." Gerry summed it up. "To be one of the advocates of Republicanism these times is to be the subject of abuse, there being a party extended throughout the Union, both active and powerful, & utterly devoted to a monarchical system." And Gerry was supposedly a confidante of Adams!

Proving that Jefferson was not the only Republican to fear Hamilton's use of the federal army, Gerry warned that the "anti-revolutionists" might join the "war-faction" to "inflame the two, to excite them, if possible to hostilities." Hamilton and his allies would then drop the hammer on the Republicans and the Constitution.

Jefferson opined in a May 14, 1800, letter to Thomas Mann Randolph that some of the Federalists were supporting Pinckney and expected "with the Aid of S. Carolina, to give him the preference" over Adams.

Federalists struck at Republicans by enforcing the Sedition Act. First, Congressman James Lyon of Vermont who earlier had fought Congressman Griswold on the House floor was arrested and convicted.

Then, in early 1800 Jefferson's man James Callender found himself indicted and jailed for sedition after writing *The Prospect Before Us* in which he unmercifully castigated the president. "The reign of Mr. Adams had, hitherto, been one continued tempest of malignant passions." Callender wrote. "As president, he has never opened his lips, or lifted his pen, without threatening and scolding. The grand object of his administration has been to exasperate the rage of contending parties, to calumniate and destroy every man who differs from his opinions. Mr. Adams has labored, and with melancholy success, to break up the bonds of social affection, and, under the ruins of confidence and friendship, to extinguish the only beam of happiness that glimmers through the dark and despicable farce of life."

Callender charged that members of the Adams administration "love English supremacy and hate American Independence." Historians will ask," posited Callender, "why the United States degrades themselves to the choice of a wretch whose soul came blasted from the hand of nature, of a wretch that has neither the science of a magistrate, the politeness of a courtier, nor the courage of a man?"

After Callender had sent Jefferson a draft of the essay, he not only told Callender that the essay "cannot fail to produce the best effect," the vice president gave him more money to finish writing and publishing the tract. Callender was arrested and jailed in Richmond. In May he was tried, convicted, and sentenced to jail. Yet the sedition trials did not gain support for the Federalists. Only the Republicans gained strength.

The bitterness and anger that Adams felt toward the vicious attacks continued for decades.

Years later Abigail remained furious over Callender, particularly when Jefferson freed him from jail. During a long and angry exchange of letters, Abigail told Jefferson on July 1, 1804. "One of the first acts of your administration was to liberate a wretch who was suffering the just punishment of the Law due to his crimes for writing and publishing the basest libel, the lowest and vilest Slander, which malice could invest, or calumny exhibit against the Character and reputation of your predecessor."

When it appeared things couldn't get much worse, Adams finally became fully frustrated with his cabinet. McHenry, Pickering and Wolcott had remained loyal to Hamilton and continually tried to undermine Adams and his policies. When McHenry and Pickering conspired to prevent Adams's mission to France, Adams in a burst of temper summarily fired McHenry on May 5. McHenry had been taking orders from Hamilton— "the greatest intriguant in the World," "a man devoid of every moral principle," "a bastard" and "a foreigner," charged Adams. Adams then charged McHenry with conspiring with Hamilton to suspend Adams's peace mission to France, withholding public papers, nepotism and squandering public money. "You cannot, sir, remain longer in office," McHenry recorded Adams as saying in his recalled notes of his firing.

Five days later Adams asked Pickering for his resignation. Pickering refused, forcing Adams to fire him too. Upon hearing the news, Hamilton declared that the time had come for men of "real integrity" to unite against all "charlatans." The struggle within the Federalist Party had now become a backyard brawl.

Jefferson saw Adams's cabinet shakeup as an attempt "to court a little popularity that they may be afterwards allowed to go on 4 years longer in defiance" of the will of the people.

Adams also wanted to disband the army, which had been ineffectually led by Hamilton. Before he could, Congress voted to disband the army.

The presidential couple did not stay in Philadelphia. The nation's capital was scheduled to remove to the new city of Washington in the District of Columbia on the Potomac River. Abigail decided to set off for home in Massachusetts. John headed for the new national capital on the Potomac.

As the presidential election of 1800 approached, Jefferson expressed faith in the innate republican principles and sense of fairness among Americans. Even if the election were close, Americans would support the winner. "No mortal can foresee in favor of which party the election will go. There is one supreme consolation," Jefferson opined in a March 26, 1800, letter to his friend and financial backer William Short. "That our people have so innate a spirit of order & obedience to the law, so religious an acquiescence in the will of the majority, and deep conviction of the fundamental importance of the principle that the will of the majority ought to be submitted to by the minority, that a majority of a single vote, as at the last election, produces as absolute & quiet a submission as an unanimous vote."

He could not know how close the election would be!

Both sides tried gaming the electoral system. Every state had electoral votes equal to the total of its senators and congressmen. Each elector cast two votes without indicating the office intended for each person voted for. Constitutionally, electors could cast their votes for whomever they wanted. Each state legislature determined the manner electors would be chosen. They could be elected either individually or on a ticket slate by the state legislature or by the people in districts or on a statewide basis. Thus, the real election for president was determined by the election of representatives and senators in the states. Clearly, there were many opportunities to try to influence the outcome. Both parties sought to manipulate the system to their advantage.

In New York Burr engineered elections for the state legislature that gave vital votes to Jefferson. Governor Jay, although a decided Federalist, refused to switch the choice of electors from the legislature to district voting thus guaranteeing extra votes for Jefferson.

Worried that the Federalists might win some electors in district voting, Stevens Thomson Mason urged Madison to secure Jefferson's election by manipulating the electoral system in Virginia. "Unless you can ensure a general sufferage there, the thing is jeopardized. Will not the political expediency, the strong necessity of the case justify our State in adopting (in self-defense) some mode which will secure so important an object."

In Pennsylvania Jeffersonians gained control of the lower house and Federalists the Senate leading to a stalemate. The delay nearly cost Pennsylvania its electoral votes before a compromise allowed each house to choose half of the electors.

On a positive note, the election of 1800 saw the publication of America's first presidential campaign biography, *Address to the People of the United States with An Epitome and Vindication of the Public Life and Character of Thomas Jefferson.* Instead of castigating Adams, John Beckley, the former Republican clerk of the House and a campaign manager for Jefferson, wrote what is considered the first campaign biography as an antidote to the numerous attacks against Jefferson's character appearing in the public press. Thousands of the pamphlets were distributed throughout the country and extracted in newspapers.

On the negative side, the election of 1800 was one of the most verbally vicious campaigns in American history. All of the old charges were restated with greater hyperbole. Adams was a monarchist who couldn't be trusted to preserve the Republic. Adams was now blamed for the standing army, war with France and the Alien and Sedition Acts.

Jefferson's supporter, Edward Livingston told Jefferson on April 11, that until we win the election for president "the head of our body politic will always be affected with delirious dreams of royal & aristocratic Visions until a republican Energy is given to the System." And the nastiness went on and on and on.

Jefferson avoided any blame for the administration's actions, but was castigated as a coward, a slave monger, a Francophile, a democrat, and worst of all a deist if not an atheist.

Adams found himself under attack from the Hamilton branch of the Federalist Party as well as the Republicans. In a day when the anonymous or pseudonymous essays were the norm, Hamilton decided to openly and viciously attack the candidate of his own party. Hamilton had been viciously attacking Burr and the New York Republicans (Ultimately Burr would kill him for these attacks.). Now he verbally assaulted Adams.

Abigail had long ago warned her husband of Hamilton who she called the "spare Cassius"--a reference to Gaius Cassius Longinus a chief instigator of the plot to assassinate Julius Caesar. Now at the height of the election, Hamilton decided to go public with his overwhelming dislike, even hated, "for the man he considered unfit for the presidency." Always a gifted writer, Hamilton spent months preparing an essay, which in the fall of 1800 he published. The "Letter from Alexander Hamilton, Concerning the Public Conduct and Character of John Adams Esq. President of the United States" detonated like kegs of black power in the final days of the campaign.

In more than fifty pages Hamilton pointed out all the actions which could "be traced to the ungovernable temper of Mr. Adams" and proved Adams's "unfitness for the station of Chief Magistrate." Adams was "often liable to paroxisms of anger which deprive him of self-command and produce very outrageous behavior." He was weak, vacillating, eccentric, egotistical and prone to "bitter animosity." It was almost as if Hamilton were mirroring his inner self.

It was no secret that Hamilton had opposed Adams's candidacy in 1796 and now in 1800. But this was too much for many Federalists and they began to rally around Adams. Federalist writers, such as Noah Webster, quickly responded to Hamilton's charges, describing Adams as "a man of pure morals, of firm attachment to republican government, of sound and inflexible patriotism." Hamilton was a "would be Caesar," accused Webster. But the damage was already done. By the time he was finished Hamilton had ruined Adams's hope for reelection and his own future within the Federalist Party.

Adams laughed away some of the charges in letters to his friends and relatives. Jefferson even stopped writing to his friends in France in hopes of deflecting charges of being a Francophile.

Sometimes to their credit, they stood their ground. Adams stoically awaited word from France that would prove his decision to negotiate rather than declare war was correct. Much later Adams would declare that he wanted his gravestone engraved only with the words: "Here lies John Adams who took upon himself the responsibility of peace with France in the year 1800."

Jefferson refused to state a religious association and declared to Benjamin Rush in a September 23, 1800, letter that he still opposed organized religion. "I have sworn upon the altar of god, eternal hostility against every form of tyranny over the mind of man."

"I have a view of" Christianity "which ought to displease neither the rational Christian or Deist," asserted Jefferson. He still feared that Episcopalians and Congregationalists hoped to obtain "an establishment of a particular form of Christianity thro' the US." Jefferson added "they believe that any position of power confided to me will be exerted in opposition to their schemes, and they believe truly, for I have sworn upon the altar of god eternal hostility against every form of tyranny over the mind of man." This is enough to "cause their printing lying pamphlets against me," Jefferson complained.

Just when everyone believed tension could not rise higher, Virginia Governor James Monroe reported a slave revolt. If there was anything to tighten the tension of southerners it was this. Gabriel Prosser had organized a slave conspiracy to march on Richmond, seize the state arsenal, slaughter innocent white people, and fight their way to freedom, reported Monroe. Fortunately for the public safety, according to Monroe, the militia had been called out in time to stop the revolt.

In November 1800 Adams finally received some good news from America's minister to France. Murray had reached agreement with Bonaparte on October 3. Gifts were exchanged and all proclaimed peace and goodwill forever. The Treaty of 1778 was abrogated, but they agreed to free passage for neutral goods. Favored Nation status in trade was established; all captured public ships were to be returned; and in case of future hostilities citizens of each nation would have six months to remove their goods and money from the other. In short, America got peace and some concessions from France.

Adams had been proven right to take the diplomatic and political risks necessary to peacefully end the Quasi War, but it was too late. By a the time an official copy of the Convention or Treaty of Mortefontaine reached the United States in December the votes had been cast. Adams was right, but defeated.

The president did not even have the pleasure of announcing the results of the negotiations in his final speech on the state of the union on November 22. Instead he could only tell Congress that he hoped the negotiations would "meet with a success proportioned to the sincerity with which they have so often been repeated."

The results of the New York election had probably cost Adams the presidency.

At this point Jefferson went to meet with Adams on some business. According to Jefferson in a January 16, 1811, letter to Rush, the president "accosted me with these words: 'Well, I understand that you are to beat me in this contest, and I will only say that I will be as faithful a subject as you will have.' Mr, Adams said I, 'this is no personal contest between you and me. Two systems of principles on the subject of government divide our fellow citizens into two parties. With one of these you concur, and I with the other. As we have been longer on the public stage than most of those now living, our names happen to be the more generally known. One of these parties, therefore, has put your name at its head, the other mine. Were we both to die today, tomorrow two other names would be in the place of ours, without any change in the motion of the machinery. Its motion is from its principle, not from you or myself. 'I believe you are right,' said he, 'that we are but passive instruments, and should not suffer this matter to affect our personal dispositions.' But he did not long retain this just view of the subject."

After Republicans captured the legislature in South Carolina the outcome was certain. Jefferson would win, but would Adams, Pinckney or Burr be the vice president. By December 12 when he wrote to his son-in-law Thomas Randolph, Jefferson was certain he would receive more than the required 70 votes and he was certain that at least one elector in Georgia would not vote for Burr.

Many Americans, later called centrists by some historians such as George Billias and Ronald Formisano, hoped to avoid open warfare during and/or after the 1800 election by having Adams and Jefferson continued in their respective offices. Gerry was one such political leader in Massachusetts, telling Jefferson in a January 15, 1801, letter. "I must candidly acknowledge, that I tho't the best policy to re-elect Mr. Adams & yourself; because in that event, you would have united your respective parties in suppressing the feudalists, & at the next choice there was little reason in my mind to doubt that Mr. Adams would retire, & with his friends support your election to the chair and administration whereas the danger is now, that many of his adherents will again unite with the Hamiltonians & embarrass your administration, if you should succeed him, to avenge what they consider an act of ingratitude to the object of their choice." Jefferson did not reply.

Jefferson insisted to Robert R. Livingston of New York on December 14 that the election would restore the government of the United States to its true republican principles, rather than the administrations of Washington and Adams that had seen monarchists masquerading in Republican garb. "The constitution to which we are all attached, was meant to be republican, and we believed it to be republican according to every candid interpretation, yet we have seen it so interpreted and administered, as to be truly, which the French have called it, *a monarchie masquée.*"

Full of confidence in his victory, Jefferson went so part as to offer Livingston the post of Secretary of the Navy, because "to put it on her republican tack will require all the skills, the firmness & the zeal of her ablest & best friends."

The next day Jefferson sought to find common ground with Burr to ensure their success and prevent the Federalists from usurping the presidency. Jefferson was fearful that Burr would be elected president in the House of Representatives with the help of Federalist votes. Jefferson hoped to preempt the Federalists by getting Burr to commit to support Jefferson's candidacy. "I understand several of the highflying federalists have expressed their hope that the two republican tickets may be equal, & their determination in that case to prevent a choice by the H. of R. (which they are strong enough to do) and let the government devolve on a President of the Senate."

Burr promptly privately assured Jefferson of his support in a December 23 letter. "As far forth as my knowledge extends, it is the unanimous determination of the republicans of every grade to support your administration with unremitted Zeal: indeed I should distrust the loyalty of any one professing to be a republican who should refuse his services." Publicly, Burr was content to let the Federalists' plans roll on.

Upon hearing the news from South Carolina that the state had voted solidly for Jefferson and Burr, Abigail knew her husband would lose the election. Writing to her son Thomas on November 13, she said. "The consequence to us personally is that we retire from public life: for myself and family I have few regrets." She bravely thought she would "be happier in Quincy." She had no regrets. "I have little to mourn over" my husband's defeat. For Abigail there was a bright side to her husband's loss.

On December 3 the electors met in each state to cast their votes as required by the constitution. There they were to "vote by Ballot for two Person of whom one at least shall not be an Inhabitant of the same State with themselves." And therein lie the rub.

The votes would not be officially opened until February 11, when the vice president presiding over the Senate would count the votes for his own election. There were no secrets.

Given the state of communication in 1800 it took many days before the outcome of the voting was widely known.

Jefferson and Adams were both in Washington when the voting occurred. Adams believed or hoped that Pinckney would win. Jefferson feared mostly that he and Burr would receive the same number of votes throwing the election into the House of Representatives.

By Christmas Eve newspapers were reporting that the presidential present went to Jefferson. Unfortunately, his running mate Burr held in his hands the ribbon to unwrap the present.

Both Jefferson and Adams were wrong. Jefferson and Burr both had seventy-three votes. Adams had sixty-five and Pinckney sixty-four. The Federalists received no votes in South Carolina and no votes in New York. At least no one had to solve the problem of a sitting president being chosen as vice-president.

Jefferson and Burr greatly benefited from the three-fifths rule, which gave the southern slave states sixteen extra electoral votes. Some Federalist wags at the time and historians since labeled Jefferson "the first negro president." The Massachusetts General Court went so far as to propose a constitutional amendment that would have eliminated the three-fifths rule.

Efforts to game the electoral system had worked. There was no revolution in the presidential election of 1800, only political slight of hand. The real election had occurred in the choices for state legislatures and in political leaders' manipulations of the voting system. The authors of the constitution had sought to take political manipulations, shenanigans, and possible corruption out of presidential elections. They had failed.

The Republican majority in the House even tried to establish a new rule for the challenge of Electoral College votes. The Federalist Senate defeated the plan to have a majority of the Congress determine the legitimacy of disputed electoral votes.

Virginia's switch to a statewide vote for electors gave all the votes to Jefferson and cost Adams eight votes.

Governor Jay's decision not to change from legislative selection to district voting for electors cost Adams many New York votes. The decision in Pennsylvania to allow the Senate and the House to split the vote for electors cost Jefferson votes. South Carolina's decision to allow the legislature to choose electors cost both Adams and Pinckney. Massachusetts like Virginia switched from a district to a general ticket format and went one better by allowing the Federalist legislature to choose the electors rather than the general voting populace. This decision to change to a general ticket format probably cost Jefferson a few votes.

Jefferson told his son-in-law Thomas Randolph, the only reason the Federalists ran "Genl. Pinckney in conjunction with Mr Adams" was to secure votes from South Carolina. It didn't work.

The victory belonged to the party managers, such as Beckley in Pennsylvania, Charles Pinckney in South Carolina, Burr in New York and Madison in Virginia.

Adams blamed the loss on Hamilton, Pickering and other Federalists who opposed him.

Adams accused them of being "old Torries" or "British agents" in a February 15, 1801, letter to his son Thomas. "Is this principle or Passion? Reason or Madness? Some who were neither old Torries nor British Agents, united with both from other motives. A long War with France, for a pretext to raise a regular Army, was desired by Some, for the purpose of Patronage and Influence, and by others to assist in forcing on the People a change of Some sort in the Constitution," said Adams echoing the sentiments of Jefferson.

The only constitutional change brought about by the election was the Twelfth Amendment to the constitution requiring the casting of separate electoral votes for president and vice-president.

The only satisfaction for Adams was that Hamilton had had his eggs scrambled and the men Hamilton most envied were now president and vice-president. "Mr. Hamilton has carried his eggs to a fine market," crowed Adams to William Tudor on December 13. "The very man-the very two men of all the world that he was most jealous of are now placed above him."

When it was clear that Adams had lost and most believed that Jefferson had won, the Adams family was in a deep depression. Abigail's sister, Elizabeth, wrote to her son William on December 27, 1800, that the election results had "rubbed very hard" and made her husband "quite sick."

John blamed the entire problem on political parties and the "dexterous gentleman" from New York. "How mighty a power is the spirit of party! How decisive and unanimous it is!," exclaimed Adams in a December 30, 1800, letter to Gerry, who managed to back Jefferson while remaining a confidante of

Adams. "In the case of Mr Jefferson, there is nothing wonderful; but Mr Burr's good fortune surpasses all ordinary rules, and exceeds that of Bonaparte. All the old patriots, all the splendid talents, the long experience, both of federalists and antifederalists, must be subjected to the humiliation of seeing this dexterous gentleman rise, like a balloon, filled with uninflammable air, over their heads. And this is not the worst. What a discouragement to all virtuous exertion, and what an encouragement to party intrigue, and corruption." Adams wondered. "What course do we steer, and to what harbor are we bound?"

The problem was no one knew whether Jefferson or Burr would be president or vice-president. People who thought 1796 had brought a political odd couple to these offices were now temporarily dumbfounded by the new result. Opportunities for political deals and outright corruption abounded. Could the new Republic solve the conundrum and survive?

The nation appeared to be balancing on a razor's edge between civil war and acceptance of a constitutionally elected president. Electors cast two votes without discriminating between president and vice president. In 1796 this had resulted in the election of Adams as president and his opponent Jefferson as vice president. This time the results were more insidious and potentially more explosive. Because Jefferson and his running mate Burr had received the same number of electoral votes, the contest would be decided in the House of Representatives with voting done by states. There was opportunity for mischief because Federalists held the balance of power in the House. They could not constitutionally elect Adams, but they could deny Jefferson the presidency by supporting Burr.

Some Federalists even suggested they could delay or prevent the election of either Jefferson or Burr until the required inauguration date of March 4. Then so the reasoning went, the Federalist president pro-tem of the Senate would be acting president or there might be a call for a new election and a new opportunity to retain the presidency.

Jefferson anticipated these moves in a December 19, letter to Madison. The Federalists would seek to name a temporary president by merely stretching the constitution, feared Jefferson. "There will be an absolute parity between the two republican candidates. This has produced great dismay & gloom on the republican gentlemen here, and equal exultation in the federalists, who openly declare they will prevent an election, and will name a President of the Senate pro tem by what they say would only be a *stretch* of the constitution."

Some Federalists thought they could capitalize on rumored voting irregularities in Georgia and South Carolina to upend the election. But cooler heads realized that the months of turmoil might just upend the republic not just the election. In the end Vice President Jefferson simply counted their electoral votes without any challenges in Congress. And so their twenty-four electoral votes equally went to Jefferson and Burr.

Some Federalists, as could be seen in an article in the January 20, 1801, issue of *The Mercury and New England Paladium of Boston*, declared Adams and Pinckney had been chosen by a majority of white freemen. Jefferson had only won because of the constitutional provision that counted three-fifths of the slaves in apportioning members of the House of Representatives. The author of a Plain Fact openly declared that Jefferson did "ride into the temple of Liberty on the shoulders of slaves."

And then mysterious fires in the offices of the War Department and the Treasury Department kindled fears of civil unrest. Many Americans feared that a revolution like in France or Haiti was about to break out in the United States. Some Republicans raised the fear that the Federalists were fomenting violence to justify using military force to control the government. Others, such as Mathew Clay, thought the fires were arson designed to destroy the records of public corruption under the Federalists. In a January 21, 1801 letter to Monroe he said that people agreed the fires were arson and "who can doubt when they are told that Dexter is Secretary to both the treasury and War departments such is the fact."

While waiting for Congress to settle the tied presidential election, Jefferson received many panicked letters from his supporters. Gerry wrote from Federalist Massachusetts that there was an "insidious plan" of the "feudalists" to support Burr for president in order "to promote that division among the people which they have excited & nourished as the germ of a civil war."

While the Republican governors of Pennsylvania and Virginia talked of calling out the militia to install Jefferson as president, other Republican moderates assured Jefferson that neither the Federalists nor the Republicans planned to overthrow the constitution.

Abigail worried that there was danger in the deadlocked election for her husband. She warned the president through her nephew and the president's private secretary, William Shaw, on February 14, that Adams should "be upon his guard. And keep Silence for every word, look and thought are Strictly watchd & Scrutinized-tho we have nothing to hope, or to fear, yet I know it is best, that no advantage be gained of any of us."

Moderates, like Pennsylvania's Hugh Brackinridge, tried to assure Jefferson that both the Federalists and Republicans did not plan to step into "the opening abyss of a probable suspension of the federal government, from the non-election of a President."

Jefferson was worried enough about the plan to have the Senate President pro-tem act as president that he went to meet with Adams to secure his aid.

He later explained in a January 16, 1811, letter to Rush to have made a visit to Adams to secure his promise "to have this desperate measure prevented by his negative." According to Jefferson, Adams "grew warm in an instant" and answered, "with a vehemence he had not used towards me before."

"When the election between Burr and myself was kept in suspense by the federalists, and they were mediating to place the President of the Senate at the head of the government, I called on Mr. Adams with a view to have this desperate measure presented by his negative. He grew warm in an instant, and said with a vehemence he had not used towards me before, "Sir, the event of the election is within your own power."

Adams insisted that Jefferson could be "instantly" president if he would agree to support Federalist policies. "You have only to say you will do justice to the public creditors, maintain the navy, and not disturb those holding offices, and the government will be put into your hands. We know it is the wish of the people it should be so." Jefferson then angrily replied. "Mr Adams I know not what part of my conduct, in either public or private life, can have authorized a doubt of my fidelity to the public engagements. I say however I will not come into the government by capitulation. I will not enter on it but in perfect freedom to follow the dictates of my own judgment."

Adams countered that "things must take their course." Jefferson said he then turned the subject to another matter and the meeting was over. The fight would go on. Jefferson would believe that for "the first time in our lives we had ever parted with anything like dissatisfaction."

Adams, of course, had his own account of this ill-fated meeting, which was not very flattering to either man. Edward Coles, Jefferson's friend and Madison's private secretary, met with Adams in the summer of 1811. Coles later told this story to historian Henry S. Randall in a May 11, 1857, letter. Coles recalled to Adams. "Mr. Jefferson said knowing Mr Adams sensitiveness, and wishing to do nothing to arouse it, he deliberated much as to the proper time for making his usual call on the President; fearing if he called very soon, it might have the appearance of exulting over him, and if on the other hand he delayed it any longer than Mr Adams thought was usual his sensitive feelings might construe it into a slight, or the turning the cold shoulder to him, in consequence of his having lost his election. But the first glimpse of his convinced Mr Jefferson he had come too soon." As Jefferson approached Adams rushed toward Jefferson in "a hurried and agitated step." Adams shouted. "you have turned me out, you have turned me out!" Jefferson replied. "I have not turned you out, Mr. Adams." The voters decision was not "one of personal character" but of a choice between systems of government, according to Coles. There was no talk of a deal mentioned.

According to Coles, Adams agreed Coles "could not have given a more sensitive account of what passed." Adams added "Mr. Jefferson said I was sensitive did he well I was sensitive. But said I never heard before that Mr. Jefferson had given a second thought as to the proper time for making the particular visit described."

Ironically, the 1811 meeting between Coles and Adams would set the stage for the reunion of Jefferson and Adams when Coles conveyed his conversation to Jefferson.

Federalist Party leaders, such as Hamilton and James Bayard, consulted about whether to support Jefferson or Burr. Bayard insisted in a January 7, 1801, letter to Hamilton that "Mr. Burr it is distinctly Stated that he is willing to consider the Federalists as his friend & to accept the office of President as their gift. I take it for granted that Mr. B would not only gladly accept the office, but will neglect no means in his power to secure it."

Hamilton disliked Burr more than Jefferson. Burr's "politics are tinctured with fanaticism, that he is too much in earnest in his democracy." Moreover, "he is not scrupulous about the means of success, nor very mindful of truth, and that he is a contemptible hypocrite." Talk about projecting yourself!

Jefferson at least was "not so dangerous a man; and he has pretensions to character," argued Hamilton.

Abigail as usual got to the heart of the matter in a February 1801 letter to her sister Mary. "Never were a people placed in more difficult circumstances than the virtuous part of our Countrymen are at the present Crises." Abigail herself could not decide between Jefferson, whose "age, succession and public employments" gave "the prior Right," or Burr, "the more bold, daring and decisive Character."

The decisive point to Hamilton was. "If the antifederalists who prevailed in the election are left to take their own man, they remain responsible, and the Fœderalists remain *free united* and without *stain* in a situation to resist with effect the pernicious measures. If the Fœderalists substitute Burr, they adopt him and become answerable for him." In other words, the Federalists should take the long view.

Adams too was taking the long view by appointing as many Federalist judges and officials as he could. A new judiciary act increased the number of federal judges except at the Supreme Court where the number was reduced from six to five. Adams then nominated John Marshall to the vacant chief justice post and the Senate confirmed him in late January. Adams continued to appoint a series of "midnight judges" and "midnight appointments" to other Federal offices even as Congress was trying to select the new president.

Jefferson condemned the law as a "parasitical plant engrafted at the last session on the judiciary body." Federalists saw the "judiciary as a stronghold," according to Jefferson, and "from that battery all the works of republicanism are to be beaten down and erased."

To make an oft-told tale short, the House of Representatives began deadlocked on February 11 and remained deadlocked through thirty-five ballots.

As early as February 12 Jefferson recorded reports that "there was shadowy talk of deal making." Delaware Federalist James Bayard, who was related by marriage to Jefferson's supporter Samuel Harrison Smith, was circulating among Republican leaders, such as Samuel Smith and Edward Livingston, probing for grounds for a deal. Federalists were willing to offer Republican congressmen cabinet positions and other federal posts to support Burr, noted Jefferson.

Adams had already given Jefferson the terms that would guarantee him the presidency.

Jefferson informed his daughter Mary on February 15, "after 4 days of balloting, they are exactly where they were on the first. There is a strong expectation in some that they will coalesce tomorrow: but I know no foundation for it."

John was very circumspect in reporting to Abigail on February 16. "The Election will be decided this day in favour of Mr Jefferson as it is given out by good Authority." The authority was not so good, as the House did not settle on Jefferson until the next day.

Meanwhile, Adams kept busy tidying up his affairs and making numerous "midnight appointments." Ironically, what Jefferson saw as an unforgivable grasp to retain Federalist power, Adams saw as a necessary burden. "The Burden upon me in nominating Judges and Consul and other officers," Adams added, "is and will be very heavy." Finally, Adams had to "give a feast today to the Indian Kings and Aristocrats."

Jefferson would greatly resent the last minute appointments. Jefferson spoke angrily about them more than decade later in a January 16, 1811, letter to Rush. "And then followed those scenes of midnight appointment, which have been condemned by all men. The last day of his political power, the last hours, and even beyond midnight, were employed in filling all offices, and especially permanent ones, with the bitterest federalists, and providing for me the alternative, either to execute the government by my enemies, whose study it would be to thwart and defeat all my measures, or to incur the odium of such numerous removals from office, as might bear me down."

The next day the impasse began to weaken when James Bayard of Delaware went to Jefferson's supporters with a new deal. If Jefferson would not remove all Federalist officeholders, particularly judges, promise to maintain the navy and the national bank, then some Federalists (in Maryland, South Carolina, Delaware and Vermont) would abstain from the voting for Burr in the House thus allowing Jefferson to be chosen president. Ironically, the terms of Bayard's "deal" were basically those that President Adams had reportedly offered to Jefferson and Jefferson reported he had rejected out of hand.

A Federalist Congressman from South Carolina, Robert Goodloe Harper, claimed in a February 24, 1801, letter that the Federalists conceded because "the supporters of Mr. Jefferson had come to a determination which was known to have been solemnly made, and was publicly avowed, to rick the constitution and the union rather than give him up, and that no probability existed of a change in any of them; those who had voted for Colonel Burr, and who preferred the constitution and the peace of the country to their own wishes, thought it time to preserve those great and invaluable objects, by suffering Mr. Jefferson to be chosen; conceiving that union, even under him, was better than a separation of the states; and that the government might survive a bad or weak administration, but must be greatly endangered, if not certainly destroyed, by being left without a head. They therefore gave up their opposition."

Jefferson would later protest his innocence in the proffered deal. "No proposition of any kind was ever made to me," claimed Jefferson. "Nor any answer authorized by me." Talk about maintaining deniability.

Still Jefferson seemed to acknowledge the bargain in a July 1 letter to his long time friend Elizabeth Trist. Jefferson turned aside a request for a political appointment by pointing to "a conciliation plan" that has kept Federalists in office and reduced the number of offices open to new appointments. "I must observe that such is the effect of our conciliation plan, & so strongly has it operated on the minds of our former adversaries, that not one of them has refused to continue in service under the new administration. There has not been one single resignation from them: and as our principles do not admit much removal, the vacancies are few in proportion to the candidates. In truth it is the case of one loaf, and ten men wanting bread." So Jefferson was not above citing his bargain to fend off office seekers. I'd love to help, but!

February 17 brought the thirty-sixth ballot and an end to the crisis.

Jefferson became the third president of the United States. The new Federal government had survived a constitutional crisis. American politicians had proven that in a Republic contesting parties could peacefully resolve a disputed presidential election.

Jefferson could achieve his wish "to see our government brought back to it's republican principles."

Abigail greatly resented Jefferson's election. Her February 21 letter from Philadelphia (which turned out to be her last letter written to her husband) to John was not very circumspect. "I have heard Some of the democratic rejoicing Such as Ringing Bells and fireing cannon; what an inconsistency Said a Lady to me to day, The Bells of Christ Church ringing peals of rejoicing for an Infidel President!"

And there was still more vitriol in her tank. "The People of this city have evidently been in terror, least their Swineish Herd should rise in rebellion and seize upon their Property and share the plunder amongst them; they have permitted them really to overawe them." Forgetting Shays's Rebellion in Massachusetts, Abigail could "foresee some day or other N England will be obliged to march their militia to preserve this very state from destruction." And then no doubt they would rue the day they had elected Jefferson instead of her husband.

Adams informed Jefferson on February 20 that he was leaving seven horses and two carriages in the presidential stable. Adams was right in saying "These may not be suitable for you."

Very early in the morning of Jefferson's inauguration on March 4, Adams took the public stage out of Washington, leaving the day and the city to Jefferson. Was Adams graciously getting out of the way of the incoming president, or was he sulkily sneaking out of town? We will never know.

Like two scorpions in a bottle, one has to go or die.

Jefferson did not give tribute to Adams at the end of his term. Adams did not graciously offer his support to his successor.

# Tom On Top

*"We are all republicans, we are all federalists."*
THOMAS JEFFERSON, MARCH 4, 1801

*"I wish Jefferson no ill; I envy him not. I shudder at the calamities which I fear his conduct is preparing for his country, from a mean thirst of popularity, an inordinate ambition, and a want of sincerity."*
JOHN ADAMS, TO WILLIAM CUNNINGHAM, JANUARY 16, 1804

*He has been alienated from me, by belief in the lying suggestions contributed for electioneering purposes, that I perhaps mixed in the activity and intrigues of the occasion."*
THOMAS JEFFERSON TO BENJAMIN RUSH, JANUARY 16, 1811

THE MORNING OF March 4 his supporters and the local militia escorted Jefferson from his room at the Conrad and McMunn boarding house under a clear and beautiful sky to the Senate Chamber in the Capitol. For the first time the Marine Band played for the presidential inauguration. Also for the first time the inaugural address was published in a newspaper (William Bayard Smith's Jeffersonian Republican paper, *The National Intelligencer*) the morning of the inauguration.

At noon Jefferson, "dressed as a plain citizen" according to newspaper accounts, entered the small crowded Senate Chamber to deliver his inaugural address before he was sworn in as president. Vice President Burr introduced Jefferson while Chief Justice Marshall waited on the dais to swear him in. Jefferson delivered his thirty-minute speech in a tone so low, that Margaret Bayard Smith, a supporter and ardent admirer, described it as "almost

Gerard W. Gawalt

femininely soft." This was not the rousing start of the "second American Revolution" anticipated by his supporters.

Jefferson hoped for a new start "on high ground." It was time for the nation to "unite in common efforts for the common good." Jefferson then called for the restoration of "social intercourse that harmony and affection" because without it "liberty and even life are but dreary things."

In his inaugural address he conveyed a unifying message. "We are all republicans, we are all federalists." One has to wonder whether the people in the audience understood the president to mean political parties or the federal republican form of government. If they guessed door number two, they would have been right.

Jefferson went on to explain. "If there be any among us who would wish to dissolve this Union or to change its republican form of government, let them stand undisturbed as monuments of the safety with which error of opinion may be tolerated where reason is left free to combat." He asserted: "I believe this, on the contrary, the strongest government on earth."

To those would be monarchists he asked. "Or have we found angels in the forms of kings to govern him?"

Jefferson promised a "wise and frugal Government" that would be compressed "within the narrowest compass."

Then, in an enduring symbol of national unity Jefferson was administered the oath of office by his archenemy and federalist Chief Justice John Marshall.

Afterwards Jefferson went to his boarding house and then to the new President's House.

Adams stayed on the stagecoach to his own house in Quincy.

The day after Jefferson's inauguration Robert Goodloe Harper, a Federalist Congressman from South Carolina, issued this hopeful statement. The change of administration "took place yesterday at 12 o'clock; when Mr. Jefferson, the new President, took the oath of office, in presence of the Senate, which men pursuant to a summons from his predecessor, of such members of the late House of Representatives as were still in the city, and of a numerous concourse of spectators. The whole ceremony was conducted with the utmost propriety. As on the part of those who had supported the new President in the election, there was no unbecoming exultation; so his imposers manifested by their behaviour, a cheerful acquiescence in the decision of the majority. They attended the ceremony [Harper made no mention of the absent President Adams.] and after it concluded they paid a visit to the President, to express their respect for him as Chief Magistrate of the nation, and their readiness to support him in the proper exercise of his authority. The speech which he delivered previous to taking the oath, was well calculated to inspire these sentiments, and to afford the hope of such an administration as may conduce to his own glory and the public good. Before the evening all was quiet, as if no change had taken place. Should Mr. Jefferson conduct the government on rational principles, and with steadiness vigour and prudence, his elevation will prove a public blessing."

Then it was back to politics as usual.

Soon Jefferson was condemning Adams for nepotism. No doubt referring to the diplomatic appointments of his son John Quincy and the former president's appointment of William Stephens Smith, his son-in-law, as surveyor of the Port of New York in 1800, Jefferson turned down a distant relative on March 27, with this swipe at Adams. "The public will never be made to believe that an appointment of a relative is made on the ground of merit alone, uninfluenced by family views. Nor can they see with approbation offices, the disposal of which they entrust to their president for public purposes, divided out as family property," said Jefferson. "Mr Adams degraded himself infinitely by his conduct on this subject," accused Jefferson.

Still Jefferson did not remove Smith from his post until he was arrested in 1806 for violating the Neutrality Act of 1794 by attempting to ship men and military supplies to support Venezuelan Revolutionary Francisco de Miranda.

Jefferson thought his election saved the republican ship of state from the winds of aristocracy and monarchy. "However, the storm is over," Jefferson assured Samuel Adams on March 29, 1801," and we are in port. The ship was not rigged for the service she was put on. We will shew the smoothness of her motions on her republican tack. I hope we shall once more see harmony restored among our citizens, & an entire oblivion of past feuds."

To paraphrase a popular song from the 1950's--Life would be a dream, Mr. Jefferson.

Having been dissuaded by Madison from sending a conciliatory letter to Adams after their first election duel in 1796, Jefferson again ducked the opportunity to do so in 1801. When some mail for Adams arrived at the President's

House after his departure for Boston, Jefferson forwarded it with a strictly formal note that mentioned neither the election loss nor the recent death of Adams's son Charles.

Frustration, sorrow and anger all boiled over in Adams's bitter reply of March 24.

"Had you read the Papers inclosed they might have given you a moment of Melancholly or at least of Sympathy with a mourning Father. They relate wholly to the Funeral of a Son who was once the delight of my Eyes and a darling of my heart, cutt off in the flower of his days, amidst very flattering Prospects by causes which have been the greatest Grief of my heart and the deepest affliction of my Life." Adams then gratuitously asserts to the sonless Jefferson. "It is not possible that any thing of the kind should happen to you, and I sincerely wish you may never experience any thing in any degree resembling it." Adams concluded with another self-serving statement. "This part of the Union is in a state of perfect Tranquility and I see nothing to obscure your prospect of a quiet and prosperous Administration, which I heartily wish you." In other words, I left the nation in great shape, and if things go wrong it is all on you. And there the relationship of Adams and Jefferson remained for more than a decade.

John claimed that he paid little attention to national or world events in retirement. Abigail told her son Thomas. "Your father appears to enjoy tranquility and a freedom of which he has never before experienced. His books and farm occupy his attention."

However, a month later on July 11, 1801, John was revealing a still seething resentment of Jefferson and a deep interest in foreign affairs. Adams agreed with Jefferson's decisions to maintain a strong navy, and might even have agreed with his decision to send a squadron of ships to confront the Barbary pirates.

Still, his judgment of Jefferson was harsh. "The only misfortune of it is that Mr. Jefferson's sayings are never well digested, often extravagant, and never consistently pursued. He has not a clear head, and never pursues any question through. His ambition and his cunning are the only steady qualities in him. His imagination and ambition are too strong for his reason."

Jefferson's administration had a strong beginning. Jeffersonian Republicans replaced many but not all Federalists in appointed positions. For example, as early as a March 8 cabinet meeting, Jefferson decided to replace the federal attorney for the district of Maine, John Davis, with Jeffersonian Silas Lee. Some of his comments reflected the bitterness of the contest. Jefferson noted that "John Lee, Collector of Penobscot, bror of Silas, a refugee a royalist & very violent [Federalist] to be removd when we appoint his brother Atty." And so he was on July 27, 1801.

In his first year Jefferson replaced nearly fifty percent of incumbent office-holders. Jefferson explained his philosophy in a March 24, 1801, letter to William Findley, anti-federalist Irish political leader near New Cumberland, Pennsylvania. "Mal-conduct is a just ground of removal; mere difference of political principle is not. The temper of some states requires a stronger procedure, that of others would be more alienated even by a milder course." He particularly targeted Adams's appointments made after he knew he had lost the election. "The nominations crowded in by Mr. Adams after he knew he was not appointing for himself, I treat as mere nullities," Jefferson told Findley.

His administration's refusal to honor the appointment of William Marbury as Justice of the Peace for the District of Columbia resulted in one of our most famous Supreme Court cases. In Marbury v. Madison Jefferson's old nemesis and Adams's midnight appointment as chief justice, John Marshall, established the corner stone of federal judicial review, much to Jefferson's chagrin.

The old whiskey tax was repealed. The Alien and Sedition Acts were allowed to expire; in fact an extension of the Sedition Act had been defeated in the House of Representatives before Jefferson was sworn in. Men jailed under the Sedition Act, including the infamous James Callender, were freed. The navy was allowed to shrink even as it was sent to battle the Barbary pirates. The army was reduced and the number of federal employees shrank. The terms for purchasing federal land were eased for settlers. Only the Bank of the United States escaped unscathed.

Jefferson did his best to limit the power and extent of the federal government and to foster the growth of an agrarian society and curb the growing commercialism in America. He lived to learn he had fought a losing battle.

Life was quiet in Quincy.

The political harmony was broken by Callender's vicious attacks on Jefferson. Angered because Jefferson did not provide him with sufficient funds and a political appointment after his release from jail, Callender turned on his longtime supporter and became editor of a Federalist newspaper, *The Recorder*, in Richmond.

Jefferson confided to Madison. "I am really mortified at the base ingratitude of Callender."

His most sensational accusation was that Jefferson "for many years has kept, a concubine, one of his slaves." The "apostate" Callender elaborated. "By this wench Sally, our President has had several children." And furthermore, "The AFRICAN VENUS is said to officiate as housekeeper at Monticello."

Federalist newspapers gave the story full play. Some supporters of Jefferson, such as William Burwell sprang to his defense. But unlike a summer thunderstorm, which passes violently but quickly clears the air, this storm still clouds Jefferson's reputation.

Adams's judgment was belated but harsh. Writing to Joseph Ward on January 8, 1810, Adams blamed Jefferson. "I give him up to censure for this and I have a better right to do so, because my conscience bears me witness that I never wrote a line against my enemies nor contributed one farthing to any writer for vindicating me or accusing my enemies."

As to Sally Hemings and Jefferson, Adams was a believer of Callender. "Callender and Sally will be remembered as long as Jefferson as blots on his character. The story of the latter is a natural and almost unavoidable consequence of that foul contagion in the human character, Negro slavery."

Jefferson created sensations of his own by urging his supporters, such as Joseph H. Nicholson of Maryland, to impeach Federalist judges for verbal attacks on the administration. So much for Jefferson's faux anger at the Alien and Sedition Laws.

United States judge John Pickering of New Hampshire, a noted Federalist as well as an alcoholic was the first the go—impeached and convicted in the Senate.

After United States Supreme Court Associate Justice Samuel Chase repeatedly denounced Jefferson's policies from the bench, Jefferson vowed he should not go unpunished. Republicans were particularly aggrieved by Judge Chase's behavior during the trial and conviction of Jeffersonian political writer, Thomas Cooper, for sedition in April 1800. Chase staved off conviction in the Senate, but the Republicans had made their point. They could certainly play political hardball.

Fortunately, Jefferson did not broaden his attacks on Federalist officeholders by seeking retribution in the legal system against all his political opponents.
Perhaps, he remembered reading how the Roman use of the courts against
their political opponents helped bring down the Roman Republic.

Perhaps he was diverted by planning his western expeditions.

Jefferson had a life-long commitment to supporting western exploration
and asserting American claims to western lands. More than most of his contemporaries, Jefferson realized that the American West was not an empty des-
ert, but a land crowded by conflicting nations and claims of sovereignty. Even
before holding national office Jefferson tried on several occasions to organize
expeditions to the West.

First he had tried at the end of the American Revolution to talk George
Rogers Clark into leading an expedition to the Pacific, then John Ledyard in
1786, and then André Michaux in 1793.

Jefferson had been planning an expedition to the Pacific Ocean for more
than two decades. Now he had his chance to send one forth.

Once he became president he was able to secure support and funding for
the project in 1803. Final preparations for the adventure up the Missouri River
were underway, when the stunning news that France had sold the United States
the entire Louisiana Territory from New Orleans to the Rocky Mountains
reached Jefferson. Now Meriwether Lewis and William Clark would be trying
to find a water route to the Pacific through American not French or Spanish
territory. For Jefferson this was the highlight of his administration. For Adams
the Lewis and Clark expedition was only a brief report in the Boston newspapers. In fact after Adams and Jefferson resumed their correspondence in 1812,
the Lewis and Clark Expedition warranted only a brief mention by Jefferson
and no response from Adams.

Jefferson dreamed of an "empire for liberty' stretching from the Atlantic
to the Pacific even if it required wars. Just after leaving the presidency he told
his successor, James Madison, in an April 27, 1809, letter that the Napoleonic
Wars offered the United States a chance to seize Canada and all the lands
west of the Mississippi River. "We should then have only to include the north
in our Confederacy, which would be of course in the first war, and we should
have such an empire for liberty as she has never surveyed since the creation; &

I am persuaded no constitution was ever before so well calculated as ours for extensive empire & self-government."

Indeed when the next war began, the United States tried on several occasions to seize Canada. Jefferson told Adams on June 11, 1812, that the war will end the Indian problem. The Indians who do not surrender will be driven "into the Stony Mountains." But there "they will be conquered however in Canada." Adams's June 28 response spoke only cynically of "the contumacious spirit that appears around me."

Jefferson had taken a giant leap toward his "empire for liberty" with the purchase of the Louisiana Territory from France in 1803. Seeking just to gain access to the sea through New Orleans or at best purchase New Orleans, the Jefferson administration was presented with a golden opportunity to purchase all of France's territory west of the Mississippi River.

Federalists and Jefferson himself were not sure that the constitution allowed for the purchase of foreign territory. Jefferson prepared drafts of a constitutional amendment that would have allowed for the acquisition of Louisiana, but Madison convinced him that the constitution could be stretched to include the addition of new territory because, as John Quincy Adams told his father, they were afraid that they did not have the votes to pass it.

John Adams, of course, had no say in the matter, but his son John Quincy, a United States Senator from Massachusetts did. John Quincy favored the acquisition but wanted to prohibit slavery in Louisiana. John Quincy told his father on January 31, 1804, that "The Prohibition of the admission of slaves into Louisiana is like the drawing of a jaw tooth."

John told his son in a February 25th reply. "I leave the national affairs to the Administration and to Congress." Former President Adams said nothing directly about slavery, instead giving his son this supportive advice. "I do not disapprove of your Conduct in the Business of Louisiana. I think you have been right, though I know it will become a very unpopular Subject in the Northern States, especially when they See the Account of Expences which must be occasioned by it."

When John Quincy left the Federalist Party line to support Jefferson's acquisition of Louisiana, he came under fire in his home state. John no doubt agreed with his son's unsuccessful efforts to limit the spread of slavery in Louisiana. One Federalist accused John Quincy of bi-partisanship and dragged John into the struggle by accusing the son of imitating the father. "Curse the stripling, how he apes his sire."

In seeking to establish, what he called "an empire for liberty," Jefferson influenced the country's policies toward Native Americans and the extension of slavery into the West. Jefferson had a life-long interest in Native American culture, but he believed that Native Americans must adopt Euro-American culture including agriculture and formal education or be pushed further west beyond the Mississippi River.

If the Indians did not adopt American culture and ally themselves to America, or worse sided with the English, Jefferson told Adams in 1812 "these will relapse into barbarism and misery, lose numbers by war and want, and we shall be obliged to drive them, with the beasts of the forest into the Stony mountains." But we still admire them!

Adams still remained publicly quiet in Quincy, perhaps because of embarrassment over his own financial difficulties. Despite John's aversion to banks, he agreed with his son John Quincy to route much of the money John had received from the redemption of United States bonds in Holland through the hands of a South Carolina banking house operating in London and Charleston, Bird, Savage & Bird, which was also a fiscal agent of the United States Treasury in London. When the bank house failed in 1803, the Adamses suffered a devastating loss of about $13,000.

John Quincy informed his parents of the loss on April 2, and reported that although "They felt it severely," they "bore it with proper firmness and composure."

The crisis occurred because John had agreed to purchase Cotton Tufts' share of a Quincy estate for $7,000 by writing a bill drawn on the London firm. The bill was protested with severe fines. They could not withdraw from the purchase of the land but they could not pay for it. As Abigail told her son Thomas on May 8, 1803. "Mr Tufts had sold his part of the Farm to your Father for seven thousand dollars so that he was Lord of Mount W[ollasto]n.

John Quincy had also used the banking house and also was forced to sell property to meet his bills of exchange amounting to hundreds of pounds sterling that he had drawn on the bank. The firm of former United States consul in London Samuel Williams honored some of the bills, which Abigail acknowledged "will be the saving of Some thousand of dollars." Bird, Savage & Bird eventually repaid their losses in installments, but by the time the last install-ment was paid Adams was dead.

John Quincy who according to Abigail was in "no way to blame in the business," tried to ameliorate his parents' financial suffering. Declaring "the error of judgment was mine and therefore I shall not refuse to share in the suf-fering," John Quincy, apparently without consulting his unhappy wife Louisa, sold his Boston house and dipped into his own liquid assets to bail out his par-ents by purchasing their houses and farms and giving them life tenancies. John Quincy then moved his family from Boston to Quincy before leaving in the fall of 1803 for Washington to serve in the United States Senate.

This was wrote Abigail "A catastrophe so unexpected to us, and at a time when we had become responsible for so large a sum has indeed distrest us, at no other time of our lives could we have been equally affected by it."

Jefferson learned of the failure of Bird, Savage & Bird in the spring of 1803, because the United States had used it as a bank in London. No direct evidence that Jefferson knew of Adams's misfortune has been found, but it is hard to believe that such a juicy piece of gossip about the former president would have escaped Jefferson's ears.

Adams would have been horrified, although perhaps with a tinge of grati-tude, had he known Jefferson had conceived a plan to bail him out of his finan-cial problems with a federal sinecure. Jefferson asserted in a January 16, 1811, letter to Rush that he tried to arrange for a patronage position in Massachusetts for the former president "to ease his retirement" because "it was understood he was not rich." The timing of Jefferson's original plan is unclear but it is pos-sible he had heard of Adams's disastrous investment in a failed British bank-ing house. It is also possible Jefferson's failure to remove Adams's son-in-law William Stephens Smith from his post of collector of the port of New York became a part of Jefferson's plan after Massachusetts Republicans nixed his original idea.

Here is the pertinent part of Jefferson's letter. "And my first wish became that of making his retirement easy by any means in my power; for it was understood he was not rich I suggested to some republican members of the delegation from his State, the giving him, directly or indirectly, an office, the most lucrative in that State, and then offered to be resigned, if they thought he would not deem it affrontive. They were of opinion he would take great offence at the offer; and moreover, that the body of republicans would consider such a step in the outset as arguing very ill of the course I meant to pursue. I dropped the idea, therefore, but did not cease to wish for some opportunity of renewing our friendly understanding."

In private Adams remained critical of Jefferson and his administration. "I wish Jefferson no ill; I envy him not. I shudder at the calamities which I fear his conduct is preparing for his country, from a mean thirst of popularity, an inordinate ambition, and a want of sincerity," wrote Adams in a January 16, 1804, letter to his cousin William Cunningham Jr., who had mistakenly identified Jefferson as the author of *Thoughts on Government*.

Neither the president nor Adams was moved to publicly comment when their old antagonist, Hamilton, was fatally wounded by Jefferson's vice president and political opponent, Aaron Burr, in a duel at Weehawken, New Jersey. Burr survived but his political life and reputation were in tatters. George Clinton of New York would replace Burr in the next victorious Jeffersonian campaign.

Adams had no sympathy for Hamilton, whom he liked to call "the bastard Bratt of a Scotch pedlar." He would not "suffer my character to lie under infamous calumnies because the author of them with a pistol bullet in his spinal marrow, died a penitent." The cause of Hamilton's ambitions and immoral behavior, according to Adams, was a "superabundance of secretions which he could not find whores enough to draw off." Adams added, "the same vapors produced his lies and slanders by which he totally destroyed his party forever and finally lost his life in the field of honor." Ouch!!

Hamilton's political partisans used his death to attack the old Whigs, Adams later commented to Jefferson on September 3, 1816. "His party made the most of it, by Processions, Orations, and a Mock Funeral. And Why? To glorify the Torys, to abash the Whiggs, and maintain the Reputation of Funds, Banks and Speculation. And all this was done in honour of that insignificant Boy, by People who have let a Dana a Gerry and a Dexter go to their Graves without notice." Jefferson could not have said it better.

Jefferson had already decided to remove Burr from his presidential campaign in 1804, but he would not speak critically of Hamilton. To Jefferson Hamilton would always be a "singular character" and, perhaps forgetting the sordid Reynolds affair, a man marked by "virtue in private life."

During this turmoil the indomitable Abigail tried to reconnect with Jefferson when his daughter, Mary Jefferson Eppes, died of childbirth complications (most likely of infection and puerperal fever) on April 17, 1804. Abigail recalled the time when she cared for young Mary in London on her trip to join her father in France. And expressed sympathy and sorrow "over the departed remains, of your beloved and deserving daughter." "Had you been no other than the private inhabitant of Monticello, I should e'er this time have addrest you," Abigail wrote on May 20. "But reasons of various kinds withheld my pen, until the powerfull feelings of my heart, have burst through the restraint, and called upon me to shed the tear of sorrow over the departed remains, of your beloved and serving daughter, and event which I most sincerely mourn."

Had Jefferson merely accepted this letter of condolence as he wrote Mary's widower, John Eppes, as "proof that our friendship is unbroken," all would have been well.

But in his June 13 reply Jefferson could not resist making a political and personal attack on John despite his determination "to make an effort towards removing the cloud between us." "I can say with truth that one act of Mr. Adams's life, and one only, ever gave me a moment's personal displeasure. I did consider his last appointments to office as personally unkind." Jefferson continued his assault. "It seemed but common justice to leave a successor free to act by instruments of his own choice." Jefferson's biting accusation of Adams's violation of trust in several "midnight appointments" angered Abigail.

Abigail was still angry about the adminstrations failure to reappoint her son John Quincy to his post as a commissioner of bankruptcy. There is no evidence in Jefferson's papers that John Quincy was considered for the appointments under the new law. Jefferson's man in Massachusetts, Levi Lincoln, did inform Jefferson: "John Quincy Adams is made the most prominent character for federal promotion." Lincoln added in his July 24, 1802, letter: "They even borrow popularity from his father, as little as he may have to spare, to bestow upon the son." Jefferson's disingenuous explanation that congressional action had terminated the appointments and leaving out that John Quincy was not considered for the renewed appointments seemed to mollify Abigail.

Good thing she didn't know of Jefferson's nasty comments on nepotism and his predecessor. Although had she known of Jefferson's plan to bail them out of financial hot water she might have been somewhat mollified even if humiliated.

Jefferson did not appoint John Quincy to any other Federal post.

Abigail and the president then exchanged several long letters. Abigail defended John's actions as following the precedent of George Washington and subsequently accused Jefferson of violating the constitution by declaring laws unconstitutional on his own authority. Jefferson then asserted that the president had as much right as the Supreme Court to judge the constitutionality of a law. The result was a brilliant example of Abigail's courage and intellect. Both hardened political veterans debated some of the most contentious political and constitutional issues of the day, including the vicious nature of political campaigns, the evolving political spoils system, Jefferson's pardons of people convicted of seditious libel against Adams, and the Supreme Court's sole right to be the final arbiter of the constitution. All students of American political life should read the exchange of correspondence. Unfortunately, the exchange ended when John discovered the correspondence and made it plain he did not approve.

In fact John appended the following note to the letter-book copy of Abigail's final letter to Jefferson dated October 25, 1804. "Quincy Nov. 19. 1804. The whole of this Correspondence was begun and conducted without my Knowledge or Suspicion. Last Evening and this morning at the desire of Mrs. Adams I read the whole. I have no remarks to make upon it at this time and in this place." No doubt John and Abigail had some additional words to say to each other.

Abigail and John did not have to debate its continuance because Jefferson did not respond to Abigail's letter of October 25, because he sensed her desire to end the correspondence. Abigail said she would "close this correspondence by my Sincere wishes, that you may be directed to that path which may terminate in the prosperity and happiness of the people over whom you are placed, by administering the government with a just and impartial hand."

Jefferson later noted he took Abigail's wish to heart. "I soon found from the correspondence that conciliation was desperate, and yielding to an intimation in her last letter, I ceased from further explanation," Jefferson told Rush on January 16, 1811.

Gerard W. Gawalt

Years after the correspondence had ended Jefferson sent the letters to Rush and tried to explain to his friend why he and the Adamses could not remove their "misunderstanding." "Indeed," Jefferson claimed in a January 16, 1811, letter, "I thought it highly disgraceful to us both, as indicating minds not sufficiently elevated to prevent a public competition from affecting our personal friendship."

Still he couldn't resist adding. "He has been alienated from me, by belief in the lying suggestions contributed for electioneering purposes, that I perhaps mixed in the activity and intrigues of the occasion."

Jefferson later acknowledged in a December 5, 1811, letter to Rush that he overreacted to Abigail's criticism of him and "wronged" both John and Abigail by not believing Abigail's assurances that John had not known of "these jaundiced sentiments of hers." He believed he could not forgive them without admitting to her criticisms.

Jefferson's re-election campaign was much easier than that of 1800. Still, the future of the nation was unsettled and thoughts of secession still floated in the New England air. Senator Timothy Pickering queried Massachusetts Federalist Theodore Lyman. "And must we submit to these evils. Is there no remedy?" A new nation north of the Susquehanna was the solution, according to Pickering.

The Massachusetts General Court thought the problem was the sixteen extra congressmen and electoral votes the southern states received because of the three-fifths rule, and proposed a constitutional amendment to rectify the problem.

Jefferson told Elbridge Gerry on March 3, 1804, that he had planned to retire after one term, but "the unbounded calumnies of the Federal party have obliged me to throw myself on the verdict of my country for trial." In Jefferson's mind, "They force my continuance."

Then Burr killed Hamilton throwing the entire Federalist world into turmoil.

Adams's former 1800 vice-presidential candidate, Charles Cotesworth Pinckney, and Rufus King of New York carried the Federalist standard. With the new Electoral College system in place, Jefferson and George Clinton crushed Pinckney, 162 to 14.

Jefferson carried every state except Connecticut and Delaware.

The defeat was overwhelming. Adams's son, John Quincy, summarized the dire straits of the Federalists. "The power of the Administration rests upon the support of a much stronger majority of the people throughout the Union than the former Administrations ever possessed since the first establishment of the Constitution."

Jefferson rode from the President's House to the Capitol on March 4, 1805, for his second inauguration.

"He was in high spirits, dressed in black and even in black silk stockings," wrote Augustus John Foster, British diplomat. Jefferson apparently declined to wear his new blue wool coat tailored by Thomas Carpenter of Washington.

There were no memorable lines or grandiose thoughts in his speech, which Jefferson, delivered in his very soft public speaking voice. The people have "pronounced their verdict, honorable to those who had served them, and consolatory to the friend of man, who believes he may be intrusted with his own affairs."

Much of Jefferson's second inaugural address concerned Native Americans. He warned them to beware of leaders who "inculcate a sanctimonious reverence for the customs of their ancestors."

They must abandon "the hunter's state" and adopt the farming civilization offered them. "We have therefore liberally furnished them with the implements of husbandry and household use; we have placed among them instructors in the arts of first necessity; and they are covered with the aegis of the law against aggressors from among ourselves." They must overcome "prejudice of their minds, ignorance, pride and the influence of interested and crafty individuals among them, who feel themselves something in the present order of things, and fear to become nothing in any other." In short, they must become Euro-Americans.

Jefferson offered "sincere congratulations" to the country and returned to the President's House—his house for another four years.

America's relationship with Europe hit rock bottom after 1804. The Napoleonic Wars pushed both France and Great Britain to the brink. America's trade with France infuriated the English and they had the navy to take out their anger on the United States.

In 1806 Jefferson and the Republican Congress tried to use economic weapons against the warring powers. The administration tried to limit trade with Great Britain and France. First passing a Non-Importation Act on April 18, 1806. Jefferson exulted to Monroe on March 18, that the Congress was "never more solidly united in what they believed to be best for the public good." The prohibition of the importation of some British goods was lucky to last the year and then was suspended.

In the midst of these international difficulties, former vice president Burr attempted to establish an independent empire including New Orleans and the Spanish Southwest. As early as August 6, 1804, British minister Anthony Merry had warned Jefferson that Burr planned "to effect a separation of the western part of the United States from that which lies between the Atlantic and the mountains."

Jefferson tracked Burr's activities for two years. Then, having been informed of the filibuster by General James Wilkinson, who was secretly in the pay of the Spanish, Jefferson issued a proclamation on November 27, 1806, condemning those "conspiring and confederating together" to attack the Spanish.

Burr surrendered to authorities and was charged with treason and transported to Richmond for trial. On January 22, 1807, Jefferson declared that Burr's "guilt is placed beyond question." One Jefferson supporter, Senator William Branch Giles, even forced a measure through the Senate to suspend Habeas Corpus for three months. The House wisely defeated the measure on January 26, 1807.

Adams was very "anxious to see the progress of Burr's trial: not from any love or hatred I bear the man, for I cannot say that I feel either." Adams concluded. "But I hope his innocence will be made to appear, and that he will be fully acquitted."

The government's treason case was based on the word of co-conspirators and fell apart before the strict interpretation of the treason clause in the constitution and the rulings for evidence of treason made by Chief Justice Marshall sitting as Circuit Judge.

After the acquittal a furious Jefferson wrote Federal Attorney George Hay. "The criminal is preserved to become the rallying-point of all the disaffected and worthless of the United States, and to be the pivot on which all the intrigues and conspiracies which foreign governments may wish to disturb us with, are to turn."

A still fuming Jefferson in a January 24, 1814, letter to Adams, accused Chief Justice Marshall of finding "many sophisms" "to "twist Burr's neck out of the halter of treason." In his reply Adams made no mention of Burr's "treason" or even Burr.

In the midst of this turmoil Republicans began to urge Jefferson to run for a third term. According to his former secretary and now congressman, William A. Burwell, Jefferson turned to Burwell to decide how to answer an April 13, 1807, address from the Pennsylvania Senate and House asking Jefferson to seek a third term. Jefferson "observed" to Burwell "that addresses from Individuals had never embarrassed him but he could not treat the address of one of the states with apparent indifference," Burwell noted in his journal. Jefferson couldn't decide when to answer even though "it was generally known he would decline reelection." Burwell and Jefferson feared "that the moment he officially announced his determination intrigues would ensue and mingle itself with every measure before [Congress]." Burwell recommended a delay, and Jefferson held his noncommittal response until December 10, 1807.

Then on June 22, 1807, HMS Leopard attacked USS Chesapeake off Cape Henry on the Virginia coast. Three American sailors lay dead and seventeen including the captain, James Barron, were wounded. Then the British fired on a revenue cutter carrying Vice President George Clinton.

The nation prepared for war. Jefferson and Congress did not. John Adams's son, John Quincy, then a United States Senator, believed that "procrastination includes the whole compass of Mr. Jefferson's policy."

Jefferson told his son-in-law Thomas Mann Randolph on October 26, 1807, that Congress "will be more disposed to combat" Great Britain's "practice of impressment by a nonimportation law than by arms." He was right.

Even after France banned British exports to all nations and George III ordered the seizure of British subjects from all merchant and naval ships, including the United States navy, the peace party prevailed.

Then Jefferson in a fit of a pox on all your houses and ships turned to an embargo on all American shipping to counter British seizures of American ships and sailors. There would be no importation or exportation of goods in American ships—only intra-country coastal trade. Jefferson argued that the embargo on American shipping "gives time." And "Time" Jefferson believed "may produce peace in Europe."

Congress agreed and the infamous embargo, so ruinous to American commerce and especially to the shipping industry of the Northeast, went into effect on December 22, 1807. Jefferson's plan was a disaster for Federalist New England. Even the Republican Governor of Massachusetts, James Sullivan, warned Jefferson the embargo strengthened the pro-British party and led to talk of secession. But it did delay war for five years. His Secretary of State and his successor, James Madison, would have to pick up the burden of war.

Adams condemned the action to Benjamin Rush. Jefferson was guilty of "imprudence" in reducing the American navy, asserted Adams. The embargo was worse—it was "a cowardly measure." Adams remained publicly silent, telling Rush he would "raise no clamor" because he was "determined to support the government in whatever hands as far as I can in conscience and honor."

John's son, John Quincy, supported the embargo. For "his apostacy" the Federalist Massachusetts legislature removed him from the Senate.

Sixteen days before his presidency ended, the embargo was lifted in favor of a Non-Intercourse Act prohibiting commerce with British or French ports. It was a sad note for Jefferson to hear as he limped out of office.

On the eve of leaving office, Jefferson feared "the monarchists of the North" were trying to lead New England and New York into disunion. "A line seems now to be drawing between the really republican Federalists and the English party who are devoted, soul and body, to England and monarchy," asserted a worried Jefferson in a January 2, 1809, letter to Thomas Mann Randolph. His handpicked successor, James Madison, would have to deal with the destruction from the whirlwind, named The Embargo.

In his final days in office, President Jefferson tried to imitate Adams with some last minute appointments. Chief among these was his nomination of his former secretary, friend, and creditor, William Short, to be American minister to Russia. The Senate turned down Jefferson and in an ironic twist Adams's son John Quincy was nominated to that post by President Madison possibly in an effort to send John Quincy to political oblivion and approved by the Senate.

Certainly, John Adams enjoyed that turn of events, even if Abigail thought her son should not accept.

Rush congratulated Adams in a July 26, 1809, letter. "I rejoice in your son's mission to Petersburgh. He deserved it." He would miss his son's weekly visits, John told Rush, but "I would not advise him to refuse to serve his country when fairly called to it."

# Reconciliation And Death

*"And now, my dear friend, permit me again to suggest to you to receive the olive branch which has thus been offered to you by the hand of a man who still loves you. Fellow laborers in erecting the great fabric of American independence!"*
BENJAMIN RUSH TO JOHN ADAMS, DECEMBER 16, 1811

JEFFERSON'S ACOLYTE OR some might say puppeteer, James Madison, was inaugurated president on March 4 sending Jefferson, if you could believe his lifelong protests against public life, into happy retirement.

Jefferson's longtime friend and Adams's nemesis, Samuel Harrison Smith sang Jefferson's praises in his *National Intelligencer*. "Never will it be forgotten as long as liberty is dear to man, that it was on this day that Thomas Jefferson retired from the supreme magistracy amidst the blessings and regrets of millions." If Adams read this tribute, he no doubt wished the retirement had come eight years sooner.

Even on the verge of Jefferson's retirement, Adams could offer his protagonist but a ray of good will. "Mr. Jefferson has reason to reflect upon himself," wrote Adams to their mutual friend Rush on April 18, 1808. "How he will get rid of his remorse in his retirement I know not. He must know that he leaves the government infinitely worse than he found it, and that from his telescopes and mathematical instruments, however, he may secure his felicity. But if I have not mismeasured his ambition, he will be uneasy and the sword will cut away the scabbard. As he has, however a good taste for letters and an ardent curiosity for science, he may, and I hope will, find amusement and consolation from them for I have no resentment against him, though he has honored and salaried almost every villain he could find who had been an enemy to me."

Then the next year Adams went public in a three-year rant of essays defending his administration in the *Boston Patriot*. Despite Abigail's best efforts to curb his boiling anger, Adams threw down a verbal gauntlet. "Let the jackasses bray or laugh at this, as they did at the finger of God. I am in a fair way to give my critics food enough to glut their appetites." Jefferson, whom he accused of duplicitous behavior, was no doubt one of the critics Adams had in mind. The volcanic eruption of anger and verbal vindictiveness against old friends, such as Mercy Otis Warren, and long time rivals like Jefferson, Hamilton and Franklin, was Adams at his self-justifying worst.

Jefferson, too, harbored similar suspicions and thoughts of Adams, as can be seen in two letters he wrote to Rush in 1811. Referring to Adams, he wrote on January 16, "I think it a part of his character to suspect foul play in those of whom he is jealous, and not easily to relinquish his suspicions." Still, he claimed to "have the same good opinion of Mr. Adams which I ever had."

But as Rush worked to bring his two old friends together, Jefferson began to mellow but not very quickly.

Even from the perspective of nearly another decade and after the resumption of their conversational friendship, Jefferson continued to pummel Adams and his administration in his 1818 memoir, called his *Anas*. Adams had "conformed as a good citizen to the will of the majority," but the Federalists used the French Revolution as "a raw head and bloody bones." According to Jefferson, "nothing rescued us from their liberticide effect, but the unyielding opposition of those firm spirits who sternly maintained their post in defiance of terror, until their fellow citizens could be aroused to their own danger, and rally and rescue the standard of the constitution." Jefferson then condemned Adams with faint praise, saying that his old companion "would now, I am persuaded, maintain" the "republican structure" of the government "with the zeal and fidelity belonging to his character."

Wow! And this man was his "friend."

Adams too was unwilling to give Jefferson credit for the prosperity of much of his administration. "The halcyon days of New England prosperity were the first six years of Mr. Jefferson's administration." But Adams asked James Lloyd in 1815. Was this due to the "wisdom, the virtue, or the energy of Mr. Jefferson?" Or postulated Adams was it "the natural, necessary and unavoidable effect of the universal peace and tranquility abroad and at home, and with universal nature, civilized and savage, entailed upon him by his predecessor, in spite of friends and enemies?" The unspoken answer was clear to Adams.

As the nation teetered toward war with Great Britain, Rush, who had maintained a lively exchange of letters with Jefferson and Adams, finally succeeded in enticing both men to renew their friendship through letters. A visit to Adams from Edward Coles, Jefferson's friend and Madison's private secretary, in the summer of 1811 helped set the stage.

Coles and Adams discussed the final meeting of Adams and Jefferson. According to Coles, Adams was ripe for reconciliation. When told Jefferson thought he was overly sensitive, Adams replied that he "was sensitive." Adams then went on to tell Coles, "I always loved Jefferson, and still love him."

"That is enough for me," Jefferson told Rush in a December 5, 1811, letter after hearing the report from Coles. "I only needed this knowledge to revive towards him all the affections of the most cordial moments of our lives, changing a single word only in Dr. Franklin's character of him, & knew him to be always an honest man, often a great one, but sometimes incorrect and precipitate in his judgments: and it is known to those who have ever heard me speak of Mr Adams that I have ever done him justice myself and defended him when assailed by others with the single exception as to his political opinions, but with a man possessing so many estimable qualities, why should we be separated by mere differences of opinion in politics, religion, philosophy or anything else?"

Rush passed on Jefferson's comments in a December 16, 1811, letter to Adams adding—"And now, my dear friend, permit me again to suggest to you to receive the olive branch which has thus been offered to you by the hand of a man who still loves you. Fellow laborers in erecting the great fabric of American independence! Fellow sufferers in the calumnies and falsehoods of party rage! Fellow heirs of the gratitude and affection of posterity! And fellow passengers in a stage that must shortly convey you both into the presence of a Judge with whom the forgiveness and love of enemies is the condition of acceptance! Embrace—embrace each other!" Rush continued on to tell both Adams and Jefferson "were I near you, I would put a pen into your hand and guide it while it composed the following short address. Friend and fellow laborer in the cause of the liberty and independence of our common country, I salute you with the most cordial good wishes for your health and happiness."

Adams responded positively to Rush's report of Jefferson's favorable response to reports of the Adams-Coles meeting.

Both men knew Rush's game. "I perceive plainly enough, Rush, that you have been teasing Jefferson to write to me, as you did me some time ago to write to him," Adams cracked to Rush on Christmas 1811. Even though he asked Rush "what use can it be for Jefferson and me to exchange letters?" Adams had almost certainly already decided to take the plunge.

On New Year's Day of 1812, Adams wrote to Jefferson enclosing "two Pieces of Homespun" and wishing Jefferson "Many happy new Years."

When Jefferson received the letter he thought Adams had sent pieces of cloth without seeing the accompanying two-volume set of *Lectures on Rhetoric and Oratory* by John Quincy Adams. Jefferson quickly responded on January 21 with a written lecture on the virtue of homespun cloth and the raising of sheep. Then he moved on to recall the times "we were fellow laborers in the same cause, struggling for what is most valuable to man, his self-government."

Ever the slippery one, Jefferson informed Rush in a letter written the same day that he was careful to avoid any mention of family or sensitive subjects. ""To avoid the subject of his family, on which I could say nothing, I have written him a rambling, gossiping epistle which gave openings for the expression of sincere feelings, & may furnish him ground of reciprocation, If he merely waited for the first declaration; for so I would construe the reserve of his letter." It was enough.

Jefferson encouraged Adams to write about his health and personal life. "I should have the pleasure of knowing, that in the race of life, you do not keep, in it's physical decline, the same distance ahead of me which you have done in political honors and achievements." Even here the competitive fires still burned.

And the two friends were back on track. Both old men turned to each other for written companionship because they were bored and their correspondence stimulated them while reminding them of their glory days fighting for independence and the founding of the American nation.

They would never meet again, but their written conversations renewed a friendship and provided a venue for frank exchanges of views on everything from literature, to lifestyle, to Native Americans, to American expansion, and even to politics.

They didn't have telephones, emails, or any electronic connections so they made the most of simple letters.

Two subjects seldom mentioned in their letters were slavery and the misfortunes of some of their children and grandchildren. Adams would never mention the return home of a broken but bullying Thomas Adams. Jefferson would never mention the spousal abuse of Martha Randolph and Anne Bankhead and the vicious physical confrontation between Anne's husband Charles and Martha's son Thomas Jefferson Randolph.

Adams explained to young Josiah Quincy why he could now be a friend of Jefferson. An explanation Quincy recorded in his diary. "I do not believe that Mr. Jefferson ever hated me. On the contrary, I believe he always liked me: but he detested Hamilton and my whole administration. Then he wished to be President of the United States, and I stood in his way. So he did everything that he could to pull me down. But if I should quarrel with him for that," noted Quincy, "I might quarrel with every man I have had anything to do with in life." So concluded Adams, "I forgive all my enemies and hope they may find mercy in Heaven. Mr. Jefferson and I have grown old and retired from public life. So we are upon our ancient terms of goodwill." Adams still retained a friendship for Jefferson. The reciprocation was not always so evident.

Differences still remained. Adams told Jefferson on May 1, 1812, "in measures of Administration I have neither agreed with you or Madison. Whether you or I were right Posterity must judge. I have never approved of Non Importations, non Intercourses, or Embargoes for more than Six Weeks. I never have approved and never can approve of the Repeal of the Taxes, the Repeal of the Judiciary System, or the Neglect of the Navy. You and Mr. Madison had as good a right to your Opinions as I had to mine, and I must acknowledge the Nation was with you. But neither your Authority nor that of the Nation has convinced me. Nor, I am bold to pronounce will convince Posterity."

War with Great Britain--known in this country, as the War of 1812 or the second war for independence—was an early test of their newly restored friendship. Jefferson eagerly anticipated war in a June 11 letter. The capture of Canada would end the Indian threat and "secures our women and children for ever from the tomahawk and scalping knife." Jefferson expected "that the doors of Congress will re-open with a Declaration of War. That this may end in indemnity for the past, security for the future and compleat emancipation from Anglomany, Gallomany, and all the manias of demoralized Europe."

Adams was more realistic and couldn't resist a jab at Jefferson and Madison's small navy policies in his June 28 reply. "We have War in Earnest. I lament the contumacious Spirit that appears about me. But I lament the cause that has given too much Apology for it: the total Neglect and absolute Refusal of all maritime Protection and Defence."

But neither man could anticipate the bitter course of the war, the nation's capital in flames, and New England on the verge of secession.

After the British had burned the capitol and the Library of Congress in 1814, Jefferson sold his more than 6000-book collection to the government for the congressional library. Jefferson's 1814 library has now been reassembled at the Library of Congress. Jefferson used the twenty-three thousand nine hundred and fifty dollars that he received to pay more than twenty thousand dollars of his ever -present debts --$4,870 to Kosciuszko, $10,000 to Short, and on and on. Then he promptly began a new library of several thousand books with some of the remaining $6,340.

Upon hearing that Jefferson's library would be part of the Library of Congress, Adams wrote of his envy in an October 23, 1814, letter to Jefferson. "By the Way I envy you that immortal honour: but I cannot enter into competition with you for my books are not half the number of yours: and moreover, I have Shaftesbury, Bolingbroke, Hume, Gibbon and Raynal, as well as Voltaire."

Strangely, the end of the war in 1815 earned barely a mention in the men's correspondence even though John Quincy Adams was involved in the peace negotiations. Adams mentioned it not at all. Jefferson heralded "Peace, God bless it! has returned to put us again into a course of lawful and laudable pursuits." It was the restoration of the Bourbon monarchy in France that seemed of most interest to Jefferson, but not the least to Adams.

The eight- year administrations of Jefferson's acolytes, Madison and Monroe, passed through the avid and interested minds and written conversations of the two ex-presidents.

Jefferson's long time plan for a university in Charlottesville began to come together in 1818. At Jefferson's urging the Albemarle Academy had secured legislative approval to establish a Central University, but this was just a tactical maneuver. On February 21, 1818, the Virginia legislature authorized the founding of a university. In August Jefferson and the state commissioners met at Rockfish Gap and decided on Charlottesville for the location of the university.

Even though he had attended the College of William and Mary and studied law with Professor Wythe in Williamsburg, Jefferson was determined to establish a new university near Monticello. Jefferson's plan for the diffusion of knowledge in the 1780's had included a plan for a public university at the pinnacle of an educational pyramid.

There was also an element of provincial pride, as Jefferson told Joseph C. Cabell on January 22, 1820. "If our legislature does not heartily push our University we must send our children for education to Kentucky or Cambridge. The latter will return them to us fanatics and tories, the former will keep them to add to their population." Fortunately, for Jefferson and the tens of thousands of graduates from the University of Virginia, the legislature did not shirk from the burden.

During the remainder of Jefferson's life his main outside activity was the establishment of the university. From Monticello he could view the progress of construction with his telescope on the days he did not ride into town for a direct examination.

Adams offered Jefferson encouragement and verbal support. Jefferson confided to Adams. "I am comforted and protected from other solicitudes by the cares of our University." Jefferson told Adams he feared the delays in construction "may render It doubtful whether I shall live to see it go into action."

Adams was pleased for Jefferson, but added a note of criticism.

"Your university is a noble employment in your old Age," Adams told Jefferson on January 22, 1825, "and your ardor for its success, does you honour, but I do not approve of your sending to Europe for Tutors and Professors. I do believe there are sufficient scholars in America to fill your Professorships and Tutorships with more active ingenuity, and independent minds, than you can bring from Europe."

Adams was echoing criticism from within Virginia, when he added. "The Europeans are all deeply tainted with prejudices both Ecclesiastical and Temporal which they can never get rid of; they are all infected with Episcopal and Presbyterian Creeds, and confessions of faith."

Jefferson had to back down on several faculty appointments, but his plans gained momentum.

Jefferson had little life left when the first session of the university was finally held in the fall of 1825.

Both Jefferson and Adams experienced money problems in their retirement. Adams thought that there should be a pension plan for defeated public officeholders. "I think that when a people turn out their old servants, either by legal suffrages or from complaisance to a vulgar opinion, they ought to grant them, at least an outfit; for by making them conspicuous, and multiplying their acquaintances, they expose them to expences heavier than when in office," Adams wrote Jefferson on July 12, 1822. "To turn out such men to eat husks with the prodigal or grass with Nebuchadnezzar ought to be tormenting to the humanity of the Nation; it is infinitely worse than saying 'go up thou Bald Head'," concluded Adams. Jefferson made no response.

For Adams there was that one-time disaster. Immediately after his retirement, Adams became caught in a financial crunch when he contracted to purchase land from Cotton Tufts and the bill he drew on the London banking house of Bird, Savage & Bird failed to clear. Unbeknownst to John and his son John Quincy the firm declared bankruptcy soon after nearly $13,000. of John's money was sent there from bonds in Holland.

The Adamses faced a financial disaster. Fortunately for them, John Quincy came to their rescue by slowly purchasing their properties and giving them life tenancy.

No wonder, Adams could tell John Taylor. "I have never had but one opinion concerning banking, from the institution of the first in Philadelphia, by Mr. Robert Morris and Mr. Gouvernour Morris, and that opinion had uniformly been that the banks have done more injury to the religion, morality, tranquility, prosperity, and even wealth of the nation, than can they have done or ever will do good."

"This System of Banks begotten, hatched and brooded by Duer, Robert Morris, Governeur Morris, Hamilton and Washington, I have always considered as a System of national Injustice. A Sacrifice of public and private Interest to a few Aristocratical Friends and Favourites," Adams told Jefferson on November 15, 1813.

Jefferson, on the other hand, had had chronic financial problems for most of his life. Just two days before his March 4, 1809, retirement, Jefferson explained to his daughter Martha that he had a management plan. "If I can sell the detached tracts of land I own, so as to pay the debts I have contracted here (about ten thousand Dollars) and they are fully adequate to it, my wish would be to live within the income of my Albemarle possessions." His rented property would bring in $2000. and he would have the "profits of the lands and negroes of Monticello and Tufton, the toll mill, and nailery." Jefferson calculated that the "income about 2000 to 2500 dollars" from his Bedford lands "would then be free to assist the children as they grow up and want to establish themselves."

Not even the ever-doting Martha believed that Jefferson could live within the income of just his plantations, when he couldn't live on the twenty-five thousand dollar presidential salary plus the income from his plantations.

The expenses of a lifestyle that always exceeded his income, coupled with debts inherited by his wife and then a disastrous co-signed bank loan of $20,000 for a bankrupt friend and relative kept Jefferson mired in debt. His friend William Short loaned him tens of thousands of dollars and periodic loans from banks (five from Richmond banks and two from the "hated" Bank of the United States), kept him afloat but mired in debt. When he died, Jefferson was more than 100,000 dollars in debt. Throughout his life Jefferson had used his own and his friends' money to keep juggling his many loans and debts and when he died he left them to sort out the financial chaos.

In his reply to Adams's November screed against banks, Jefferson announced. "I have ever been the enemy of banks; not those discounting for cash; but of those foisting their own paper into circulation, and thus banishing our cash. My zeal against those institutions was so warm and open at the establishment of the bank of the U.S. that I was derided as a Maniac by the tribe of bank-mongers, who were seeking to filch from the public their swindling, and barren gains." Jefferson was wisely concerned about inflation and the flood of paper money.

Adams no doubt would have agreed with Jefferson when he concluded. "You might as well, with the sailors, whistle to the wind, as suggest precautions against having too much money. We must scud then before the gale, and try to hold fast, ourselves, by some plank of the wreck."

Finances soon became even more difficult for debtors. Fortunately for Adams, his son had rescued him. Unfortunately for Jefferson there would be no rescue.

Gerard W. Gawalt

When the bank failures of 1818 ushered in the nation's first financial crisis, called the Panic of 1819, Jefferson faced disaster. First his own debts were called and loans had to be renegotiated. Then his friend Wilson Cary Nicholas for whom Jefferson had endorsed a $20,000 loan died with insufficient assets to cover the debt, leaving Jefferson responsible for its payment.

Jefferson tried to rescue his finances with a lottery scheme. The Virginia legislature only reluctantly approved the plan to sell tickets for Monticello, Shadwell Mills, and one-third of his Albemarle lands. His friends pressured Jefferson to put off the lottery, hoping to raise enough money through private subscriptions. In the months before Jefferson's death more than sixteen thousand dollars were subscribed, but more than one hundred thousand dollars were still needed. After his death family members and friends tried to revive the lottery, but within a year it had failed and Jefferson's properties, slaves, and personal properties went up for sale.

The world for both men continued to shrink. Jefferson still took his twice-yearly eighty-mile trips to his plantation, Poplar Forest, in Bedford County. Adams seldom left the confines of his farm and the town of Quincy and his ability to read and write began to deteriorate.

Then came the shock of Abigail's death.

Abigail's death of typhoid fever on October 28, 1818, send Adams into depression and ensured a lonely final eight years even though he was often surrounded by his children and grandchildren.

John warned Jefferson of the impending doom in an October 20 letter. "Now Sir, for my Griefs! The dear partner of my Life for fifty four Years as a Wife and for many Years more as a Lover, now lyes in extremis, forbidden to speak or be spoken to."

Jefferson learned of her death from the newspapers and penned Adams an emotional letter. Jefferson too, like Adams, had lost his wife and children. "Time and silence are the only medicines," Jefferson wrote. "I will not therefore, by useless condolances, open afresh the sluices of your grief nor, altho' mingling sincerely my tears with yours, will I say a word more, where words are vain." The only comfort, Jefferson remarked, is knowing that "the term is not very distant" when we shall "ascend in essence to an ecstatic meeting with our friends we have loved and lost and whom we shall still love and never lose again."

Still life went on in Quincy, at Monticello and in the United States.

The expansion of slavery was the major issue of the time. Northerners and some southerners had long feared the spread of slavery and even Jefferson had tried to prohibit slavery in the old northwest through a Congressional resolution in 1784. By 1819 the issue was at full boil. Missouri wanted admission as a slave state. The northerners who controlled the House of Representatives refused to assent.

Jefferson feared "the Missouri question is a breaker on which we lose the Missouri country by revolt, and what more God only knows." Jefferson knew even a compromise would only postpone the battle. "I thank god that I shall not live to witness its issue."

Adams too seemed to peer into the future and see darkness and destruction. "The Missouri question I hope will follow the other Waves under the Ship and do no harm," wrote Adams on December 21. "I know it is high treason to express a doubt of the perpetual duration of our vast American Empire, and our free Institutions." But continued Adams. "I am sometimes Cassandra enough to dream that another Hamilton, another Burr might rend this mighty Fabric in twain, and perhaps into a leash, and a few more choice Spirits of the same Stamp, might produce as many Nations in North America as there are in Europe."

Jefferson too saw the enormity of the question. But as a slave owner he feared that if Congress had the right to regulate slavery in any state, they might choose to end slavery entirely. "The real question, as seen in the states afflicted with this unfortunate population is Are our slaves to be presented with freedom and a dagger?" Jefferson asked Adams on January 22, 1821. For if Congress has a power to regulate the conditions of the inhabitants of the states, within the states, it will be but another exercise of that power to declare that all shall be free. Are we then to see again Athenian and Lacedemonian confederacies? To wage another Peloponnesian war to settle the ascendancy between them? Or is this the tocsin of merely a servile war? That remains to be seen: but not I hope by you or me. Surely they will parley awhile, and give us time to get out of the way. What a Bedlamite is man!"

Ultimately a temporary political compromise was arranged. Missouri would be the only slave state allowed north of the 36th parallel, all states would have to return runaway slaves, and Maine, that northern section of

Massachusetts which chaffed under the conservative politics of Boston, would be admitted as a non-slave state to balance Missouri in the Senate.

Fortunately, for Adams and Jefferson they were long dead before the civil war over slavery nearly tore the nation in two.

Adams still had enough vigor to rejoice at his 1820 election to the convention to revise the Massachusetts' constitution, which he had written forty years before. The delegates greeted the eighty-five year-old Adams with applause when he arrived at the convention. The reception of his bold proposal to provide for complete religious freedom in the state was not quite so wholehearted. His proposed amendment failed.

Jefferson "was quite rejoiced" to see that Adams "had health and spirits enough to take part in" his state's convention. Jefferson had hoped that Adams's proposed amendment would lead to "moral emancipation" to match the physical liberty that they already enjoyed.

Adams told Jefferson his performance at the convention was embarrassing. After a total desuetude of 40 years without public debate "I bogged and blundered more than a young fellow just rising to speak at the bar." Adams confided, "I attempted little and that seldom." Still he had attended and he had tried.

Both men worried about posterity and their place in the history of the founding of the United States.

Jefferson still preferred, as he told Adams in 1816, "the dreams of the future better than the history of the past." Even though Jefferson told Josephus Stuart in 1817 that accurate history would "not to be found among the ruins of a decayed memory," he set about to write his own autobiography. Neither Jefferson nor Adams would complete their autobiographies.

"Who shall write the history of the American revolution?" Adams queried Jefferson on July 30, 1821. "Who can write it? Who will ever be able to write it?" Both were inclined to believe, as Jefferson stated in his August 10 reply. "Nobody; except merely it's external facts. All it's councils, designs and discussions, having been conducted by Congress with closed doors, and no member, as far as I know having made notes of them, these, which are the life and soul of history must for ever be unknown."

As the fiftieth anniversary of the Declaration of Independence approached both men and their supporters sparred about the authorship and originality of that iconic document. Jefferson annotated his personal "rough draught" of the Declaration and Adams tried to assert his participation in the writing of the Declaration.

Political opponents of the Jeffersonian Republicans and personal critics of Jefferson sought to minimize Jefferson's role in its writing. Timothy Pickering, a former Federalist secretary of state and an ancient political enemy of Jefferson and quondam supporter of Adams, led the attack in a July 4, 1823, public address.

Based on an August 6, 1822, letter from Adams, Pickering charged that the ideas of the Declaration were "hackneyed" by 1776 and had been first clearly stated by James Otis of Massachusetts in his 1764 pamphlet *The Rights of the British Colonies Asserted and Proved.*

Acting on a request from Pickering, Adams had written at length about the drafting of the Declaration in which he openly declared Jefferson to be "the author of the Declaration of Independence."

It is worth quoting at length from both Adams's letter and then Jefferson's response to Pickering via Madison.

The aged Adams wrote:

"You inquire why so young a man as Mr. Jefferson was placed at the head of the Committee for preparing a Declaration of Independence? I answer; it was the Frankfort advice [i.e. advice given to Adams by Pennsylvania leaders during a 1774 overnight stay in Frankford, Pennsylvania, designed to keep Massachusetts radicals in the background in Congress and push Virginians to the forefront.] to place Virginia at the head of every thing. Mr. Richard Henry Lee might be gone to Virginia, to his sick family, for aught I know, but that was not the reason of Mr. Jefferson's appointment. There were three committees appointed at the same time. One for the Declaration of Independence, another for preparing articles of confederation, and another for preparing a treaty to be proposed to France."

"Mr. Lee was chosen for the Committee of confederation, and it was not thought convenient that the same person should be upon both. Mr. Jefferson came into Congress, in June 1775, and brought with him a reputation for literature, science, and a happy talent of composition. Writings of his were handed about, remarkable for the peculiar felicity of expression. Though a silent member in Congress, he was so prompt, frank, explicit, and decisive upon committees and in conversation, not even Samuel Adams was more so, that he soon seized upon my heart; and upon this occasion I gave him my vote, and did all in my power to procure the votes of others. I think he had one more vote than any other, and that placed him at the head of the committee. I had the next highest number, and that placed me second. The committee met, discussed the subject, and then appointed Mr. Jefferson and me to make the draught, I suppose because we were the two first on the list."

"The sub-committee met. Jefferson proposed me to make the draught. I said 'I will not.' 'You shall do it.' 'You! No.' 'Why will you not? You ought to do it.' 'I will not.' 'Why.' 'Reasons enough' 'What can be your reasons?' 'Reason 1st—You are a Virginian, and a Virginian ought to appear at the head of this business. Reason 2d—I am obnoxious, suspected, and unpopular. You are very much otherwise. Reason 3d—You can write ten times better than I can.' ' Well,' said Jefferson, 'if you are decided I will do as well as I can.' 'Very well. When you have drawn it up, We will have a meeting.' A meeting we accordingly had, and conned the paper over. I was delighted with its high tone and the flights of oratory with which it abounded, especially that concerning Negro slavery, which, though I knew his Southern brethren would never suffer to pass in Congress, I certainly never would oppose. There were other expressions which I would not have inserted, if I had drawn it up, particularly that which called the King a Tyrant; I thought this too personal, for I never believed George to be a tyrant in disposition and in nature; I always believed him to be deceived by his courtiers on Both sides of the Atlantic, and in his official capacity only, cruel. I thought the expression too passionate, and too much like scolding, for so grave and solemn a document; but as Franklin and Sherman were to inspect it afterwards, I thought it would not become me to strike it out. I consented to report it, and do not now remember that I made or suggested a single alteration. We reported it to the committee of five. It was read, and I do not remember that Franklin or Sherman criticized any thing. We were all in haste. Congress was impatient, and the instrument was reported, as I believe, in Jefferson's handwriting, as he first drew it. Congress cut off about a quarter of it, as I expected they would; but they obliterated some of the best of it, and left all that was exceptionable, if any thing in it was. I have long wondered that the original draught has not been published. I suppose the reason is, the vehement philippic against negro slavery. As you justly observe, there is not an idea in it but what had been hackney'd in Congress for two years before. The substance of it is contained in the declaration of rights and the violation of those rights, in the Journals of Congress, in 1774. Indeed, the essence of it is contained in a pamphlet, voted and printed by the town of Boston, before the first Congress met, composed by James Otis, and I suppose, in one of his lucid intervals, and pruned and polished by Samuel Adams."

Jefferson did not respond directly to Pickering or Adams, but in an August 30, 1823, letter he poured out his thoughts to his best friend and confidant, James Madison.

"You have doubtless seen Timothy Pickering's 4th of July Observations on the Declaration of Independence. If his principles and prejudices personal and political, gave us no reason to doubt whether he had truly quoted the information he alledges to have received from Mr. Adams, I should then say that, in some particulars, Mr. Adams' memory has led him into unquestionable error at the age of 88, and 47 years after the transactions of Independence, this is not wonderful, nor should I, at the age of 80, on the small advantage of that difference only, venture to oppose my memory to his, were it not supported by written notes, taken by myself at the moment and on the spot. He says, 'the committee (of 5 to wit, Dr. Franklin, Sherman, Livingston, and ourselves) met, discussed the subject, and then appointed him and myself to make the draught; that we, as a subcommittee, met, and after the urgencies of each on the other, I consented to undertake the task; that the draught being made, we, the subcommittee, met, and conned the paper over, and he does not remember that he made or suggested a single alteration'."

"Now these details are quite incorrect. The committee of 5 met, no such thing as a subcommittee was proposed, but they unanimously pressed on myself alone to undertake the draught. I consented; I drew it; but before I reported it to the committee, I communicated it *separately* to Dr. Franklin and Mr. Adams, requesting their corrections, because they were the two members of whose judgments and amendments I wished most to have the benefit, before presenting it to the Committee; and you have seen the original paper now in my hands, with the corrections of Doctor Franklin and Mr. Adams interlined in their own hand writings. Their alterations were two or three only, and merely verbal. I then wrote a fair copy, reported it to the Committee, and from them, unaltered to Congress. This personal communication and consultation with Mr. Adams, he has misremembered into the acting's of a sub-committee. Pickering's observations, and Mr. Adams' in addition, 'that it contained no new ideas, that it is a commonplace compilation, it's sentiments hackneyed in Congress for two years before, and its essence contained in Otis's pamphlet' may all be true. Of that I am not to be the judge."

"Richard Henry Lee charged it was copied from Locke's treatise on government. Otis's pamphlet I never saw, and whether I had gathered ideas from reading and reflection I do not know. I know only that I turned to neither book or pamphlet while writing it. I did not consider it as any part of my charge to invent new ideas altogether and to offer no sentiment which had ever been expressed before. Had Mr. Adams been so restrained, Congress would have lost the benefit of his bold and impressive advocations of the rights of revolution. For no man's confident and fervid addresses, more than Mr. Adams's encouraged and supported us thro' the difficulties surrounding us, which, like the ceaseless action of gravity, weighed on us by night and by day. Yet, on the same ground, we may ask what of these elevated thoughts was new, or can be affirmed never before to have entered the conceptions of man?"

"Whether also the sentiments of independence, and the reasons for declaring it which make so great a portion of the instrument, had been hacknied in Congress for two years before the 4th of July '76, or this dictum also of Mr. Adams be another slip of memory, let history say. This however I will say for Mr. Adams, that he supported the Declaration with zeal and ability, fighting fearlessly for every word of it. As to myself, I thought it a duty to be, on that occasion, a passive auditor of the opinions of others, more impartial judges than I could be, of its merits or demerits. During the debate I was sitting by Dr. Franklin, and he observed that I was writhing a little under the acrimonious criticisms on some of its part; and It was on that occasion that, by way of comfort, he told me the story of John Thompson, the Hatter, and his new sign."

"Timothy thinks the instrument the better for having a fourth of it expunged. He would have thought it still better had the other three-fourths gone out also, all but the single sentiment (the only one he approves), which recommends the friendship to his dear England, whenever she is willing to be at peace with us. His insinuations are that altho' 'the high tone of the instrument was in unison with the warm feelings of the times, this sentiment of habitual friendship to England should never be forgotten, and that the duties it enjoins should *especially* be borne in mind on every celebration of this anniversary.' In other words, that the Declaration, as being a libel on the government of England, composed in times of passion, should now be buried in utter oblivion to spare the feelings of our English friends and Angloman fellow citizens. But it is not to wound them that we wish to keep it in mind; but to cherish the principles of the instrument in the bosoms of our own citizens: and it is a heavenly comfort to see that these principles are yet so strongly felt, as to render a circumstance so trifling as this little lapse of memory that Mr. Adams worthy of being solemnly announced and supported at an anniversary assemblage of the nation on its birthday. In opposition however to Mr. Pickering, I pray God that these principles may be eternal."

A prayer Adams would no doubt have joined.

Life for both men continued to constrict. Jefferson made his last visit to Poplar Forest in 1823. Both men had difficulty writing --Jefferson because of his long injured wrist and Adams because of "my blindness and Palsy."

In their twilight years both men could exult in the election of John Quincy over Andrew Jackson as president. Adams generously included Jefferson in the shared experience of the election of "our John", writing to Jefferson on January 21, 1825. "The presidential election has given me less anxiety than I, myself could have imagined. The next administration will be a troublesome one to whomso-ever it falls. And our John has been too much worn to contend much longer with conflicting factions. I call him our John, because when you was at Cul de sac at Paris, he appeared to me to be almost as much your boy as mine."

Jefferson probably looked back on his own election in the House of Representatives in 1801 as John Quincy won his showdown with Andrew Jackson on the same field.

"I sincerely congratulate you on the high gratification which the issue of the late election must have afforded you," responded Jefferson on February 15. "It must excite ineffable feelings in the breast of a father to have lived to see a son to whose education and happiness his life has been devoted so eminently distinguished by the voice of his country."

Adams was so touched by Jefferson's congratulatory letter, that when he misplaced it he told Jefferson it was "the most consolatory letter I ever received in my life." "What would I not give for a copy," lamented Adams. His wish was apparently never fulfilled, because the editors of the Adams Papers have never recovered the original copy.

One month later Jefferson's granddaughter Ellen Randolph married Joseph Coolidge, Jr. of Boston and moved to the Bay State. Later that year they visited Adams prompting Adams to tell the proud Jefferson. "Mrs Collidge deserves all the high praises I have constantly heard concerning her."

Their friendship deepened with the passage of time. By the last full year of their lives, Adams was assuring Jefferson he would be "Your friend to all eternity." Ever the skeptic, Adams hedged on whether they would meet in death. "We shall meet again, so wishes and so believes your friend, but if we are disappointed we shall never know it."

Jefferson's colitis confined him to his house except for a few days "which I could get on horseback." Adams was nearly blind by 1825 and had to have someone read to him and help write his letters.

As life began to ebb for both men, Adams looked defiantly to the future while Jefferson looked to the past. Ellen Coolidge told Adams "she had heard you say you would like to go over life again." Adams strongly disagreed in a December 1, 1825, letter to Jefferson. "In this I could not agree; I had rather go forward and meet whatever is to come. I have met in this life with great trials. I had a Father, and lost him. I have had a Mother and lost her. I have had a Wife and lost her. I have had Children and lost them. I have had honorable and worthy Friends and lost them—and instead of suffering these grief's again. I had rather go forward and meet my destiny."

Jefferson's December 18 reply was equally defiant. "You tell me she repeated to you an expression of mine that I should be willing to go again over the scenes of past life. I should not be unwilling, without however wishing it. And why not? I have enjoyed a greater share of health than falls to the lot of most men; my spirits have never failed me except under those paroxysms of grief which you, as well as myself, have experienced in every form: and with good health and good spirits the pleasures surely outweigh the pains of life. Why not then taste them again, fat and lean together. Were I indeed permitted to cut off from the train the last 7 years, the balance would be much in favor of treading the ground over again."

Old age was overtaking both men. They knew it. Each prepared for the future.

"I am certainly very near the end of my life," wrote Adams on January 14, 1826. "I am far from trifling with the idea of Death which is a great and solemn event. But I contemplate it without terror or dismay,'" Adams continued. Either there is life after death or there is not, Adams wrote. "If finit, which I cannot believe, and do not believe, there is an end of all but I shall never know it, and why should I dread it, which I do not; If transit I shall ever be under the same constitution and administration of Government in the Universe," Adams added, "and I am not afraid to trust and confide in it."

Just a month later in the midst of his final winter with personal and public financial problems hovering over his head like a cloud of doom, Jefferson as usual confided his problems and hopes in a February 17, 1826, letter to Madison, whose friendship had "subsisted between us, now a half a century, and the harmony of our political principles and pursuits, have been sources of constant happiness to me through that long period." He closed with this plaintive cry. "To myself you have been a pillar of support thro' life. Take care of me when dead, and be assured that I shall leave with you my last affection."

In their final letters Jefferson took pride in their revolutionary struggle that allowed their children to enjoy "the Halcyon calms succeeding the storm which our Argosy had so stoutly weathered." Adams in reply railed against the "perpetual chicanery" and "personal abuse" being heaped on his son, President John Quincy Adams. "Our American Chivalry is the worst in the World. It has no laws, no bounds, no definitions, it seems to be all a Caprice."

With that their correspondence ended.

The two old warriors were battling their foes until the end.

Americans planned great and glorious celebrations for the fiftieth anniversary of the Declaration of Independence.

Pressed to provide words of wisdom on the great occasion of the fiftieth anniversary celebrations, both men left us lasting thoughts.

When the Rev. George Whitney asked for a message to be delivered at Quincy, Adams reportedly replied. "I will give you, 'Independence Forever'!"

Jefferson replied by a June 24, 1826, letter to a similar request from Roger Weightman, the mayor of Washington. "May it [The Declaration of Independence] be to the world, what I believe it will be (to some parts sooner, to others later, but finally to all) the Signal of arousing men to burst the chains, under which monkish ignorance and superstition, had persuaded them to bind themselves, and to assume the blessings & security of self-government. that form which we have substituted, restores the free right to the unbounded exercise of reason and freedom of opinion."

With great and enduring symbolism, death came to Adams and Jefferson on July 4, 1826, the fiftieth anniversary of the Declaration of Independence. Jefferson died about 1 p.m. and Adams lingered until around 6 p.m. expressing the hope that "Jefferson still lives."

# Select Bibliography

## Printed Works

W. W. Abbot et al., eds., *The Papers of George Washington.* 49 vols. Charlottesville, Va.: University of Virginia Press, 1983-.

Charles Francis Adams, ed., *Memoirs of John Quincy Adams.* 12 vols. Philadelphia: J. B. Lippincott, 1874-1877.

Edwin M. Betts and James A. Bear, Jr., eds., *The Family Letters of Thomas Jefferson.* Columbia, Missouri: University of Missouri Press, 1966.

George A. Billias, *Elbridge Gerry: Founding Father and Republican Statesman.* New York: McGraw-Hill Book Company, 1976.

Julian P. Boyd et al., eds., *The Papers of Thomas Jefferson.* 37 vols. Princeton: Princeton University Press, 1950-.

Patricia Brady, *Martha Washington.* New York: Viking Press, 2005.

Ray Brighton, *The Checkered Career of Tobias Lear.* Portsmouth, N.H.: Portsmouth Marine Society, 1985.

Andrew Burstein, *Jefferson's Secrets. Death and Desire at Monticello.* New York: Basic Books, 2005.

Lyman H. Butterfield et al., eds., *Diary and Autobiography of John Adams.* 4 vols. Cambridge: The Belknap Press of Harvard University Press, 1962.

Lyman H. Butterfield et al., eds., *Adams Family Correspondence.* 10 vols. Cambridge: The Belknap Press of Harvard University Press, 1963-.

Lyman H. Butterfield, ed., *Letters of Benjamin Rush.* 2 vols. Princeton. N.J.: American Philosophical Society, 1951.

Lester Cappon, ed., *The Adams-Jefferson Letters. The Complete Correspondence Between Thomas Jefferson and Abigail and John Adams.* Chapel Hill: The University of North Carolina Press, 1959.

310

Alan Pell Crawford, *Twilight at Monticello. The Final Years of Thomas Jefferson*. New York: Random House, 2008.

Noble E. Cunningham, *Circular Letters of Congressmen to Their Constituents, 1789-1829*. Chapel Hill: The University of North Carolina Press, 1978.

John Patrick Diggins, *The Portable John Adams*. New York, Penguin Books, 2004.

Joseph Ellis, *American Sphinx. The Character of Thomas Jefferson*. New York: Vintage Books, 1996.

Joseph Ellis, *First Family. Abigail and John Adams*. New York: Alfred A. Knopf, 2010.

John Ferling, *A Leap in the Dark. The Struggle to Create the American Republic*. New York: Oxford University Press, 2003.

John Ferling, *Adams vs. Jefferson. The Tumultuous Election of 1800*. New York: Oxford University Press, 2004.

John Ferling, *Jefferson and Hamilton. The Rivalry that Forged a Nation*. New York: Bloomsbury Press, 2013.

James Thomas Flexner, *George Washington: The Indispensable Man*. Boston: Little, Brown & Co., 1974.

Claude Fohlen, *Jefferson á Paris*. Paris: Perrin, 76, rue Bonaparte, 1995.

Worthington C. Ford, ed., *Writings of John Quincy Adams*. 7 vols. New York: The Macmillan Company, 1913-1914.

Gerard W. Gawalt, *Circle of Friends: Thomas Jefferson and His Women Correspondents*. Charleston, S.C.: Create Space, 2010.

Gerard W. Gawalt, "Drafting the Declaration," in Scott Douglas Gerber, ed., *The Declaration of Independence. Origins and Impact*. Washington, D.C.: CQ Press, 2002.

Gerard W. Gawalt and Ann G. Gawalt, *First Daughters: Letters Between U.S. Presidents and Their Daughters*. New York: Black Dog & Leventhal, 2004.

Gerard W. Gawalt, *George Mason and George Washington: The Power of Principle*. Charleston, S.C.: Create Space, 2012.

Gerard W. Gawalt, *My Dear President: Letters Between Presidents and Their Wives*. New York: Black Dog & Leventhal, 2005.

Gerard W. Gawalt, " 'Strict Truth': The Narrative of William Armistead Burwell," *The Virginia Magazine of History and Biography* 101, (January, 1993): 103-132.

Gerard W. Gawalt, revised edition, Julian Boyd, *The Declaration of Independence. The Evolution of the Text*. Washington, D.C.: The Library of Congress and Thomas Jefferson Memorial Foundation, 1999.

Edith B. Gelles, *Abigail & John. Portrait of a Marriage.* New York: William Morrow, 2009.

Annette Gordon-Reed, *The Hemingses of Monticello.* New York: W. W. Norton & Company, 2008.

James Grant, *John Adams: Party of One.* New York: Farrar, Straus and Giroux, 2005.

Margaret A. Hogan and C. James Taylor, eds., *My Dearest Friend. Letters of Abigail and John Adams.* Cambridge, Ma.: The Belknap Press of Harvard University Press, 2007.

William T. Hutchinson et al., *The Papers of James Madison.* Series 1, 17 vols. Chicago and Charlottesville: 1962-.

Walter Isaacson, *Benjamin Franklin: An American Life.* New York: Simon & Schuster, 2003.

John P. Kaminski, ed., *The Quotable Jefferson.* Princeton: Princeton University Press, 2006.

Roger G. Kennedy, *Burr, Hamilton and Jefferson. A Study in Character.* New York: Oxford University Press, 2000.

Roger G. Kennedy, *Mr. Jefferson's Lost Cause.* New York: Oxford University Press, 2003.

Cynthia A. Kierner, *Martha Jefferson Randolph, Daughter of Monticello. Her Life and Times.* Chapel Hill: University of North Carolina Press, 2012.

Adrienne Koch and William Peden, eds., *The Life and Selected Writings of Thomas Jefferson.* New York: Random House, 1944.

Michael Kranish, *Flight from Monticello. Thomas Jefferson at War.* New York: Oxford University Press, 2010.

Leonard Levy, *Thomas Jefferson and Civil Liberties. The Darker Side.* New York: Quadrangle Books, 1973.

J. Jefferson Looney et al., eds., *The Thomas Jefferson Papers. The Retirement Series.* 9 vols. Princeton, N.J.: Princeton University Press, 2005-.

Edgar S. Maclay, ed., *Journal of William Maclay. United States Senator from Pennsylvania, 1789-1791.* New York: D. Appleton & Company, 1890.

Pauline Maier, *American Scripture: Making the Declaration of Independence.* New York: Vintage Books, 1998.

Pauline Maier, *Ratification. The People Debate the Constitution, 1787-1788.* New York: Simon & Schuster, 2010.

Gerard W. Gawalt

Dumas Malone, Thomas Jefferson. 6 vols. Boston: Little, Brown and Company, 1948-1981.

David G. McCullough, 1776. New York: Simon & Schuster, 2005.

David G. McCullough, John Adams. New York: Simon & Schuster, 2001.

John Meacham, Thomas Jefferson: The Art of Power. New York: Random House, 2012.

Frank C. Mevers, ed., The Papers of Josiah Bartlett. Hanover, N.H.: University Press of New England, 1979.

Stewart Mitchell, ed., New Letters of Abigail Adams, 1788-1801. Worcester and Boston: Houghton, Mifflin, 1947.

Paul C. Nagel, Descent from Glory: Four Generations of the John Adams Family. New York: Oxford University Press, 1983.

Paul C. Nagel, The Adams Women: Abigail and Louisa Adams, Their Sisters and Daughters. New York: Oxford University Press, 1987.

Old Family Letters: Copied from the originals for Nicholas Biddle. Philadelphia: Lippincott, 1892.

Merrill D. Petersen, ed., The Portable Thomas Jefferson. New York: The Viking Press, 1975.

Jack Rakove, Revolutionaries: A New History of the Invention of America. Boston: Houghton Mifflin Harcourt, 2010.

Harry Rubenstein, Barbara Clark Smith, and Janice S. Ellis, The Jefferson Bible. Washington, D.C.: Smithsonian Press, 2011.

James M. Smith, ed., The Republic of Letters. The Correspondence between Thomas Jefferson and James Madison 1776-1826. 3 vols. New York: W.W. North & Company, 1995.

Paul H. Smith, Gerard W. Gawalt et al., eds., Letters of Delegates to Congress 1774-1789. Washington, D.C.: Library of Congress, 1976-1999.

Lucia Stanton, "Those Who Labor for My Happiness." Slavery at Thomas Jefferson's Monticello. Charlottesville: University of Virginia Press, 2012.

Harold C. Syrett et al., eds., The Papers of Alexander Hamilton. 27 vols. New York: Columbia University Press, 1961-1987.

Robert J. Taylor et al., eds., Papers of John Adams. 16 vols. Cambridge: The Belknap Press of Harvard University Press, 1977-.

Lynne Withey, Dearest Friend. Life of Abigail Adams. New York: Simon & Schuster, 1981.

Gordon S. Wood, The Creation of the American Republic, 1776-1787. Chapel Hill: Published for the Institute of Early American History and Culture, 1969.

Gordon S. Wood, *Empire of Liberty: A History of the Early Republic, 1789-1815*. New York: Oxford University Press, 2009.

L. Kinvin Wroth and Hiller B. Zobel, eds., *Legal Papers of John Adams*. 3 vols. Cambridge: The Belknap Press of Harvard University Press, 1965.

Andrea Wulf, *Founding Gardeners. The Revolutionary Generation, Nature and the Shaping of the American Nation*. New York: Alfred Knopf, 2011.

## Manuscripts

Adams Family Papers, Massachusetts Historical Society (microfilm)
Adams Family Papers, Library of Congress
William Cranch Papers, Library of Congress
Elbridge Gerry Papers, Library of Congress
Thomas Jefferson Papers, Library of Congress

## Internet

Adams Family Papers, Online Catalog, Massachusetts Historical Society
The American Founding Era, The Rotunda
American History from Revolution to Reconstruction
American Memory, Library of Congress
The Avalon Project, Yale University
Corliss Knapp Engle, "John Adams, Farmer and Gardener," posted on Harvard University site.
Creating the United States, Library of Congress Exhibit (Gerard W. Gawalt, Curator)
Founders Online, National Archives
Thomas Jefferson, Library of Congress Exhibit (Gerard W. Gawalt, Curator)
Thomas Jefferson's Monticello
Thomas Jefferson Papers, University of Virginia
Massachusetts Historical Society, Digital Editions
OpenLibrary.org

Gerard W. Gawalt

Made in the USA
Lexington, KY
02 January 2017